Discourse and Language Education

T0204442

CAMBRIDGE LANGUAGE TEACHING LIBRARY

A series covering central issues in langauge teaching and learning, by authors who have expert knowledge in their field.

In this series:

Discourse and Language Education

Evelyn Hatch

Professor Emerita
University of California, Los Angeles

CAMBRIDGE
UNIVERSITY PRESS

Published by the Press Syndicate of the University of Cambridge
The Pitt Building, Trumpington Street, Cambridge CB2 1RP
40 West 20th Street, New York, NY 10011-4211, USA
10 Stamford Road, Oakleigh, Melbourne 3166, Australia

© Cambridge University Press 1992

First published 1992
Second printing 1994

Printed in the United States of America

Library of Congress Cataloging-in-Publication Data
Hatch, Evelyn Marcussen.
Discourse and language education / Evelyn Hatch.
p. cm. – (Cambridge language teaching library)
Includes bibliographical references and index.
ISBN 0-521-41582-9 (hardback) – ISBN 0-521-42605-7 (paperback)
1. Discourse analysis. 2. Communication. 3. Speech acts
(Linguistics) 4. Language and languages – Study and teaching.
I. Title. II. Series.
P302.H39 1992
401'.41 – dc20   91-23795
                                                            CIP

A catalog record for this book is available from the British Library

ISBN 0-521-41582-9 hardback
ISBN 0-521-42605-7 paperback

Contents

Contents

Practice exercises

Preface

Discourse and Language Education was originally one of four manuals prepared for an introductory course in linguistics at the University of California, Los Angeles. Gathering material for that course was a cooperative endeavor involving myself, my teaching assistants, and my students. Over time, a separate class in discourse analysis was added to the UCLA curriculum, and *Discourse and Language Education* became a separate course book with its own independent organization.

Given this history, there are many people – all the collaborators who offered data and analyses – to thank. Their names are given in the text along with their examples. Special thanks go to Charlotte Basham, Joanna Brunak, Sara Cushing, Carla Eardley, Margaret Early, Eleanor Fain, Vanessa Flashner Wenzell, William Gaskill, Barbara Hawkins, James Heaton, Karen Hribar, Thom Hudson, Marilyn Hulquist, Larry Hunt, Tom Kaiser, DeYoung Lee, Dan Lennon, Linda Ronkin, Christine Salica, Robin Scarcella, and Nora Villoria for allowing me to use examples from their unpublished work.

I especially want to thank Vanessa Flashner Wenzell. As a teacher of introduction to linguistics and introduction to discourse analysis classes, she has had a substantial impact on this project. Palmer Acheson, Barbara Hawkins, Gabriele Kasper, Anne Lazaraton, and Teresa Pica have made numerous suggestions on ways to improve this book, all of which are acknowledged with appreciation.

Ellen Shaw and Suzette André of Cambridge University Press provided encouragement and assistance. Their suggestions were offered in the spirit of collaboration and improved the text immensely. The index was provided by Diane Avis of Hatch & Henessey. I appreciate her assistance and accuracy. The errors that remain are mine alone.

Discourse and Language Education

Introduction

Language has often been defined as a *system* of arbitrary symbols used for human communication. The purpose of this book is to help you discover system in the ways we use language for communication in social contexts. A secondary goal is to convince you that language is not just some entity we *use* in communication, but that much of what we call language "use" is part of language, part of the system of arbitrary symbols.

Discourse analysis is the study of the language of communication – spoken or written. The system that emerges out of the data shows that communication is an interlocking social, cognitive, and linguistic enterprise.

While it is commonplace to talk about system in our linguistic descriptions of phonology, syntax, and semantics, the search for system at the discourse level is still evolving. There is no agreed-upon set of analytic procedures for the description of discourse. The units and processes defined in an analysis depend on the goals of the study. For example, if we want to know how writers show the relation between the claims they make and the evidence for those claims, the analysis will differ from that used to describe the signals children use to interrupt teachers in the classroom. If we are concerned with modeling the language of tutorial sessions, the analysis will differ from that used to study children's narratives. If we want to compare how people complain, gripe, and share their troubles across various languages or study how such communication is carried out by bilinguals or by language learners, the analysis will differ again. If we want to describe how advice is given on radio call-in programs, the analysis will differ from that used in a speech act analysis of advice-giving directives. Given all the ways in which communication is accomplished, it is difficult to see how one and only one "best" method of analysis might apply.

In this book, system in discourse is shown in a series of hierarchically arranged levels. A glance at the table of contents will show you what these are; a chapter is devoted to each. Chapter 1 describes the highest level, or tier – the structure of communication systems. The relation of system signals to conversational analysis is also included in this chapter. Chapter 2 demonstrates the ways in which communication components are realized in specific languages to allow for smooth and appropriate social interaction. Chapter 3 looks inside the communication system at the system of scripts we develop to meet our many different communication goals. In Chapter 4, communication goals are analyzed again, first as speech acts and then as speech events. By using these different analyses, variability is shown not only in analysis but also

1

within the system and across languages. In Chapter 5, classical rhetorical models are used to analyze written and spoken data. The data described here are largely monologues produced by one person and communicated to others. The chapter also includes a brief introduction to rhetorical structure theory.

Chapters 1 through 5 show the layers, or tiers, of structure in communication. These structures serve as flexible templates that can be used to carry out our communication goals. Chapter 6 shows that specific linguistic devices such as cohesive ties and deictic markers can also be used to make the discourse more coherent. Chapter 7 explores the dimensions of oral and written discourse and the various dichotomies proposed to account for such differences. Chapter 8 gives an overview of pragmatics and of contextual analysis, an analysis that highlights the ways in which specific questions about grammar, lexicon, and prosody can be answered by reference to discourse goals. Finally, Chapter 9 summarizes the many methods of analyzing and interpreting discourse structure.

Each chapter includes sections labeled "Practice." These were included for several purposes: to raise your awareness of systematicity in language at the discourse level, to give practice in analysis by "hands-on" involvement with data, and to offer suggestions to start you on your own independent research. You may want to start a journal for your answers, ideas, and observations. Practice items can also be used as study group assignments; each member can carry out part of the research, and the study group can combine the results for a short research paper. Given these goals, it's not surprising that there is no key with "right" or "wrong" answers to practice items. The Practices are meant to stimulate thought and start you on what I hope will be an adventure in discourse analysis.

There are references at the end of each chapter. They are preceded by a Research and Application section, which presents brief summaries of research similar to that discussed in the chapter and asks for your analysis and comments. You are not expected to complete all of the Research and Application items. Select the topics that interest you most. You may only wish to read through them at this point. Perhaps they will form a basis for a paper or future research activities. Again, the intent is to encourage your involvement in discourse analysis.

Discourse and Language Education was prepared specifically for people with strong interests in language and language acquisition. The book will not tell you "how to teach discourse" to language learners. Nevertheless, if you believe that language learners are, in the best sense of the term, "language researchers," you will find that many of the practice activities can be used with language learners to heighten their awareness of the system behind discourse.

Typically, the people in my courses have been communications and linguistics majors, EFL (English as a foreign language) and ESL (English as a second language) teachers, ASL (American Sign Language) and foreign language teachers, and teachers whose schools enroll students from many language and ethnic backgrounds. Because their students represent all age levels (preschool to senior citizen classes), all proficiency levels, and a wide range of first languages, an attempt has been made to include examples from an equally wide range of learners.

The majority of the examples given in the book are from data collected in the United States and, most frequently, in Southern California. Examples from other areas of the world and for other languages are also given, but these are limited by my experience and travels. To broaden the scope, your help is requested. When you complete a practice exercise or an activities project and are pleased with the results, I invite you to share your data and your analysis with me. Although no promises can be made that your examples will appear in the next revision of this book, as many as possible will be included. I envision this as a text that has been cooperatively built and collaboratively completed.

In preparing *Discourse and Language Education,* my overall objective has been to reveal system in discourse. This overall objective has been divided into several course objectives.

Objectives

1. You should know the universal system constraints on human communication. (Chapter 1)

   Evidence: List system constraints with an example of each.

2. You should understand that ritual constraints influence the way that system constraints are realized in different languages. (Chapter 2)

   Evidence: Select any of the system constraints and show how ritual constraints of two languages might lead speakers of those languages to misunderstand or misjudge each other.

3. You should be able to relate system constraints to the components of conversational analysis. (Chapter 1)

   Evidence: Given a transcript, identify conversational features that match the system constraints.

4. You should understand the structure of communication shown in script theory. (Chapter 3)

   Evidence: Given any particular communication goal, identify the actors, props, and the actions of the script.

5. You should know how scripts are organized as "pointers" to memory. (Chapter 3)

   Evidence: Given any particular script, identify the higher-level script to which it "belongs." Demonstrate the shared structural units, and explain how these might point to higher levels of memory organization.

6. You should be able to discuss the connection between speech act functions and sentence syntax. (Chapter 4)

    Evidence: Label any particular English sentence with its possible speech act functions. Given any particular speech act, list examples that vary in sentence structure.

7. You should understand the relation between speech events and speech acts. (Chapter 4)

    Evidence: Given a speech event, list its structural components. Then list the major speech act function shown in the speech event, and list other possible speech acts that could fall within the speech event.

8. You should understand the relation between speech events and scripts. (Chapters 3 and 4)

    Evidence: List the structural components of a given speech event. List the corresponding goal, plan, and script components (e.g., actors, props, actions). Compare the outcome of the two analyses.

9. You should be aware that the structure of speech events may vary across language groups. (Chapter 4)

    Evidence: Give examples that show differences in the components of one speech event in different languages.

10. You should know something of rhetorical genre analysis. (Chapter 5)

    Evidence: List the structural components of narrative, procedural, descriptive, and argumentative prose. List insights regarding syntax that are linked to rhetorical form.

11. You should understand that the organization of rhetorical genres differs across language groups. (Chapter 5)

    Evidence: Give examples to show which genres are most universal in structure and which are least. Or, select one genre and show how it differs across languages.

12. You should understand the goals and methods of rhetorical structure analysis. (Chapter 5)

    Evidence: Given a short text, identify the relation between spans of text within it. Explain the effect of the relation (i.e., the possible goal of the author in selecting specific clauses in that particular relation to each other).

13. In addition to the structure supplied by system constraints, scripts, speech events, and rhetorical genre, text coherence can be improved via prosody and syntax. You should be able to relate linguistic signals of reference and deixis to cohesion in text. (Chapter 6)

    Evidence: Given a text, demonstrate how reference is established via deixis and how tracking is accomplished with both cohesive ties and deictic markers.

14. You should know that speakers and writers use syntax and phonology to carry out many discourse tasks. (All chapters)

    Evidence: Show how prosody (stress, pitch, intonation) and syntax (tense/aspect, articles, passives, existentials, adverbial clauses) can be used for discourse functions that may or may not relate to specific genres.

15. You should know the ways in which organization of discourse texts vary across modes and the ways dichotomies (planned versus unplanned, oral versus written, contextualized versus decontextualized, BICS versus CALP) purport to capture these differences. (Chapter 7)

    Evidence: Given two versions of a text, demonstrate the differences in terminology typical of these dichotomies.

16. You should know that the structure of classroom discourse varies according to culture, content, and course activity. (All chapters)

    Evidence: Compare data from two different classrooms. This comparison should reflect your understanding of system constraints; scripts, plans, and goals; speech events; and so forth.

17. You should consider how a theory of language that includes the discourse system would necessarily differ from a theory of language that centers on syntax (plus phonology and semantics). (All chapters)

    Evidence: No evidence is required at this point. However, thoughtful consideration of this objective is important if you believe that linguistics should include the study of the use of language for human communication.

You will notice that there is no objective that asks you to recount the historical development of discourse analysis because such a history would require a book itself. Perhaps this is an error, for you may complete this manual without a real appreciation for all the work on analysis of texts that took place before the more recent renewal of interest in discourse analysis. You might read van Dijk's (1985) introduction to the field as a way of setting a historical framework for this book.

These, then, are *my* objectives for this book. You, or your instructor, may have quite different goals. As you draw up your own goals and objectives for the course, list them in your journal. Consider, too, how meeting the objectives might be useful when the knowledge obtained is applied to language learning, to intercultural communication, and to common, everyday classroom issues, materials development, language testing, or in applied linguistics research.

Reference

van Dijk, T. A. (1985). Introduction: Discourse analysis as a new cross-discipline. In T. A. van Dijk (Ed.), *Handbook of discourse analysis, Vol. 1: Disciplines of discourse* (pp. 1–10). London: Academic Press. Each chapter in this particular volume of the handbook gives background regarding discourse analysis within a particular discipline, so you might wish to browse through the entire volume.

1 Communication theory: system constraints and conversational analysis

In his study of human communication, Goffman (1976) claimed that there is a set of *universal constraints* on all communication. Since the constraints are universal, they should appear in all types of communication and in all languages. Each language, of course, would differ in exactly how the constraints are met, and the ways in which the constraints are met should vary according to the communication channel.

Goffman divided these communication constraints into two types: *system constraints,* the components required for all communication systems, and *ritual constraints,* the social constraints that smooth social interaction. Together they provide a systematic framework for our description of discourse, even the discourse of everyday, mundane communication. For example, researchers such as Duncan, Jefferson, Sacks, and Schegloff, among others, have investigated system constraints – the ways we open and close conversations, our conversational turn-taking signals, how we repair messages to make them interpretable, how bracketing is done, and so forth. A discussion of all these system constraints follows. System constraints also apply to more formal channels of communication. We can look, for example, at how we open or introduce topics and conclude or close topics in written text as well. We can use the universal system constraints as a framework to describe classroom discourse (the openings, how teachers organize who talks when), our telephone conversations, or even the personal letters we write.

Before turning to a description of communication systems, though, we need to think about the discourse data that systems are meant to describe. If we wish to describe the system of, say, conversation, we are required to collect and transcribe natural conversational data – language produced by users in ordinary, everyday ways.

Many communication specialists work from videotaped data because nonverbal information such as eye gaze, body orientation, hand movements, and head tilt may serve as communication signals. However, transcriptions are also needed for detailed analysis of the discourse system.

Although there is no set method for transcription of such data, the examples throughout this book display transcription conventions developed by Jefferson (see Atkinson and Heritage 1984) for conversational analysis (variations appear in Schegloff and Sacks 1973; Brown and Yule 1981):

/ / or / indicates that the next speaker overlaps at this point:

P: but umm in the high school ummm/ /they
R: / /Don't they use 'em?

An alternative is to use a bracket at the point of overlap:

P: but umm in the high school ummm ⌐ they
R: ⌊ Don't they use 'em?

Brackets also show when two speakers start simultaneously:

R: ⌐ I mean it's not time.
P: ⌊ We can go.

An asterisk or right bracket shows the point at which overlap ends:

M: It's very /very
H: /interesting*
M: yes interesting uh.

= is used for "latching," to show there is no gap between utterances:

M: mmhmm (.2) ye:s =
H: = like saffron

Numbers in parentheses (.2) usually indicate elapsed time in tenths of a second. A (.) stands for a micropause. Some researchers prefer to use + for a short pause, + + for a somewhat longer pause, and + + + for a long pause. These are then keyed to the number of seconds represented by each +. Others prefer to use such symbols to stand for the number of syllables or beats in the ongoing rhythm of the conversation.

Punctuation is used for intonation rather than grammatical function. A question mark, for example, indicates strong rising intonation while a comma indicates a slight rise. A colon means the syllable is lengthened. Multiple colons indicate a more prolonged syllable.

M: at school? annna university? is difficult.
J: Wo:::::w (held equivalent of five syllables)

Uppercase type is used for stress (pitch and volume):

A: to my BOYfriend ann NOTHING else.

A (°) indicates that the following talk is said softly:

S: (°) hn I don't get it.

(h) indicates explosive aspiration; h without parens means audible breathing. A dot (·) indicates in-breath:

S: · h h oh

Single parentheses may be used when the transcriber is unsure of accuracy. Double parentheses indicate nonverbal sounds such as ((cough)).

S: to do a (chef) or ((hiccough)) hh gosh.

7

A right arrow (→) or an underline may be used to point to parts of the transcript relevant to the analyst's description.

In transcripts, the spellings of words are altered to try to capture some of the detail of natural speech. However, accurate representation of speech sounds is not the focus of the research, and so phonological or phonetic transcriptions of data are not used. "See you in ten minutes" might be transcribed as "see yuh 'n ten minutes," and "give me the key" might be shown as "gimme the key."

One final note regarding the transcribed data that occurs throughout this manual. It's important that the data be accurately transcribed, because the analysis depends on the transcription. This is true of written data as well as oral data. In all examples, the written data are presented exactly as they were written. That is, misspellings and other "errors" are not corrected even when misspellings or error type are not at issue. Sometimes these "errors" may be more interesting than the issues that are being discussed, but I hope they will not distract you from the basic content – the analysis of discourse.

Now that you are familiar with transcription conventions, let's turn to an examination of system in communication beginning with the first of Goffman's types of constraints: system constraints.

System constraints

There are eight system constraints that Goffman claimed to be universal in all human communication. They are channel open and close signals, back-channel signals, turnover signals, acoustically adequate and interpretable messages, bracket signals, nonparticipant constraints, preempt signals, and a set of Gricean norms.

Channel open/close signals

In all communication, there must be ways to show that communication is about to begin and then begins, and ways to show that it is about to end and then ends. These channel open/close signals will differ according to the channel (e.g., phone calls, letters, meetings, classrooms). The description of these signals and how they vary across mode, channel, and setting is part of the analysis of discourse.

Consider how you project channel opening signals when you meet a friend on the way to class. What do you think you do (nonverbal signals)? What do you think you say (verbal signals)? Simultaneously, the friend must also make opening response signals. What do you think the friend does (nonverbal signals)? And what do you think the friend says (verbal signals)?

Since our intuitions about language may have been shaped in part by written text dialogues (e.g., those used in language instruction or those of plays), it is important to check intuition against real language data. Let's look at such data now. These data are from American telephone conversations, a channel that has quite formalized openings and closings:

```
((phone ringing))
Marcia:  Hello.
Tony:    Hi Marcia,
Marcia:  Yeah?
Tony:    This is Tony
Marcia:  HI Tony
Tony:    How are you,
Marcia:  OHhhh hh I've got a paper b- (0.2) the yearly paper due tomorrow.
Tony:    How about that.
Marcia:  heheheh hh I can tell you a lot ab(h)out th(h)at . . .
```
(Data source: Wong 1984)

This particular example shows the four basic parts of phone conversation openings described by Schegloff (1968): (1) summons-answer sequence, (2) identification sequence, (3) greeting sequence, and (4) how-are-you sequence. In other words, phone openings consist of more than a simple "hello."

SUMMONS-ANSWER SEQUENCE

The ringing of the telephone represents the summons, and the answer is a response to that summons. In American phone conversations, the most frequent response is "hello." If the person answering knows ahead of time to expect a call, the response may be a "hi" or even "yeah?" Self-identification responses such as "Acme Computers" or "Dr. Jones's office" more often mark the communication as business rather than personal. (If you were trained to answer the phone as "Smith residence" or whatever, you will object to this last statement. But, if you monitor your calls, you will soon find that the preceding generalizations are true for most American phone calls!)

IDENTIFICATION SEQUENCE

We are very often able to identify the caller or the answerer from minimal voice samples. A caller who recognizes the answerer by the initial "hello" may show that recognition has taken place and invite a reciprocal recognition by simply answering "hi."

```
((phone ringing))
E:  Hello:,
S:  Hi.
E:  Hi, Sue.
```

9

If the answerer and the caller are both recognized from such minimal voice samples, all is well. However, there are sequences where the names of answerers and callers are given in the identification sequence:

((phone ringing))
E: Hello:,
C: Dr. Hatch?

((phone ringing))
E: Hello:,
S: hhMom?

Sometimes the intonation is exclamatory or given with falling intonation.

((phone ringing))
E: Hello?
B: EV-lyn!

((phone ringing))
E: Hello:,
S: MOM-my, you're home.

Callers, too, may give an immediate self-identification.

((phone ringing))
E: Hello:,
S: Hi mom, it's me.

((phone ringing))
E: Hello?
A: Hi Gran'ma this is Arien eatin' popcorn. Yuh hear it?

According to Schegloff (1979), these resources for identification are graded in American phone conversations so that identification from the voice sample alone is "preferred." If a name is given, a first name rather than first and last name is "preferred." It appears that the less information needed for identification, the better. When identification falters even for an instant, however, self-identification is forthcoming, often in the second turn.

((phone ringing))
S: hh Hello,
D: Hi Sue,
S: Hi. =
D: = It's Denise. =
S: = ohh HI, Denise.

GREETING SEQUENCE

We've already seen that much of the work of the identification sequence can be accomplished by an exchange of greetings. However, these opening exchanges do not necessarily constitute a greeting. In the following exchange, the first set is part of the identification sequence, and the second set forms the greeting.

((phone ringing))
E: Hello?
S: Hi,
E: Hi, Sue.
S: Hi, Mom,

The one distinguishing characteristic of a "hi" as a greeting versus that of identification is that greetings are not repeated. However, one "hi" can serve both purposes – recognition and greeting.

HOW-ARE-YOU SEQUENCE

Finally, the opening may include a "how-are-you" sequence. The default response is usually "okay" or "fine." A neutral response allows the caller to conclude the opening and provides an anchor point for introduction of the topic or reason for the call. If the default is not used, the how-are-you sequence expands and may become the first topic of conversation if, in fact, it was not the reason for the call.

((phone ringing))
E: Huh-lo?
S: He-LO!
E: Hi Sue, How are yuh.
S: Fine, how're you.
E: hhhh Oh, not so good. I hadda a run-in with B.

In other words, the how-are-you gives the answerer the opportunity to capture the first topic of conversation. In some instances, the answer to the question leads to a multitude of sequences and to a closing before the caller ever gets around to the real reason for the call!

The form of openings to the communication channel varies across oral versus written modes, according to the channel (i.e., phone conversation openings differ from face-to-face communication), and according to the setting (i.e., classroom openings may differ from those of boardroom meetings or dental appointments). Although there is variation across mode, channel, and setting, each type of communication will have an opening sequence that can be systematically described.

Practice 1.1 Openings

1. Check the dialogues in a language teaching text with which you are familiar. What opening signals are used? If there are

any phone call examples, how similar or different are the openings to the four-part system just described?

2. Have you heard the comedy routine where a mother carries out a long advice-giving phone conversation only to discover in the end that it's not *her* daughter on the line? The daughter says something like "Does that mean you're not coming over to baby-sit?" What do you do when you're not quite sure who callers are and they do not immediately identify themselves?

3. In face-to-face communication, are there times when you would open communication with "Excuse me"? If so, what does "excuse me" signal?

4. Think about how you begin letters to your friends. What kinds of opening signals do you use? In what circumstances might you use "Dear Sir or Madam," "To Whom It May Concern," "Your Excellency"?

5. Academic textbooks must also contain opening signals. Look at the opening of this book. What signals are used to open the text?

Now think for a moment about how you close the channel in telephone conversations. It is *not* a simple "good-bye." What series of moves do you make at the end of a social evening to signal the close of that event? Consider how a teacher signals that the class is finished and students are free to leave. How might the system be described?

It is not always easy to determine precisely where closing signals begin. *Preclosing signals* such as "well," "so," and "okay" used with falling intonation are among the signals given by each participant when he or she is ready to close the communication channel. However, a "so" uttered by one party that is not followed by a reciprocal "mmm" or another precloser from the other party cannot constitute a preclosing. Preclosings are cooperatively accomplished.

E: Okay. so::
S: Yeh.
E: Yeh. so I'll call yuh tomorrow then.
S: Okay mom, talk to you later.
E: bye.
S: bye.

In fact, once such preclosing moves are made, it is difficult to stop the closing of the channel without some other signal such as "Oh, wait a minute," "Oh, just a minute," or "Oops, I forgot."

A: ... Okay an then mmm-I'll ask my mom if she'll pick us up at the mall.

J: (.5) Okay. Wait a mn – (.4) hh what's the street you turn on to get to the bike shop?

Certain types of written discourse such as personal and business letters have conventionalized openings and closings (e.g., Dear Dion, Dear Sir:, With love, Sincerely,). With a computer modem, it is possible to send messages around the world via electronic mail. If you use such a system, you probably have already noticed that the style of such messages is somewhere between that of phone and letter communication. The system itself may automatically generate a memo-style opening as it "mails" the message.

Date: Tue, 05 Jan 88 12:24 PST
To: Evelyn Hatch <icm2erh>
From: David Walter <ihw1abc>
         TESL and Applied Linguistics
         3300 Rolfe, UCLA
         Los Angeles, CA 90024
Subject: ANOVA

No automatic closing, however, is provided. The sender may or may not provide an additional opening, but will have to generate a closing. Frequently the sender's message has openings and closings that more closely emulate phone messages than written memos.

Hi Evelyn,
Could you rerun the GLM ANOVA on the GAPS with NS-NS vs. NS-NNS? I'd really appreciate it. Okay? Talk to you later,

                                                              Dave

Needless to say, such messages look strange following a formal, machine-generated opening.

Practice 1.2   Closings

1. Observe the ways openings *or* closings are done in several situations (e.g., when you go to see a professor during office hours, at the doctor's office, meeting friends, with family members). If possible, compare your findings with those of your study group or class. How would you account for differences in the data?

2. We have described openings and closings of ordinary phone conversations. If you work with or can observe deaf students who use a TDD (telecommunications device for the deaf), describe the ways that openings and closings are done in TDD calls.

3. During the next few days, try to stop some of your telephone closings when you've already gone through the preclosing moves. (If it's too hard to talk and do this too, listen for instances in which other people add a last-minute piece of information that stops the final closing.) What happens? How is the closing then renegotiated?
4. Note the ways that parents help young children use openings and closings (e.g., "say bye-bye"). What kinds of instructions do parents give to ensure appropriate greetings and leave-takings?
5. The following activity asks you to collect data that you will be able to use for many other activities in this book. Record a full class period (turn your tape recorder or videocam on before class begins and do not turn it off until everyone has left). Locate the opening and closing segments. Transcribe these portions of the data. At the end of the class, the teacher must use preclosing moves to show that time is almost up. Final closing markers must also be given. How is this done? Compare your data with that of others in your class or study group. Do teachers use the same openings and closings? How much similarity or difference do you find? List your preliminary findings for the project.

Backchannel signals

Goffman's second system constraint is that there have to be signals that a message is getting through. Eye contact, head nods, smiles, and body alignment all help to tell us whether or not the recipient has answered our summons and is attending to our message.

During conversations, even when it is not our turn at talk, we may nod or make noises like "umhmm," "uhhuh," "yeh," "yerright" – backchannel feedback that encourages the speaker to continue. These signals do not take the turn away from the speaker.

L: Here's a little girl.
E: Uhhuh
L: She was walking with flowers in the grass.
E: mmhmm
L: And then she saw the ice cream and she told a lady can she have some.
E: yeah
L: And then the lady, the lady gave her some.

In this example, the "listener" gives signals that show the message is being received and that the listener is aligned with the speaker in terms of that message. The listener does not capture the communication channel – does not get a full talk turn – with these contributions.

Teachers give feedback signals, but they also watch for and interpret the feedback their students offer them. When a student does not offer feedback, silence ensues and the teacher diagnoses a problem:

T: And you probably have some way of remembering that already.
(1.3)
((Student stares blankly at tutor))
T: Maybe not

(Data source: Fox, in press)

The actual verbal or nonverbal forms we use to signal message reception differ according to setting. The signals used by friends in conversations differ from those given by students in classrooms. In teacher-training programs, teachers are told not to ask students if they understand. Rather, they are encouraged to watch feedback signals given by students and adjust the presentation in accordance with those signals. Smiles and head-nodding behavior encourage the teacher; bored looks prompt the teacher to switch gears, and looks of puzzlement call for message clarification and elaboration.

In some settings, feedback has become ritualized. An example of this is in religious services. The congregation may give choral feedback responses. In some services, individual, spontaneous responses may be possible, but when they can occur and the form they will take are usually set. Ritualized feedback is also part of most spectator events. Think, for example, of the feedback the audience gives at a symphony concert, at a ballet, or at a high school basketball game. Performance events have space and time built in for audience feedback.

Backchannel or feedback signals differ across settings and according to the roles of speakers. Cultures may differ in the type or placement of the feedback, but all cultures and languages have a backchannel component in their system of communication.

Practice 1.3   Backchannel signals

1. Check the feedback signals in the classroom data you taped for Practice 1.2. Transcribe these sections. What signals are used? Do some of these signal receipt of "news" as well as show that the message is being received? Do any of them work to cause the teacher to shift the topic? Compare your findings with members of your class or study group.
2. The backchannel signals used differ across languages. What are the typical backchannel signals in the languages

you use? If you teach international students, collect examples from as many languages as you can. Do you ever notice students using these in place of English backchannel signals?

3. If you are a teacher (or if you can observe a class), describe what happens when students do not give encouraging feedback signals. Which signals do they use to show lack of understanding? Which signals indicate disagreement? Which show boredom?

4. What feedback signals are used in deaf communication to show the speaker that the message is being received while allowing the speaker to continue with the message?

5. Observe people reading in the library. What kinds of feedback signals (verbal or nonverbal) do they give as they read "silently"? As an alternative, watch people working at computer terminals. Record their verbal and nonverbal feedback to the computer and to themselves.

6. Select one type of performance event (e.g., a play, a concert, a sports event, or a religious service) and describe the feedback given by the audience. Where and when does feedback occur? How much freedom in terms of time, place, and type of response do individual audience members have in making their contributions? If you select a religious service, you might wish to compare your description with that of Rosenberg (1975) and Bauman (1974).

Turnover signals

In communication, there must be a set of signals that allow for a smooth exchange of turns. Sometimes these signals are ritualized, as in the "roger" and "over" signals of airline communication or the GA (go ahead) of TDD phone calls of the deaf. In face-to-face communication, it would be a bit strange to say "over" or "go ahead" each time we reached the end of a turn. Speakers have a variety of signals to project the end of a turn. The signals cue the next speaker to begin a turn. Since speakers must come in on cue, they must be able to recognize the signals that show that the previous speaker is ending a turn. Slowing of tempo, vowel elongation, and falling intonation all help to signal the end of a turn, a place for an exchange in turns. This is sometimes called a *transition-relevant place*, or TRP (Schegloff's term). Although turns are usually nicely timed, overlaps do happen. In fact, overlaps (*not* interruptions) are thought to show alignment between the communication partners. Notice, however, where the overlap occurs in the following example:

A: Well, I wanna bring somethin diffrunt //y'know.
B: //yeh me too.

The overlap is placed so as not to interfere with the content of the message. It also fits in at a syntactic boundary, between the end of the clause and the tag question ("y'know").

Syntactic completion can also signal a transition-relevant place. For example, assume that the speaker says, "If you try to use that program, you'll run into trouble." The speaker has a slight pause after "program," and the listener may give some backchannel signal (e.g., "umhmm"). The speaker, though, has projected the end of the turn with the use of an "if." Until the "then" is finished, the next speaker won't normally try to take a turn. Nonverbal signals, too, may serve this function. A change in gaze direction (at or away from the listener) can indicate the end of a turn (Goodwin 1981). Or, if the speaker begins to raise his or her arms at a possible transition place, listeners can project when the turn will end. Again, the next speaker won't normally try to take a turn until the speaker's arms are lowered.

Well-aligned speakers may, in fact, complete turns in a collaborative fashion. Overlaps that show collaboration are "good" overlaps. In the following example, Sherry (a Chinese student of English) is talking with a friend about her fear of giving parties:

S: But (.) especially if (.) if I'm inviting people from . . . (.) for example from school, from work, an' y'know my old friends and then they don't know each other then (.4) I 'ave got the added task of y'know (.3)
NS: In/troduce-
S: /uh-introducing one to another.
NS: Yea/h (Tha-)
S: /An' you don't know whether they will mix and they will talk or whether it will be a flop.
NS: Yeah, I know, I know. That's always /That's always
S: /The fear
NS: Yeah.

(Data source: Riggenbach 1989)

In the preceding example, Sherry uses a pause (.3), inviting the native speaker (NS) to help her complete the turn about introducing people. Toward the end, the NS begins "That's always" and Sherry completes the turn "the fear" in an overlap of collaborative completion.

Teachers and tutors often invite collaborative turn completions as a way of checking students' comprehension. This is projected with rising question intonation followed by a pause, with the hope that the listener can chime in:

T: Who did that land already belong to?
Ss: Spain ((a few Ss respond at the same time))
→T: And now + explorers coming + and claiming it for?
Ss: England ((several Ss respond at the same time))

(Data source: Hawkins 1988)

Language learners also use rising intonation as a projection marker to get help from native speakers. Rising intonation and a pause elicits a collaborative completion, as in the following example about the dangers of horseback riding.

M: Mmhmm sometimes it dangerous because if you go out of chair = chair is name of it?
S: Yeah the saddle
M: Maybe you die because if you (pause)
S: Yeah you hit your head. ((completes turn for Miguel))

(Data source: Scarcella)

When the invitation to complete the turn fails, we find pauses after which the speaker resumes the turn. In the next example, the tutor wants the student to understand that exponential functions are always positive. Notice the number of pause points where the student could have produced, but didn't, a collaborative completion with this information.

T: Okay, and here's a time (.2) when you can drop the absolute value. (2.7) 'kay .hh because, again as long as the inside stuff is always positive you can get rid of it. .hh and exponential functions (.7) are always po//sitive =
S: Right. yeah.
T: = .hh so you can if you want to: drop this out, (1.5) since ummm exponentials (.4) are always positive.

(Data source: Fox, in press)

While most talk is turn by turn, the amount of overlap can vary a great deal across language groups and according to the amount of involvement among the participants. In family conversations or conversations among close friends, we may talk at the same time as a way of encouraging the speaker. We may give special feedback signals, adding sound effects, appreciative exclamations, or collaborative completions.

In conversations, the length of each turn is usually fairly short. This gives each participant the right to a fair share of turns. In more formalized communication – for instance, in classrooms, faculty meetings, or business meetings – the turns are distributed less evenly; they are controlled and distributed on a differential basis, and they tend to be longer. However, even in informal conversations, a speaker can claim very long stretches of talk time in one turn. For example, a child may say "y'know what?" and once you've responded "What?" the child has permission to hold the floor for a long storytelling sequence. If someone says, "Want me to tell you how to do this?" and you assent, that person has claimed the floor for an extended period of time. The phrases that get us an extended turn to talk are sometimes called *tickets*. We need to obtain "permission" via such a ticket or a preannouncement, such as "Did you hear what happened down at the pier?", when we claim more than our fair share of time.

Because Goffman's system constraints are claimed to operate in all communication, let's consider turn taking in written text. There are many ways that authors give readers turns. Textbook writers, for example, have subtle ways of taking the reader's contribution into account – assuming that the reader would have objected to X, or assuming that the reader has a question Y and the textbook writer answers it. Summaries at the end of units serve the function of answering the reader's unspoken question, "What have I been reading, and why is it important?" Conversely, in composition classes, teachers instruct novice writers to consider their readers as if they were about to ask not just for summaries but also for definitions, for examples, or other evidence, and even as if they were about to argue with the writer. That is, written communication is a reciprocal transaction between the writer and the reader.

Practice 1.4   Turnover signals

1. Just as there are turn signals in two-party talk and in written text, there are conventions for turn taking in group interactions. In groups, the turns at talk (who talks next) have to be regulated in some way. In meetings you attend, who controls the turns? How does this person nominate others to take a turn? How do people nominate themselves to talk (i.e., capture a turn)?

2. Examine the turn-taking system in the classroom data you collected for Practice 1.2. Are there any examples of students passing the turn on to other students? If so, transcribe those segments. Count the number of times the turn ping-pongs back to the teacher. What kinds of activities promote an equitable distribution of turns at talk for the participants?

3. In class, we frequently do "group work." In addition to accomplishing the task set for the group, the group will have to work out the openings/closings and the turn-taking system for accomplishing their work. If your data includes group work, how is this done? Does one person (or several people) take over the "teacher" role, opening and closing the session, allocating turns to speakers? Is there one person or several people to whom the turn to talk "returns"? Has the teacher included instruction on how the group is to organize to carry out their communication? If not, how might you argue for such instruction?

4. When teachers lecture (rather than verbally interact with students), they often use the sequence "Okay? Okay." Do you think this okay exchange is an "empty turn" for the students, signals a change in topic of discussion, or fulfills

both functions? If students want to ask a question, how would they decide whether this was a good place to claim a turn?

5. List two tickets or preannouncers that give you the go-ahead to take an extended period of talk.

6. Consider the following example from a State Bar pamphlet ("Do I need a lawyer?" 1980).

    1. Do I need a lawyer?
       You might. Basically, legal advice is like medicine: You can take it to cure problems and to prevent them.
       You need legal advice to cure problems if you are accused of commiting a crime, if you are being sued or if you want to sue someone. A lawyer also can help you if you want to get a divorce or if you need to file bankruptcy.
    2. How do I find a lawyer?
       California has more than 67,000 practicing lawyers. So you should not have trouble finding the right one – once you know where to look. . . .
    3. Do lawyers specialize?
       Just like doctors, some lawyers specialize and some do not. Many lawyers are "general practitioners." Like family doctors, they handle a wide range of problems and cases. . . .
    4. How will I know which lawyer is best for me?
       Before you choose a lawyer, you may want to do some "comparison shopping." If so, make a list of several lawyers. Then, telephone the lawyers on your list and ask them for information that will help you make a decision.

    What turn-taking signals are used? What identifies the reader as the source of the questions? Frank (1989) has looked at question-answer sequences in sales letters (e.g., questions answered by the reader, such as "How many other banks can make this promise?" and questions answered by the writer, such as "Will it work? We guarantee it!"). You might compare these patterns across different types of sales letters or look for such examples in sales literature in other languages.

7. If you can observe a mother interacting with her very young infant, note the turn taking that occurs as the mother, for example, bathes or feeds the infant. What is the pattern of turn-taking vocalizations in these contexts? How does the mother cue the baby (e.g., touching it, shifting it) to take a turn at "talk"? Are many of the baby's turn-taking signals nonverbal rather than verbal? Compare your findings with those presented in Freedle and Lewis (1977).

8. Eye gaze can play an important role in the timing of ends of turns. Eye gaze aversion in English, according to Williams (1979) and Goodwin (1981), signals the end of turns. The same behavior in ASL (American Sign Language) shows an intention to continue talking (Cokely and Baker 1980). If the camera has picked up clear examples of eye gaze shifts at ends of turns of talk in your classroom data (from Practice 1.2), check to see whether eye gaze aversion is, indeed, a typical signal of the end of a turn.

Acoustically adequate and interpretable messages

The fourth system constraint identified by Goffman is that communication requires an ungarbled message. In order for communication to take place, messages have to be interpretable. They also have to be "hearable." We have all been at cocktail parties or receptions in crowded rooms where the noise level prohibits message reception. If messages are garbled, they must be "repaired." If they are not, then other parts of the communication system break down, and communication grinds to a halt.

The question is, What constitutes a clear message? Just how acoustically accurate must a message be to be "adequate," and what makes a message "interpretable"? How clear must messages be in order to serve communication?

In the following example, the language learners (H, Persian, and M, Japanese) make many phonological and syntactic errors, and yet communication takes place.

H: Do you-do you spend uh (.4) some drugs =
M: mmhmm
H: = in your food?
M: mm hm (.2) ye:s =
H: = like saffron, or salt, or pepper something like that?
M: mmhmm oh: I: see. Yes mm (1.0) Japanese?
H: Yes, in Japanese food.
M: o:h in Japanese food mmm Japanese food no:t spi-cy: (.2) almost =
H: What does it mean? spicy?
M: Spicy means uh mm (1.0) mm mm mm not-do you know spice? (.2) spicy meaning uh sometimes with seed with uh tree seeds or uh: nuts.
H: yes
M: mm example umm tabasuko? And uh, muhstad mm and pepper.
H: Yes, I got it.
M: Not spicy Japanese food. (.2) Very soft taste.
H: Yeah.
M: Yeah mm.
H: It's different from u:h Indian food.

(Data source: Schwartz 1980)

21

Much of this exchange appears to be acoustically inadequate, and at times comprehension seems difficult. Nevertheless, Gumperz (1979: 15) says that "participants need not agree on the details of what was meant in any utterance, so long as they have negotiated a common theme or focus."

When people are learning languages, they may have difficulty interpreting messages not negotiated to their level of competence. There are many ways to deal with this. Some learners "fake it," pretending to understand and continuing to interact in the hope that they will catch the theme or focus of the conversation. Scarcella's subject, Miguel, was extremely good at keeping the burden of conversation on the native speaker. Consequently, native speakers often judged Miguel's competence as quite high, when in reality he did not understand much of what was said. Notice his skilled use of backchannel signals and *Wh-* questions to accomplish the interaction:

M: (pointing to a picture on Joe's wall) What about this?
J: Well it's called "The Broken Bridge and the Dream." I uh I'm not sure what it means. But ya know this is the broken bridge and it kinda looks like =
M: = uhhuh
J: The more real everything is, everything is solid but as you get closer here (pointing) like man's hopes or his aspirations everything becomes a little more transparent less real
M: yeah
J: Dali would say I'm wrong. He says everybody's wrong.
M: Very strange. What's that?

(Data source: Scarcella)

In this case, "faking it" soon resulted in a barrage of talk that Miguel did not understand. Obviously, there are pluses and minuses to the use of faking strategies. Communication can continue fairly smoothly, but it may also break down completely since information that allows the participants to build a common theme or focus is missing.

Other learners use backchannel cues to let the speaker know they do not understand. The speaker then repairs the message. As the talk is negotiated, repairs and readjustments are made, and the talk becomes simplified to (hopefully) an appropriate level. There are advantages and disadvantages to this strategy too. The message becomes comprehensible during the repair process, but both the native speaker and language learner may find the need for constant negotiation of repairs too burdensome to make the conversation worthwhile. The learner may then be denied the extended interaction with native speakers that could facilitate language learning.

In the following example, the native speaker (NS) is a typist; M is a Japanese student at an American university. The typist wants to know whether the material that M wants to have typed is in final or initial draft form. Because this information determines whether or not there is time to complete the job, the NS continues an extended repair sequence. In other circumstances, both might have given up much quicker.

NS: Is this the final?
M: Uhh, it's un mmm pardon?
NS: Is this your final?
M: Fi::ne?
NS: Are you filing or is this the rough draft + + or the final?
M: Oh, I see. Final you mean last one.
NS: Right. Is it the last one?
M: Yesss ((sounds unsure))
NS: Yeah, last copy?
M: Mmhmmm ((still sounds uncertain))
NS: Right + + is it all typed now?

There is, as you might imagine, a whole body of research that looks at the types of adjustments we make when our messages are not acoustically adequate or interpretable. In conversational analysis, this includes the study of the "repair" system (Sacks, Schegloff, and Jefferson 1974; Schegloff 1979). In research on language learning, the repairs often lead to special registers such as "foreigner talk," "teacher talk," or (in the case of language disorder research) "clinician talk."

These registers have many similarities. All show an increase in acoustical accuracy. This is accomplished by slowing the rate of speech so that there are fewer reduced vowels, fewer contractions, little consonant cluster simplification, and so forth. Heavy stress is placed on important content words, and there is a longer break at syntactic boundaries. The slower rate not only increases acoustical accuracy but gives the learner more processing time.

The need to repair utterances to make them interpretable shows up in these special registers – in vocabulary selection and syntactic change as well. There is less slang, fewer idioms are used, and the vocabulary choices are toward high-frequency items. Definitions are more explicitly marked either by formulas (e.g., "This means X," "It's a kind of X") or by intonation (e.g., "a nickle? a five-cent piece?"). Along with a slower speech rate, we find short, simple syntax, less pronominalization, and simpler noun phrases.

The discourse itself is also simplified in these special registers to make it possible for learners to carry on conversations. To help learners participate, their conversation partners may avoid asking questions for which the learner must offer considerable information. For instance, they may use an or-choice or yes-no question [e.g., "Did you want to buy a computer? (.2) I mean, did you want to buy a computer or just rent one? (.2) You want to rent one?"]. The learner need only make a choice of answers offered as candidate responses, or simply respond "yes" or "no." Teachers may "fill in the blank" when learners search for words or expressions. In a helpful conspiracy, they may offer hints and finally even answer their own questions to make the communication easier for the learner. This lightens the burden on the learner, and it also supplies a good deal of incidental instruction:

T: Would it be: easier for you to go through thi(hh)s pipe, (.9) or this pipe.
(1.6) 'kay. 'cause we stretched it out to three times its length.
S1: Yeah.
S2: Yeah.
T: It'd be a hell of a lot easier to crawl through this pipe (than if it had) to go
through this pipe. =
S1: (P-)
S2: = Right.

(Data source: Fox, in press)

In addition, questions from native speakers (whether teachers or other conversation partners) form a temporary "scaffold" or format so that learners can participate in conversations. In the following example, notice the modeling that the teacher and other students do that allows Mileka (M, a speaker of Hawaiian English) to finally produce the pronoun "it." (Note that "om" is an accusative case pronoun in Hawaiian English.)

M: No, get the knife and put that in. ("That" refers to a knife)
T: Oh, all right. I stuck it in the peanut butter. ("It" replaces "that")
M: Then put 'om in on there. ("om" refers to knife)
T: You have to tell me what to do with the knife.
J: Put it in. (Peer models "it")
T: I did put it in. (Teacher models "it")
K: Put it in. (Peer models "it")
M: Now put it on the bread. (Mileka uses "it" for knife)
(one minute later)
M: Rub it on the bread. (Uses "it" with no immediate model)

(Data source: Speidel 1987)

Finally, to make the ongoing conversation clearer, native speakers and teachers may remodel the output of the learner into a more grammatical form, as in these exchanges with Rafaela, a native speaker of Spanish.

NS: You're not working right now?
R: No.
NS: No?
R: Ahhh + + + for one week + + I::: the::: comp-any? Is inventory +
Inventory + aha + for one week.
NS: Oh.
R: Monday I work + + I work + Monday.
NS: You're going to start working Monday again.

R: I like men American but I no no + + I no + + have nothing.
NS: Oh, I see. You don't have a boyfriend here.
R: No boyfriend American.

R: Before here 3 + 2 months + + I live my mother.
NS: For two months you lived with your mother.

(Data source: Brunak, Fain, and Villoria)

It seems unlikely that teachers or other native speakers are taught to do this kind of modeling. It is more likely that they have learned to be responsive to each student's contribution, and modeling is a by-product that can serve an unintentional instructional purpose.

In this section we have looked at ways in which we attempt to make our messages acoustically adequate and interpretable. When communication begins to break down, repairs and adjustments are made. Such repairs are common in all communication. They are even more common in conversations involving learners. To overcome communication breakdowns when one partner is not yet proficient in the language or in the content of the material being talked about, we may use a fill-in-the-blank cooperative completion, rephrase questions so that less language is demanded of the learner, supply answers, model the learner's response, or model better forms of answers. All languages have a variety of repair mechanisms that can be used to reframe messages in more acoustically adequate and interpretable forms.

Practice 1.5 Acoustically adequate and interpretable messages

1. Tape-record an interaction with a beginning language learner (or tape yourself as a beginning learner of another language). Afterward, ask the learner to comment on what was and was not understood in the conversation. What cues of (non)comprehension appear on the tape? Which were truly cues of (non)comprehension?

2. How much restatement and remodeling does the native speaker do on these tapes? Does it help? If so, how?

3. Examine the classroom tape you recorded for Practice 1.2. Transcribe a section that shows how the teacher adjusts the complexity of his or her talk. Which adjustments do you believe were necessary in order to meet the requirement of acoustically adequate and interpretable messages?

4. What types of repairs do the students make? Transcribe these sections. Are the repairs clearly due to language proficiency? If possible, interpret the cause (e.g., word searches or gain in planning time) of the repair.

5. Do you believe you can consciously control your "foreigner talk" or "teacher talk" in conversing with language learners? What kinds of simplification (phonological, lexical, syntactic, discourse) do you find most difficult to control? How do you explain this?

6. If you teach ASL or are a learner of ASL, videotape your class. What examples of "foreigner talk" do you find in the

tape (e.g., slower signing, more careful articulation of signs, repeats and repairs)?

Bracket signals

In all communication, there must be signals to show that parts of the message, "side sequences," are not right on-line with the message of the moment. Goffman calls these *bracket signals.* The brackets are like instructions for putting the ongoing talk or text on hold (don't forget about it) so that you can return to it later if you wish. (See Jefferson 1972 for more about the analysis of side sequences.)

During the next few days notice the verbal signals used to start a bracket. How many times do you hear "by the way," "incidentally," or other bracket signals? How often do speakers use "well, anyway(s)" as a bracket to return to the original topic?

There are, of course, many different signals – both verbal and nonverbal – that can be used as bracket signals. Intonation and shifts in body position, for example, often mark asides:

LF: (reading a lecture paper). . . to the tota:l – ((looks up and directly at audience)) I'm reading this as fast as I can because I bet you're as hungry as I am. I didn't eat any breakfast this morning – ((audience laughter; looks back down and continues reading the text)) . . .

VF: (during public lecture). . . as the main topic – ((gestures with hand)) I've forgot the instructions on how to use this microphone Oh, there we go ((drops hand to podium)) – So, the main topic . . .

One easy way to notice nonverbal bracketing signals is to turn down the sound on your television set. (If you tape a TV program with your VCR, it will allow you to replay the tape many times.) With the volume off, the non-verbal signals used to show bracketing become clear.

Sometimes we get lost in our side sequences and forget how they relate to what went before. So, we have special formulaic expressions to handle such problems – "How'd I get off on this?" "I forgot why I started to tell you about this. Sorry. Well, anyways . . ."

In written material, punctuation marks may be used to set bracketed material apart from the rest of the text. Parentheses and dashes are often used; footnotes also serve as bracket signals. Many manuals that are formatted on personal computers use a little flower symbol for paragraphs; these symbols are meant to be read as "by the way" notes, pieces of text that are not completely in line with the ongoing text.

Some signals for side sequences are clear; others are not. Language learners, for example, often comment that they do not know a joke is about to be told and, therefore, do not understand that the bracketed material is an aside – a joke – until other students laugh. In this case, nonverbal signals or intonation alone may not be adequate bracket cues. Bracket signals in written text, however, are much more overt.

While asides can occur in all kinds of communication, nonverbal and verbal bracketing signals are not the same across languages. Still, we know that all languages have bracket signals to cue readers and listeners that parts of the communication are not directly in line with the rest of the message.

Practice 1.6   Bracket signals

1. Check your classroom videotape (from Practice 1.2) for the bracketed asides used by teachers (and any used by students too). What functions do these particular side sequences appear to serve? What makes asides more or less successful in terms of the functions you propose?
2. Observe how speakers bracket jokes. What signals do they use as a ticket to tell the joke? Are the signals ever nonverbal? If you have observed that international students worry about missing jokes in class, determine whether it is the bracketing or the appropriateness of telling jokes in classroom discourse that contributes most to missing the joke.
3. Compare the brackets that appear in written compositions of native and nonnative speakers. How many brackets are used in each composition? Are they marked in the same way (e.g., with parentheses, dashes, brackets, separate paragraphs, footnotes)? Would you consider including instruction on bracketing side sequences as part of a composition course in academic English? Why or why not?
4. If you have access to a large data base (e.g., the Brown or Lund corporus), check the frequency of use of parentheses and dashes across text genres. What predictions can you make about the frequency of asides and the choice of parentheses versus dashes in different text types? (If you do a corpus check using a computer concordance program, be sure to check the entries so that you include only the parentheses and dashes that serve as bracket signals.)

Nonparticipant constraints

In order that messages be interpretable, it is necessary to keep other competing messages out of the channel. We have already mentioned how difficult it can be to attend to messages when the noise level is high (e.g., at a reception or cocktail party). For successful communication, Goffman therefore proposed a seventh system constraint: All languages must have some way of blocking nonparticipant noise from the communication channel. There are a variety of strategies that can be used to keep the noise of nonparticipants in the background and out of focus.

Conversely, there are times when we are at a party and want to join a group in which a conversation is already under way. The problem, then, is how to move from nonparticipant to participant. There must be signals – verbal and nonverbal – to allow or prevent entrance of nonparticipants into the communication channel.

One strategy used to move from nonparticipant to participant status is to repeat parts of what one overhears in the ongoing communication. Often, a reason is added to explain why one has a right to overhear.

(Setting: A coffee shop; two men are speaking together, and a woman is seated at the next table "listening in.")
A to B: . . . like someone from California.
B: yeh
C: Someone from CaliFORnia? I mean, I'M from California and . . .

Other signals may be nonverbal. For instance, laughter can be used as a cue. In the following example, J and M are Mayan speakers; g is an English speaker. All speak Spanish as a second language.

J, M: (Maya talk) (laughter)
g: ¿Que es, que es broma?

(Data source: Jordan and Fuller 1975)

A response of "What's so funny?" when we hear laughter from a group of conversants works well to let us into conversations. When we feel a special right to enter the conversation (as in the case of the woman from California speaking up when something is said about her state), we can gain admittance to the communication channel.

J, M: (Maya talk)
J: (Maya talk) Estados Unidos (Maya talk)
g: Hey, we're getting talked about over there. Hablan de nosotros, ¿uh?
J: Eso oigo.

(Data source: Jordan and Fuller 1975)

The classroom is another setting where the form of nonparticipant constraints can be observed. For example, how do individual students break into already-established groups? Or, if a teacher wants to include someone who is on the periphery of a discussion, how is this accomplished? Students, particularly in elementary schools, vie for teacher attention. When the teacher is working with one group of students, how does another student get included in the group? If the teacher or the other students do not want the communication channel opened for this individual, how is this managed? All these questions could be researched in the classroom. In addition, if you have been a student in a language class (or any other class, for that matter), there undoubtedly were times when you did *not* want to be called on. Typical signals of American nonparticipants include averted eye contact. Of course, averting one's eyes is not a universal signal that one wants to remain a nonparticipant. Nor is hand waving a universal signal to gain access to communication in the classroom. Nonparticipant constraint signals differ across settings and language groups. Still, each language or culture group must have some way of signaling nonparticipant versus participant status in communication.

Practice 1.7   Nonparticipant constraints

1. At the next large party you attend, note the ways in which nonparticipant constraints are shown. How do nonparticipants gain admission into a group where communication has already been established?
2. Study the ways in which students approach teachers to claim admission to the communication channel during class time and during break time. Are students more likely to approach the teacher to talk if he or she stays in the teacher post or leaves it? Why? If the teacher is busy preparing notes for the next hour, how does he or she signal nonparticipant status to the approaching students? If the teacher welcomes chat, how do other students gain entrance to the communication channel?
3. We assume that people who have a headset on (listening to music or the news) want to be nonparticipants in any other communication. But could a Walkman actually be used to promote communication? If so, how?

Preempt signals

In addition to nonparticipant constraints, there also have to be ways for participants to interrupt an ongoing channel message. Emergencies come up when speakers must interrupt each other. There need to be ways to do this. Imagine that a friend has called and has been telling you his or her troubles for an extended period of time while you really have work you must do. How would you interrupt the ongoing message?

During the process of writing, we may also receive preempt signals, such as ringing doorbells or school buzzers. In the last few minutes, for example, two messages have flashed on my computer screen that electronic mail has come in. When this happens, I can stop and check the "mailbox" for the content of these messages (so the preempt strike worked), or I can ignore the preempt attempts. It would, however, be strange to try to stop an overly long troubles-sharing conversation by suddenly saying "message waiting"! So instead, we use nonverbal signals (such as leaning forward, shifting forward in our seats, opening our eyes wide and raising eyebrows, waving a pencil in the air, and so forth) or verbal signals, such as "Oh the cookies! The cookies are burning!" (the "oh" is a particle that signals an unexpected event).

In addition, there are times when we need to preempt the talk in order to request repairs or message clarification. Notice the overlap and the signal "E-e-e" used by the tutor to interrupt and redirect the student's plan of operation.

     S: And then the mass. (.8) I need the mass of an electron.
         (.2)
     T: Mhm
         (1.8)
     S: And that's in my book (1.7) And th//en
→T: E-e-e- what units are you going to put that in? This is the main thing I'm
         worried about.

                                        (Data source: Fox, in press)

While the signals, verbal or nonverbal, may differ across setting or culture groups, there are always ways that the communication message can be preempted.

Practice 1.8   Preempt signals

1. On television, news flashes sometimes preempt regular television programs. How is this done? Does the importance of the news flash determine whether the picture is disrupted (rather than have a message run across the bottom of the screen)? Commercials also preempt programs, but the switch to the commercial seems not to be a true preemption of the communication. How would you classify this switch from program to commercial (e.g., turn-taking, bracketing, preempting)?
2. How do ASL speakers interrupt each other? What are the preempt signals? Do they differ from regular turn-taking signals? If so, how?
3. At conferences, speakers are warned that if they run over their allotted time, they will be interrupted. To avoid this problem, the chairperson may hold up a sign that says "one minute left."

     VF: . . . as we might like. ((Timer shows card)) OK. In SUM-
            mary, then . . .

RNC: . . . a teacher training program. ((Timer shows card)) I
     have two minutes more, folks! ((Audience laughs))

How do preempt signals work in other types of meetings? If
a nonparticipant comes into the meeting room with a
message for a participant, how is the preempt
accomplished? If a member attempts to do a preempt and
the chairperson does not wish to allow the preempt, how is
this done? (If you are unsure, think about televised political
conventions and the ways in which the chairperson
recognizes or does not recognize attempts to preempt the
ongoing communication work.)

4. At public events (such as basketball games or symphony
concerts) it is sometimes necessary, in the case of an
emergency, to do a preempt to ask for someone in the
audience. How is this accomplished?

5. Examine your classroom tape (from Practice 1.2) for
instances of preempt signals. Transcribe these segments.
What signals are used? Does the preempt interrupt only for
a moment (for example, students ask clarification questions)
or does it completely change the course of the
communication?

Gricean norms for communication

Goffman also noted that communication cannot truly work unless participants generally observe four major norms of cooperation: relevance, truthfulness, quantity, and clarity. These norms, called *maxims*, were proposed by
Grice (1975) as criteria for cooperative communication.

RELEVANCE

The first maxim for cooperative conversation is to "be relevant." That is, each
person must make a contribution relevant to the topic. Communication messages cannot be random, but must relate to what has gone before. It is difficult,
for example, to see how a communication message could consist of the two
following contributions:

A: Would you like coffee or tea?
B: My daddy says so, that's why!

However, since we know that responses are usually relevant, we can interpret
the following service encounter exchange:

A: Do you do buttonholes?
B: She'll be back in an hour.

Because we assume the response is relevant to the question, we infer that there is a person who does buttonholes and that the person will return in an hour.

Service encounters are infamous for questions being answered by questions:

A: Do you have orange juice?
B: Large or small?

The requester infers that orange juice comes in either large or small contain-ers. If the requester replied "Large or small what?" the service person would be surprised. We can see, then, that contributions need not be relevant to the previous utterance but, rather, relevant to the negotiated common theme or focus of communication.

Look now at the following fragment from a coffee-break chat. The data were collected in an Australian hospital staff lounge during break time. Can you identify the topic of conversation?

Gary:	well, I got pictures tomorrow night-boy, I I love that that State Theatre
Pauline:	Oh, isn't it beautiful
Gary:	//yeah
Bronwyn:	//yeah
Gary:	//yeah
Pauline:	//I relly love it – my favorite
Pat:	I've never been there
Bronwyn:	//oh, it's beautiful
Pauline:	//oh it's beautiful – it's got chandeliers and things
Pat:	I've been to the one in Wollongong
Bronwyn:	//oh no – look nothing beats the State really
Bronwyn:	it's beautiful
Pauline:	I've always loved it
Bronwyn:	this has been restored and everything
Pat:	What's on there?
Gary:	ah Monty Python

(Data source: Slade and Norris 1986)

The topic is the State Theatre, and the relevant contributions about the topic concern its attributes (it's beautiful; it's got chandeliers; it's been restored; and it is loved – at least by Gary and Pauline). This topic is embedded in another topic "going to the movies" and the identification of the movie as a Monty Python special.

The topic, however, need not be the same for each participant. While we try to make our contributions relevant to the topic of conversation, we may have our own personal topics that we try to weave into the conversation. Personal topics are often introduced through a first-person referent. In this transcript there are several contributions that begin with "I." When Pat says "I've been to the one in Wollongong," that attempt to move toward Pat's personal agenda of talking about adventures in Wollongong is rejected by

Bronwyn and Gary, at least for the moment. The point is that there might be single or multiple versions of a conversation topic. Topics in a conversation are dynamic and are negotiated as a conversation progresses. For this reason, we cannot really say that a discourse has a topic; only speakers and writers do.

In the following segment of the "chat" transcript, we can clearly see where the topic shifts: Bronwyn succeeds in moving to her personal narrative on seeing the movie *E.T.*, noting that it was at the State Theatre. Pat, again, does not seem very effective in switching the focus from Bronwyn's experience to her own.

Gary: no, no, no – but um even that – they put second rel- or late release – like really low sort of movies //on
Pauline: //yeah
Gary: but – oh well, Saturday night//Monty Python
Bronwyn: //well, I went and saw *E.T.* at the State Theatre and when I took the kids I thought – oh there's thousands of kids here – it's going to be so noisy – I won't even be able to hear what the movie's about – so the kids yapped and yapped all thousands of them//until *E.T.* started
Others: //mmm
Bronwyn: and then honestly you could've heard a pin drop
Gary: mm yeah
Pat: I thought it was great – I bawled my eyes out
Bronwyn: yeah, these kids were rapt – it didn't matter whether they were little or //big
Pauline: //mmm
Pat: I went with my sister, Michell, Christopher and Joanne and Jo – it took Joanne an hour after we'd walked out to stop crying
Bronwyn: because it was so sad
Gary: I didn't want to see it at all
Pauline: no, neither did I
Pat: it was really funny and really sad in parts

(Data source: Slade and Norris 1986)

To make the messages "cohere," contributions must be relevant to what goes before and what one expects might follow. In writing, only one person is building the text, trying to put information into an appropriate sequence so that the pieces most highly related to each other come together. Writers can use paragraph markers to do some of this work. Each new paragraph shows a slight shift in focus so that the sentences within it relate more directly to each other. Each paragraph in turn relates in some organized way to the overall topic of the discourse.

In writing and in speaking, there are times when we want to add material but realize that our contribution is not directly relevant to the ongoing communication. In some cases, this material can be bracketed as a side sequence.

In other cases, there is a small shift in topic as the result of the contribution. In any event, if contributions are not directly relevant, there need to be special signals (such as "This is a little off the subject, but ..." or "Doesn't that remind you of ...") to show the topic shift.

TRUTHFULNESS

A second Gricean maxim is that contributions "be truthful." This does not mean that you cannot tell a lie, but simply that a cooperative conversationalist does not usually say other than what he or she believes to be true.

When we violate truthfulness, we often do so using special intonation for sarcasm, for teasing, or for playfulness, as in the following examples from Gough (1984). The first exchange shows a father diverting a child's attention from an argument with his sibling by pretending a muffin can fly:

F: Do you wanna half of a muffin? Here it comes (makes loud airplane noises as he flies the muffin plane around the kitchen). Flyin'. (more airplane noises, then lands the muffin plane on child's plate)

When the truth maxim is violated, speakers may, in fact, say so – that it's "just pretend."

P: Mommy?
M: Mmhmm
P: How old are you for pretend?
M: Ohh (.8) I'm about 12 years for pretend.
P: Ah. You're older.

(Data source: Gough 1984)

The ability to take on another role in pretense appears very early in child development. Learning how to move in and out of "truthfulness" with appropriate marking may be acquired early in life, but the successful execution and recognition of irony, teasing, and joking is not an easy matter even in adulthood. We assume, according to Grice's maxim, that contributions will be truthful unless marked as deviations from that norm. The markings are not always easy for language learners to recognize. Pretense, teasing, and joking may be quite difficult for many learners.

QUANTITY

The maxim of quantity is one which is difficult for many people. In conversations, everyone should have his or her "fair" share of talk time. No one should "hog" the floor without special permission. In writing, some of us are very long-winded, while others are too brief. It is difficult to judge exactly how much inferencing or "reading between the lines" we can ask our readers to do. We want to be brief, but not so brief that our message isn't clear.

CLARITY

Finally, Grice notes that we should "be clear." We should avoid obscurity and ambiguity. Our message should be constructed in an orderly way. This, of course, overlaps with the system constraint on interpretable messages. Here, however, the emphasis is not just on comprehensibility but on clarity of messages.

All four of Grice's maxims are important for effective communication. Controls on manner (clarity), quality (relevance and truthfulness), and quantity (enough but not too much) of contributions are important for communication to run smoothly among cooperative participants. You might, however, think for a moment about instances where the maxims are flaunted. For example, a recommendation letter that is two sentences long flaunts the maxim of quantity. And there are instances of noncooperative communication, sometimes called *crosstalk,* in which participants have their own agendas. Questions may be answered with apparently irrelevant responses. Not only may the responses be unrelated to the question, but they may be misleading rather than truthful. The quantity maxim may also be violated in crosstalk. Opponents may pile on irrelevant facts and details or refuse to give any details or supporting information at all. Finally, the clarity of the message may be intentionally distorted so that each side can claim that the other has sabotaged the communication. The study of crosstalk shows how violations of maxims can distort communication.

Practice 1.9   Grice's maxims for communication

1. Read the following directions for a falafel pie lunch. Then divide it into paragraphs. Justify your paragraph breaks using Grice's maxim of relevance.

   In a large bowl, beat 3 large eggs, ¾ cup nonfat milk, and one 8-ounce package of falafel mix. (Falafel mix is a seasoned garbanzo meal that you can find in your supermarket in the section for rice and rice mixes or in the section for fancy foods.) In another bowl, mix 1 pound of turkey sausage or ground turkey and a small (4-ounce) can of diced green chilies. Add ½ cup of the falafel mixture to this and stir to mix well. Smoothly spread the turkey-falafel mixture in an 8-by-12-inch oval casserole. Spread the remaining falafel over the meat mixture. Bake in a 350-degree oven until well browned, about 45 minutes. While the pie bakes, make a salad of 2 cups of diced, peeled jicama and 2 cups of diced cucumbers. Season to taste with rice vinegar and salt. To serve, spoon falafel pie from the casserole and offer low-fat plain yogurt and lime slices with it. You can serve the salad on crisp lettuce leaves. This lunch is so easy to prepare that even small children can do it. It became a favorite Mother's Day lunch in our family for that reason. Strawberries are ripe at that time, so you can make the lunch special by serving strawberries sprinkled with powdered sugar for dessert. Iced tea or a light zinfandel wine are perfect beverages for this lunch.

2. Grice's second maxim is "be truthful." How do you show that you are uncertain of the truthfulness of something you are about to say? Are such signals different from those you use as a teacher or student when you are unsure of your facts? If you use different signals in different contexts, how do you account for the change?

3. If you are not an expert conversationalist, in which direction regarding Grice's maxim of quantity do you think you err – too much or too little information or talk per turn? How different in this respect are your contributions in the classroom from those in an informal family setting? If there is a difference, how do you account for this?

4. Teachers often mark students' compositions as "unclear." Can you give a precise definition of "clarity"? How does your classroom definition compare with Grice's maxim of clarity?

5. Examine your classroom data (from Practice 1.2) for instances that illustrate each of the maxims (relevance, truthfulness, clarity, quantity). Transcribe an example of each. If there are examples in which Grice's maxims are flouted, transcribe these as well. If you work in a study group, discuss your findings. If there are sufficient data and the topic interests you, you might want to expand this into a research paper.

Conclusion

This chapter has presented the eight system constraints that Goffman claimed to be universal in all human communication. If you collected classroom data as a course project, you have data that could be used to support that claim in a special setting. We have also looked at the ways people use signals to regulate communication. (You may find the term "gambit" used in place of "signal" in some books, particularly in language teaching textbooks – see, for example, Edmondson 1981; Edmondson and House 1981; Faerch and Kasper 1982.)

In addition to system constraints, Goffman identified a second type of constraint on human communication: that which deals with the ritual or social constraints on communication. We have already touched on these in some of our examples in this chapter. This second constraint is examined in more detail in the next chapter.

Research and application

A. Transcription

1. Crookes (1990) and Ochs (1979) discuss the importance of determining the basic units in discourse analysis and using a transcription system that reflects such units. Review these articles and explain why this is an important issue.

B. Openings/closings

2. Godard (1979) shows that openings of French phone calls differ from those of American English. For example, French callers check to see if they have reached the *number* they are calling immediately after the "hello" response to the ringing of the phone. In addition, Godard found it necessary to distinguish between types of calls (marked for business, marked for intimacy, and unmarked calls) in order to determine the sequence of moves. Summarize the article and then explain why differences in openings and closings do not challenge the notion of system constraints.

3. The contrastive rhetoric hypothesis originates with Kaplan (1966, reprinted 1972). In addition to talking about ways in which students from different L1 (first language) groups develop compositions, he talks about the introductory sections of such compositions. Read this classic and then develop a preliminary research plan to investigate the contrastive rhetoric hypothesis as it relates to the introductions to *oral* presentations by the L1 groups represented in your classroom (or one you can observe). How might you collect data to see whether the introductory sections of talks of L2 (second language) learners are the same or different from those of native speakers? How might you determine whether their introductions are more similar to those used in the L1 groups?

4. Atkinson, Cuff, and Lee (1978) describe the ways in which meetings are called back to order. Compare the data in this study with those of your own meetings or data or your classroom following a break. Do the data agree with those of this study?

C. Backchannel signals

5. Martirena (1976) analyzed certain types of interaction signals in four conversations among speakers of Rioplatense Spanish. If you teach Spanish or have students whose first language is Spanish, you might read this article and compare Martirena's description of Spanish signals to the signals you teach in your classroom.

D. Turnover signals

6. Baker (1977) notes that there is a strong tendency for hearing persons to use the turn-taking signals of their oral language when communicating in Sign. Her article describes the turn-taking signals used in the ASL interactions she videotaped. Students of ASL, she states, have to learn these signals "the hard way" if they hope to have effective communication with native signers. As is the case in most language instruction, little if any attention is paid to this part of the language system. If you teach ASL, do you include instruction on the signals for each of Goffman's system constraints? If you teach English or another language to deaf students, describe any instruction you offer on the signals of system constraints.

7. Nystrand (1986) talks about the structure of written text as a reflection of the reciprocal needs of writer and reader. In a sense, there are turn-taking points throughout written text. These result when the author sees a possible trouble point for the reader. They are places where the writer may choose, for example, to offer definitions, examples, or elaboration to answer the "silent turn" of the reader. Writers do take their readers into account as they develop text. Nystrand's research shows that different types of readers have different needs; and so the choice of elaboration can become difficult if the writer does not have a specific group of readers in mind. Expert readers, Nystrand shows, want elaboration of details, and nonexperts want elaboration of the main idea. Look at the way in which Nystrand elicited data to show this difference. Does this difference of need for elaboration of detail versus need for elaboration of main ideas occur in your own reading? If so, document which you

need most in understanding course materials for your classes. Or, prepare a preliminary research plan to substantiate this expert/nonexpert difference with language learners.

E. Acoustically adequate and interpretable messages

8. Yule (1990) divided learners into two groups: more fluent, which he called "outer circle" students, and less fluent, the "inner circle" group. One student from each group formed a pair with the task of giving and receiving route descriptions (how to get from the post office or a bookstore to ten delivery points on a grid board). Yule found that pairs were better able to negotiate messages so that they were adequate and interpretable when the weaker (less fluent) student had control of the process (i.e., when the weaker student asked questions to get information on the route). Explain why the pairs should have better negotiation and cooperative strategies in the case where the weaker student controls the interaction. Is there any reason to believe that the difference attributed to proficiency might be to the language background of the students? (Students in the "outer circle" group were all from India, and those in the other group were from China and Korea.) After reading the article, design a research plan to replicate this study with your own students in such a way that language and proficiency level are not confounded. Or, design a project with native and nonnative pairs and describe the types of negotiation you expect to find.

9. Hatch (1983) lists the many features of foreigner talk register and the possible benefits of each. However, many people believe that such simplifications are not only unnecessary but unhelpful. In the following two examples, the first is a dialogue in which the native speaker avoids collaborative completions (i.e., does not supply lexical items the learner seems to be searching for). In Example 2 the learner manages to get collaboration in a very roundabout way. In each example, the learner is a native speaker of Spanish. Consider the positive and negative aspects of this register. How would you advise teachers to respond in such interactions? Should they use a simplified register? Give your rationale for this advice. Chaudron (1983) is a good source to check in making your decision.

Example 1
R: Saturday, Sunday ((eliciting "last weekend"?))
    me
    how do you say . . .
    Saturday, Sunday.

me in . . .
in car of my father.

NS: Where? In your father's car? Where did you drive?

R: Capistrano
me
my mother me go for my mother watch.
She watch house.
Me ((gesture of driving))

NS: Oh, are you looking at a house in Capistrano?

R: Yeh.
Mama say me
Mama say me
Mama no understand car.
You know?

NS: Yes, so she didn't want to drive.

R: Mama say me . . .
"Ricardo, you me go de Capistrano."
Me . . .
"Fred. Fred, please, keys for car.
Me a this for police (+ gesture)

NS: But you don't have a license, you just have a permit, right?

(Data source: Butterworth and Hatch 1978)

Example 2

NS: Oh, that's a beautiful plant!
I like that.
Did you buy that?

R: Excuse me
this is the . . .
October 24.
The how you say . . . the ((writes 1974))
year, ah?

NS: 1974. Last year.

R: Ah, last years.

NS: One. ((correction of plural))

R: Last year.
Last year a friend gave me it.

NS: Oh gave it to you! That's a nice gift!
Do you like plants?

R: Yes I like
This is my . . .
Miss Fain give me.
In October 24.

(Data source: Brunak, Fain, and Villoria)

10. Palmberg (1979) used Tarone's categories to investigate the ways that Finns, Finland Swedes, and Swedes made their English messages "acoustically adequate and interpretable."

Three concepts – avoidance, paraphrase, and transfer – were needed to account for the strategies these speakers used when they encountered difficulty in talking about a series of cartoon pictures (a couple quarrels as they wait for a bus; they board the bus and the woman gets a seat; when the seat next to her is vacated, the husband sits down; they resume their quarrel). The Finns tended to avoid or paraphrase difficult concepts rather than utilize transfer. The three strategies were equally employed by the Finland Swedes. The Swedes paraphrased as the first alternative, followed by transfer and avoidance. Palmberg notes a study by Ickenroth where less advanced Dutch learners of English used paraphrase much more than advanced learners, while advanced learners used many lexical substitutions. He concludes that not only the L1 but also the proficiency level and individual preference factors need to be considered in such studies. Do you think that the strategies used in this experimental task would be the same as that required in ordinary conversation? You might investigate this by taping students in a storytelling task and in conversation. After you have taped the conversation, ask the students to listen to the tape and talk about the problems they encountered in the conversation and the strategies they used to formulate comprehensible messages. Compare your findings with those of Hawkins (1984).

F. Grice's maxims

11. Kasermann and Altorfer (1989) suggest that a *noncooperative principle* might be needed to supplement Grice's maxims for cooperative conversationalists. They suggest that the maxims break down when dealing with conversations involving more than two participants. They call for research to show what types of factors determine behavior that deviates from the expected and an analysis of differences in amount and type of participation in conversations that occur when more than two parties are involved. After reading Kasermann and Altorfer's article, decide which of Grice's maxims is most seriously challenged and whether the challenge is sufficient to call into question the inclusion of the maxims as a universal system constraint.

G. Other communication signals

12. The prosodic system plays an important role in turn taking and also in preempt signals. If you are interested in phonology, you

will want to read Duncan (1972); the French and Local and the Cutler and Pearson articles in Johns-Lewis (1986); Brasil, Coulthard, and Johns (1980); and Crystal (1969). Each includes a substantial bibliography of studies that links prosodic features with components of the communication system. Prepare a paper that reviews the literature on this connection for one system component.

13. For accurate transcription, laughter in the data is transcribed. Although Crystal (1969) discusses the universality of laughter, very little has been written on the function of laughter in second or foreign language communication. Palmberg (1982) analyzed data from fifty-three Finns collected as they commented on a series of pictures that told a funny story. All instances on the "laugh-giggle continuum" were analyzed. Thirty-two speakers laughed. More than half of these were ignorance/ embarrassment signals: "Then he takes a bow and shots something ((laugh)) . . . er . . . er . .'Hjalp' . . . What is it?" Next in frequency were laughs signaling that the speaker was guessing about an expression: "A man comes out from a . . . from a house (= cave) ((laugh))." Other laughs signaled delight, as when the learner remembered a difficult vocabulary item. Still others signaled relief when they had finished the task; thus, tension could be dissipated with laughter. One speaker used laughter as a joke signal in his response to a question:

E: What did you call these? ((points to ants)) Did you say anything about those?
L: No unfortunately not.
E: What would you call them?
L: For example his cousins ((laugh)).

Palmberg poses a number of important questions that you might consider in your research: When does one actually laugh? Can a hierarchy of functions be established? Does laughing behavior change according to the language being used? There are many other questions that could be asked: When and how is laughter elicited? Are age, gender, status, and L1 differences related to choice of laughter form (the "laugh-giggle continuum")? How might laughter be used in opening/closing, backchanneling, as a preempt signal, as a relevant reply, and so forth? Look at laughter in your transcripts. Form a research plan to explain the occurrence of laughter in your data.

14. Saville-Troike (1985) talks about the significance of silence in the interpretation of talk. She suggests a broad classification that

includes functions or events relating to social action. The framework includes:

a. institutionally determined silence (*location:* libraries, temples; *ritual:* funerals, operas; *memberships:* monks with vows of silence; *hierarchical:* lower versus higher class; taboos)
b. group-determined silence (*situational:* access to speaking allocated by group decision; *normative:* differential allocation of time to children; *symbolic*)
c. individually determined silence (by social context, by linguistic context, or psychologically determined), and noninteractive (contemplative/meditative) silence.

Saville-Troike suggests that elaborating and testing such a taxonomy would give us a fuller appreciation of the complexities and universal characteristics of the human communication system. Study Saville-Troike's framework carefully and decide just how it might fit with Goffman's proposal for describing human communication systems. Can silence be appropriately used as a communication signal for any of Goffman's system components, or does it relate entirely to his social, ritual constraints on communication?

References

Atkinson, M. A.; Cuff, E. C.; and Lee, J. R. E. (1978). The recommencement of a meeting as a member's accomplishment. In J. Schenkein (Ed.), *Studies in the organization of conversational interaction* (pp. 133–153). New York: Academic Press.

Atkinson, J., and Heritage, J. (1984). *Structures of social action: Studies in conversational analysis.* Cambridge: Cambridge University Press.

Baker, C. (1977). Regulators and turn-taking in American Sign Language. In L. Friedman (Ed.), *On the other hand: New perspectives on American Sign Language* (pp. 215–236). New York: Academic Press.

Bauman, R. (1974). Speaking in the light: The role of the Quaker minister. In R. Bauman and J. Scherzer (Eds.), *Explorations in the ethnography of speaking* (pp. 144–160). Cambridge: Cambridge University Press.

Brasil, D.; Coulthard, M.; and Johns, C. (1980). *Discourse intonation and language teaching.* London: Longman.

Brown, G., and Yule, G. (1981). *Discourse analysis.* Cambridge: Cambridge University Press.

Butterworth, G., and Hatch, E. (1978). A Spanish speaking adolescent's acquisition of English syntax. In E. Hatch (Ed.), *Second language acquisition: A book of readings* (pp. 231–245). Rowley, Mass.: Newbury House.

Chaudron, C. (1983). Foreigner talk in the classroom – an aid to learning? In H. Seliger and M. Long (Eds.), *Classroom oriented research in second language acquisition* (pp. 127–145). Rowley, Mass.: Newbury House.

Cokely, D., and Baker, C. (1980). *American sign language: A teacher's resource text on curriculum, methods, and evaluation.* Silver Spring, Md.: T. J. Publishers.

Crookes, G. (1990). The utterance, and other basic units for second language discourse analysis. *Applied Linguistics,* 11, 2: 183–199.

Crystal, D. (1969). *Prosodic systems and intonation in English.* Cambridge: Cambridge University Press.

Cutler, A., and Pearson, M. (1986). On the analysis of prosodic turn-taking cues. In C. Johns-Lewis (Ed.), *Intonation in discourse* (pp. 139–155). San Diego, Calif.: College Hill Press and London: Croom Helm.

Duncan, S. (1972). Some signals and rules for taking speaking turns in conversation. *Journal of Personality and Social Psychology,* 23, 2: 283–292.

Edmondson, W. J. (1981). *Spoken discourse: A model for analysis.* London: Longman.

Edmondson, W. J., and House, J. (1981). *Let's talk and talk about it.* Munich: Urban & Schwarzenberg.

Faerch, C., and Kasper, G. (1982). Phatic, metalingual, and metacommunicative functions in discourse: Gambits and repairs. In N. Enkvist (Ed.), *Impromptu speech: A symposium* (pp. 71–103). Turku, Finland: Abo Akademi.

Fox, B. (in press). *Human tutorial dialogue.* Hillsdale, N.J.: Lawrence Erlbaum Associates.

Frank, J. (1989). On conversational involvement by mail: the use of questions in direct sales letters. *TEXT, 9,* 2: 231–259.

Freedle, R., and Lewis, M. (1977). Prelinguistic conversations. In M. Lewis and A. Rosenblum (Eds.), *Interaction, conversation, and the development of language* (pp. 157–185). New York: John Wiley & Sons.

French, P., and Local, J. (1986). Prosodic features and the management of interruptions. In C. Johns-Lewis (Ed.), *Intonation in discourse* (pp. 157–180). San Diego, Calif.: College Hill Press.

Godard, D. (1979). Same setting, different norms: Phone call beginnings in France and the United States. *Language in Society,* 6, 2: 209–219.

Goffman, E. (1976). Replies and responses. *Language in Society,* 5, 3: 254–313.

Goodwin, C. (1981). *Conversational organization: Interaction between speakers and hearers.* New York: Academic Press.

Gough, J. (1984). Play: A case study of language and pretense play within a family setting. Unpublished Ph.D. dissertation, Applied Linguistics, University of California, Los Angeles.

Grice, H. P. (1975). Logic and conversation. In P. Cole and J. Morgan (Eds.), *Syntax and semantics, vol. 3* (pp. 41–58). New York: Academic Press.

Gumperz, J. 1979. The sociolinguistic basis of speech act theory. In J. Boyd and S. Ferrara (Eds.), *Speech acts ten years after.* Milan: Versus.

Hatch, E. (1983). *Psycholinguistics: A second language perspective.* Rowley, Mass.: Newbury House.

Hawkins, B. (1984). Is an appropriate response always so appropriate? In S. Gass and C. G. Madden (Eds.), *Input in second language acquisition* (pp. 162–178). Rowley, Mass.: Newbury House.

(1988). Scaffolded classroom interaction and its relation to second language acquisition for language minority children. Unpublished Ph.D. dissertation, Applied Linguistics, University of California, Los Angeles.

Jefferson, G. (1972). Side sequences. In D. Sudnow (Ed.), *Studies in social interaction* (pp. 294–338). New York: The Free Press.

(1973). A case of precision timing in ordinary conversation: Overlapped tag-positioned address terms in closing sequences. *Semiotica, 9,* 1: 47–96.

Johns-Lewis, C. (1986). *Intonation in discourse.* San Diego, Calif.: College Hill Press and London: Croom Helm.

Jordan, B., and Fuller, N. (1975). On the non-fatal nature of trouble: sense-making and trouble managing in lingua franca talk. *Semiotica, 13,* 1: 11–32.

Kaplan, R. (1966). Cultural thought patterns in inter-cultural education. *Language Learning, 16:* 1–20. Reprinted In H. B. Allen and R. N. Campbell (1972), *Teaching English as a second language: A book of readings* (pp. 294–310). New York: McGraw-Hill.

Kasermann, K., and Altorfer, A. (1989). Obstruction in conversation: A triadic case study. *Journal of language and social psychology, 8,* 1: 49–58.

Martirena, A. (1976). A study of interaction markers in conversational Spanish. In W. McCormack and S. Wurm (Eds.), *Language and man. Anthropological issues* (pp. 269–286). The Hague: Mouton.

Nystrand, M. (1986). *The structure of written communication: Studies in reciprocity between writers and readers.* New York: Academic Press.

Ochs, E. (1979). Transcription as theory. In E. Ochs and B. Schieffelin (Eds.), *Developmental pragmatics* (pp. 43–72). New York: Academic Press.

Palmberg, R. (1979). Investigating communication strategies. In R. Palmberg (Ed.), *Perception and production of English: Papers on interlanguage. AFTIL, vol. 6* (pp. 45–68). Publications of the Department of English, Åbo Akademi, Turku, Finland.

(1982). Laughing matters – a look at some foreign-language communication data. *Scandinavian Working Papers on Bilingualism, 1,* 12–18.

Riggenbach, H. (1989). Nonnative fluency in dialogue versus monologue speech: A microanalytic approach. Ph.D. dissertation, Applied Linguistics, University of California, Los Angeles.

Rosenberg, B. (1975). Oral sermons and oral narratives. In D. Ben-Amos and K. Goldstein (Eds.), *Folklore: Performance and communication.* The Hague: Mouton.

Sacks, H.; Schegloff, E.; and Jefferson, G. (1974). A simplest systematics for the organization of turn-taking for conversation. *Language, 50,* 5: 696–735.

Saville-Troike, M. (1985). The place of silence in an integrated theory of communication. In M. Saville-Troike and D. Tannen (Eds.), *Perspectives on silence.* Norwood, N.J.: Ablex.

Schegloff, E. A. (1968). Sequencing in conversational openings. *American Anthropologist, 70,* 6: 1075–1095.

(1979). The relevance of repair to syntax-for-conversation. In T. Givon (Ed.), *Syntax and semantics. Vol. 12: Discourse and syntax* (pp. 261–286). New York: Academic Press.

Schegloff, E. A., and Sacks, H. (1973). Opening up closings. *Semiotica, 8,* 4: 289–327.

Schwartz, J. (1980). The negotiation of meaning: Repair in conversations between second language learners of English. In D. Larsen-Freeman (Ed.), *Discourse analysis and second language acquisition* (pp. 138–153). Rowley, Mass.: Newbury House.

Slade, D., and Norris, L. (1986). *Teaching casual conversation: Topics, strategies, and interactional skills.* Adelaide, Australia: National Curriculum Resource Center.

Speidel, G. E. (1987). Conversation and language learning in the classroom. In K. E. Nelson and A. van Kleeck (Eds.), *Child language, 6* (pp. 199–213). Hillsdale, N.J.: Erlbaum.

State Bar Pamphlets (1980). "Do I need a lawyer?" Communications Division, State Bar Pamphlets, 651 Brannan Street, San Francisco, CA 94107.

Williams, E. (1979). Elements of communicative competence. *ELT Journal, 34,* 1: 18–21.

Wong, J. (1984). Using conversational analysis to evaluate telephone conversations in ESL textbooks. Master's thesis, Applied Linguistics, University of California, Los Angeles.

Yule, G. (1990). Interactive conflict resolution in English. *World Englishes, 9,* 1: 53–62.

2 Communication theory: ritual constraints

In addition to system constraints, there is a second system of universal constraints on communication, which Goffman (1976) calls ritual (or social) constraints. These constraints smooth social interaction and interact with the system constraints. While the system constraints give us the components required for all communication systems, ritual constraints reveal the system of social markers that allow communication to flow in an appropriate way. For example, if we greet someone, we expect that our greeting will be welcome and that we will be greeted in return. When we contribute to a conversation, we expect that our contribution will be valued. We expect to receive our fair share of talk time and will, ourselves, allocate a fair share of turns to others. When we move to join an ongoing conversation, we expect that the move will seem reasonable and be granted. If we preempt a communication channel, we expect that our reasons for doing so will be judged as adequate rather than rude. When our talk is not clear, we expect listeners to give us some cues so that we may patch up the trouble ourselves. We don't expect others to point out our faults or fix them for us. Such ritual expectations form the fabric of social life. We try, throughout our interactions, to show that we and our communication partners are people of social worth. That is, the ritual constraints reveal the ways in which we present ourselves as competent members of our particular society. While ritual constraints govern communication of all social groups, the ways they operate vary from group to group.

Ritual constraints and system constraints

Let's begin by showing how ritual and system constraints interact, and highlight cross-cultural differences in discussing the interaction.

Ritual constraints in openings/closings

In all cultures, greetings are given and returned. If the greeting is not returned, something has gone wrong in the social interaction. Didn't the person see us? Was it inappropriate to greet this person? Is the person angry with us? *Why* wasn't the greeting sequence completed? Even if the greeting is returned, the opening must be of appropriate length so that both parties are given due recognition. In some cultures, Americans are often seen as rude and uncaring because their opening greetings are fairly short. Conversely, Americans who have learned languages where openings are lengthy often report

47

feeling uncomfortable asking about the health of family members whom they have never met, or being asked about their own relatives. Closings also differ across languages and cultures. In some languages, every person in the group must be spoken to in the closing. In other social groups, one can take leave with mainly nonverbal signals. If our openings and closings are too abrupt, we may be thought rude or angry, as though we did not wish to enter into communication and rushed to get out of it. If our openings and closings are too extended, we may be thought of as fawning, long-winded or boring, or self-centered – we have not considered the demands we make for time and attention. However the leave taking is done, it should be accomplished so that no one appears rude, unappreciative, or demanding of undue attention.

The conventions for openings and closings in written communication also differ across languages and social groups. Kaplan (1972), for example, has discussed variations in the openings to academic discourse papers written by international students from a number of first language groups. The differences in the students' expectations about how openings and introductory sections of papers should be done show quite clearly, he claims, in their English compositions. There are large differences also in expectations about what introductions to theses and dissertations are meant to establish. Students from other language groups who are writing their theses and dissertations in English often wish to fulfill the expectations of their first language regarding what must be shown in introductions – for example, that the writer has found and has reported on what every previous author has said about the subject and is, therefore, an authority on the subject too. However, their American academic advisors often object that such writing is pedantic, irrelevant, and self-serving. They insist that students highlight the basic questions and an evaluation of the solutions as background to the new research; the focus should be on questions and ideas, not on a listing of every piece of research previously undertaken.

Americans attempting to write their theses and dissertations in foreign language departments are often faced with the reverse. Their advisors complain that they have not shown the necessary scholarship to cover all the literature in detail and, thus, have not demonstrated that they have a solid base from which to undertake the research. Again, differences in how openings and closings are to be done in order to show that participants have demonstrated social and intellectual worth differ, and perceptions regarding these differences can have important social consequences.

Practice 2.1 Ritual constraints in openings/closings

1. If you have lived in or visited another country, you may have found that openings of phone conversations were carried out differently. What differences did you find?

2. Kasper (1982) gives an example in which a German EFL student used the following opening at a party where people were speaking English: "Excuse me please, may I ask whether you are alone here?" What might a native speaker say as a similar opening in this setting?

3. Inexperienced writers sometimes use inappropriate closings in their compositions. In the following examples written by university students, it is possible that the closings were meant to be friendly notes to unknown readers, rather than genuine closing statements! The first three examples are from Scarcella (1976); the final example is from Urzua (1989).

   a. But time is up and let me stop here. Thank you!
   b. So, my country has been developed economically. . . . I hope that the change should be plus rather than minus. Thanks for reading!
   c. The people of my country is happy and hopeful. They have jobs and enjoy the life. I just came from there and wish you'll have a chance to take a look.
   d. [Concluding an essay that describes a special English program for chemical engineers.] If in the future you would like to visit Mexico, don't forget you'll find a lot of friends here in U de G. And if you need a hand, here mine.

   Collect papers from two language learners and determine how you would conclude each paper. What changes, if any, would you make? (Discuss these revisions with members of your study group.) Why, or in what way, are your closings more "appropriate"? What suggestions do you have for sharing these ideas with the papers' authors?

Ritual constraints and backchannel signals

When we begin a conversation, we expect that others wish to converse with us and will value what we have to say. In part, we judge this willingness in terms of backchannel signals. If backchannel signals differ across cultures (and they do), we may misjudge the value placed on our participation. An anecdote may make this clear: A group of Soviet teachers of English came to my university. Many of them used the English word "well" as a backchannel signal rather than "mmhmm," "uhh," or other common English backchannel signals. The American teachers, reacting to this inappropriate (for English speakers) backchannel signal, felt that the worth of what they were saying was continually being challenged, while the Soviet teachers thought they had signaled interest and support for the speaker.

Nonverbal backchannel signals may also vary. In classroom lectures, American students usually nod and smile to signal that they are following the lecture, understand it, and find it interesting. Students from other language groups may use such head nods and smiles to indicate that they are listening but not necessarily following or appreciating the lecture. Frowns and lack of eye contact may be signals to lecturers that the material is not clear and needs to be revised or that the material is already known and the lecture is therefore boring. Teachers become disoriented if they find that their reading of such signals is wrong. For example, I have misread frowns as meaning lack of understanding and have revised and revised only to find out that the frowning students were trying to tell me they already knew the material and wondered why I should drone on about it forever!

Practice 2.2   Ritual constraints and backchannel signals

1. If backchannel signals are withheld even after an initial repair, we usually believe the silence is a request for another repair. We may believe the person withholding the backchannel signals disagrees with us but, because confrontations are unpleasant, decides to say nothing. In the following examples, what does the speaker do when the backchannel signals are withheld?

   > B: . . .an' that's not an awful lotta fruitcake.
   > (1.0)
   > Course it is. A little piece goes a long way
   > (Data source: Pomerantz 1984)

   > E: I really don't like it.
   > (.8)
   > I mean – well, it's not so:: bad, I guess.

2. Tao and Thompson (1991) give examples where fluent English-Mandarin bilinguals still use English backchannel signals (aha, um, yeah, uhhuh) instead of Mandarin ones (ao, a, ei, dui/shi) when speaking Mandarin:

NS:	. . . Suoyi beifang ren na, zhuyao jiushi chi "mianshi.	The northerners mainly flour-food.
Bilingual:	/Aha	
NS:	/Nanfang jiu shi dami.	The southerners rice.
Bilingual:	Aha.	

   Consider the backchannel signals you use in speaking your second language (particularly if you teach that language). Are they typical of native speakers of that language, or are they more like those of your first language? If you are an

English teacher, do you ever notice your international students using the backchannel signals from their first language in place of English backchannel signals? What difference does it make whether L1 or L2 signals are used? Does it matter if backchannel signals are used more often or less frequently than in the second language?

3. Sometimes, communication partners do backchannel *exchange* sequences. The listener may say "yeh," the speaker contributes a "right," and the listener another "umhmm," before the speaker picks up the turn again. It's been suggested that Spanish speakers tend to exchange backchannel cues (as shown in the following example) more often than English speakers.

P: Y e ¿te gusta aquí? ¿la USC?
J: Sí. Me gusta. Hay cosas que me gustan y cosas que no me gustan.
P: ¿Cómo cuál?
J: que las clases están muy difíciles
P: Uhum sí
J: Sí
P: Uhum.
J: Para mí han sido muy difíciles.

(Data source: Scarcella 1983)

Review the backchannel signals in the classroom data you taped for Practice 1.2. Are there exchanges of backchannel signals such as those described by Scarcella for Spanish?

4. Erickson (1985), analyzing videotaped job interview data, showed that cultural differences in nonverbal feedback caused stress during an interview. The interview began as the applicant of Italian-American background and the interviewer of German-American background sat down. The interviewer glanced at the application form and began the interview by saying "Just got your degree . . . one year in Rome huh." The applicant began his explanation happily: "Right . . . Loyola University offers a junior year abroad program and," but then produced a series of disfluencies, "ah . . . at the moment of . . . ah . . . accepting or not I . . . ah . . . decided to go . . . ah," and finally finished the turn smoothly, ". . . it was a great experience." Over the following weeks, the applicant and the interviewer reviewed the videotape, and each commented on this segment of the interview. By looking at the nonverbal cues, frame by frame in this segment, Erickson noted that at the beginning of the

disfluent section, the interviewer looked away and began drinking from his coffee cup. The interviewer returned eye gaze at the end of the turn, when the speaker resumed fluent speech. The applicant felt the interviewer wasn't interested in what he had to say. His cultural assumptions were that if he were interested, the interviewer would not just sit there, but move while listening and say something. The interviewer stopped the tape at the same place, but his interpretation was that the applicant was nervous and, therefore, should be allowed to continue talking about Rome in the hope that he would calm down. By being less animated kinesthetically, the interviewer meant to put the applicant at ease, but only ended up making him more nervous. Fortunately, the applicant got the job, but clearly the expectations caused the interviewer and the applicant to become progressively more distant rather than closer during the interview.

Mismatch in feedback signals can cause difficulties in communication. This is true of nonverbal signals too – in this case, ethnic differences in nonverbal signals. Do you think there is any difference in the communicative power of verbal versus nonverbal feedback signals? Are there any instances of nonverbal feedback in your classroom videotape? If so, check your interpretation of the signals with the students who made them.

Ritual constraints and turnover signals

In communication, we expect to receive our fair share of turns at talk. What is "fair" differs across cultures. Power among participants is often reflected not just by length of turn but also by who introduces topic switches at the beginning of a turn. If status differences are heavily coded in language behavior, turns, turn length, and topic shifts may differ according to gender, role, and social status.

The gaps, or small silences, between turns at talk also differ across language and culture groups. Although overlaps and collaborative completions occur in American conversations, more frequently the turn is exchanged "on cue," with only a tiny gap between turns. However, in Scandinavian languages, gaps between turns are relatively long. In other languages, turns may be tightly latched; that is, the gap is so slight that speakers almost overlap.

Zimmerman and West (1978) claim that Americans interpret overlong pauses before a turn is taken up as a signal of feigned involvement, lack of understanding, lack of interest, unwillingness to continue the topic of conversation, and lack of desire to interact. In learning another language in which the gap between turns is shorter than their own, Americans may feel they are being rushed (that what they have to say is inconsequential) or that speakers of this language are being pushy or aggressive. Some researchers have found that the gap between turns of English speakers in various parts of the United States also differs. People in urban areas of the Northeast, for example, tend to have shorter gaps and more overlaps than people in rural areas of the Northeast. And they, in turn, have shorter gaps and more overlaps than those living in rural areas of the Midwest and South. What's important is not differences in length of gaps but the social interpretation made of this small difference. (Another personal example may make this clear: I have very long gaps between turns at talk; a colleague has very short gaps. He tries to hurry me along, but, being obstinate, I wait an even longer time. He tries valiantly to add some spark to the conversation, moving it along at his rate. This mismatch of gaps distorts the rhythm to such an extent that we always end up irritated with each other.)

Overlaps, as noted in Chapter 1, seem to occur most frequently in the conversations of family and close friends, where overlaps signal encouragement, where there are lots of collaborative completions, and where everyone "chimes in" as a story is told. Such overlap of talk has been reported for personal talk among many ethnic groups. As long as the message does not become garbled, overlaps help create a great deal of camaraderie. Overlaps let the speaker know that he or she is not talking to the wall – everyone is participating.

Practice 2.3   Ritual constraints and turnover signals

1. Conversations are supposed to be *symmetrical* – that is, each party should receive a fair share of turns at talk. However, we know that in conversations between language learners and native speakers, native speakers often take a more active role. To illustrate, Holmen (1985), working from 20 videotaped conversations between Danish upper-secondary school students and a native speaker of English, found that the learners would fall somewhere between "passive" and "very passive" on the chart in Figure 2.1. Note the criteria used for rating the degree of activity.

   The features in the chart suggest that conversations between language learners and native-speakers might more resemble an interview. The turns and turn lengths are not symmetrical. How could you use this chart to characterize the difference between a conversation and an interview?

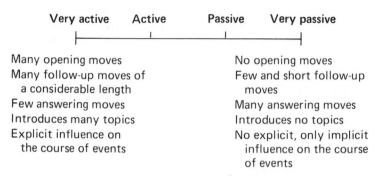

| Very active | Active | Passive | Very passive |

Many opening moves

Many follow-up moves of
a considerable length

Few answering moves

Introduces many topics

Explicit influence on
the course of events

No opening moves

Few and short follow-up
moves

Many answering moves

Introduces no topics

No explicit, only implicit
influence on the course
of events

Figure 2.1

What other features would you want to use to differentiate the two? If you use an oral interview as a measure of communicative competence, do you think "communicative competence" means "conversational competence" more than "interview competence"? If so, what suggestions might you make to turn the interview into something closer to a conversation?

2. Sato (1990) looked at turn taking in ESL classrooms. She was particularly interested in whether teachers distributed turns equally and whether students from different language groups took equal numbers of turns. Sato found that Asian students took fewer turns on their own initiative than non-Asian students. If possible, observe one class and determine whether ethnicity makes a difference in the number of turns students take. If there are large differences, ask students in the class to collect similar data. Note whether their findings agree with yours. Ask them to explain their findings. (You could follow this with a study of whether such awareness leads to changes in turn taking in the classroom.)

3. Overlaps in turn taking can be either good or bad. In the following conversation, Julie (JU), a Chinese student, and a friend have been discussing a birthday party that both attended. The NS has just said that at the end of the birthday song, people sang "and many more."

NS: That means you should have lots m//ore birthdays.
JU: //Oh I see. I see. I see. In our country we:: (.8) is a (.4) people (.8) uh (.6) when they (.3) have a birthday (.3) we just family cel- celebration. Not like Amer//ica.
NS: //No friends?
(.7)

JU: Yeah:h. No. They just-uh neat-eat-uh noodle. Means the:: (.)
they live the long long time. Like the noodles. Very//long
NS: //uh::
JU: Not like here. Here is-uh they =
NS: = well she had – a lot of her family here. Her daughter (.3)
who lives in Washington (.) //I dunno if you remember.
JU: //Oh: I see.
NS: seeing her. Very pretty young woman. =
JU: = Uh-huh.

(Data source: Riggenbach 1989)

While a common theme of "birthday celebrations" is clear in the transcript, neither speaker is really collaborating with the other. Each appears more concerned with her own message than with collaborating on the message of the other. Comment on the overlaps and feedback signals given by each speaker. Notice the number of long pauses in Julie's first turn. What might the NS have done at these points to assist Julie to build her message about birthday celebrations in her country?

4. It is said that Americans cannot stand silence in conversations, and rush in to fill the gap whenever it occurs. Language learners complain that they never get a chance to talk because Americans ask a question and then answer it themselves! What does this suggest about differences in the timing of turn taking?

5. Can you think of other languages or language groups where the gap between turns seems to be longer than for American English? Can you think of languages or language groups where the pause between turns seems to be shorter than in American English? What cross-cultural misunderstanding do you believe might result from the mismatch?

Ritual constraints and acoustically adequate and interpretable messages

While all communication operates under the system constraints of acoustically adequate and interpretable messages, there is a good deal of leeway as to what constitutes an adequate message. Social consequences are obvious when messages are either too acoustically adequate or acoustically inadequate. For example, in ordinary conversation, friends use a relaxed register of speech where careful enunciation is not demanded. In fact, if they enunciate each word clearly, or if they are unable to match the general articulation patterns of those around them, there are sure to be social consequences. Beebe and Giles (1984) is a good source to consult regarding Giles' accommodation theory – a theory which shows that people try to match the language of those with whom they interact as much as possible in order to show that they are aligned or identify with that social group. On the other hand, for those who wish to separate themselves in some way from the social group – perhaps to obtain autonomy – adjustments and matching may be much less strong.

In Chapter 1, we discussed the adjustments that take place when we talk with people who are less expert in the language or the content material being discussed. Foreigner talk, clinician talk, teacher talk, and baby talk are thought to be registers that, if pitched at the right level, may help learners take a more effective role in communication. On the other hand, such registers may have deleterious social consequences. Most language learners are quite aware that these adjustments are being made. Depending on how they view the person making the adjustments, they may see them as helpful or as insulting. All of us have probably been infuriated when teachers or parents or strangers treated us as incompetent either because they misunderstood our contributions or because they just looked at us and decided we couldn't possibly understand. And all of us have heard of people who speak very loudly or even yell when they decide foreigners do not understand them. When registers are used in a thoughtful, helpful manner, however, both partners take part in a benevolent conspiracy to mask any inadequacies that take place during communication. The goal is to show that each values the other as a person of social worth.

Practice 2.4   Ritual constraints and adequate messages

1. Examine your classroom videotape from Practice 1.2 for instances where you believe students attempted to show solidarity by "accommodating" their physical gestures or their language to each other (or to the gestures or language of the teacher). Transcribe or view these sections and share them in your study group. How might this accommodation be helpful, and how might it impede language learning?

2. Conversational analysts categorize repairs as speaker-initiated or listener-initiated and as speaker-corrected or listener-corrected. We don't expect others to point out our faults or to fix them for us, so self-initiated repairs and self-corrections are much to be preferred. We've noted before that even silence is one way of getting the speaker to notice that something is wrong and needs to be repaired:

   NS: Where have you traveled (0.5) besides Iran and here?
   → (3.0)

NS: Whe- which countries have you traveled in.

(Data source: Gaskill 1980)

If your classroom data has a large number of repairs, attempt to divide them into repairs made by learners and those made by native speakers. Then divide each according to whether the repairs are self-initiated – that is, not prompted by others – or initiated by others. Are the repairs completed by the speaker or the listener? Do you think this subdivision of types of repair is helpful for your data? If so, what does it reveal?

3. According to your classroom data, do the students use English pause fillers (e.g., "umm," "uhh") or those of their first language? Faerch (1979) gives examples of Danes using Danish pause fillers "erm" and "er" in their English repairs: "I'll start erm ((sigh)) er – I learn erm shirts and er ((laugh)) can't explain that." Gaskill's (1980) data, on the other hand, shows a Farsi speaker using the same pause fillers as native speakers of English: "That film wa- uh (1.4) tis starts- its stars.hh uh was uh (4.2) Peter uh::: Robert Edford and. . . ." Lehtonen (1979) says that Finns keep quiet – they use unfilled rather than filled pauses. Once you have identified the pause fillers, ask the students to listen and comment on them too.

4. In conversations with friends, learners often solicit correction, particularly in vocabulary searches. Sometimes these invitations for repair are successful, and sometimes not.

L: Yeh .hhh uh (1.0) ss: some movies from America or other countries. (.8) that (1.0) comes to Iran

NS: mhm

L: in double. Y'know double. T-translate?
(1.6)

NS: Uhh:: oh yeh in trans-translation – Whadiya mean (.4) a double
(.2)

L: Do//ouble

NS: Dou- Yeh:::: I-I don't know I don't (.4) //know what that is.

L: //that is (.8) hhh uh I don know, we say double?

NS: Uhun.

(Data source: Gaskill 1980)

Can you guess what English word L wanted the NS to supply? Notice the 1.6 pause. Why was it difficult for the NS to supply the repair? Did you find similar repairs in your classroom data? Would you expect to find more such invitations to repair in the classroom? Why or why not?

Ritual constraints and bracket signals

Bracket signals differ across language groups, and the appropriateness of allowing asides, or side sequences, also differs. In academic discourse, for example, some language groups allow for what might be called a very ornate style, where personal comments, anecdotes, and illustrative side sequences are valued. In other language groups (or even in other disciplines), no such diversion is allowed. Footnotes or notes may be used, but side sequences and the markers that provide ways of tracing back to the original thesis are not allowed.

Moreover, in many language and social groups, it is a mark of excellence to offer as little connection between mainline and side-sequenced materials as possible. The inference is that if one is an educated person, the allusions given in side sequences are easily processed, their connection to the ongoing text is clear, and it is insulting to the listener to overtly draw the connection by use of bracket signals. Even in languages where bracket markers are common, it is difficult to say "Huh, I don't get it. How does that relate to what we were talking about?" To admit that we don't understand is tantamount to saying the speaker hasn't carried off the side sequence well enough for us to understand. We show ourselves to be incompetent and at the same time challenge the social competence of the speaker – neither of which we wish to do.

Practice 2.5   Ritual constraints and bracket signals

1. L. Haynes (personal communication) has noted that in Guyanese social discourse, asides are given without overt bracketing, and participants are challenged to make quick connections. Can you think of another language or social group for which this is also the case?
2. Have you ever missed brackets (e.g., didn't know that a joke was being told in a bracketed side sequence until everyone laughed) and felt "left out" of the social group? Or, have you ever had participants in a social group suddenly switch to a language you don't know and then back again? What other types of brackets can have the same social effects?
3. If you found few bracket signals in the compositions you used in Practice 1.6.3, ask the writers why they seldom use bracket material. Do they prefer to use footnotes rather

than parentheses? Is their choice of bracket signals a
matter of length, of formality, or an effect of instruction?
4. You may have noticed the large number of parenthetical
comments in this book. Do these "asides" give a more
informal, conversational tone to the writing? Do you think
women use such comments more often than men in their
writing? Are asides appropriate for an academic textbook?

Ritual constraints and nonparticipant signals

Most of us do not feel entirely comfortable attending a party where we know
practically no one. We may stand around hoping that someone will approach
and engage us in conversation rather than try to join a group that is already
conversing. Though we may know the conventional signals for joining the
group, we may not be sure our entry into the group will be seen as valuable.
When our host draws us into a group, introduces us, and tells us something
about the others, he or she is trying to build a bridge by establishing that we
do indeed belong to the group and that each member of the group has something of worth to contribute.

Imagine, now, that you are a beginning language learner and that you are
not sure of either the language or the social constraints linked to moving into
a group already engaged in conversation. (Recall the example given by Kasper
where German EFL students said "Excuse me, please, may I ask whether you
are alone here?" or "Would you like to drink a glass of wine with me?" as
ways of opening a conversation with someone at a party.) Even though you
may know how to move from nonparticipant to participant status in your
first language, you may not know how to do so in your second language. Not
knowing the forms and worrying that the use of an inappropriate form might
cause members of the group to reject you can make this a painful task.

Practice 2.6   Ritual constraints and nonparticipant signals

1. Design a role play where students must move from
nonparticipant to participant status. If you work in a study
group, compare the role plays and select the best. What
signals, in addition to those we discussed in Chapter 1 (e.g.,
joining in during laughter, repeating part of what a speaker
has said, and giving a "reason" for commenting on it), could
language learners use in these role plays? (You might like to
run an experiment to compare how well learners carry out
such role plays with and without prior discussion of the
signals.)

2. There are times when teachers must talk to some students but not to others (who may want to be included). How would you go about assigning nonparticipant status without being rude? Would you use particular bracketing signals to do this?

3. Whispering seems to be an "exclusion" nonparticipant signal. Small children whisper to keep things secret from others in the immediate environment. In the computer room where I work, students working at other terminals often whisper as a way of not disturbing others. I am seldom aware of people talking while I'm working, but as soon as they whisper, I immediately pay attention. What is the social role of whispering? Is it the same in other languages? If possible, ask international students for help with this. Would they ever whisper, rather than speak in a low voice, to avoid disturbing others?

4. Does passing notes serve the same function as whispering in the classroom? At what age (if ever) do these behaviors seem less appropriate? How does doodling, writing notes to yourself, and subvocalizing differ in function from whispering and passing notes?

Ritual constraints and preempt signals

When we give a preempt signal, we expect those already engaged in a conversation will judge that we have a right to interrupt the conversation – that we will not be seen as rude. Again, what counts as an acceptable interruption differs across language and culture groups. As an example, I have on occasion taught in universities outside the United States, and I was amazed to learn that, although professors were certainly placed at a high status level in most of these countries, all sorts of preempts could take place during my faculty lectures. I have been interrupted by tea servers coming by to take orders for tea, cigarettes, and biscuits; by office people wanting to distribute materials for other courses; by family members wishing to talk with students (and did so in the classroom); and by other faculty and even deans wishing me to leave class to have a conference with them. None of these preempts would be appropriate in the United States, and, to my shame, my reactions let the preempter know I thought the behavior inappropriate. In each case, I was angry but, once I became more familiar with the cultures, I too looked for the entrance of the tea server as a socially and personally necessary part of the lecture session. And I understood why all the other interruptions were appropriate, given the time and transportation constraints working in the social system. Nevertheless, my initial reaction was to interpret these preempts as disrespectful.

Practice 2.7   Ritual constraints and preempt signals

1. Observe the ways that very young children interrupt conversations. How "socially acceptable" are the interruptions? How do parents or elementary school teachers make the interruptions (or attempts to become participants in conversation) more acceptable?

2. Most research studies show that men account for between 75 and 95 percent of the interruptions (overlaps where the other speaker then yields the turn) in male-female conversations. We've already noted that overlaps can be "good" in terms of showing solidarity if the overlaps are collaborative completions. However, they can also be "bad" if the initial speaker loses the floor and the interrupter shifts to a new topic. If status is used to explain why men account for most of the interruptions, and if teachers have higher power status than their students, one would expect to find a somewhat different pattern in a classroom with a female versus a male teacher. Identify all the overlaps that work as interruptions in your classroom data (from Practice 1.2). What is the ratio of teacher to student interruptions and of the male to female interruptions?

Ritual constraints and Grice's maxims

We expect that listeners will judge our talk not only as *relevant* but also as a valuable contribution to the theme of the conversation. Sometimes, we later realize that what we said to someone (or in class) was really not relevant, and we feel embarrassed. We call our own competence into doubt. Teachers sometimes have to work hard to make all the contributions of their students seem relevant to the ongoing theme of the discussion. Not to protect students in this way is seen as poor teacher behavior. This, however, is not the case in all cultures: When the maxim of relevance is violated, students are brought to task.

We also expect that contributions to a conversation be *truthful* – the speaker says what he or she believes to be true. If we are not very good at discerning the intonation of irony or sarcasm – which is often so when we are learning a language – we may misunderstand the speaker's intent completely. When, however, people tell us untruths, we may feel hurt if we think we are being misled. But there are ways to get people who are telling us untruths to stop and correct themselves. For example, silence, as every parent knows, is a powerful backchannel signal that leads children to rethink and revise their statements.

The maxim of *quantity* differs greatly among language and social groups. The allowable quantity of talk relates, of course, to turn taking. Some people, because of their social roles, receive more turns and are allowed longer periods of talk. For example, in religious services, only a limited number of people are allowed to talk for any length of time. The people who conduct the service, because of their special roles as priest, rabbi, minister, and so forth, produce the greatest quantity of talk. These same people in other roles and settings – for example, in their homes or as guests at a party – receive only their "fair" share of talk time. The quantity maxim, however, also relates to the amount of information given in talk. We all know people who are boring because they tell us too much, give us too much detail. We also know people who seem to delight in giving too little information; in this case, we may feel that the person is trying to show his or her superior knowledge by making us ask for clarification. Neither is a "cooperative conversationalist," and such behavior has social consequences within our society.

There are also social consequences linked to the notion of *clarity*. All of us have our own view of what is needed for clarity. For example, in American academic prose, it is customary to use headings to promote clarity – to help the reader remember the writer's focus or theme. Many believe these are helpful and important signals. Others feel they are insulting to the reader; the reader is not given the option of discovering or creating his or her own clarity in the message. Different standards of clarity are also found cross-culturally. International students at American universities often protest that an academic style with headings and numbers is too childish and, even when instructed to use this system, refuse to do so. So much clarity, they feel, trivializes the message.

Ritual constraints relate to clarity in yet another way. When an American's talk is not clear, the listeners are expected to give the speaker cues so that he or she can repair the message. Listeners are not expected to overtly correct the speaker. In some cultures, this is not the case. Bald corrections are offered without any fear of appearing rude. Most Americans, receiving such bald corrections, would view the speaker as rude, perhaps aggressive, and attempting to establish dominance (i.e., "She's such a know-it-all").

Practice 2.8   Ritual constraints and Grice's maxims

1. Examine your classroom videotapes (from Practice 1.2). Does the teacher ever attempt to make a student response more relevant? How is this signaled? Compare these signals with those found by others in your class or study group.
2. List situations for which you think irony and sarcasm might

be effectively and appropriately used. Describe the ways that irony and sarcasm might be shown nonverbally as well as verbally.

3. Check your language textbooks to see whether there are lessons on the use of intonation to mark irony or sarcasm. If you are a teacher, ask your native speaker friends or colleagues to tape-record examples of irony and sarcasm in your lessons and play these back for your students. Can they always identify the intended irony?

4. "Appropriate" quantity of talk can vary from culture to culture. If you speak another language, have you noticed differences in the *amount* of talk that seems appropriate per turn? Are there differences in appropriate length of turns for males versus females? for older persons versus young people?

5. In Practice 1.9, you were asked to think about what teachers mean when they mark "unclear" on students' compositions. From a ritual constraint viewpoint, what difference would it make if a teacher wrote this at the top of a student's paper versus beside a small circled section of the paper? To find out, you might do this on a sample composition (written by someone not in the class) using an overhead projector. Ask students what difference it makes, and have them comment on how they would feel if they received such feedback.

6. Johnson (1989) looked at how students comment on "trouble points" – places where improvement is needed to make the message clear – in each others' compositions during peer correction. When we write, we hope our work will be viewed as interesting, important, informative, and well written. Critically analyzing someone else's message is always a face-threatening act and so suggestions for improvement must be offered with care. In Johnson's study, the students first offered compliments ("I learned a lot about . . . from your paper"), then the softened criticism ("Perhaps . . .," "I have some small suggestion to make here"), and then gave a final message of cooperation or solidarity ("I hope my observations have been helpful," "Good luck, and let's hang in there"). If you use or have observed peer correction (whether notes written on a composition or letters to the writer), examine how these requests for clarity also show an awareness of the need to avoid embarrassing the writer. (You may want to prepare a

preliminary research plan if you have sufficient data and find this an interesting topic. You may also want to consider asking students for their reactions to teacher and peer correction as Smith (1989) did in the article "It Doesn't Bother Me, But Sometimes It's Discouraging.")

Summary

Ritual expectations form the fabric of social life. When these expectations are not met, we feel hurt, rejected, and unhappy. According to Goffman (1955, 1967, 1969, 1972, 1974), we want to show ourselves as worthwhile and competent, and we also want to show that we value our interactors as people of social accomplishment. We do not always succeed or perform as smoothly as we'd like, even when we communicate with another native speaker. And, as language learners, we know that misunderstandings occur even though we may be proficient speakers of the language.

Consider an exchange between an Indian industrial worker and an English staff person, an example discussed by Gumperz (1982). In the exchange, Gumperz notes that the worker was attempting to sign up for a class for professional people, assuming it was appropriate for him to apply. The staff person, however, knew that the worker did not qualify and thought it inappropriate for him to apply.

The participants later listened to themselves on tape and made comments about the exchange. The Indian worker said he thought the staff person's tone of voice was impolite because it was so high. He also said that the staff member constantly interrupted, showing she was not paying attention to him. The interruption pattern made the worker lose his turn, and, to show he wanted to regain it, he raised his voice. The staff member did not understand that the worker wanted a turn to talk, but simply thought he was angry and shouting.

In Gumperz's example, part of the misunderstanding could be attributed to mismatch in turn taking. Part could be attributed to a mismatch of social meanings of pitch, stress, and volume. And some part of the misunderstanding must be attributed to mismatch in ritual expectation regarding the class application processes (i.e., if applications are announced, applications can be made; if application forms are filled out, application forms are to be accepted). In any case, neither side succeeded in showing the other person that he or she was a worthwhile and competent interactor, a person of social worth. (For further examples drawn from interethnic communication, see also Gumperz 1977, 1990, and Gumperz and Tannen 1979.) To present ourselves favorably and, at the same time, to accommodate others is not a simple task. Nevertheless, it is crucial if the communication is to be successful.

Practice 2.9 Summary practice on ritual and system constraints

1. As learners of another language, we worry about presenting ourselves as competent persons. The native speakers of that language with whom we interact may also concern themselves with protecting us – a benevolent conspiracy to mask our shortcomings. Think about your own learning experiences and how each of the system constraints is overlaid with ritual constraints that govern how they are carried out in a socially appropriate way in the new language. List each component (i.e., opening/closing, backchannel signals, and so forth) and then the differences you have noticed for each in the languages you have learned. In which have you been most and least successful in presenting yourself as a competent person? What social judgments did you make about your native speaker partners because of these differences? What social judgments do you suppose they made about you?

2. Review the classroom data you taped and transcribed for each of the system constraints. How have ritual constraints interacted with these? If some were carried out in an inappropriate manner, what types of instruction might be used to highlight this interaction of ritual and system constraints?

Social competence and face

In his analysis of ritual constraints, Goffman suggests that each of us has to learn social conventions for "presentation of self" and "presentation of other." In presenting ourselves, we want to project a demeanor of modesty yet behave in a competent manner. When we blunder, we want to recover with poise. Think of the many times when you have mulled over "what I should have said" or "what I should have done." Our new version of the interaction somehow shows us to be a more modest, more competent, or more caring person than we actually were.

There are many stereotypes about men and women that have to do with demeanor – one is that women are more concerned with showing modesty and men are more concerned with appearing competent. However, what is considered an appropriate show of competence or modesty differs according to gender. For example, men are considered less modest because of their willingness to interrupt others in order to say what they think – and what they think demonstrates competence. It was noted in Practice 2.7 that in business meetings and in male-female conversations, men take longer turns and interrupt more frequently than women. This seems strange because people who have power can control the turn-taking system; they do not need to interrupt. If those without power are to have a chance to display competence, they may need to steal turns by interrupting others. Thus, interrupting in order to gain a turn demonstrates a lack of power. It might be interesting to see how we judge interruptions according to gender. Is an interruption a display of appropriate assertiveness and competence, or is it inappropriate aggressiveness and lack of modesty?

To behave in a modest way, we should (usually) be circumspect in self-reference. As small children, we are warned not to brag. Older writers are told to use passive voice instead of always referring to themselves as the agent. In everyday conversations, we may court the spotlight (e.g., in sharing our troubles, in telling what happened to us) but then soften the focus in various ways. Of course, there are times when a healthy dose of lusty swaggering and bragging is also appreciated.

Butler-Wall (1986) suggests that modesty can be established in conversations with disfluency markers such as false starts, repetitions, "uhh," "y'know," "I mean," "I think," and so forth. In the following example, Mark (M) shows modesty regarding his abilities as a super salesperson as much by disfluency markers and laughter as by lexical choice:

M: yeah (.8) but is it it's not I don't know it's (.8) not that hard =
L: = mmhm
M: just have to learn to DO it take just (.9) learn your PITCHES (.9) ((Laugh)) and how to deal with people I guess it's not that bad at ALL.

Even in direct bragging, some of the claims to glory are softened by disfluencies. These are shown in Butler-Wall's transcript of Pete (P) as he brags about his high school class.

P: That's good I (don't) know my my class (.8) for (1.3) for (our) CLASS we were a GREAT class because we were like I was state champion in dramatic interpretation of LITERATURE we had my class there was also the (1.1) um state (1.7) VOCALIST the best male vocalist in the //state
X: //mmhmm =
P: was in my class the best FEMALE vocalist was in my class we were (1.1) champions of our league. . . .

Language learners, too, are "fluent" in use of disfluencies as markers of modesty.

D: (1.5) so I'm kinda know a lot of WEAPONS stuff ((laugh)).

The use of self-deprecating laughter, disfluencies, and the softening of technical vocabulary (note D's use of "weapons stuff" rather than technical munition terms) all help portray speakers as modest persons.

66

In presentation of self and of others, sports stars may be an exception! Listen to sports stars as they are interviewed on television. They are less concerned with modesty than with claims to prowess. Since most of our concepts are regulated through metaphor, you might think of sports contests as "war." In war, we do not usually try to show that our enemies have social worth. We are seldom modest about how competent, right, or strong we are.

All of us, of course, do a great deal of self-presentation or *self-staging,* to use Goffman's term. For example, in the preceding transcript about "our class," P put on a dramatized show while the listener was primarily obliged to show audience appreciation. When we dramatize stories, tell what happened to us, or engage in complaints about the actions of others, we may become an animator, a figure who seldom seeks a simple answer to a question or compliance with a request but rather most often desires an appreciation of the show put on. Still, the self-displays in such talk are supposed to get audience appreciation of the figure animated, not the animator. Goffman was very interested in the nature of self. For him, self was "not an entity half concealed behind events, but a changeable formula for managing oneself during them" (1974: 573). Individual and social constraints play a very important role in our understanding of ourselves and our roles in discourse.

Ritual constraints on communication include not only ways of presenting self, but the ways we give face to others. In everyday discourse, we often defer by avoiding delicate topics, we reassure our partners, and we avoid open disagreement. We ask permission to tell tales. When we realize our messages are not clear to the listener, we highlight important items and mark background information and asides. When we don't understand the other person, we given nonverbal or nonthreatening feedback to that effect. We allow the other person to correct or repair troublesome messages. We offer hints or act doubtful rather than challenge errors. Even in teenage confrontation where self-staging is most important, the other side is insulted and challenged in what may appear to be a demeaning way, yet the challenge recognizes the opponent as someone worthy of that challenge. (Teenage bragging, insult hurling and rejecting, and swaggering give us evidence of a whole series of cultural and social values as well as the ways in which we do self-staging. See, for example, Mitchell-Kernan and Kernan 1977, or just listen to the content of rap music.)

Ritual constraints can help override breakdown in communication content. Even when we know (and everyone else knows) that we are beginners learning a new language or beginners learning new content, we are aware of the stigma attached to incompetence. As learners, we try to disguise this incompetence in many ways. Our teachers and friends also engage in a benevolent conspiracy to avoid embarrassing us. They help us smooth over or cover up our incompetencies. Of course, not all learners have fragile self-esteem, yet corrections and repairs, if offered at all, are usually done with great tact. For example, more fluent speakers may protect the face of less fluent learners by accepting "off target" comments as "on target," resulting in radical topic shifts. The conversations may also take on an interview quality as the more fluent speaker tries to find a safe topic that will allow the less fluent speaker an opportunity to take part. This can result in a series of mundane topics of little interest to either party. In fact, the question asker may even know the answers to the questions.

The following exchange is between two immigrant students, a Spanish student, Jose, and a Vietnamese student, Vinh. Notice the strategies each student (particularly Jose) uses to protect the other and to move the conversation along.

J: Well uh + + how was you vacation?
V: Uhh vacation vacation very good
J: very good.
V: and you?
J: good too. How many places do you uh you meet? A new places?
V: Oh I – I /gwen/ the /ple/ + + Long /bi?/ + + San Diego.
J: Long Beach and San Diego?
V: and you?
J: Well, I go to-to the church, I go + to the beach the mornings + an I go + billard pool, y'know? b-big tables? many balls?
V: Yesss
J: Yeh. (1.) You make a drawings? a new drawin's?
V: Yesss
J: Uh in a color or black and white?
V: Yesss
J: Uhhuh. You gonna be a millionaire o famous maybe.
V: Yesss. Where do you work?
J: What kinda work I have? I have a a I made a plas-uh parts for airplane + an the rubber /bens/ fo:r – but bigger.
V: Big. Yesss.
J: Yeh annn uh a many things of plastic like uh the microphones? o the airphones?
V: oh yesss
J: Uhhuh and air conditioner too.
V: Yeh. Where do you work?
J: In uh Hawthorne El Segundo
V: Yes
J: I /tuka/ freeway.
V: Yes. Freeway. Yes. Yes.
J: Yep. Yep. You have a car ah right now?
V: Yes, now I don't have a car here. I do::: buy car /nek/ week.
J: Next week uh espensiv one? O?
V: Yes /pensiv/

(Data source: Brunak, Fain, and Villoria)

After Jose asks about his vacation, Vinh politely asks Jose about his. They ask and respond to each other's questions in a conspiracy of understanding.

When Vinh replies "yesss," a sure sign he does not understand, Jose continues right on as if the response were entirely appropriate. Vinh's immodest reply to Juan's prediction that he will one day be rich and famous is overlooked as he expresses an interest in Jose's work. Each has worked hard to advance the conversation along and to present himself as a competent conversationalist.

There are many situations where the presentation of "self" and presentation of other take on special importance. Some of these are formal situations, such as when we are called on to introduce someone. When we introduce people to each other, we must give them face and also show that we are competent at introductions. The stress this causes often makes us forget each other's names! The introduction must be sensitive to status and setting. Think for a moment of the difference between introducing professional friends at business meetings and introducing friends who have just dropped in to see you. The introduction must be just right for the occasion and the people involved. Success (your vision of yourself as a competent person) is sometimes as difficult in these first-language situations as it is in another language or culture.

In some sense, our demeanor or modesty in presenting ourselves as competent individuals, and our use of deference in presentation of the other, is bound up with other interpersonal needs. Tannen (1985) suggests that, as we communicate with others, we are faced with decisions on how to resolve our conflicting interpersonal needs of being connected with and yet of staying autonomous from others. To show connectedness, we indicate involvement, friendliness, and solidarity. To maintain autonomy, we recognize distances between people, being deferential and considerate. In each encounter, we may adjust the weight given to each of these needs. Certainly there are cultural norms as well. That is, the degree of connectedness or independence is set, in part, by the social expectations of our own cultural group. There is a good deal of variation within cultural groups. Tannen suggests that over time we develop a conversational style (or a series of styles) that shows in the choices we make as individuals. For example, connectedness is shown in our choices of personal rather than impersonal topics. In conversations with high connectedness there is a great tolerance for loosely associated topics. The "point" of the talk may be implicit rather than explicit.

Our multiplicity of roles and shifting personal needs for connection and autonomy can be shown through a discourse analysis that focuses on ritual as well as system constraints.

The following excerpt illustrates the tolerance for loosely associated topics and the implicit rather than explicit point of conversations among close friends. In this example, three friends are discussing a personal topic – their reactions to a wedding reception at which vegetables rather than flowers were used to decorate the tables.

1   MD: Actually I would not have chosen vegetables . . . for my wedding either
            . . . but they were interesting.
       BH: Did you LIKE them?
       MD: Mmmm I wouldn't have picked them
4   BH: I didn't think they were::: (5.0)
       MD: I mean, I wouldn't, I wouldn't have requested them.
       BH: Besides which, what're y'gonna do with five million chilis – five million
            green chilis?
7   MD: ((laugh)) I wanna //go in there.
       GD: //Y'could have a chili* bakeoff.
       BH: Yeah, right – MY mother have a chili bakeoff! ((loud laughter))
10 GD: ((loud laughter)) Mrs. Lee's Chili Bakeoff!
       MD: I wanna go into Silver Birches someday. Never been in there.
       BH: It's kind of a neat store.

Notice that MD gets overlapped in turn 7 as she first says she wants to go "in there" and again in turn 11 when she says she wants to go to Silver Birches, the store that does wedding and party decorating. The association to the decoration scheme is not made explicit. Mention of the store is quickly accepted as implicitly "relevant" to the topic. At this point, there is a sound in the background.

((Whistle sound in the background like a cherry bomb falling))
13 GD: What was that?
       MD: ((Whistles in imitation))
       GD: Are we being bombed?
16 MD: Picolo Pete.
       BH: Yeah, //that's what it sounds like.
       GD: //Have you been* listening . . . to W's reports?
19 B: Haven't heard 'em in a long time.

The sound of a cherry bomb reminds GD of bomb sound effects (turn 15), which in turn reminds her (turn 18) of such sound effects on a local early-morning radio show that features comedy routines based on current events. "W" is a character in one such routine, a woman reporter, who is always being sent off with no help to cover the news. She usually gets as far as the local gas station. The trail of associations that sets off this loosely associated topic shift is never called into question. Rather, it is greeted with a giggle from MD (line 21), an encouraging backchannel signal.

20 GD: Well she got down there, and of course –
       MD: ((giggle))
       BH: Last I heard// – W: (high pitch voice) "I don't wanna go to San
                 Salva – I don't wanna go to El Salvador," and then she says, but
                 well, y'know, (low pitch voice) "Go down and make your
                 reservations" (high pitch) "Well, give me the money." (low
                 pitch) "We – WE're not paying for it!" (high pitch) "Well, I bet
                 Connie Chung got HERS paid for."

23 GD and MD: ((loud laughter))
    BH: //"No!" (low pitch)
    GD: //(low pitch) "No!* That's the way ALL radio stations deal
                  with their workers" =
26 BH: = She went down in the interest of . . . good reporting. (low
                  pitch) "Now, W, I don't ((laughing while talking)) wanna hear
                  anything more about it."
    GD and MD: ((laughter))

Notice the collaborative storytelling. GD began the story (turns 18 and 20);
BH took up the narrative (turn 22); GD and BH alternate the telling (turns
24, 25, and 26), and GD then concludes the story (turns 28 and 30).

28 GD: Well, she was down there and you could hear 'er in the phone
                  booth – 'course they won't accept a collect phone call.
    BH and MD: ((laughter))
    GD: k-k-k-kkk ay-yay-yay-yay-Ay! Ay! Ay! ((static sound effects))
                  then she says – y'can hear 'em saying,' (low pitch) "Can't you tell
                  them to keep it down in there?" n' she says, (high pitch) "I tried,
                  but they don't understand me!" n then she says that she had t'
                  get a job, cuz she couldn't afford t'stay in the hotel. (low pitch)
                  "Well, what are you doing?" She says . . ., (high pitch) "I'm
                  picking bananas – six foot, seven-foot, eight-foot bunch – Uunh!!"
31 MD and BH: ((loud laughter))
                  (3.0)

Now, the topic shifts from W to other characters on the radio show (turns 32
to 35) to some known plan to make up a contest game for the show (turn 36).
There is no attempt to say "Remember that idea we had once?" The only clue
is the "I still wanna write." The topics are loosely related.

32 BH: I think I like W one of the best of their characters.
    MD: I tell ya, I still wanna write t' them, or call them someday, and ask them
                  for a list of their characters, cuz one ti – a list of their "staff." One time I
                  hada list //of their staff.
    BH: //Well, Mary*just DO it – that's all!
35 MD: I:: kno::w.
    GD: But I still want them to have the contest.
    BH: Well, I think what we oughta – what you oughta do t'get this contest
                  going is that . . . you oughta write for the list – Mary, this is your job –
                  you write for the list, and once you get the list, we'll start either drawing
                  or collecting pictures, OK? and then we'll get it together and we'll send it
                  in 'n then say, "Have a contest."
38 MD: Alright.
    BH: Now, Mary, DO THAT!!
    MD: ALRIGHT – I WI::LL!!
41 BH: Oh – you've said THAT before. //((laughter))
    MD: //((laughter))

                                                    (Data source: Hawkins)

The discourse is performed in a collaborative style by the friends. There are frequent overlaps and even shouts of laughter, response cries that urge each other on. Academicians all, their talk in an education setting would call forth a very different, more autonomous and less connected style.

Practice 2.10 Presentation of self and of other

1. One task that many people find difficult to do is preparing a résumé (curriculum vitae, or CV) for job applications. Here the task is to suppress modesty and display competence. Prepare a résumé for yourself. Examine it for displays of modesty. Compare it with those of your study group members. What kinds of things did you neglect to mention that might have made you appear more competent? How can you state your experience in a stronger way? Do you feel these changes constitute unwarranted bragging?

2. One way teachers establish self and protect others is by the use of disfluencies. Examine the classroom videotape data you collected for Practice 1.2 for disfluencies on the part of the teacher. How do these help portray him or her as both a competent and a modest person? How do they work to protect students in the classroom? How important are these disfluencies in establishing rapport between the teacher and students?

3. One way we protect others, at least to some extent, is by not pointing out their errors. In the following transcript, I is a native speaker of English and H is a student whose first language is Farsi. I and H are talking about how difficult it is to find a good apartment near campus. Identify instances where the native speaker accepts a topic shift and where he offers a correction. How do these give face to the nonnative speaker?

    I: but you have to take TIME to look for them.
    H: (.5) Y//eh
    I: D'ya*-d'you have ti:::me?
    H: hhh (.4) a little
    I: Not too much //hmm-hm h* -mmmm hhh
    H: //No.* (1.) hhh (.4) uh: (1.0) I took two class in graduate
    I: Mhm
    H: (1.) I am graduate
    I: Uhuh. What ary-what are you studying?
    H: (1.0) m:athematics.
    I: Uhuh (1.0) and uh two classes (.4) and and arya taking English?

H: An' English class, yes.
I: Mhmm. That's three class//es*?
H: //Ye*ah.

(Data source: Gaskill 1980)

Compare these with face-saving moves in corrections offered by the teacher or students in your videotaped classroom data.

3. You may have noticed that people from other countries often introduce themselves in terms of their professional affiliation – "I belong to Sumitomo Bank." This provides information that might otherwise be casually asked for later in conversation – "And what do you do?" How often, and in what circumstances, do American English speakers give their affiliation in self-introduction or in their introductions of others?

4. As a class experiment, let's see how we present self and others in formal introductions. Look at the following fictitious résumé. Decide how you want to introduce this person as a speaker to one of the following groups: speaker on stuttering of bilingual children at a meeting of the American Speech and Hearing Society; speaker on careers in art for women to students at a local city college; speaker at a clinic for beginning runners at a sports store in a shopping mall. Decide whether you know the speaker well (as a childhood friend) or whether you only know of her. In your study group, have one person introduce the speaker to the others in the group. Tape-record the introduction.

Elizabeth Simone

Education

M.A., Language Disorders – California State University, Northridge
B.A., Philosophy – University of California, Los Angeles
A.A., Art – Santa Monica College
High school diploma – University High, with honors program in History, University of California, Los Angeles
Nondegree program in Art – California Institute of the Arts

Professional Experience

• Editor, *Scrambler,* a magazine for runners, 1981 to present
• Free-lance writer and illustrator, *City Sports, Ultrarunner,* and *Audubon,* 1980 to present

- Volunteer assistant coach, women's cross-country running, California State University, Northridge, 1987 to present
- Accountant (part-time), AvCom, Pearblossom, California, 1981 to present
- Instructor (language pathology clinic), California State University, Northridge, Summer 1980
- Speech pathologist, Los Angeles Unified School District, 1978–1980
- Speech pathologist, Veterans' Hospital, Los Angeles, 1976–1978

Publications and Honors
- Articles for *City Sports* on triathlon training and women in athletics, 1985–1986
- Illustrations for *Audubon* and *The Tanager* (a Los Angeles newsletter), 1980 to present
- "Clinician's talk," *Journal of Speech and Hearing,* 1980
- *Three Lines,* a children's novel, Doubleday, 1978
- "Women in Art," art show, Santa Monica College, 1981
- American age-group record holder, TAC, 15K
- Overall woman 10K, six races
- First in division, 10K, twenty-eight races

Travel
- U.S., India, Middle East, and Europe

Memberships
- ASHA (American Speech and Hearing Association)
- San Fernando Track Club
- Santa Monica Track Club

Hobbies
Running (road and cross-country), biking, swimming, painting, writing, bird-watching

(a) What information did the introducer select for the introduction? What information was left out? Why? (b) What information did the introducer give about himself or herself during the introduction? (c) What parts of the introduction are concerned with showing the professional competence of the speaker? (d) Are there parts which present the nonprofessional side – the special unique qualities – of the person? If so, how do these enhance the presentation of other?

5. Think about the different ways in which you interact with other teachers or students. How differently do you show

connectedness versus autonomy in your interactions during coffee breaks or lunchtime and during teacher meetings?

6. In the next few days, note the kinds of topics you raise in communicating with others. Prepare a list and the setting in which each topic was raised. Can you classify the topics as personal versus impersonal? Can you classify them in terms of connectedness or autonomy? Does the setting influence the type of topic? Do your topic choices in family conversations differ drastically from those with your professional colleagues? Can you discern a personal style (or range of personal styles) regarding connectedness versus autonomy in your choice of topics?

Conclusion

In Chapter 1, we examined systematicity in discourse in terms of the components of communication. Although the system constraints are universal in all human communication, each language uses its own particular form of signals to meet these constraints. In this chapter, we have looked for systematicity in discourse in terms of ritual constraints. Ritual constraints are also common to all languages, but the ways in which they are reflected in language differ widely across language and social groups. Together the system and ritual constraints provide a starting point for discourse analysis and research on cross-cultural communication.

Research and application

A. Openings/closings

1. Scarcella (1984) contrasted the opening sections of compositions written by students from different L1 groups with those of native speakers of English. After you have read her article, compare the types of openings used by Scarcella's subjects with those of your own students or those you have observed.

B. Backchannel signals

2. Tao and Thompson (1991) contrasted the forms and functions of backchannel signals in Mandarin and English, and described data from two highly fluent English-Mandarin bilinguals speaking with native speakers of Mandarin. According to this study, Mandarin speakers use relatively fewer backchannels in conversations than English speakers. The backchannel signals

overlap more often in English; in Mandarin there is a noticeable pause before the signal. The functions also differ in that the signals are used most frequently to show understanding, confirmation, or acknowledgment of agreement rather than to urge the speaker to continue. In spite of their fluency in Mandarin, the two bilinguals used English backchannel signals rather than Mandarin forms. One example was given in Practice 2.2; here is another.

Bilingual 2:	Neige yingyang meiyou. Yingyang yao shao de duo.	That thing doesn't have much nutrition.
NS:	Meiyou ying yang.	No nutrition.
Bilingual 2:	<u>Yeah.</u>	
NS:	<u>Ao</u>	
Bilingual 2:	Yingyang bu hao.	Not good in nutrition.

Not only did the bilinguals use English backchannel signals, but they used more signals, and often overlapped – evidence for L1 transfer. Design a preliminary research plan that would consider the question of automaticity of such signals. It has been claimed that one reason phonological transfer is stronger than lexical or syntactic transfer is that these are highly automatized patterns. The same might be true of the form and timing of backchannel signals. How might you investigate this question?

3. Fishman (1978a) found that the backchannel comments of men and women differ. In cross-sex conversations, she found that women use frequent exclamations of appreciation tightly latched to the male's talk.

M: I saw in the paper where Olga Korhut Korbut=
F: =yeah=
M: =went to see Dickie.
F: You're kidding! What for?
M: I don't know.

Women also "worked harder" to maintain the flow of conversations. For example, they used more "tickets" to get attention to the topic and asked questions to get responses from men. In the following exchange, the woman is reading a book in her field and the man is making a salad. Notice the minimal backchannel signals and the lack of any expression of appreciation or collaboration signaled by the relatively long (4.0) pause before the male introduces a new topic.

F: I didn't know that.

M: Hmmm?

F: Um you know that ((garbage disposal on)) that organizational stuff about Frederick Taylor and Bishopgate and all that stuff?

M: UhHmm ((yes)) =

F: = in the early 1900s people were trying to fight favoritism to the schools

(4.0)

M: That's what we needed. (18.0) I never did get my smoked oysters.

Consider the issue raised by Fishman (1978b): Since this work is related to what a woman *is,* the idea that it *is* work is obscured. The work is seen not as something women do but as part of what they are. Do you think that one could determine what it means to be male or female in a particular society by studying each of Goffman's system components in cross-sex communication? Give an example to support your answer.

C. Turnover signals

4. Rawlinson (1986) tape-recorded natural conversations of native speakers and nonnative speakers and then lengthened the pauses or gaps between turns (a pilot study showed no effect for shortened pauses but strong effects for lengthened pauses). The taped voices (with normal and lengthened pauses) were judged for social and intellectual characteristics by American university students. When pauses were longer than normal, speakers were judged more negatively in regard to ambition, cheerfulness, attractiveness, and confidence regardless of gender or nationality. There was no difference in calmness, unselfishness, or adjustability. Male speech with longer pauses was judged even more negatively than female speech with longer pauses on intelligence, warmth, kindness, and acceptingness. According to Rawlinson, this implies that males involved in same-sex conversations may be expected more than females involved in same-sex conversations to fill a gap between turns. "Men may simply be expected to be more aggressive" (p. 100). In an earlier discussion about interruptions, I noted that men interrupt more often than women, and I viewed this as a negative trait. Here, Rawlinson suggests that language learners may want to observe the timing and overlaps of native speakers and think about how speakers are judged if they lengthen time between turns. Discuss this issue with members of your study group and also with your students. What consensus can you get on the importance of matching time between turns to that of native speakers?

5. Blum-Kulka (1990) discussed "metapragmatic comments" –
   including talk about turn taking – of Hebrew-English bilinguals
   (in Israel). She found that more talk about turn regulation
   occurred in the English data, and more talk about behavior
   occurred in Hebrew. Here is an example with Marvin, age 7, and
   Daniel, age 6; the data are dinner table conversations:

   Marvin: Can I say something? Is it my turn?
   Mother: I don't know.
   Daniel: No! You have to wait until I finish!
   Marvin: You had a long turn, so there.
   Daniel: You had a longer one.
   Marvin: No, I didn't.
   Daniel: Yes, you did.
   Father: Daniel, are you finished saying what you were saying?

   The bias for one language or another for specific tasks has often
   been noted in bilingual classrooms. If you teach in such a
   program or can tape dinner table conversations in your bilingual
   home, examine the data for instances of talk about the system
   constraints. Is one language rather than another used more often
   to talk about these constraints? You may want to compare your
   findings with those of Blum-Kulka.

6. Volk (1990) looked at the allocation and acknowledgment of turns
   by four-year-old bilingual children in peer conversations, and
   noted that the children used self-selecting allocators such "ay
   dios" or "pero" in taking turns.

   N: (to Patricia) Pero Kathy
      Yo voy para casa de Kathy.
      (to Kathy) Right, Kathy?
      I'm going to your house?
   K: (nods yes) You're gonna come next week.

   If your taped data for Practice 1.2.5 is from a bilingual
   elementary school, read Volk's article and then categorize the
   types of moves used by the children to claim turns or nominate
   others to take turns. How similar are your findings to those in
   Volk's study?

D. Repair

7. Gaskill (1980) gave examples in which the language learner,
   Hamid, did a self-repair without any apparent cues from the
   native speaker that there might be some trouble with the
   utterance. The self-correction shows that the speaker is capable

and competent enough to do this work – thus demeanor is preserved.

Example 1
H: . . . I can:: (1.5) uh (1.0) I can to get a job in (0.6) uh (0.4) at a:: (2.0) somewhere dat uh (1.0) has a computer:

Example 2
H: . . . I tink ah (0.7) I can::: (0.3) correct de pa::per (1.0) uh homework (0.4) uh (0.4) coin- (0.2) students' homework.

In the first example, Hamid changes "in" to "at" and then moves to "somewhere," which does not require a preposition (such repairs, of course, are not really attempts to correct grammar but rather to find a better way to express his hope of finding a job). In the second example, Hamid's repairs result in a more specific definition of the types of papers he might correct if he obtained a job as a tutor. In Example 3, Hamid repairs the native speaker's question into his own form prior to formulating an answer to the question.

Example 3
NS: What would HAppen if you went back HOme and did not get your degree::?
    (2.8)
NS: What?=
H: = Uh IF (1.0) if I can't get degree? and (0.8) uh:: (1.3) I come back (1.0) to my country?

Hamid self-initiates and self-corrects his repair in the first two examples; in the third, he initiates repair on the native speaker's question – rephrasing it to see if this is what he was asked. Other-initiated repairs where the speaker goes ahead to correct himself are shown in the following example from Dittmar and von Stutterheim (1985):

NS: Haben Sie auch schon mal Arger gehabt?
    (Did you already get into trouble?)
L: ja, ja, hab ich schon Arger gemacht
    (yes, yes, I caused already a lot of trouble)
NS: nicht Arger gemacht, sondern Arger
    (not caused trouble, but you got)
L: gehape, gehape, gehab
    (got, got, got)

You might investigate which settings and kinds of interaction get repairs that are self-initiated and self-repaired, and which are face threatening – other-initiated and other-repaired. In what settings are repairs that preserve demeanor or give face less important than those that instruct or correct?

8. McHoul (1990) looked at repair in high school geography classes and found that there were instances within turns where students self-initiated repairs (e.g., in word searches). However, the most prevalent pattern was for the teacher to use "clues" or question reformation as a repair initiator and for students to self-repair the trouble source. Other-corrections occurred but only after the teacher tried for, but failed to get, the student to make the correction. That is, other-correction was a last resort. Thus, McHoul concluded that there is no difference in preference for self-repair in classroom and ordinary conversational interactions. Read this article and compare McHoul's findings with the repairs you located in your classroom tape (from Practice 1.2). If you are especially interested in this topic, ask the members of your study group to share their data so that you can research this topic in depth. Consider sharing your findings by sending your paper to one of the journals listed in the appendix.

E. Other communication signals

9. The analysis of system and ritual constraints provided in Chapters 1 and 2 covers openings and closings but does not look at mini-openings and closings within one communication unit. Each time there is a topic shift within a conversation, there are small closing and reopening moves. You may notice this in teachers' use of "Okay"-"Okay" sequences. These "okays" mark the end of one topic and the start of another. Other second signals are "(okay) so" and "(okay) now." In conversations, native speakers of English are more likely to use the preclosing moves of "yeh, so, umm" to signal the end of a topic. These signals differ across languages, and, as shown in the following personal note, they cannot be translated verbatim from the first language.

While living in Spain, an English-speaking friend and I noticed that many times, after we had been talking at length with Spaniards, they would say "Pues nada." At first, we felt a little insulted, since translated, it meant "Well, nothing," as if what we had been saying was worth nothing. Due primarily to our aggravation, which slowly turned into curiosity, we decided we were going to figure out what it meant. We therefore began taking mental notes of the times when we heard it, and reported back to each other our findings. We finally narrowed it down to the fact that it was used whenever there was a lengthy pause in a conversation. Having realized this, we decided that the next time we were out with Spaniards, we would say it whenever such a pause occurred. When we did, the mystery unravelled itself, for every time we used it, without fail, a new topic of conversation was begun. "Pues nada" was a way of closing one topic and moving on to another.

(Data source: Hribar)

Give this note to your international students and ask them for the topic-shift signals used in their language. Prepare a research plan to discover whether these signals are presented in the textbooks used to teach these languages. If you are motivated to carry out this project, consider sending your report to the *MLA Journal* for publication.

10. Along with laughter and other nonverbal signals that accompany speech, weeping can have a function within discourse that relates to the portrayal of "self" in Goffman's definition of that term (i.e., "Self is not an entity half concealed behind events, but a changeable formula for managing oneself during them.") Hill (1990) analyzed the incidence of weeping in a story told by a Mexicano woman. She found that sobs, gasps, and sniffles occurred at phrase boundaries, so weeping did not disrupt the syntax of the message. However, weeping did disrupt the intonation contours that were an important part of the "fidelity" of the woman's portrayal of characters in her story. Weeping also "flooded" across episode boundaries and thus might have disrupted comprehension of the story. However, Hill argues that weeping and tears are important markers of openness and sincerity in this culture and, thus, were coherent with the central theme of the woman's story – portraying her "good" selfhood in spite of life's trials and tribulations. The weeping served an expressive function underscoring and paralleling the storyteller's verbal portrayal of self. Read Hill's article and think about how her method of analysis might be applied to the study of either laughter or weeping in a second or foreign language context. What important new questions could be asked about "face" and such nonverbal signals in the second or foreign language context?

References

Beebe, L., and Giles, H. (1984). Speech accommodation theories: A discussion in terms of second-language acquisition. *International Journal of the Sociology of Language, 46,* 5–32.

Blum-Kulka, S. (1990). You don't touch lettuce with your fingers: Parental politeness in family discourse. *Journal of Pragmatics, 14,* 2: 259–288.

Butler-Wall, B. (1986). The frequency and function of disfluencies in native and non-native conversational discourse. Ph.D. dissertation, Applied Linguistics, University of California, Los Angeles.

Dittmar, N., and von Stutterheim, C. (1985). On the discourse of immigrant workers. In T. van Dijk (Ed.), *Handbook of discourse analysis. Vol. 4: Discourse analysis in society* (pp. 125–152). London: Academic Press.

Erickson, F. (1985). Listening and speaking. In D. Tannen and J. Alatis (Eds.), *Language and linguistics: The interdependence of theory, data, and application* (pp. 294–319). Georgetown University Round Table, Washington, D.C.: Georgetown University Press.

Faerch, C. (1979). Describing interlanguage through interaction problems of systematicity and permeability. Paper presented at the 17th International Conference on Polish-English Contrastive Linguistics, Boszkowo, Poland. See also articles in E. Glahn and A. Holmen (1985), *Learner discourse.* Anglica et Americana 22, Department of English, University of Copenhagen, Denmark.

Fishman, P. (1978a). Interaction: The work women do. *Social Problems, 25,* 397–406.

(1978b). What do couples talk about when they're alone? In D. Butturff and E. Epstein (Eds.), *Women's language and style* (pp. 11–22). Akron, Ohio: L & S Brooks.

Gaskill, W. (1980). Correction in native speaker–non-native speaker conversations. In D. Larsen-Freeman (Ed.), *Discourse analysis in second language research* (pp. 125–137). Rowley, Mass.: Newbury House.

Goffman, E. (1955). On face-work: an analysis of ritual elements in social interaction. *Psychiatry, 18,* 213–231. Reprinted in J. Laver and S. Hutcheson (Eds।., *Communication in face to face interaction* (pp. 319–346). Harmondsworth: Penguin.

(1967). *Interaction ritual: Essays on face-to-face behavior.* New York: Anchor Books.

(1969). *Strategic interaction. Conduct and communication, no. 1.* Philadelphia: University of Pennsylvania Press.

(1972). Alienation from interaction. In J. Laver and S. Hutcheson (Eds.), *Communication in face to face interaction* (pp. 347–363). London: Penguin.

(1974). *Frame analysis.* New York: Harper & Row.

(1976). Replies and responses. *Language in Society, 5,* 3: 254–313.

Grice, H. P. (1975). Logic and conversation. In P. Cole and J. Morgan (Eds.), *Syntax and Semantics, vol. 3* (pp. 41–58). New York: Academic Press.

Gumperz, J. (1977). Sociocultural knowledge in conversational inference. In M. Saville-Troike (Ed.), *Language and anthropology. Monograph series on language and linguistics* (pp. 191–212). Washington, D.C.: Georgetown University Press.

(1982). *Discourse strategies.* Cambridge: Cambridge University Press.

(1990). The conversational analysis of metaethnic communication. In R. Scarcella, E. Andersen, and S. Krashen (Eds.), *Developing communicative competence in a second language* (pp. 223–238). New York: Newbury House.

Gumperz, J., and Tannen, D. (1979). Individual and social differences in language use. In C. Fillmore, D. Kemplar, and W. S. Wang (Eds.), *Individual differences in lan-*

guage ability and language behavior (pp. 305–326). New York: Academic Press.

Hill, J. (1990). Weeping as a meta-signal in a Mexicano woman's narrative. *Journal of Folklore Research, 27,* 1/2: 29–49.

Holmen, A. (1985). Distribution of roles in learner–native-speaker interaction. In E. Glahn and A. Holmen (Eds.), *Learner discourse* (pp. 70–89). Anglica et Americana 22, Department of English, University of Copenhagen, Denmark.

Johnson, D. M. (1989). Politeness strategies in L2 written discourse. *Journal of Intensive English Studies* (University of Arizona, Tuscon, Arizona), *3,* 71–90.

Kaplan, R. (1972). Cultural thought patterns in inter-cultural education. In H. B. Allen and R. N. Campbell (Eds.), *Teaching English as a second language: A book of readings,* second edition (pp. 294–310). New York: McGraw-Hill.

Kasper, G. (1982). Pragmatische Defizite im Englischen deutscher Lerner. *Linguistik und Didaktik, 10,* 370–379.

(1982). Teaching-induced aspects of interlanguage discourse. *Studies in second language acquisition, 4,* 2: 99–113.

La Barre, W. (1972). The cultural basis of emotions and gestures. In J. Laver and S. Hutcheson (Eds.), *Communication in face to face interaction* (pp. 207–224). Harmondsworth: Penguin.

Lehtonen, J. (1979). Speech rate and pauses in the English of Finns, Swedish-speaking Finns, and Swedes. In R. Palmberg (Ed.), *Perception and production of English: Papers on interlanguage. AFTIL, vol. 6* (pp. 27–44). Publications of the Department of English, Åbo Akademi, Turku, Finland.

McHoul, A. W. (1990). The organization of repair in classroom talk. *Language in Society, 19,* 349–377.

Mitchell-Kernan, C., and Kernan, K. (1977). Pragmatics of directive choice among children. In S. Ervin-Tripp and C. Mitchell-Kernan (Eds.), *Child discourse* (pp. 189–208). New York: Academic Press.

Pomerantz, A. (1984). Agreeing and disagreeing with assessments: Some features of preferred/dispreferred turn shapes. In J. Atkinson and J. Heritage (Eds.), *Structures of social action: Studies in conversational analysis* (pp. 57–101). Cambridge: Cambridge University Press.

Rawlinson, M. W. (1986). The interpretation of timing between conversational turns: A study of native speakers and nonnative speakers of English. Master's thesis, Brigham Young University, Provo, Utah.

Riggenbach, H. (1989). Nonnative fluency in dialogue versus monologue speech: A microanalytic approach. Ph.D. dissertation, Applied Linguistics, University of California, Los Angeles.

Sato, C. (1990). Ethnic styles in classroom discourse. In R. Scarcella, E. Andersen, and S. Krashen (Eds.), *Developing communicative competence in a second language* (pp. 107–119). New York: Newbury House.

Scarcella, R. (1976). Watch up! Prefabricated routines in second language acquisition. *Working Papers on Bilingualism* (Toronto: OISE), *17,* 79–88.

(1983). Discourse accent in adult second language performance. In S. Gass and L. Selinker (Eds.), *Language transfer in language learning.* New York: Newbury House.

(1984). How writers orient their readers in expository essays: A comparative study of native and nonnative English writers. *TESOL Quarterly, 18,* 4: 671–688.

Schegloff, E.; Jefferson, G.; and Sacks, H. (1977). The preference for self-correction in the organization of repair in conversation. *Language, 53,* 362–382.

Smith, E. (1989) "It doesn't bother me, but sometimes it's discouraging": Students respond to teacher's written comments. *Journal of Teaching Writing* (Indiana Teachers of Writing, Indiana University and Purdue University at Indianapolis), 253–265.

Tannen, D. (1982). Oral and literate strategies in spoken and written narratives. *Language, 58,* 1: 1–21.

(1985). Relative focus of involvement in oral and written discourse. In D. Olson, N. Torrance, and A. Hildyard (Eds.), *Literacy, language, and learning* (pp. 124–148). Cambridge: Cambridge University Press.

Tao, H., and Thompson, S. (1991). English backchannels in Mandarin conversations: A case study of superstratum pragmatic "interference." *Journal of Pragmatics,* 16, 3: 209–223.

Urzua, A. (1989). The reading-writing connection: Evidence from the L2 context. Master's thesis, Applied Linguistics, University of California, Los Angeles.

Volk, D. (1990). Allocation and acknowledgment in young bilingual children's conversations. *Linguistics and Education, 2,* 91–107.

West, C., and Zimmerman, D. (1985). Gender, language, and discourse. In T. van Dijk (Ed.), *Handbook of discourse analysis: Discourse in society, vol. 4* (pp. 103–124). London: Academic Press.

Zimmerman, D., and West, C. (1978). Sex roles, interruptions, and silences in conversation. In M. Lourie and N. Conklin (Eds.), *A pluralistic nation: The language issue in the United States* (pp. 255–274). Rowley, Mass.: Newbury House.

3   Scripts and communication theory

In everyday life, we have many *goals*. For example, when hungry, our goal might be to obtain food. To fulfill that goal, we might go to the kitchen, a restaurant, or a grocery store. Suppose we decide on the grocery store but have never gone grocery shopping before. We would need to design a *plan* that might involve going to the store to find out what we must do to get food. We could observe others, ask questions, and try out options to accomplish the goal. After that, each time we shopped, we could rely on what we had already learned about shopping – the plan would become refined, producing a full-fledged *script*.

In his many publications, Schank has attempted to characterize the knowledge that people have of the structure of stereotypic event sequences such as grocery shopping. He uses the term "script" to represent this knowledge. One of Schank's goals has been to describe such knowledge in a formal way so that it might serve as a theory of how humans process natural language. A second goal has been to make the description so explicit that it can be programmed and tested on a computer. Schank's theory is called the *conceptual dependency theory*.

The script

Schank and Abelson (1977) have shown that the structure of a script includes a set of actions in temporal sequence to meet a goal. Within a script may be scenes. For example, a restaurant script would include an ordering scene, an eating scene, and a paying scene. The script also contains *roles*. In the grocery shopping script the roles would be played by the customer and important others (e.g., the cashier, the baggers, and so on). And the script includes a series of *props*. In the grocery shopping script, the props would be the signs, scales, checkout registers, and so on.

The essentials of the grocery shopping script might be:

Goal: to obtain food
Script: grocery shopping
Actors (roles):
– customers
– checkout clerks

– baggers (box persons)
– various clerks, stock persons, store manager
Props:
– basket/shopping cart
– groceries on display for purchase (by food group)
– signs (directory and price)
– scales and bags in produce area
– checkout counter
– register
Actions:

– go to market	ARRANGE
– select basket/shopping cart	
– select food	
– choose food	
– weigh and bag food if necessary	DO
– place food in basket/cart	
– take basket/cart to checkout counter	
– unload basket/cart	
– pay for groceries	PAY
– exit store with groceries	EVALUATE

In Schank's (1984) conceptual dependency theory, the script is formalized in a way that allows us to build a model that can be tested. This formalization is accomplished in part by identifying "semantic primitives" that specify actor roles, props, and actions within and across scripts. (Semantic primitives are typically capitalized in discussions of script theory.) Now let us look at some of the semantic primitives in relation to the grocery shopping script.

Actors (roles)

All scripts have actors, which are the typical roles exhibited by individuals in the script. Actor roles are independent of the individual person who plays the role. That is, a "customer" is a role. If I go shopping, then I am an "instance" of a CUSTOMER ("CUSTOMER" is a formal concept, or semantic primitive, and therefore capitalized). This relation can be formalized as "Evelyn ISA CUSTOMER" where ISA is the link that assigns the qualities of CUSTOMER to the individual.

Actor roles may be revealed not only by what actors do in the script but also by what they wear. For example, hospitals usually have very strict rules about the types of uniforms different people wear. The clothes, as well as the badges, define each person as having a particular role. In the grocery shopping script, clerks may wear special uniforms (as well as operate special machines at the checkout counter). Again, the relation between the actor and what he or she wears (or operates) can be formalized as, for instance, "CLERK HASA

UNIFORM" or "JUDGE HASA ROBE" where HASA is a link assigning the clothing (or machine) to the role.

Certain stereotypic verbal expressions go with participant roles within specific scripts. For example, the checkout clerk may greet us, ask about our preference for plastic or paper bags or boxes, and, in closing, may tell us to "have a nice day." These expressions "belong" to the clerk role in the grocery shopping script. A classic example from another script is "I now pronounce you husband and wife," which can only be said by someone authorized to marry people!

The roles people play within a script are also tied to role motives. For example, if we know that an actor is a football player, we make assumptions about him in terms of the role and the motives and goals of football players within a football game script. If, in another script, we mention that a person ISA football player, we still assign at least some of the motives and goals of football players to the person as an actor within this new script. If we know an actor is a computer hacker, we make other assumptions. If we know an actor is a hacker *and* a football player, we make still other assumptions. That is, the definition of roles includes information on motives, and these motives can be assigned to persons identified by that role even within other scripts.

Props

The props in some scripts are more important than in others. For example, in a "going for a walk" script, props are neither numerous nor essential. In scripts such as the grocery shopping script, the props are extremely important. In the grocery shopping script, the items for sale, the checkout counter, the register, and the basket or shopping cart are important to the script.

We have already said that an actor HASA prop when we mentioned badges or uniforms that, at least in part, identify the role. Much of the knowledge we share about roles includes the props that are controlled by a particular role. For instance, the role of CLERK also includes the prop: "CLERK HASA REGISTER." The CLERK controls that prop within the script. The customer role includes temporary possession of some means of transporting purchases: "CUSTOMER HASA CART." In other scripts, we might find "DOCTOR HASA STETHOSCOPE," "JUDGE HASA GAVEL," or "TEACHER HASA DESK." These props are important for the role and also for actions carried out in the script.

The relationships between roles and props quickly become "givens," so we don't need remark on them in normal communication. Because the information is known, shared information, there is no reason for anyone to say that the shopper has a cart, or the clerk has a register, or the store has food items. Nothing new or interesting there. (But I might say that Ralph's has cherries on sale because cherries are a seasonal fruit, and special prices are always big news to my friends!)

Actions

Each actor carries out a series of actions to meet his or her goal within the script. In a sense, we could say that these actions, too, belong to the actor, but, in fact, they are a series of sequentially ordered actions determined by the demands of the script itself. So, the clerk cannot use the register until the customer brings the purchases to the checkout counter. And the customer cannot pay for items until they have been tallied by the clerk.

The sequence of actions within the script may be grouped in terms of *plans*. For example, our first subplan in the grocery shopping script might be to USE a basket or shopping cart. Within the USE subplan, we find three semantic primitives: to KNOW where the carts and baskets are, to PROXimate (i.e., locate) them, and to take CONTrol of one of them. You can see that this USE subplan occurs many times in the grocery shopping script as groceries are located and placed in the basket.

If you think about all the possible actions in the grocery shopping script, you will notice that some are indispensable. For example, "select food" is an indispensable part of the grocery shopping script, one of several actions that the CUSTOMER must DO. To DO the selection, the USE subplan is put in motion. "Talking to the butcher" is an optional part of the script. PAY is an indispensable part of the script. The CUSTOMER must PAY, but the options for paying (with cash, by check or credit card, or by charging it to our account) may vary. In addition, some actions are distinctive to a particular event. The DO of "select food" doesn't occur in many other scripts (except within some larger event such as preparing a meal). In contrast, the PAY sequence occurs in many different scripts (similar PAY sequences occur in service-type encounters – for example, at a restaurant); it is not distinctive.

Many actions in scripts require movement. The movement of body parts as the shopper walks through the store involves the semantic primitive of MOVE. In shopping, actors also move objects. Therefore, there is a semantic category of "transfer" in Schank's conceptual dependency theory. The movement may be physical (PTRANS stands for physical transfer), as in the grocery shopping script, where we gain CONTrol of objects by moving them from shelves into shopping carts. The ownership or control of items may also be transferred from actor to actor (ATRANS stands for abstract transfer of ownership). In the grocery shopping script, ownership is officially transferred at the checkout counter as we pay for the merchandise. In other instances, the transfer may involve verbal information. When we ask the clerk where to find yogurt and are told it is in aisle 6, information (rather than an object) is transferred (MTRANS stands for mental transfer) from person to person.

Once we get home from the grocery store, we may MOVE to the kitchen, GRASP each article in turn, and PTRANS them to the refrigerator, to shelves, or onto plates. If we are good shots, we can PROPEL the trash into the garbage can. Once the food is available, we can INGEST it, satisfying our hunger.

You'll notice that the grocery shopping script has an EVALUATE segment. In evaluation, to use Schank's terminology, we mentally build (MBUILD) a positive or negative mental judgment and assign "good," "bad," or whatever as a trait of this encounter. As we make our purchases, we may EVALUATE the quality of the products, the fairness of the price, and the friendliness of the clerks. Our major evaluation, however, is whether or not we have met our goal of acquiring food to satisfy our hunger. Thus, the evaluation is global in terms of the goal but also particular to parts of the script as well.

The underlying structure of scripts is represented in a schematic form using semantic primitives such as those just described. Schank (1984) illustrates these schematics in detail, so to learn more about the formal explication of conceptual dependency theory, please consult this source. In case you are curious about how syntax is incorporated into conceptual dependency theory, the semantic primitives are represented in a canonical order – for example, Chris ↔ INGEST ← candy. You will find displays for most of the basic sentence types in Schank (1984).

Scripts, then, have actors, props, and actions that meet a goal. Once we have formed a plan to meet a goal and have used that plan many times, the script that is formed seems entirely unremarkable. However, when we move to another country or are functioning in another language, we may find that our scripts need to be radically amended. For example, if you move to a culture where the grocery store is not a supermarket but an enormous outdoor market that stretches for blocks and is made up of stalls for fruit, fish, grains, cereals, and spices, and where each customer must bargain for purchases, the scripts no longer match. New variants must be formed. So, the form of many scripts is language- or culture-specific (a source of potential "language shock" for learners who identify language as only syntax and phonology!).

Practice 3.1   Scripts

1. Actions in scripts may or may not be indispensable or distinctive. In the grocery shopping script, can you identify one action that is indispensable *and* distinctive, one that is neither indispensable *nor* distinctive, one that is not distinctive *but is* indispensable, and one that is not indispensable *but is* distinctive?
2. List as many MOVE, PTRANS, ATRANS, MTRANS, and MBUILD acts as you can think of that might occur in the grocery shopping script. In which cases are objects being transferred among actors according to their roles? In which cases are objects simply being moved from one

place to another? What common verbs are used for these "semantic primitives"?

3. How different is the grocery shopping script described in this chapter from that of another culture group you know? What are the differences in props, actors, and actions? Is there a difference between the bagger in the U.S. script and the person who bags or boxes purchases in your script? If so, how does this change the script? Is the verbal interaction different? In what way? Using as a model the grocery shopping script at the beginning of this chapter, write out the script for grocery shopping in your culture or another culture you know well.

4. In some service encounters, prices are not given but must be negotiated by the seller and buyer. This negotiation becomes part of the PAY sequence. If you have some experience with bargaining, list the moves. Is it clear whose role encompasses the offerer in this sequence – the seller of the merchandise or the offerer of the money? Which do you believe is the offerer in this sequence (and why)?

5. The roles of actors are also set in the script. If an actor (for example, a waiter) refuses to carry out his or her role, does this change the script or only become part of the evaluation of this particular instance of the playing of the script? Give an example of such a refusal and its effect.

6. We play many roles in life. Sometimes we use one role to explain why we can't take part in another script. For example, a child playing "Sleeping Beauty" refuses to come to dinner: "I can't. I'm the princess. I'm asleep." An adult says, "I can't. I have to go to work." List the roles that you play. Is there a hierarchy of importance to these roles? If so, in what ways do the roles determine who you are and in which scripts you will participate?

7. In some scripts, props are very important. Assume your goal is to paint a room. The props – the objects used to paint the room – assume high focus. If you say you spent a lot of time looking at color chips, but then got all the stuff together and painted the room, what must be included in "all the stuff"?

8. The study of system in language scripts leads us to wonder how we go about learning social communication. For example, when first taken out on a trick-or-treat venture for Halloween, a child's goal may not be well formed. The goal may be to have fun or to get candy or to

dress up and scare people. The child may not know the "trick-or-treat" opening or the "thank you" that comes at the end of the script. Parents or older siblings walk the child through the script from beginning to end many times during the evening. If you know this trick-or-treat script, write it out (include roles, props, actions, and stereotyped utterances used at points in the script). If possible, compare the stereotyped utterances with those described in Berko-Gleason and Weintraub (1976). If you do not know the trick-or-treat script, think of a holiday or birthday script in which young children participate, and outline the script (actors and roles, props, actions, stereotyped utterances).

9. If you have contact with very young children, document the amount of script teaching that adults do. For example, do they give the child a toy phone and instruct her to "say hello to daddy"? Are they the ones who link actions to motives or states ("Oh, he went back to sleep. Guess he's tired."). In your examples, is the teaching directed at the script components or at the language needed for the script? Do older children coach, model, or specifically teach younger children the language needed for the script?

10. How often do children pretend to be (i.e., play the roles of) mother, father, big sister, or pets? What role features do they assume in this play? If you observe boys of different ages, at what age do boys refuse to play the role of "baby"?

11. What scripts do young children practice (e.g., ironing, cleaning house, going to the store, going to the doctor, driving the car, shooting robbers, going to school, playing teacher)? Do they also use correct gestures or other nonverbal signals that go with the role? Von Raffler-Engel (1977) has studied the early emergence of language or culture-specific gestures in young children. For example, a 27-month-old Japanese child playing with a toy phone bows to her listener. Have you observed similar language-specific gestures in the play of young children?

12. Do children show a knowledge of all parts of the scripts they practice or play? For example, when my daughter was a young child, she "ran away" to the ice cream shop, ordered a cone, accepted it with thanks, and began to eat it. Why do you think she "forgot" to pay?

13. The ability to play a role in a second-language script is often seen as showing communicative competence.

Obs: Do you guys want to play doctor?
Juan: I wanna be the doctor.
Carlos: ((on phone)) Allo doctor, I'm sick.
Juan: Come.
Carlos: OK, I be right there.
Juan: 'Bye.
Carlos: ((hangs up phone and pretends to knock at door))
Juan: Come in.
Carlos: ((turns to observer with a proud grin)) Hey, he knows a lotta English!

Heidi: Here, you take this car. ((playing service station))
Nora: You no do dese. I be! ((= I'll be the attendant))
Heidi: She talks good now, huh? She knows everything now.
                                    (Data source: Wong Fillmore 1976)

One of my friends was judged as having excellent colloquial Arabic because of her ability to play the customer bargaining role very well at the market. Some people learn particular scripts very well ("safe islands"). Are there special scripts in which you or other language learners either excel or fail?

14. If you are a teacher, videotape your students as they role-play a script of your own choosing. How much of the script has the learner successfully acquired? Which role(s) can the learner successfully assume? What props can the learner successfully incorporate into the performance? What obligatory and optional script actions does the learner use? What special script language can the learner use? Does the learner view the L2 script as different or similar to his or her L1 scripts (and in what way)? (You might want to do this exercise as a study group activity where each person asks a student from a different L1 group to perform the chosen role play. Compare the outcomes for similarities and differences.)

The classroom script

As teachers and as students, we participate in many school-related scripts. We have a general idea of what the goal of the classroom is (to offer instruction and to obtain learning) and a general script in mind for meeting that goal. We have, at least, some idea of what language classrooms are like, the scripts of student-teacher tutorials, teacher-parent meetings, and teachers' meetings. Some of these scripts – such as the language classroom script – build on our early experiences as students in such classrooms. As we switch roles from student to teacher, our perceptions of the script, our role in the script, and the motives of actors in the script also shift. Our teacher training, our experience as novice teachers in practicums, and our years of experience teaching different students in different cultures also affect the details of the script and the way we play the script. Once we become parents and participate in educating our children, we also change our ideas about instruction. That is, we evolve our personal style for playing our roles within scripts in response to our experiences within the script.

The actors in a classroom script include the teacher and the students and possibly teacher aides. In some schools, students may wear identifying uniforms as part of their role. Characteristically, there are special places and props within the classroom for the actors. While teachers and students may both have desks, the teacher's desk is usually larger and placed in a position where it can be seen by all students. The area around the desk is space that "belongs to" its owner. Some of the props in the classroom are seen as belonging mainly to the teacher (e.g., the blackboard and chalk, the overhead projector, the doors and windows!) and others to the students (e.g., the books and papers on or within the students' desks, student computers).

The teacher and students MOVE from place to place and DO a series of actions within the classroom. Some of these are PTRANS as the students place their books on desks, others are ATRANS as the teacher collects and returns papers, and some are MTRANS as ideas are exchanged among students and teachers. MBUILD affective states are developed and shift as the script unfolds.

There are a variety of ways in which classroom activities may be organized, but four are typical of elementary classrooms. The most common is the teacher interacting with all the students as a class. The teacher determines whether his or her talk will be to all the students or to individuals. The teacher may elicit individual or chorus responses, and may allow students to volunteer or call on them. The second most frequent type of interaction is for the teacher to meet with some students as a group (as in reading or writing groups). In this context, the students must respond individually since the teacher's purpose is often to evaluate individual performance. The third type of activity is for students to work independently at their desks with the teacher available for help. Students must approach the teacher or raise a hand to obtain this help, and the interaction is not heard by the other students. The fourth type of interaction consists of group work that students themselves run with little supervision from the teacher.

Phillips (1972, 1983), who worked with Warm Springs Indian children in Oregon, notes that although the first two types of interaction occur most frequently in American elementary schools, they are also the types of interactions in which the Indian children felt most uncomfortable. The children were more talkative and relaxed in the last two types of interaction because, Phillips explains, those ways more closely match how learning is done in the home: by observation, listening, supervised participation, and private self-initiated self-testing. A number of educators have been concerned about the home-school mismatch of the scripts for teaching and learning. The work of teachers at the Kamehameha project in Hawaii (see Jordan, Tharp, and Vogt 1985) shows that home learning styles can be implemented in the school environment.

Language classrooms differ, at least in some ways, from ordinary classrooms. Depending on the methodology adopted for instruction and the age and proficiency level of the students, there may be a great deal of small group work, there may be much project work, or there may be teacher-fronted instruction or even choral drills. Whatever the techniques, however, teachers are in charge of the DO actions – directing and assisting students or carrying out the actions themselves.

In the classroom, the DO actions may occur in a set sequence. For example, the teacher moves to the teacher space to begin many of the DO actions. He or she DOes an "opening" sequence to which students may or may not be expected to respond, and then DOes the first "structuring move" (these are sometimes called "regulatory moves") – a move that sets the task(s) students are to carry out.

T: Okay, three activities. One is I will tell you about a wedding. And then I will show you a picture of a different wedding. And then we're going to play a game. OK?

(Data source: Richards 1987)

Notice that teachers use "okay" for at least two separate functions. First, they may use it to mark the end of a structuring move. Second, they may use it to signal that they are DOing a topic shift. The task itself may then be carried out in a series of teacher questions – student answers – teacher evaluates moves, or the task may be carried out by students working on their own or in small groups. The teacher determines when the first task is complete and, moving to a teacher space, DOes a subclosing and structures the next task. As the teacher notes the end of an activity, a period, or the end of the class day, new closing moves must be structured, and the students participate in the closing.

T: OK, time to stop.
    (To S1) Put away the game, please.
S2: ((Points to puzzle)) (in Korean) Ah! I have to finish!
T: (To S1) Time to stop. (Rising intonation)
S3: ((to S2, using teacher's intonation)) Time to stop.
S2: ((looks at S3 threateningly))

(Data source: Saville-Troike et al. 1984)

Teachers DO often ask questions, particularly those to which they know the answer. These "display questions" in language classes often check on vocabulary or require students to produce sentence syntax, so teacher can check that students have learned the lesson content or have the necessary background to understand new material:

T: Do you know what this is?
M: Egg.
T: This is an egg. An egg.
And what do we do with an egg?
M: You crack it. In a bowl.
T: You crack it. In the bowl.
G: (In Korean) We eat that.
T: Right. And we call this an egg.
G: (In Korean) If we don't use a refrigerator, there will be a little bird coming out.
T: Right. That's an egg.

(Data source: Saville-Troike et al. 1984)

The teacher does not understand the student's more interesting Korean responses but reinforces them with "right" as though the student has told her that, indeed, the object is an egg.

When students are unable to take a turn, the teacher or other students use a set of moves known as *scaffolding* to help the learner along:

Juan: teacher
           lookit ((holds up a quarter))
NS child: mmhmm a quarter
Juan: quarter
NS child: for what?
Juan: for Monday ((the day milk money is due))
NS child: on Monday? for what?
Juan: for milk

(Data source: Young 1974)

With this series of questions, the native-speaker child builds a scaffold that lets the learner, who is at the beginner stage, build an equivalent to the utterance "Lookit, teacher, I have a quarter for milk."

Teachers' questions serve as a scaffold. They offer cues that help students arrive at a solution for problems:

T: Okay. "You have a quarter and a dime. How many seven-cents stamps can you buy?" What's the FIRST thing you have to do to get the answer to the problem? + + Okay, Vicente?
V: Add?
T: Yes! What do you have to add?
V: uhm A - + either a quarter + a quarter and a dime
T: Good! //and how*
V: //and seven cents?
T: How much is it?
V: Uhm + + quarter, dime
T: How many cents in a quarter?

95

V: Quarter? twenty-five.
T: Twenty-five. And how many + cents is in a dime?
B: Five? No, I mean ten?
T: Ten! Okay, so all together we have?
Ss: Thirty-five. ((Several Ss answer at once))
T: Thirty-five cents. Okay. So let's say if you have a quarter and a dime, in other words you have thirty-five cents + + how many seven-cent stamps can you buy?

(Data source: Hawkins 1988)

In high school foreign language classes, the practices or drills, themselves, may encourage the teacher to use a series of display questions, and whatever scaffolding is used is most often in the first language of the learners:

T: Um . . . kak skazat' po-russki (how do you say in Russian) "Let's go to the movies"?
(Chorus of student answers)
T: Let's go to the MOVIES.
S1: How do you say, "Let's go"?
S2: V teatr (to the theatre)
T: Well, that's "to the theatre," like to see plays . . . how about . . . "to the movies"?
S1: V kino
T: Da, xorošo (Yes, that's good) Do you want to go to the movies.
S1: Pojdjomte
T: No, that means "Let's go." How about "do you want to"? "Do you want to go." If you say-if you have a verb like xotite (do you want) or možete, you have to follow it with an infinitive verb, like idti (to go) or rabotat (to work). All right . . .
S1: So . . . idti?
T: Yeah, so how about, "I can read Russian"?
S1: Ja mogu citaju russki jazyk (I can, I read Russian) or something like that, I don't know.

(Data source: Eardley 1985)

There are a number of ways in which the actions of the classroom have been described aside from script theory. Sinclair and Coulthard (1975) divided the discourse into *lessons,* which include *transactions,* which include *exchanges* made up of *moves,* which include *acts.* These could be integrated into scripts using the DO segment of the script and the primitives of MTRANS, MBUILD, PTRANS, ATRANS, and so on. That is, teachers and students together DO the lesson, and they contribute to transactions, exchanges, moves, and acts according to their roles.

In Sinclair and Coulthard's system, the lesson is made up of transactions. These transactions include preliminary, medial, and terminal exchanges. The preliminary and terminal exchanges are concerned with boundaries between transactions while the medial exchanges concern teaching. There are several subtypes of teaching exchanges that could be classified as DO or MTRANS in script theory. These include, among others:

Teacher informs:	luckily the French could read Greek
Teacher directs action:	I want you to take your pen and I want you to rub it hard on something woolen.
Teacher elicits verbal:	What's the name of this?
Pupil elicits:	Are the number for le – for the letters?
Pupil informs:	There's some-there's a letter's missing.
Teacher checks:	Finished Joan?
Teacher reinforces inform:	Billy, this is a "w," remember?
Teacher repeats:	We need a blue one. We need a blue one.
Pupils list:	They planted corn. No, olives! Acorns!

Each exchange, however, is not made up of single utterances but of more elaborate moves. There are five types of moves:

1. Framing moves
2. Focusing moves
3. Opening moves
4. Answering moves
5. Follow-up moves

Framing moves indicate that one stage of the lesson is ended and another is about to begin (e.g., "right, OK, well" or a stressed silence). Focusing moves tell the students what is going to happen or what has happened.

Framing:	Right (silent stress) Now,
Focusing:	what we've just done, what h we've just done is we've decided how to outline our arguments.

Opening moves get students to participate in the teaching exchange. These are often followed by an answering move.

Opening:	There were differences in who interrupted the most. Do you know who did the most interruptions? I'm sure you do. Vanessa?
Answering:	The-the men did. At least in meetings.

The answering move is then given a follow-up:

Follow-up:	The men did. That's another important finding.

Each of these moves is further subdivided into acts. For instance, in the framing move example, "Right" and "now" are marker acts. The opening move example includes a starter (the first line), an elicitation question (the second line), and prompt (the third line), and a nomination (the fourth line). The answering move is classified as a reply act, and the follow-up move includes an acceptance (the first line) and an evaluation act (the second line).

A number of different analyses have been carried out to characterize the teacher-student interaction within classrooms. Most use MOVE, rather than sentence or utterance, as the unit of analysis. These moves occur within an EXCHANGE. Transcripts may be annotated for these moves within exchanges as in the following examples. The annotations differ depending on whose form of classroom analysis the researcher uses.

Example 1
T: This is the bride. This is the groom. A bride and groom get MARRIED. ((T informs))
   WHERE do they get married? ((solicit move))   EXCHANGE
S: xxx ceremony. ((response move))
T: In a church or in a wedding ceremony. Very good.
   ((follow-up and evaluation move))

Example 2
T: Do you know how? How can you have music outdoors?
   ((T solicits and restates))
S: Singers ((volunteer response))   EXCHANGE
T: Yeah and guitar players. It was very nice.
   ((evaluation and follow-up move))

The chain of teacher solicits – student responds – teacher evaluates, however, is not the only sort of exchange found in language classrooms. Students may ask both information questions and clarification questions (e.g., "huh?" "what?"):

   T: It was on a hill in the park. You could see the ocean. A nice idea except it
      was too cold. *((T informs))*
→ S: In which month was it? *((S solicits))*
→ T: Last month. *((T response))*
      What was last month? *((T solicits))*
   S: My *((response move))*
   T: May May. *((evaluation))* It was March two months ago.
      ((follow-up))
→ S: March March. *((S follow-up))*
→ S: You want to get married there you can go? *((S solicit))*
→ T: Yeah anybody can go there. NO problem.
      ((T response))
      Yeah, it's free. It's a public park. *((follow-up))*
      So. Anyway ah *((frame))*
      have you ever been to a marriage – *((starter))*

Can you describe a marriage ceremony in your country?
((T elicit)) Have you ever been to one? *((prompt))*
You want to tell me? *((nomination))*

(Data source: Richards 1987)

Here a student asks a question that the teacher answers, but then, like many teachers, she can't resist doing a little side lesson on months of the year. The student, unlike the teacher, does not respond "good" to the teacher's answers. Instead, the student asks the teacher another question. Again, the teacher responds and then, with a "So" and "Anyway," takes control again to structure the next task for the students.

The systems used by Sinclair and Coulthard allow you to take a classroom transcript and annotate it in a way that reveals levels of structure within it. You may want to consult Sinclair and Coulthard for a fuller explication of their system to describe the classroom data collected in public schools.

Because language teachers encourage much more student talk and typically have students do a good deal of small group work, the exchanges are likely to differ from the seemingly endless teacher questions – student responds – teacher evaluates exchange cycles typical of content classes, such as those analyzed by Sinclair and Coulthard. Students ask many more questions and respond to each other as well as to the teacher:

T: Marriage and divorce. ((writes divorce on the board))
S1: And so when you divorce you don't need a lawyer.
S2: In this case yes you do.
S1: It's very expensive.
S3: xxx comes late in the United States you can ah easy divorce you don't.
T: Mm?
S3: quickly
T: It used to be a very complicated LON::G process. Ah now there are some places that offer divorces very cheap and very fast.
S2: How about Reno Las Vegas?
T: Huh
S2: How about Reno in Las Vegas?
S1: Yes I think in Las Vegas you can
S3: xx quickly you
T: Then that's one of the places you can get a quickie.

(Data source: Richards 1987)

Notice in this example that the teacher is not concerned with the grammatical form of the students' utterances but with the interpretation of their questions. She cues into the "quickly" of S3 without requesting a well-formed question, and she allows S2 to say Reno (in) Las Vegas without correction as she accepts this as a nomination of a good place to get a quick divorce. Her focus is on the message rather than on language form. At other points in the lesson, form becomes the focus of instruction and the teacher's feedback shifts to correction of form.

There are, of course, many stereotyped expressions that teachers and students use within the classroom script. We have discussed some of these in Chapter 1 in terms of the system constraints shown in classroom discourse. The opening and closing of each class period or day may include a variety of set verbal expressions for teacher and students (in addition to a bell signal). The turn-taking system is controlled primarily by the teacher, and stereotypic expressions of control and turn nomination are used. Students who are not nominated for a turn may have to use nonverbal as well as verbal signals to request a turn at talk. Students may need to request permission to enter teacher space, but teachers do not request permission to enter student space. The signals for seeking and granting permission to enter talk and space are likely to be stereotypic within the script. Structuring moves often have set verbal signals within them, such as "Turn to page 322," "Let's do exercise 3 together," or "Time to circle to your study group," or "Exchange your paper with your neighbor."

Teachers EVALUATE a great deal. In elementary school, particularly, they evaluate student behavior, because part of the often unstated goal is to teach the "rules of the game" for interpersonal interaction in school:

T: Now, Laura, do you know what you're being now?
L: What?
T: What?
L: Silly?
T: Yes.

(Data source: Christian 1980)

They also evaluate how well they and their students are meeting the subgoals of instruction in particular tasks, as well as the overall goal of offering instruction that leads to learning. Students often seem to evaluate very different goals. These may include the need for immediate feedback (are they or their classmates right?) on a point of information:

D: The "E" is an inch away from the "A." How can you make –
R: It is? ((picks up ruler to measure))

(Data source: Christian 1980)

More often, their evaluations appear to address social goals (are they having fun? are they making friends? are they successfully negotiating some status role for themselves?).

M: We're almost done making our special secret base.
D: What? I'm allowed to go in it.

(Data source: Christian 1980)

NS child: ((disgusted)) Oooh, you made a boo-boo!
Enrique: I made a boo-boo
NS child: boo-boo lookit

Enrique: So what? All up! boo-boo yep, boo-boo.
Everybody do boo-boo. I did wrong ((laugh)).

(Data source: Young 1974)

The goals and roles of students may, at various times in their careers, be less centered on that of "seeker of learning." It's not clear (at least to me) when and how students include the "seeker of learning" as a part of their goal for the classroom script.

We think of the classroom as the center of learning in school, but the school playground is another area where children must learn a series of scripts. Students must learn what areas of the playground are "assigned" to them. This is a matter of role, status, and gender. For example, in schools I have observed in the United States, girls usually walk in pairs and stay close to their grade or game area while boys may range away from the teacher and the girls to the edges of their area. Not only do students need to learn these patterns, but they also must know which games to play. Games have many set expressions attached to them (e.g., "my turn," "no way," "me first," "prove it," "how come," "I won"). In other words, there are many different scripts that learners must master: the classroom script, the principal's or nurse's office script, the playground script, and so forth. Teachers also have many scripts to learn in addition to that of their classroom: the office script, the teachers' lounge script, the teachers' meeting script, the PTA script, the parent-teacher conference script, and so forth.

Practice 3.2   Classroom scripts

1. When we play the role of teacher or student in the classroom script, we assume at least some of the attributes associated with that role. What are some of the attributes of the role of language teacher as you perceive them in your society? How do these differ from those of another culture or language group? If you are unsure, ask an international student to identify differences for you.

2. What props are important in the classroom script? At your school, how different are the props of the language classes from those of regular classroom instruction? Which props "belong to" teachers and which to students? Can teachers and students request the use of each others' property? How do they do this?

3. As a teacher, do you feel any different when you are within the teacher space and when you are in the student space? If so, do you believe students feel any different about your role when you are inside or outside the teacher space?

4. There are many set phrases that go with parts of the

classroom script. These formulaic phrases go far beyond "Open your books to page 234." Here are just a few short formulas: "Good. Right. Need any help? (Is everything) OK? Do you understand?" A few longer ones include: "Write your name in the upper right-hand corner of the page. Let's think about that. What do you think, X? Tell me what happened. There's something I forgot to mention. How are you going to do that?" Review your classroom tape (from Practice 1.2) and identify those phrases or utterances said by the teacher that you feel are formulaic. Then list formulaic utterances of students. Do these formulaic utterances relate to any special part of the script? Are any of them related particularly to language classrooms? Are they related to elementary versus secondary versus tertiary levels of instruction?

5. Richmond (1990) listed expressions teachers use to motivate students to carry out tasks (e.g., "It will be fun," "I'll give you an A," "You're the best person to do this," "It's your turn"). Check your classroom data from Practice 1.2 to see what motivational expressions are used. If you are a student, what types of motivational comments do you think work best for you? If you are a teacher, which work best with your students? Is your goal to move from extrinsic (teacher-provided) motivation to intrinsic motivation, or do you believe that motivation comments are useful in all classroom scripts regardless of student age, ability, and so forth?

6. Young children often "play school" in a way that demonstrates what they believe the teacher role and the goals of the classroom might be. If you have observed children playing "language school," what did the play reveal?

7. Elementary school children often remind each other of the "rules of the game" for classroom behavior – even to the extent of using teacher's euphemistic phrases:

Billy: Mine!! ((yelling)) Teacher!
John: Billy, don't yell! ((yelling))
　　　That's an outside voice.
　　　　　　　　(Data source: Genishi and De Paolo 1982)

If your classroom data is from an elementary school class, list any examples you have of students using "teacher talk" for the rules of the game.

8. From your classroom data, identify segments that are

teacher-fronted. What is the series of teacher-student moves in the data? What stereotypic signals do you see within these moves? Can you list a series of DO moves for the teachers and students? Which involve PTRANS, ATRANS, MTRANS, or MBUILD?

9. From your classroom data, identify the segments where small group work occurs. How does the teacher structure the task for the group? How does the group assign roles to each member of the group? (Cooper et al., 1982, claim that students are very aware of their relative understanding of material in comparison to others in groups and that they select a "teacher" who is best able to give them clear and informative feedback.) Who signals closure for the task? How is the closing completed? List any stereotypic signals used within these moves. It has often been commented that the quantity and quality of student talk during group work exceeds that shown in teacher-directed whole class sessions. How different is the structure, and how different is the quality of student talk in group work from those of the teacher-fronted segment of instruction?

10. Chapter 1 discussed system components in relation to the classroom; certainly classroom scripts include openings/ closings, preempt signals, and so forth. Salica and Early examined international students' acquisition of "interruption" in language classrooms. After looking at the actual signals used (both nonverbal – e.g., facial expression, eye contact, tapping fingers, hand raising – and verbal – overlaps, modulated "wait a minute," etc.), they also looked at the reasons for interrupting; that is, students' goals in interrupting within the classroom script. In your own words, explain why the notion of goal is important in distinguishing script analysis from the analysis of system components presented in Chapter 1.

11. Children do not necessarily come to school already equipped with the classroom script, as Mehan (1979) has shown. If you work with very young children, how long does it take them to develop the script? What "errors" do they make before they learn the script? (Are the errors primarily those revealed by an analysis of communication components – Chapter 1 – or via scripts, plans, goals?) If you have studied in another country where the classroom script differs, describe the differences and how well you adapted to the new script form.

Scripts and memory

When adults encounter a new situation, they find very little of it truly new. Memory of past plans for achieving goals must be represented in some form, perhaps as scripts, in memory. If that were not the case, we would interpret each instance as a totally unknown event. Without script information, it would be impossible to interpret many ordinary exchanges.

A: Palms Theatre.
B: I'm just calling to check the times.
A: 5:00, 6:45, 8:15, and 11:00.
B: 8:15? Okay, thanks.

Because we share a script for seeking information and the types of information that are needed regarding movies, we can easily fill in the gaps. This means that we must be able to generalize knowledge not only across different instances of the same script but across related scripts as well.

Consider your script for "going to a movie." How would the script change for "going to a play"? How does it differ from "going to a concert" or "going to a basketball game"? Do these various events, which satisfy the goal of wanting entertainment, differ in significant ways, or could these scripts all be grouped together? If scripts have evolved from plans to meet the same goal, they are likely to have much in common. If the actions of "seeking entertainment" are similar, then we should be able to form a hierarchy of scripts. Schank and Abelson (1977) suggest that scripts might be hierarchically organized in human memory. They call these higher-order representations "MOPS" (Memory Organization PacketS). It would be uneconomical if each of our entertainment scripts required a separate script in memory. MOPS are one way to group individual scripts into more general categories. With a MOP, each entertainment script could "inherit" aspects from that more general representation.

It would also be uneconomical if we could not transfer knowledge about parts of scripts (for example, paying for groceries) to other scripts that contain a similar sequence (e.g., paying for service in general).

Schank (1982), therefore, suggests that scripts serve as pointers to two types of memory – *general event memory* (e.g., your memory of visits to the dentist) and *situation memory,* which includes memory of actions common to many events (e.g., paying the bill). Thus, a visit to the dentist is no longer a script stored in one place. If it were, we could not transfer knowledge across scripts (say, from the dentist to the doctor), nor could we transfer parts of scripts (e.g., that paying a doctor for services is part of a more general contract script).

Let's see how certain scripts might be grouped together. As an example, think of all the various situations where you need to hire someone to help you solve a problem. These are called service-encounter situations. A generic service encounter might include:

ARRANGE for service
DO service
PAY for service
EVALUATE service

Whether we need to go to the dentist to have a cavity filled, to a restaurant to get food, to a tire store to get a flat tire fixed, or to a nursery to buy plants, these components of the script will still be there.

On the other hand, if we need to go to the dentist, there are parts of that service encounter that are shared only with other professional office visits. All professional office visits require an appointment. This is not necessary for many other types of service encounters. Professional office visits also include waiting in a waiting room. Therefore, we might think of the professional office visit as a subcategory of service encounters that shares many aspects of the service encounter. For example, it shares the notion of a "contract" – one contracts and pays for a service – with other service encounters, yet shares other facets only with professional office visits.

Such information can be formalized in a hierarchical manner as shown in the following example. Lytinen and Schank (1982) represent a visit to the doctor's office as calling up two other MOPS – one for the professional office visit and another for contract. The M-Contract is one that would be activated in all service encounter scripts. M-POV, below, refers to "professional office visit," a MOP activated by doctor, dentist, lawyer, or other such service visits.

M-Doctor
M-POV, M-CONTRACT
M-Contract
   negotiate + (get service) + pay
M-Professional Office Visit
   have problem + make appointment + go + enter + waiting room +
   (get service)

Lytinen and Schank show the overlap of the MOPS in diagrams such as the one in Figure 3.1 for a particular instance of a $Doctor (doctor script).

We have already noted that the roles people play within the script call for them to use language that is stereotypic. Some of these expressions generalize throughout the total hierarchy. For example, "Can I help you?" serves as an opening in most service encounters. It may appear in the professional office visit when the receptionist takes an appointment, or it may be voiced as "How can I help you?" as a variant of "What seems to be the trouble?" as an opener by the doctor, lawyer, or psychologist. Other expressions may not spread across even the local level of the hierarchy.

105

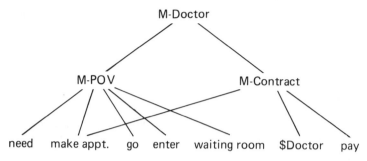

Figure 3.1

A language learner must not only be able to build scripts from general events and situation memory, but also be able to determine how language may or may not generalize across the hierarchy. Zernik (1987) gives an example that illustrates this from the learning experiences of language learners. As such a learner, assume that during a conversation with a friend, the friend complained, "Your mechanic ripped me off." The "visit to the car mechanic" memory has been successfully activated. Yet, within it, there is no ready explanation of the new term "rip off." Since the search shows no easy explanation of "rip off" in this script, the search can go to the next higher level, the "service encounter." Some few cases of "rip off" may be found at the service level, perhaps in the apartment rental or used car sales or, less likely, in the professional office visit group with a lawyer, dentist, or doctor. Within service, there are a series of normal actions such as ARRANGE service, DO service, PAY for service, EVALUATE service. In addition, there are cases of deviation from the norm such as service not done, bad service, high price, free service, excellent service. In trying to guess the meaning of "rip off," the learner may be guided by intonation and other nonverbal clues to select from the negative examples that diverge from the norm. This narrows the scope to service not done, bad service, and high price. In the script model, then, the learner would search for a known phrase that might cover these meanings – for example, "cheat" – and test the scope and generalizability of "rip off" to those of "cheat." When divergences between "rip off" and "cheat" are found, these are identified and incorporated into the new knowledge structure.

Because scripts are like templates of what *is* expected, they may seem dull and banal – tempting us to flout the expected. When a service person says "Good evening. My name is Debbie and I'll be your waitress this evening," we are tempted to reply "And my name is George and I'll be your customer this evening." But we don't (usually). We delight not so much when the template is broken as when the stereotypic language used with the template is parodied. There is a great *New Yorker* cartoon where a concert violinist turns from the symphony orchestra and the conductor on the podium to thank a jewel-bedecked audience with "Thank you, folks, thank you. And now I'd like to dedicate this next number to all my wonderful fans out there who have been so good to me over the years. It's a favorite of mine, goes by the name of Beethoven's Violin Concerto in D Major, and it sounds something like this." We almost expect him to tap his bow and add "a one an'a two an'a – " as the conductor raises his baton.

Schank (1984) has also noted that when plan violations or goal failures occur, they are extremely important because they mark points of deviation from the expected. They also trigger strong affective responses. He described a system of TOPs (Thematic Organization Points) (Dyer 1981 calls these Thematic Affect Units or TAUs) to organize memories of such failures. These are necessary in order to infer affective states of participants in the script and also to explain the cross-script remindings of similar failures or of classic stories that illustrate similar failures.

Scripts direct us, in a sense, to generic outlines in memory. When we encounter a new instance, we immediately understand much of what will happen based on the general event memory. We understand what props are involved and what roles are to be played. If each instance were exactly the same, life would be dull indeed. Someone once said that in music performance, we use past interpretations of the music to allow hearers the comfort of the known and beautiful, and add enough new of our own to shock them into really listening. Perhaps it is the same with each new instance of a script. We try to play it in our own style.

Practice 3.3   Scripts and memory

1. List the actors (and roles), props, and actions in your script for "going to the movies."
2. How does the "going to the movies" script change for "going to a baseball or soccer or basketball game"?
3. List the actors, props, and actions in your script for "going to an outdoor music concert." How similar is it to the movies and game script?
4. How does audience participation (verbal and nonverbal) change in these scripts?
5. Do you see any connection between scripts that meet the goal of seeking entertainment and the grocery shopping script? If so, what links them?
6. Think of the components of your "visit to the doctor" script. How does this professional office script differ from that of your "visit to the dentist" script (need, appointment, waiting room, examining room, doctor-patient talk, finishing, making new appointment, paying)?

7. What other professional office calls share at least some of these scenes or actions? How are they similar and different?

8. If we change roles in a script (e.g., become the dentist rather than the patient, become the teacher rather than the student), does the script change? Why or why not?

9. Zoila, an adult Spanish speaker (Shapira 1978), abstracted the English unit "pickyaup" from discourse. She used it in such utterances as "I pickyaup 3:00, okay?" "She's a little angry but I think so is because the other sister no come here mmm for ehh pickyaup her." "J say I pickyaup for beach, for dance, for go movies pero he no pickyaup." In what script would you guess "pickyaup" was first encountered? Across which scripts do you imagine it spread? Against what similar vocabulary might Zoila have checked "pickyaup"? Why do you suppose she never broke the unit into its parts?

Conclusion

Language teaching methods that relate to script theory include the "situational approach" or "contextual approach." In these programs, the syllabus is built around a series of situations (scripts) such as banking, grocery shopping, getting a driver's license, using the bus. These are selected and sequenced in such a way that the basic "survival" scripts are covered in the course. Certain types of ESP (English for special or specific purposes) courses also relate to script theory. For example, an English for hotel personnel course would involve specific scripts as would an English for flight personnel course.

You might find it interesting to check your own language textbooks for the types of scripts presented. Are the scripts grouped together in a way that will give learners the opportunity to discover how far components of scripts generalize? Just how authentic are the roles, props, actions, and language used in each script? In addition, since the conventional roles and relations (ISA, HASA, and DO relationships) of scripts are "givens," writers are not likely to pay any attention to them. For example, if the script is about getting food and the dialogue shows John going to the kitchen, opening the refrigerator, and taking out the food, we seldom stop to think that the reason the definite article is used (*the* kitchen, *the* refrigerator, *the* food) is because these are all "givens" in the script. Houses *have* kitchens, kitchens *have* refrigerators, refrigerators *have* food in them. All these are givens. Potentially, then, there is a strong link to be made between scripts and grammar and between scripts and materials development. Script theory could provide the theory underlying such approaches.

This very brief introduction to script theory is only to whet your appetite. For a fuller explication, please consult Schank (1984), Schank and Abelson (1977), Schank and Riesbeck (1981), and Dyer (1981). While much of the work on script theory has been carried out within artificial intelligence in computer sicence, the goals are similar to those of linguists – to model an understanding of scripts and, thus, find systematicity in the discourse system. In applied linguistics, such models are important not only for what they reveal about script theory but because they can be useful in analyzing cross-cultural communication. Much research is needed to support our intuition of which scripts are the more universal and which are clearly language- and culture-specific.

Next, we will look more precisely at language function within certain types of scripts as defined by speech event and speech act research.

Research and application

A. Scripts

1. It isn't difficult to find examples where script structure and the language of the script have been parodied. *Alice in Wonderland* springs to mind immediately. Actors behave in unexpected ways and say things that flout Alice's expectations. Eugène Ionesco's plays, on the other hand, abound with characters who use the most banal language in apparently mundane scripts. The effect in each is humorous and somewhat frightening. Select an example of your own and show how the author uses variations on scripts and script language to create humor or new interpretations of our social scripts. Nash (1985) might be a good source to consult for this project.

2. The programming needed to define a script is considerable. Here is a portion of the many commands from a "cooking script" developed by Cushing (1990) for an applied linguistic class project on scripts.

```
(seq *schemas*
  ((cook act
    (agent person)
    (patient food)
    (liquid water)
    (receptacle container)
    (type american)
    (heat-source heat))
  (stir-fry cook
    (receptacle wok)
```

```
          (liquid peanut-oil)
          (utensils chopsticks)
          (type chinese)
          (heat-source stove))
       (cut act
          (utensil knife
          (location cutting-board)
          (effect dismembered))
       (food nil
          (edibility t)
             (consistency)
                (taste)
                (color)
                (cookedness))
       (onion food
          (consistency crisp)
          (color white)
          (location crisper)
          (preparation dice)
          (taste hot))
       (chocolate food
          (consistency smooth)
          (preparation unwrap)
          (color brown)
          (taste sweet))
       (chicken food
          (consistency meaty)
          (location refrigerator)
          (preparation cut-up)
          (taste zesty))
```

This program (written in LISP) contains many items and types of schemas. Using the program, the computer can ask a series of questions about cooking and respond to the answers provided by the user.

Computer: What kind of cooking do you want to do today?
User: How about brownies?
Computer: You could probably find out about that in the Joy of Cooking. Please try again.
User: I'd like a recipe for stir fry.
Computer: That's a great choice. Put some peanut-oil in a wok. Do you have a wok?
User: Yes, I do.
Computer: Good. Put the wok on the stove. Then turn on the

stove but make sure the peanut-oil doesn't burn.
What kind of meat do you want to use?

User: Chicken.

Computer: Okay, cut-up the chicken. Then you should put your chicken in the wok. You must like chicken.

User: Yes, I do.

Computer: Ginger is yummy. Do you want to add ginger?

User: No, some garlic.

Computer: Press 2 cloves of garlic. Put the garlic on the chicken. What vegetables do you like?

User: Onions, carrots, celery, okra.

Computer: Green onions or white?

User: Green.

Computer: Slice the onions, slice the carrots, slice the celery.

User: What about the okra?

Computer: Yeech! Anything but okra!

User: Okay, how about apples?

Computer: Sorry, I don't know anything about apples. Put the vegetables in the wok. Stir the mixture with chopsticks. Do you have chopsticks?

User: Yes.

Computer: When the mixture is cooked, it is ready to eat. Bon appetit!

Select one of your favorite recipes. How many food items would you need to program? What attributes would you program for each food item? How many preparation methods would you need to include? When the computer doesn't recognize an entry (as with okra in the example), you can program a choice of full-sentence responses. Would you want these sentences to differ when the computer doesn't recognize (a) the type of recipe requested and (b) the name of a food item? What opening and closing signals would you use? Can you predict where communication might break down in your cooking script? Do you think such programs can serve as models of human understanding of scripts? Why can't they serve as models of *acquisition* of scripts?

3. Nemoianu (1980) gives examples of play scripts of young children. In the following example, Martin (M, English L1) instructs Sean (S, German L1) on how to play "ambulance" within another play sequence about detectives being shot.

   M: ((sings)) Hey, Sean, pretend that I got dead and you called . . . the ambulance. It goes like this. Pow! ((falls down))
   S: ((comes near Martin and falls down too))

M: You are *not* dead, *I'm* dead.
S: My dead.
M: Pretend that I was dead and you cal/led
S: /yeah ((picks up Batman))
M: That's not it. That's not the telephone, this is the telephone.
S: I want Batman. Can I have Batman?
M: ((falls down again)) Call the ambulance! You should call the ambulance.
S: What can *they* do?
M: They can get kids up. Right here is the telephone. Now call.
S: OK ((picks up the receiver))
M: No, first you have to do this. ((dials number))
S: OK. Hello? (to M) He's not there.
M: I can tell them and then I go back dead. ((takes phone and dials)) Hello, ambulance ((passes the telephone to Sean))
S: Hi, how are you? Fine . . . Good. ((hangs up)) He's not there.
M: ((calls again)) The ambulance department? Yes, they said yes. ((angry to Sean)) Here! Call the ambulance, the ambulance department, OK? . . . I'm gonna call them. Hello, the ambulance department? Yes. You are gonna come? Yes. ((lies down "dead")) Ding, ding. That's the ambulance.

(Data source: Nemoianu 1980)

In the following exchange, Martin (M) is playing with Milvia (MI, German L1). Milvia acknowledges the play topic, but then shifts roles within it:

M: Hey, I've got a, I've got an idea. We can play doctors. This is a great idea. Great idea. I get the stethoscope. Where is the . . . Here. (Give Milvia the stethoscope) You be the doctor. ((He lies down))
MI: Are you sick?
M: Yeah
MI: I have to call the doctor.
M: You *are* the doctor.
MI: I have to *call* the doctor . . . on the phone. Hello, hi doctor. Martin is sick because he didn't sleep. Okay, bye-bye. ((to Martin)) He works at the clinic tomorrow at one. The doctor's gonna come tomorrow at one.
M: Oh, after I take a bath.
MI: Yah, and you be good.

Nemoianu suggests that Milvia prefers to play the mother role because this is the register she knows best. She accepts the convention of pretend play but manages to switch to a role that she knows. Even in situations that do not call for this role, Milvia manages to change the script to include it:

M: The boat's gonna leave. The boat's gonna leave. . . .
MI: ((looking nervously around)) Where's the baby? ((gives him a baby doll)) Here's your baby. Emma, Emma!

Nemoianu believes that such chances to play roles in scripts encourage language development among young second language learners. If possible, read Nemoianu's book and consider how a theory of second language learning might incorporate learning from scripts within it. Do you think adults have as much fun "playing" with language scripts in the situational approach? How might more spontaneous play be encouraged for older learners?

4. A great deal has been written about courtroom discourse. Modeling of courtroom scripts has been discussed in artificial intelligence studies. Linguists, too, have analyzed such discourse in detail. If you have ever been so frustrated trying to find a parking place on campus that you were tempted to steal a parking permit, you may identify with one plea-bargaining case discussed by Maynard (1985). The outcome of the case (a reduction to a traffic violation from a petty theft charge) is not so interesting as the reasons for the reduction in charges. The public defender describes the offender not as playing the role of a thief but that of a student. The student doesn't consider himself a thief. The public defender tells a series of stories regarding others, including himself, who as students sometimes broke rules with impunity. When the defender worries about whether this student will be able to get a security clearance with a theft charge on the records, the district attorney relents. Role is also an issue in the article by Wodak (1985) about a judge who asks defendants questions that are not really part of their role in the trial – questions about their jobs, religion, marital status, and so forth. Can you think of instances when you could excuse your behavior or performance on the basis of not *being* a role rather than not *playing* a role (for example, not being a native speaker or not being a member of a certain society rather than playing a particular role where you made a goof)?

5. Saville-Troike (1982: 154–167) gives examples of ethnographic analysis, some of which parallel script analysis with setting, roles, props, actions, and so forth. Review these pages and other relevant sections of the book and try to determine how the goals of "ethnography" – an approach that has grown out of sociology and anthropology – differ from those of communication analysis and script theory, which have grown out of sociology and the study of artificial intelligence in computer science.

B. Classroom scripts

6. Young children learn not only how to play the student role in classroom scripts but also how to play their gender role in school. If you are an elementary school teacher, observe the roles children assume in the various activities during one day. How do these roles determine, in part, the language that the children use?

7. Carpenter (1983) compared the office-hour talk of professors with native and nonnative students. In the office-hour script with native speakers, the professor always commented on the student's progress if the evaluation was positive (e.g., "That sounds fine." "That's a good choice."). The evaluation occurred either at the end of a paper-planning discussion, at the very end of the appointment, or both. When the evaluation was not positive, nothing was said. The native students did *not* ask about how they were doing in the face of these negative cues. In the appointments with nonnative students, students who received no evaluative comments asked their professors at the end of the appointment whether or not their work was acceptable. Do you think this is the result of anxiety, or do you think that nonnative students do not recognize the negative cue of "no evaluation" within this script. How much variability is there among professors as to whether they always give a positive statement when their evaluation is positive? (I never give positive feedback to students who have excellent performances, assuming they know it and don't need it; I give many more assurances to encourage students who are struggling.) Design a research plan to investigate these questions.

8. In addition to Sinclair and Coulthard's system, there are a number of other ways that researchers have coded classroom discourse. Cooper et al. (1982) has a coding system that is especially helpful for the description of peer learning interactions. Green and Wallat (1981) and Mehan (1979) offer other helpful coding systems. Stubbs (1983) and Stubbs and Delamont (1976) provide further insights into classroom interaction. Review these different coding systems and identify their strengths and weaknesses for your own research projects.

9. Dorr-Bremme (1990) examined the relation between classroom control and the teacher's use of boundary markers. The elementary school studied had a series of well-defined activities in which students were able to behave "appropriately" – that is, made contributions that fit within the activity. To mark the shift from one activity to another, the teacher used a variety of cues

including activity formulas (such as, "Okay, let's see who's not here today" at the start of attendance; "Kim, go get a magic marker and let's see if you can do the calendar today" at the start of calendar), prosodic features such as decrease or increase in rate and shifts in loudness of voice, and framing words (such as "all right," "okay"). When there was an absence of such cues, the students took this as a signal that the teacher had no special agenda and that the floor was open to anyone. This led to a breakdown – interactional trouble where students "behaved" or "misbehaved" until the discourse was negotiated back to its regular format. Thus, when teachers did not use familiar signals to mark the end of one activity and the start of the next, there were problems in class control. Not all children in this study had acquired the meanings of these signals. Dorr-Bremme noted that when students are unaware of cues or fail to respond to them in an appropriate way, the students are ascribed undesirable personal qualities such as "immature," "strong-willed," or "out of it." If the data you taped for Practice 1.2 is from an elementary school, look for the presence or absence of boundary markers. Do you see any connection between control and the presence or absence of these markers in your data?

10. In the section on classroom scripts, we emphasized the notion of moves as units within an exchange. This notion is for analysis purposes only. It's highly unlikely that teachers or students view moves as such. Teachers and students are much more likely to think of the discourse in terms of their personal and instructional goals and to see the exchanges as evidence of a plan to carry out those goals. In summarizing the many diary studies that have been carried out by sophisticated language learners, Bailey (1983) notes the many mentions made of anxiety and competitiveness, both of which relate to the desire to be praised for one's excellence. Students' goals may, indeed, reflect their need to be recognized as good language learners – perhaps not just good, but exceptional. Bailey lists seven recurring themes in the diaries:

    a. Overt self-comparison of the language learner with classmates, with other learners, and with personal expectations

    b. Emotive responses to these overt self-comparisons, including hostility toward other learners

    c. A desire to outdo other language learners, including racing through exams to be the first finished and shouting out answers in class

    d. Emphasis on or concern with tests and grades

115

e. Desire to gain the teacher's approval, including perception of the teacher as a parent figure, and the need to meet or overcome the teacher's expectations

f. Anxiety during the language lesson, such as fear of being called on

g. Withdrawal from the language-learning experience, mentally or physically

Competitiveness can, of course, be a good thing. What kinds of activities in your classroom stimulate constructive competition? It can also be very debilitating. If competition means viewing oneself as not "the best," anxiety can result, and students may withdraw from the class. What activities in your classroom discourage competitiveness? Do you believe they help lessen anxiety? Do highly competitive students balk at such activities? (It has often been noted that many Native American groups stress cooperation and discourage competitiveness. Teachers who have been trained in highly competitive education systems may find it difficult to teach using methods based on cooperative learning techniques. How prepared are you to work in a school system where competition is no longer central to instruction and learning? There is also some disagreement about competitiveness and the need for approval. Some studies show that people with a high need of approval are either extreme risktakers or superconservative. Moderate risktakers are supposed to be better learners. See Beebe 1983 on risk taking.)

11. Nystrom (1983) examined classroom videotapes to determine teachers' goals concerning language learning for their bilingual students. She asked a series of questions:

   a. Do teachers care more about language form or about communication of meaning – that is, do they attend less to grammatical errors than to unsuccessful communication of messages?

   b. Do language teachers attend to language errors more or in different ways than teachers in nonlanguage classes?

   c. Do teachers tend to correct solicited student statements more frequently than unsolicited student statements?

   d. Do teachers correct more frequently or in different ways when other students hear the correction?

   e. Can a teacher's individual correction style be characterized to reveal his or her attitude toward language teaching and learning?

After reading Nystrom's article, look at the types of evaluative comments you or your teachers give in class and try to characterize them along the continuum described by Nystrom.

12. Sinclair and Coulthard (1975) established an analytic framework for the description of the interactions in classrooms. Review their book and apply their method to the data you collected for your classroom. Sinclair and Coulthard's analysis covers interactions rather than the intent or goal of the interactants. Other systems attempt to look at both the script and the function of moves during the interaction. You may also want to apply the system described by Gaies (1983) to your data. How different is the result? Read Long (1983), "Inside the Black Box," for a summary of many types of classroom analyses. Which method do you feel would best capture the discourse of your classroom?

C. Scripts and memory

13. Gerselman and Callot (1990) believe that there are two complementary memory processes: conceptually driven (as with scripts) and data driven (as from the specific script instance). They asked adults to recall a restaurant script story and a doctor script story. Each story included typical script statements but also some optional statements (e.g., The waitress took his order into the kitchen. The doctor read her chart with care.) The authors hypothesized that asking people to recall the stories in a forward order tapped conceptual memory and that reverse recall might bring out more specific instance recall. They compared two groups: One group did two forward recalls and the other did one forward and one reverse order recall. The second group remembered more specific instance information than the first group. Read Gerselman and Callot's article and explain why this should be so. Do you think you would get similar results with ESL or EFL learners whose scripts for the first language differ? Design a research plan to investigate this question.

14. Erickson and Mattson (1981) and van Oostendorf and de Mul (1990) show that adults will answer a question such as "How many animals of each kind did Moses take on the ark?" without noticing the Moses-Noah error. They attribute this to the semantic similarity of Moses and Noah. Both are male, biblical characters; they are both leaders and involved with water, and so forth. How might this finding relate to script theory and spreading activation in memory? Do you think that second language learners experience more or fewer such semantic illusions? How could you relate this to the notion of risk taking and tolerance for ambiguity – two factors thought to relate to success and failure in language learning?

15. Salager-Meyer (1990) examined and classified metaphors in

English, French, and Spanish medical texts. These included architectural (e.g., abdominal *wall, coupole* diaphragmique, *pilares* del corazón), geomorphical (*stellar* angioma, *plateaux* vertebraux, *campo* visual), phytomorphical (nerve *roots, racine* du *tronc* porte, *arbol* bronquial), anatomical (foreign *bodies, tête* du pancreas, *cabeza* del metatarsio), and zoomorphical (*butterfly* rash, bruit de *galop,* murmullo de *paloma*). The same categories seem to appear in all three languages. How might you relate this to spreading transfer of meanings in script theory? Do you think the same categories occur in non-IndoEuropean languages?

16. Robinson and Swanson (1990) discuss the organization of autobiographical memory. Do you think you have mental files for autobiographical scripts? If you are interested in "living histories," Robinson and Swanson's article has an excellent bibliography on the relationship of memory to autobiographical scripts. You might use this as a basis for research on "living histories" of elderly immigrants in your community.

References

Bailey, K. (1983). Competitiveness and anxiety in adult second language learning: Looking *at* and *through* the diary studies. In H. Seliger and M. Long (Eds.), *Classroom oriented research in second language acquisition* (pp. 67–103). Rowley, Mass.: Newbury House.

Beebe, L. (1983). Risk-taking and the language learner. In H. Seliger and M. Long (Eds.), *Classroom oriented research in second language acquisition* (pp. 39–66). Rowley, Mass.: Newbury House.

Berko-Gleason, J., and Weintraub, S. (1976). The acquisition of routines in child language. *Language in Society, 5,* 137–151.

Carpenter, C. (1983). "Foreigner talk" in university office-hour appointments. In N. Wolfson and E. Judd (Eds.), *Sociolinguistics and language acquisition* (pp. 184–194). Rowley, Mass.: Newbury House.

Christian, D. (1980). What do you mean, request for clarification? In R. Shuy and A. Shnukal (Eds.), *Language use and the uses of language* (pp. 128–142). Washington, D.C.: Georgetown University Press.

Cooper, C.; Marquis, A.; and Ayers-Lopez, S. (1982). Peer learning in the classroom. In L. C. Wilkinson (Ed.), *Communicating in the classroom* (pp. 69–84). New York: Academic Press.

Dorr-Bremme, D. W. (1990). Contextualization cues in the classroom: Discourse regulation and social control functions. *Language in Society, 19,* 379–402.

Dyer, M. (1981). The role of TAUs in narratives. In *Proceedings of the Third Annual Conference of the Cognitive Science Society* (pp. 225–227). Hillsdale, N.J.: Lawrence Erlbaum Associates.

Erickson, T., and Mattson, M. (1981). From words to meaning: A semantic illusion. *Journal of Verbal Learning and Verbal Behavior, 20,* 540–551.

Gaies, S. (1983). Learner feedback: An exploratory study of its role in the second language classroom. In H. Seliger and M. Long (Eds.), *Classroom oriented research in second language acquisition.* Rowley, Mass.: Newbury House.

Genishi, C., and De Paolo, M. (1982). Learning through argument in a preschool. In L. C. Wilkinson (Ed.), *Communicating in the classroom* (pp. 49–84). New York: Academic Press.

Gerselman, R. E., and Callot, R. (1990). Reverse vs. forward recall of script-based texts. *Applied Cognitive Psychology, 4,* 2: 141–144.

Green, J., and Wallat, C. (1981). Mapping instructional conversations: A sociolinguistic ethnography. In J. Green and C. Wallat (Eds.), *Ethnography and language in educational settings* (pp. 161–208). Norwood, N.J.: Ablex.

Hawkins, B. (1988). Scaffolded classroom interaction and its relation to second language acquisition for language minority children. Unpublished Ph.D. dissertation, Applied Linguistics, University of California, Los Angeles.

Jordan, C.; Tharp, R.G.; and Vogt, L. (1985). *Compatibility of classroom and culture: General principles, with Navajo and Hawaiian instances.* (Working Paper No. 18). Honolulu: Kamehameha Schools/Bishop Estate.

Long, M. (1983). Inside the black box. In H. Seliger and M. Long (Eds.), *Classroom oriented research in second language acquisition* (pp. 3–38). Rowley, Mass.: Newbury House.

Lytinen, S., and Schank, R. (1982). Representation and translation, *TEXT, 2,* 1–3: 83–111.

Maynard, D. (1985). The analysis of plea bargaining discourse. In T. van Dijk (Ed.), *Handbook of discourse analysis. Vol. 4: Discourse analysis in society* (pp. 153–179). London: Academic Press.

Mehan, H. (1979). *Learning lessons: Social organization in the classroom.* Cambridge, Mass.: Harvard University Press.

Nash, W. (1985). *The language of humor: Style and technique in comic discourse.* English Language Series, no. 16. London: Longman.

Nemoianu, A. M. (1980). *The boat's gonna leave: A study of children learning a second language from conversations with other children.* Amsterdam: John Benjamins B.V.

Nystrom, N. (1983). Teacher-student interaction in bilingual classrooms: Four approaches to error feedback. In H. Seliger and M. Long (Eds.), *Classroom oriented research in second language acquisition* (pp. 169–189). Rowley, Mass.: Newbury House.

van Oostendorf, H., and de Mul, S. (1990). Moses beats Adam: A semantic relatedness effect on semantic illusion. *Acta Psychologica, 74,* 1: 35–46.

Phillips, S. (1972). Participant structures and communicative competence: Warm Springs children in community and classroom. In C. Cazden, D. Hymes, and V. John (Eds.), *The functions of language in the classroom* (pp. 370–394). New York: Teachers College Press.

(1983). *The invisible culture: Communication in classroom and community on the Warm Springs Indian Reservation.* New York: Longman.

von Raffler-Engel, W. (1977). The nonverbal adjustment of adults to children's communicative style. In B. Laria and D. Gulstad (Eds.), *Papers for the 1977 Mid-American Linguistic Conference* (pp. 3–28). Columbus: University of Missouri.

Richards, M. (1987). Teacher talk: Experimental classroom research of the ESL teacher register. Master's thesis, Applied Linguistics, University of California, Los Angeles.

Richmond, V. (1990). Communication in the classroom: Power and motivation, *Communication in Education, 39,* 181–195.

Robinson, J., and Swanson, K. (1990). Autobiographical memory: The next phase. *Applied Cognitive Psychology, 4,* 321–335.

Salager-Meyer, F. (1990). Metaphors in medical English prose: A comparative study with French and Spanish. *English for Special Purposes, 9,* 145–159.

Saville-Troike, M. (1982). *The ethnography of communication.* Baltimore: University Park Press.

Saville-Troike, M.; McClure, E.; and Fritz, M. (1984). Communicative tactics in children's second language acquisition. In F. Eckman, L. Bell, and D. Nelson (Eds.), *Universals of second language acquisition* (pp. 60–71). New York: Newbury House.

Schank, R. (1982). *Dynamic memory: A theory of remind and learning in computers and people.* Cambridge: Cambridge University Press.

(1984). *Conceptual information processing.* Amsterdam: North Holland.

Schank, R., and Abelson, R. (1977). *Scripts, plans, goals, and understanding.* Hillsdale, N.J.: Lawrence Erlbaum Associates.

Schank, R., and Riesbeck, C. K. (1981). *Inside computer understanding: Five programs plus miniatures.* Hillsdale, N.J.: Lawrence Erlbaum Associates.

Shapira, R. G. (1978). The non-learning of English: A case study of an adult. In E. Hatch (Ed.), *Second language acquisition: A book of readings* (pp. 246–255). Rowley, Mass.: Newbury House.

Sinclair, J., and Coulthard, R. M. (1975). *Towards an analysis of discourse.* London: Oxford University Press.

Stubbs, M. (1983). *Discourse analysis.* Oxford: Basil Blackwell.

Stubbs, M., and Delamont, S. (Eds.) 1976. *Explorations in classroom observation.* London: John Wiley and Sons.

Wodak, R. (1985). The interaction between judge and defendant. In T. van Dijk (Ed.), *Handbook of discourse analysis. Vol 4. Discourse analysis in society* (pp. 181–192). London: Academic Press.

Wong Fillmore, L. (1976). The second time around: Cognitive and social strategies in language acquisition. Ph.D. dissertation: Stanford University.

Young, D. (1974). The acquisition of syntax by three Spanish-speaking children. M.A. thesis, Applied Linguistics, University of California, Los Angeles.

Zernik, U. (1987). Strategies in language acquisition: Learning phrases in context. Ph.D. dissertation, Computer Science, University of California, Los Angeles.

4 Speech acts and speech events

Chapter 1 presented the system components that outline the structure of communication. Chapter 2 discussed the ways that these components are signaled in social and cross-cultural communication. In Chapter 3 we looked at how the content of communication is organized – via script theory. In this chapter, we look at other ways of analyzing the content of communication – using speech act theory and speech event analysis.

Speech acts

Just as linguists have tried to understand how speakers might be able to produce an infinite number of sentences given a very finite set of rules for sentences, philosophers have tried to understand how an infinite number of sentences might reflect a very finite set of functions. The philosophers reasoned that since the number of things we do with words is limited, we ought to be able to assign functions to utterances.

The problem with assigning functions to sentences is that speaker intent and sentence meaning are not always the same. Speaker intent may be more or less, or actually the opposite, of sentence meaning (as in sarcasm). Thus, no utterance is completely context free in terms of meaning or function. Nevertheless, philosophers such as Austin (1962) and Searle (1969) have shown that it is possible to classify utterances into a very small set of functions. In Searle's (1969, 1976) system these include directives, commissives, representatives, declaratives, and expressives.

Directives

The starred (i.e., unacceptable) responses in the following pairs show that syntactic form alone does not tell us how to interpret the speaker's intent.

How many times do I have to tell you?
*Five times.

We need this photocopied for the 4 o'clock meeting.
*That's true.

Let's give Heidi a call three times a day.
*Yes, please do.

121

Could you do the dishes?
*Yes, I could.

Where are the matches?
*In the matchbox.

What happened to the salt?
*Nothing happened to the salt.

Is Pattilee there?
*Yes, she is here.

How would it look if you were to arrive late?
*It would look beautiful.

In each case, a request is being made so that someone will do or stop doing something. The speech act label for this function is *directive*.

In English language textbooks, two forms are usually taught for the directive function – the imperative and the polite imperative. However, the preceding examples illustrate the wide range of possible structures native speakers use for the directive function.

Social constraints suggest that when we make a request, we expect that request to be complied with. Some researchers believe that the greater the risk of refusal, the more indirect the directive will be. To account for the choice of directive forms, Ervin-Tripp (1972) found it helpful to classify directives into five types that include the relationship between the speaker and addressee roles:

1. Personal need/desire statements
   Example: I need/want X.
   Addressee: Subordinates
2. Imperative
   Example: Gimme X.
   Addressee: Subordinates or familiar equals
3. Imbedded imperative
   Example: Could you give me X (please, ok)?
   Addressee: Unfamiliar people; people who differ in rank or who are physically distant; someone who is in his or her own territory; someone whose willingness to comply is in doubt
4. Permission directive
   Example: May I have X? Is there any X left? Do you have X?
   Addressee: Someone who might not comply; also used when there is an obstacle to compliance
5. Hint (sometimes with humor)
   Example: This has to be done over. What about the X?
   Addressee: Persons with shared rules such as members of a family, people living together, and work groups

We have already noted in Chapter 2 that ritual constraints smooth social interaction, so it's not surprising to find that sensitivity to social groups is, in part, coded into our choice of directive forms. That is, all languages have directives, but the variation in directive forms within a language must be sensitive to social constraints. When we do not pay attention to these constraints, people may feel offended or think there is something wrong with the communication. Consider the following example. A colleague (not a personal friend) at another university sent me a request to collect some comparison data for him. Our universities were in different countries, and the request came at the end of the academic year when all professors are overloaded with work and the students from whom I would need to collect the data were preparing for final exams. Therefore, the ability and willingness of the addressee (me) to carry out the request was definitely in doubt. I was physically distant from the requester, but I was asked to do an action in my own territory. Yet, the request was stated in terms of imperatives: "Follow the directions . . ." "Return no later than . . ." This colleague was a native speaker of English. My reaction was, "Well of all the nerve!"

Practice 4.1   Directives

1. Supply an appropriate response to each of the following:
   a. Let's put the typewriter over there (gesture).
   b. Oh, the sugar's all gone.
   c. Sure is cold in here.
   d. What are these shoes doing here?
   e. These exams need to be graded.
   f. What happened to the beer?
   Scale the degree of politeness or directness versus indirectness of the preceding examples. How large a role might suprasegmentals such as stress, pitch, and intonation play in strengthening or softening the directive? Using Ervin-Tripp's classification, can you identify the relationship between the speaker and addressee?
2. Select one of the scripts discussed in Chapter 3. Which types of directives would actors in the script use? How might the directive form change according to actor role?
3. Look at the sequence of directive structures in a language textbook you have used. How wide a range of forms is shown? Does the sequence suggest that some linguistic forms of the directive are more central than others? How are differences in forms explained (e.g., politeness, relationship of speaker and addressee)?
4. In your classroom data (from Practice 1.2), examine the directives used by the teacher. If several members of your

study group have such data, you might investigate whether there are differences when teachers are working with adult learners rather than children. Do you notice differences in directives of male and female teachers as they work with male and female students? Our choice of directive form should reflect something about our view of the teacher role. For example, a teacher who believes teachers are facilitators ought to display different forms of the directive than a teacher who believes his or her role is that of a drill master. Do the data contain examples in support of this notion?

5. In elementary school classes, teachers often have to manipulate students to do certain tasks. What methods are commonly used? Do these reflect differences in types of directive forms?

6. Bosses complain about staff who, because of union or civil service rules, cannot be fired easily. They say that once employees have tenure, they only do what they wish to do. Deans likewise complain about college professors who receive tenure and then refuse to serve on committees or carry out other tasks when they don't want to. In these cases, what kinds of directives could be used to get employees to perform their duties?

7. Written directives may be strengthened by type size and form:

Before connecting
ANYTHING
on the Disk II or Apple II
TURN OFF THE POWER
This is a must.

During the next few days, note the print directives that you see. How and why are these directives strengthened? Do you find many such directives in the school environment? Are there any in your classroom? After you have collected the directives, ask language learners if these are typical ways of offering strong directives in their cultures as well.

8. I received the following directive from one of my Japanese students: "Dear Dr. Hatch: I will be very glad if I have your comments on my thesis in this week. Thank you very much, M." What parts of the directive are softened? What parts are aggravated? How might a native speaker have phrased this directive? Ask your international students how they

would frame such a request. Compare the results with those given by native speakers.

Commissives

A second speech act function in languages is *commissives,* which are statements that function as promises or refusals for action. Like directives, commissives vary in strength; they may be very strong or highly hedged in either positive or negative directions.

Maybe I can do that tomorrow.
I pledge to uphold the Constitution of the United States of America.
Don't worry, I'll be there.
I already gave at the office.

The forms used for commissives vary according to social relationships (ritual constraints at work again). If the President of the United States called and invited you to dinner at the White House, the form of the commissive would most likely differ from your response to your mom's invitation to drop by for supper. The commissive response I gave to my colleague who asked/ demanded that I collect data in the last week of classes was certainly different from what I would give to a friend who framed the request in a more circumspect manner.

Forms used may differ, not only across status and situation but also by gender. Women are thought to use more hedged commissives than men. It has also been claimed that women in general are not assertive. If true (and I doubt it), the validity of these claims would be evident in the types of commissives and directives women use – another interesting research possibility, especially in a cross-cultural context. In face-to-face encounters, it is fairly clear who is making the promise – that is, who is committed to the content – but in other circumstances (e.g., when we are watching television), it is not so clear. When Michael Jordan directs us to "eat our Wheaties" so that we too can bound through the air and make a slam dunk, is he (or the writers of the commercial or anyone at all) to be held accountable for the promise of such results?

All languages have commissives. When they are used and in what forms vary along social lines. The appropriateness of commissives (as well as directives) also varies across language and culture groups. Take, for example, declining invitations – a negative commissive. A language learner who does not know how to politely decline an invitation in the host language may try to transfer forms that work in his or her first language. This is true of Americans living overseas who alter their English forms to match that of the host language. For example, in Egypt I soon learned not to respond to invitations with "I'd love to (but)..." It didn't work. If I used an affirmative commissive ("I'd love to but..."), and the invitation was dropped, I felt hurt. If I used a

125

negative commissive ("I'm sorry, I can't come."), the speaker often looked surprised or offended. But once I heard an Egyptian use "I must" as a neutral commissive in English, I knew what to say. An "I must" statement allowed the invitation to be recognized as having been given and valued, and allowed the giver to receive a response. The sequence was accomplished in a way that fulfilled social expectations. If the invitation was genuine, a series of invitation and "I must" moves were negotiated to show that each side was sincere in the offer and the promise. See page 137 for an example of the reverse – where foreign students misinterpret "apparent invitations" of English speakers.

Practice 4.2 Commissives

1. If the secretary of an obnoxious office associate called to issue an invitation to dinner with the associate, how might you respond?

2. Imagine that a friend called and invited you to dinner, but you really didn't feel like being sociable. What might you say?

3. Compare the commissives you used for questions 1 and 2 with those of your classmates. Where does each of your commissives fit in a continuum of strength?

4. Given the force of social roles, it is often difficult to make a refusal. In general, we want to be helpful and do what is requested of us. (Part of the ritual constraint system is that if favors are sought, they will be granted.) List as many refusal formulas (negative commissives) as you can. Which might you use if you feel the request is unfair? If, under pressure to be helpful, you promise to do something and then must later refuse, how is this later refusal done?

5. In California, a purchaser who has signed a contract to buy a house or other substantial purchase item has three days in which to rescind the promise. In breaking a promise in nonbusiness situations, we offer explanations and excuses. Do you think a negative commissive in business transactions would also be accompanied by explanations and excuses? Why or why not?

6. The need to soften negative commissives varies according to social constraints. Again, these differ across languages. Set up a situation that calls for a negative commissive and ask your international students how they believe the commissive would be handled in their first language setting. If the commissives differ, ask if they have had difficulty with this speech act in English.

Representatives

A *representative* speech act can be judged for truth value. The preceding sentence is a representative. So are the following:

I went to the Amish quilt exhibit.
There are approximately twenty quilts on display.
Some are very old and some are new.
The old are very dramatic because they have black or dark colors for background.
Some are almost art deco in design while others are extremely angular.
The quilts contrast with the simplicity of decoration shown in the photos of Amish homes.

Representatives may vary in terms of how hedged or aggravated the assertion might be. "Darwin was partially correct" is, obviously, not as strong a statement as "Darwin was right" or "Darwin was wrong." We can soften our claims with lexical hedges. In the statements regarding the Amish quilt exhibition, notice the lexical items "approximately," "very," "almost," and "extremely," which strengthen or weaken the assertions.

Hedges are not always the same as "weasel words," which temper the directness of a statement. (The two terms reflect a different point of view. "Weasel words" is pejorative – we're trying to avoid responsibility for our claims. "Hedges" qualify, soften, or make claims more polite.) The two examples that follow show how hedges can be used to let us "weasel out" of responsibility for our statements.

Perhaps Gould overstated his argument regarding an *apparent* weakness in Darwin's notes.
The data *appear* to support the assumption of significant differences between the two groups of students.

Hedges, however, also serve a ritual function. They may act like disfluencies in smoothing over a disagreement with a conversational partner.

Maybe she *just* feels *kinda* blue.

In this last example, it is a simple matter to understand the *locutionary* force of the utterance – that is, what the sentence says. However, the *illocutionary* force of the utterance – what is intended by the utterance – is not clear unless context is taken into account. In the two earlier examples, the locutionary force is hazy because of the hedging on responsibility for the statement. There are some languages (e.g., Turkish, Japanese, Hopi) where the speaker's degree of responsibility for the truth value of what follows is marked with morphology – a discourse function is directly reflected in the grammar of the language. Fortunately or unfortunately, that is not the case in English. Hedges help us do this instead.

Practice 4.3   Representatives

1. When people do not wish to be held responsible for the truth of their claims, what range of hedges can they use? Are these mainly lexical, syntactic, or prosodic (intonation)? Can these signals be arranged along a continuum from weak to strong? If you find you can arrange them to your satisfaction, you might continue with a research project testing whether other native speakers agree with your scale.

2. Lennon logged the "uncertainty markers" that university students used to qualify their representatives. He categorized them in six groups:

   "It's hard" (It's hard to tell but I think + representative)
   "I wonder" (I'm wondering if + representative)
   "I'm not sure" (I'm not really sure, but I think + representative)
   "Don't really know" (Well, I don't really know, but isn't + representative)
   "I think" (Well, I think + representative)
   Miscellaneous (I'm getting on shaky ground here ((smile)) but + representative. Mmm ((stares wistfully into air)) + representative.)

   Log the "uncertainty markers" you or your students use (especially when not really prepared for class!). Are they the same as the hedges teachers use when they are unsure of their answers to questions students ask?

3. With your students, examine the representatives that writers produce in making claims in different types of text (perhaps a news article, an editorial, or a research article in your field). Are there differences in strength of claims from hedged to aggravated? Compare your findings to those of others in your class or study group. Do your findings agree? That is, are the differences owing to text type, or are they owing to individual choices of authors?

Declaratives

Declaratives (Austin calls these *performatives*) are speech acts that, when uttered, bring about a new state of being. When a teacher says "Class dismissed," a real change takes place – students get up and leave. The declarative "I now pronounce you husband and wife" changes the status of the couple. If a judge declares "I find you guilty as charged," the accused's status has changed from innocent to guilty. The utterance "I declare these truths to be self-evident . . ." is not a declarative if everyone thought the truths were self-evident prior to the pronouncement. If the speaker has no right – that is, no special role that allows for such a pronouncement – no real change occurred as a result of the uttering. It is an assertion about a representative.

There are special role requirements that go with the uttering of declaratives. If someone other than a certified person says "by the power invested in me," no marriage occurs. That is, the person who utters a declarative must have the power (inherited from the role in the script) to do so. Otherwise, it is all play acting.

Practice 4.4 Declaratives

1. Marriage ceremonies differ across cultures. What are the declarative statements that are similar to "I now pronounce you husband and wife" within wedding ceremonies from other cultures? Are the roles that allow one to utter the declarative the same?
2. In what circumstances would the exclamations "You won!" "You passed!" and "You're fired!" be declaratives? In what instances would they not have this function?
3. There are not many opportunities for us to use declaratives. How many declaratives can you think of? Are there examples that are not attached to a particular role in a particular script?

Expressives

All languages have utterances that can be classified as having an expressive function. Our statements of joy and disappointment, likes and dislikes are reflected in statements such as:

I'm so:: very disappointed.
What a great day!
Oh my, that's terrible!

Compliments can be expressions of like or dislike. If, during the next few days, you listen to and log the compliments that you hear, you will find only a small number of syntactic structures. Manes and Wolfson (1980, 1981) actually collected and categorized compliments and found them surprisingly formulaic. More than half of the 686 compliments they collected were formed by NP [noun phrase] IS/LOOKS (really) ADJ [adjective] – for example, "Your hair looks really nice" and "That shirt is great." Adding two other syntactic forms – I (really) LIKE/LOVE NP (e.g., "I really like those shoes") and PRO [pronoun] BE [is] (really) (a) ADJ NP (e.g., "This was really a great

129

meal") covered 85 percent of the data. Only nine syntactic patterns were needed to cover the data.

In all speech acts, we have mentioned a continuum of strength of forms from indirect to direct or from hedged to aggravated. Expressives, too, can be arranged along a continuum of strength. The range is mediated by social factors (ritual constraints again). For example, men and women are expected to use different lexical expressives in English, and the range of "acceptable" strength of expressives may differ by gender as well.

The form of expressives and expectations regarding when expressives are appropriate vary across language groups. The form and intensity of expressives may also differ. Many of our stereotypes regarding different cultures are bound up with expressives. We say language group A is so cold, so unable or unwilling to express feelings while language group B is so expressive – feelings are not only shown on faces but in the language as well. We take delight in translations of flowery compliments (expressive statements) from other languages. Wolfson (1981a) gives examples from Farsi-English bilinguals:

S: Your shoes are very nice.
A: It is your eyes which can see them which are nice.

S: It was delicious, Mom. I hope your hands never have pain.
M: I'm glad you like it.

And, perhaps, we fail to appreciate the nuances of understated expressives in other language groups.

Practice 4.5   Expressives

1. List five examples of expressives of joy and arrange them along your own strength continuum.
2. Try to use these same examples in another language. (You might ask international students to translate these into their languages.) Are there equivalent expressions? Is the strength continuum the same? Are they used by everyone regardless of gender, age, role, or status?
3. List five examples of expressives that show either sorrow or disapproval. Arrange them on a continuum of strength and compare this continuum with that for joy. What correspondences do you see?

It was noted earlier that Austin calls declaratives "performatives." *Performatives,* however, may be commissives or directives as well as declaratives. A "test" for performatives is to insert a "hereby" in the utterance. "I hereby promise, order, bet you $5.00 that . . ." sounds right. This "test" distinguishes performatives from perlocutionary verbs. "I hereby inspire, persuade you to

. . ." doesn't sound right. The distinction between performative and perlocutionary verbs is important here only in that performatives regulate social interaction. The role of the speaker determines who has the right to utter performatives. There is also an expectation that the listener will accept or follow whatever the declarative says. That's not the case with perlocutionary verbs.

Speech act functions and subfunctions

Each major speech act function can also be subdivided into a number of subfunctions. For example, in the application of speech act research to language teaching, the Council of Europe created a "notational-functional syllabus" (van Ek 1976). While the Council drew on the work of Austin and Searle, the final set of speech functions differs somewhat. Six major functions are identified. (Where possible, the speech act equivalent is given.)

1. Exchange factual information
   Example: The plane departs at 7:10.
   Speech act equivalent: representative
2. Exchange intellectual information
   Example: These arguments are correct.
   Speech act equivalent: representative
3. Exchange emotional attitudes
   Example: I'm worried about my term papers.
   Speech act equivalent: expressive
4. Exchange moral attitudes
   Example: I appreciate your help.
   Speech act equivalent: expressive
5. Suasion
   Example: Hand in your assignments.
   Speech act equivalent: directive
6. Socializing
   Example: Hi, Larry, how are you?
   Speech act equivalent: directive? (i.e., "Tell me how you are.")

In the notional-functional framework, each function is then divided into subfunctions. For example, "exchange emotional attitudes" includes like/dislike, preference/nonpreference, satisfaction/dissatisfaction, worry/confidence, fear/optimism, surprise/boredom, hope, sympathy, and so forth. Following is a list of some of the subfunctions identified in van Ek (1976). (For a complete description please see van Ek.)

1. Imparting/seeking FACTUAL information: identify, ask, report, say, think X

131

2. Express/discover INTELLECTUAL attitudes: state whether you/ask if others
   - agree or disagree
   - know or don't know
   - remember or forgot
   - consider X possible or impossible
   - are capable or not capable
   - consider X logical
   - consider (others) certain or uncertain
   - consider (others) obliged to do something
   - ask or give permission
   - accept or decline an offer or invitation
3. Express/inquire about EMOTIONAL attitudes: express your own/question others'
   - interest or lack of interest
   - surprise
   - hope, disappointment
   - fear or worry
   - preference
   - gratitude
   - sympathy
   - intention
   - want or desire
4. Express/question MORAL attitudes: express or request
   - apology or forgiveness
   - approval or disapproval
   - appreciation
   - regret
   - indifference
5. Suasion:
   suggest, request, invite, instruct
   advise or warn someone to (not) do something
   offer or request assistance
6. Socializing:
   greet, take leave
   introduce
   attract attention
   propose a toast
   congratulate
   begin a meal (e.g., bon appétit)

These lists of functions have become the basis for "threshold" level (*le niveau seuil* in French) syllabus design in language teaching where the emphasis is on teaching functions. The functions are sequenced into a syllabus so that students are taught how to apologize, express preference or disappointment, disagree, and so on.

Linguists may use different names for functions, but most descriptions do resemble each other. Halliday's system (Halliday 1975, 1976), although not incorporated into a teaching syllabus, is widely used in child language research and in other applied linguistic studies. Halliday's primary functions include:

1. *Instrumental.* The function that serves our wants or needs. The "I want" or "I need" function.
2. *Regulatory.* The function that lets us control actions. The "do this" function.
3. *Interactional.* The vocatives and other signals that get attention and allow us to interact with others.
4. *Personal.* The ways we express our individual personalities through language.
5. *Heuristic.* The "teach me" or "tell me why" function that helps us build our own worlds.
6. *Imaginative.* The "let's pretend" function that helps us build our own worlds.
7. *Informative.* The function that lets us share information with others.

It is easy to see that Halliday's classification would work well in describing functions in child language and in the elementary school classroom. The notional-functional system has been used extensively in planning syllabi for language teaching. The Austin and Searle speech act classification is more often used for analytic work in linguistics and in philosophy of language. Halliday's system might be best used to describe child language and to plan syllabi for beginning language learners.

Practice 4.6   Speech act functions and subfunctions

1. To further elaborate each function or subfunction in the notional-functional approach, a list of frequently used expressions is given. For example, under "suasion," examples of four subfunctions are listed. Add to each two examples of utterances you frequently use.
   a. Suggest a course of action *(Let's; we could)*
   b. Advise others to do something. *(Why don't you; I can recommend)*
   c. Warn to refrain. *(Be careful; look out)*
   d. Offer or request assistance. *(Can you help me? Can I help you?)*

2. In the classroom data you collected for Practice 1.2, locate any instances when students or teachers perform any of the van Ek functions. (a) Do they request and obtain *factual information?* Transcribe these portions. To whom is the request made? Does this same person give the information? (b) Are there examples of students' requesting or expressing *emotional attitudes* (such as agreeing/disagreeing, stating something is (not) possible, and so forth)? If so, transcribe these portions. Did the teacher do anything specific to obtain such language use? (c) Did the students as well as the teacher express *moral attitudes* (approving, praising, etc.) in the data? If so, transcribe these portions of the data. What prompted these expressions? (d) Transcribe sections of the data that show "suasion." What is the frequency ratio of student and teacher use of suasion?

3. Bolinger (1967) and Ervin-Tripp (1976) noted that imperatives are seldom used in conversations to command or request. In what situations do you think the following imperatives would be used?
   a. Come in.
   b. Have another drink.
   c. Shut up.
   d. Add two teaspoons of vinegar.
   e. Shove off!
   f. Take care.
   g. Get well soon.
   Are there similar expressions in another language you know or teach? Are they used in the same situations as the English expressions?

4. List any examples from your data of Halliday's functional categories: instrumental, regulatory, interactive, personal, heuristic, imaginative, and informative.

5. Many language teachers assume that a course designed around the notional-functional syllabus would not sequence syntactic structures (as in a grammar approach) or contexts (as in a situational approach). Courses can be labeled as exemplifying a grammar approach, contextual approach, or notional-functional approach, yet the best materials incorporate all three while emphasizing one perhaps more than the others. Look at a sample of different textbooks for the languages you are learning or that you teach. Can you categorize them into one of these three approaches?

Speech act analysis

Speech act analysis has provided researchers with a valuable way to look at language function and the connection between function and grammar forms. Much work has been done on children's acquisition of particular functions (e.g., comprehension of direct and indirect directives). Sociolinguistic studies have also flourished within this approach since such research could pinpoint how linguistic forms of particular speech acts might change according to the gender, age, or role of speakers and hearers. The research has not, however, been extended to look at the connection between script theory and speech acts.

In spite of the insights that can be gained from speech act analysis, a number of problems remain in applying it to language analysis. First, it is difficult to impute the function speakers intend for utterances (especially if one has recourse only to an utterance out of context). Speech act functions may overlap or a speaker may have several intentions in mind; thus, a single utterance can have more than one function. For example, if I'm looking through a file drawer and mutter, "I wonder where I put that paper," the function may be an expressive (Oh no, I've lost it again!) or it may be a directive to another person (Help me find it!). There is no one utterance – one function limitation. Most taxonomies do not allow us to pigeonhole data in several places at the same time. Even if we can solve this problem of taxonomic rigor, the assignment of speech act functions cannot be accurate unless it matches the speaker's intent. That is, the function does not reside in the utterance itself but comes from the speaker who utters the form. The study of speaker intent, called *pragmatics,* is discussed in more detail in Chapter 8.

Second, it is not clear how the subcategories relate to one another. Is a hierarchy involved? For example, are directives such as asking, begging, ordering, demanding, or suggesting just individual "branches" off directive? Or, can they be arranged in some sort of hierarchical manner? When we speak of a continuum of direct to indirect form, is this ranking unilinear? The basic problem here, of course, is how useful a taxonomy can be for either theory or teaching if it simply ends up as a "shopping list" of subcategories that are not organized in any special way.

A third problem, like the second, has to do with system. If the analysis is at the utterance level, how can it help us to understand the structure of discourse? For example, if somebody directs us to wash the dishes, that directive does not stand alone in discourse. Our response, of course, may be nonverbal, but some response (e.g., "not my job," "I don't usually wash dishes until evening," "they look pretty clean to me," etc.) is required. The analysis, at least in this form, doesn't allow us to see how speech act units combine to form a system. To do this requires more than identifying or labeling speech act units.

Speech act analysis has been of value to applied linguistics as researchers and test and materials developers have moved to include it as one of the many resources available for their work. In addition, speech act theory has led to the design of the notional-functional syllabus in language teaching, setting off a major change in language teaching methodology – away from an emphasis on linguistic form to an emphasis on language use.

Speech events

To provide a bridge between speech acts and the higher levels of the communication system (i.e., system and ritual constraints, scripts), we can turn to speech event analysis. In this work, researchers ask about how people use speech acts within a larger discourse structure called the speech event. You have already been asked to perform one speech event – the introduction. It is possible to use only one utterance ("Barbara, this is Sherry"); however, in speech event analysis, the introduction is much more than that utterance. At the very least, a follow-up move is required from Barbara. And, in most settings, the event would be even more complex. If you look back at the introduction you did in Chapter 2 (in Practice 2.10), you certainly did more than give the speaker's name to the audience. In social introductions, we hope to learn something about the speaker in the introduction ("Barbara, this is Sherry – the computer whiz I was telling you about"). Audiences, too, expect to learn something of the speaker's background, information that explains why he or she is worth listening to, and at least the topic of the speaker's talk. Optionally, there may be components that put the audience and the speaker at ease or that establish a link (and reflect glory) between the speaker and the presenter. Formulaic phrases such as "it gives me pleasure," "our speaker today," "join me in welcoming" are also attached to formal introduction speech events.

A speech event analysis, then, attempts to establish the components or templatelike parts of a functionally described interaction. To illustrate, we'll talk about three examples of speech events: compliments, complaints, and advice.

Compliments

Compliments, as speech acts, are classified as expressives – expressions of like or dislike. The speech event of compliment, on the other hand, includes not just the speech act utterance but also the entire compliment interaction. In the following example, the compliment speech act is underlined within the event.

A: Hi Marianne, how are ya?
B: //Fine

136

A: //Wha*t a beautiful scarf.
B: Oh thanks, it is, isn't it? I'm so embarrassed – Keiko gave it to me 'n you
      know these aren't cheap.
A: Oh I kno:w
B: mm so how have you been?

In American English, as you may have observed, compliments often occur between the opening and the first topic of conversation. They also occur in preclosings – a last chance to comment on something that one has noticed. Such noticings, like comments on the weather or last night's basketball game, smooth the interaction and allow a sort of "bonding" behavior between conversation partners (just as "Let's get together for lunch sometime" is a bonding preclosing rather than a true invitation, as Wolfson 1981b showed). As you can imagine, these bonding moves are not always recognized as such by second language learners. That is, learners often remark on the large number of "insincere" compliments Americans give. They also often mistake "Let's get together for lunch sometime" for a true invitation rather than a form of bonding behavior. Such tentatitve invitations need to be negotiated if a real lunch date is to be arranged (Wolfson et al. 1983).

From the preceding example, we might describe the event structure of compliments as: Compliment + acknowledgment/acceptance + bridge. However, it is also possible that the event might begin with a compliment elicitation move. That is, if we expect something to be noticed, but it isn't, we may elicit the notice. If no one noticed my new skis, I might say, "I'm so excited about my new skis." Or if no one noticed my new hairstyle, I might say "I'm not sure I like my new haircut." This should result in a noticing compliment. The compliment elicitation move is an optional element within the event structure.

In the exchange about the scarf, the compliment is acknowledged with appreciation ("thanks") and agreement ("it is, isn't it?"). In acknowledging a compliment, it is possible to deny personal responsibility without denying the compliment. For example, if we're told that our apartment looks nice, we might protest that it is small without denying that it is nice. If we're told our shoes are pretty, we may say they are old (but still pretty). Notice that in the scarf example, the compliment is accepted, agreed with, and then the credit is shifted to someone else – Keiko, the giver.

It is also possible to acknowledge but downgrade the compliment:

A: Thanks but it's just a little thing =
B: I whi//pped up in my spare time
A: //I whipped up this ((giggle))

or shift the focus of the compliment elsewhere:

A: Oh you got THOSE chairs – how great!
B: Yeh, REEEly lucked out (.) the exact same chairs at a third the price.

Acknowledging but completely rejecting a compliment is not very common – perhaps because of the ritual constraint that if we offer a compliment, we expect it will be accepted. Compliment rejection may be said in a joking manner. For example, when I complimented my daughter on a new pin she was wearing, she said "It is NOT and you can't have it!" Compliment rejection may be somewhat easier when the compliment is a noticing, such as "Oh, I really like your new haircut." It is possible to disagree: "Ugh, I hate it." Such responses may be a prelude to a narrative gripe session about the haircut event. However, if the disagreement is not immediately followed by some explanatory story, we are trapped into revoicing the compliment or into inquiring why the haircut is so bad (to convince the person it is okay). Somehow the compliment must be acknowledged and a bridge must be provided to the next topic. As long as the person continues to deny the compliment and provides no bridge, the compliment structure recycles on. The bridge, when it does appear, may seem rather rough. Here is one such instance. Note the problem with bridging to the next topic. A is a native speaker; B's first language is Japanese.

A: I really like your scarf.
B: Ohh nooo it's nothing.
A: No, I really like it.
B: It's not new.
A: I still like it anyway.
B: (.4) ((smiles))
A: Uhh, well, are you uh going to class?

Compliment structure, thus, consists of both optional and obligatory patterns: (compliment solicit) compliment act + acknowledgment (agree/deny/redirect focus) + bridge. While compliments can occur almost anywhere in communication, one very common place is in noticing positions following openings and prior to preclosing moves in communication.

Compliments have several functions. They help establish rapport and smooth the transition from greeting to the first topic of conversation. A second social function of complimenting is to reinforce and encourage good performance. That is, there is a difference between a coach saying "great shot" to an athlete and a friend saying "great hairstyle." The coach wishes to encourage the athlete to continue such performance, but that does not seem to be the motivation for complimenting someone on a new hairstyle. A third function can also be seen in the difference between a coach's saying "great shot" and someone's saying "great dinner" to the cook. The difference may be rather subtle, but it relates to thanks. If we think someone did something especially for us, our compliment pairs it with thanks. The coach is not thanking the athlete. When a teacher compliments a student on "good work," the compliment does not also express thanks. If you compliment your host on a great dinner, that compliment is also an expression of thanks. If your roommate cleans up the apartment, you may say how great it looks and the compliment does include thanks. But if, in fact, you made the mess, the compliment alone may not be sufficient. The compliment should be directly linked to an expression of thanks.

A fourth function of compliments is to soften criticism. We may say, "You're doing a great job on this but (you might want to do something else here)." There is a special intonation curve used on the compliment to show that a "but" criticism is about to follow. Listen to how you say the following utterances. Notice the pauses, word stress, and intonation curves.

Good idea. Wish I'd thought of it.
Good idea and let's think about its implications.
Good idea but let's think about its implications.

Compliment speech events have a definite structure that can be described. Parts of the event are optional (compliment elicitations, agreement, thanks). Parts are obligatory (compliment statement, acknowledgment, bridge). Compliments have several functions, and these functions relate to their position in conversations. Those that relate most strongly to smoothing the start or close of communication occur as noticings in the space between openings and the anchor topic of oral discourse or right before the preclosing moves in the conversation. Other compliments may be offered to encourage good performance, to show thanks, or to soften criticism. The functions of compliments may turn out to be very similar across language groups. When and where compliments are appropriate, however, are more likely to be language- or culture-specific.

Practice 4.7 Compliments

1. In American English, noticings are common. Given that we are usually more interested in people than in our surroundings or the weather, we often comment on anything noticeably different about the addressee's appearance. Do you think these comments are "insincere compliments"? How might you justify their use to a learner who judges Americans as insincere in their use of compliments?

2. Herbert (1990) separated compliments into two groups: those that serve as goodwill or solidarity markers, as in "noticing" types of compliment, and those that express admiration or praise felt at a particular time. The second type is most often accepted; the first type is more often not acknowledged by thanks but rather scaled down, disagreed with, questioned, or not acknowledged at all. Herbert also reported that males often ignore compliments given by

women, while females respond to compliments from males with thanks. What effect might this information have on our claim of structure within compliment speech events?

3. As a group research project, contrast the use of noticing in the languages of your students and the language you teach. Observe the opening conversational moves. How frequently do speakers give/receive noticing-type compliments? How similar or different are the noticings? Are there special social rules as to the types of noticings that one may use (i.e., are there differences in noticings used by males and females, by older and younger people, or by persons in different social roles)? In languages where openings include extended inquiry about the health of family, friends, and relatives, could one substitute a noticing instead? Do both have the same "bonding behavior" function?

4. Acceptance of compliments on skill, talent, or ability are difficult to do without appearing conceited. We may modestly claim luck ("just lucked out"), but we seldom claim talent ("it's easy if you've got my talent"). If someone complimented you on your performance as the piano soloist at a concert, what might you say?

5. As a group research project, notice how second language learners of different proficiency levels or from different language groups respond to compliments. If the total sequence is not well performed, what parts are missing? How important are the missing segments to the interaction?

6. In your classroom data from Practice 1.2 or in classes you have observed, note each teacher's use of work validation compliments and compliments used to soften criticism. How frequently is each used? Does the compliment appear to soften the criticism? Do students ever use these structures in the classroom?

7. Do young children give compliments to others, or do they only receive them? Note instances of compliments in a preschool or kindergarten classroom. Who are the compliment givers? How are compliments acknowledged? Who provides the bridge? What evidence can you find that very young children have acquired the compliment speech event?

Complaints

Complaints are meant to contrast what *is* with what *ought* to be. If your neighbors play loud music late at night, you may shout "Turn it DOWN!," but complaints seldom stand alone as such isolated speech act directives. Rather, complaints are negotiated in a larger event context.

Brown and Levinson (1978) categorized complaints as "face-threatening acts" – acts that have strong potential for disturbing the state of personal relationships. Brown and Levinson suggested three kinds of reactions to complaints:

1. Decide not to perform the complaint at all.
2. Use "off record" strategies (e.g., hints, vagueness, rhetorical questions).
3. Use bald "on record" strategies (e.g., direct, clear statements).

Brown and Levinson further categorized "on record" strategies as showing positive politeness when the listener's positive self-image is of concern, or negative politeness when the speaker's freedom of action, freedom from imposition, and the addressee's negative self-image are central. In their work on universals of politeness, they suggested that some language and culture groups are primarily "positive politeness" and others are primarily "negative politeness" languages. These patterns show up in complaint patterns.

Nash (1983), using Brown and Levinson's terms, noted that American English seems to be in the negative politeness group, while Taiwanese Chinese could be classified as a member of the positive politeness group. In the Nash study, data were elicited in a role play situation. One person was told, "A friend of yours from out of town has been staying in your home for several weeks. The friend often comes home very late at night, disturbing you and your family. You want to make the friend aware of the fact that this is a problem." The other person was told, "You have come from out of town and have been staying in your friend's house for several weeks now." Both were told,"You are sitting around talking after dinner."

In the data from Americans, negative politeness was used, but the complaints were softened with hedges:

Do you have any idea how long you'll be staying . . . *just curious.*
Uh . . . any chance of your *maybe* keeping . . . a *little bit* . . . shorter hours during
 the week *or something* . . . *maybe just* going out on the weekends.
Ummm . . . *just* a . . . we-we've been *kinda* . . . ummm . . . well . . . we go to bed
 kinda early around here.
We were *wondering if* ah . . . *if it would* . . . *if you wouldn't mind* . . . *and if you
 could manage* to come home *a little bit* earlier.

In addition to the hedges, the many disfluencies help to soften the message that the guest has not behaved properly, that things are not as they ought to be. Nash further noted that at the end of the complaint, Americans forced rather than sought agreement – another signal of negative politeness:

A: We got it all straightened out now so
B: Ya sure.
A: We don't have to say anything more about it . . . good . . . OK.

The role plays of the Chinese were classified as positive politeness, filled with statements of concern for and interest in the guest:

Pu yao . . . ma . . . kung tso nema hsin ku a tao san ching pan yeh . . . ti erh t'ien tsao shang i ta tsao yao ch'u ch'u . . . chei yang t'ai hsin ku . . . shen t'i chung yao. (Don't . . . work so hard til midnight . . . the next day go out very early . . . this way it's too hard on you . . . health is important.)

Wo shih p'a shuo ni . . . hui t'ai lei. (I'm afraid say that you . . . will be too tired.)

Wan shang a k'e neng pu fang pien . . . wan i wai mien yu shema shih ch'ing chiu fei ch'ang ma fan san ching pan yeh mei yu jen chih tao. (At night ah it might be inconvenient . . . if something were to happen (to you) outside then it would really be a lot of trouble, in the middle of the night nobody would know.)

Interestingly, both groups used impersonalization of the complaint source as a way of avoiding a direct statement that the behavior injured the complainer alone or that the offender alone was responsible for the problem. Pronouns such as "I" and "you" were not frequently used in the complaint sequences:

My wife was a little bit perturbed.

It's the kids . . . uh . . . don't want to give them a bad impression . . . when the kids wake up and my wife wakes up . . . .

Chia li yu jen yao tsao shui chiao. (There are people in the family who must go to bed early.)

Wo t'ait'ai a mei t'ien t'a yao hen tsao shang pan. (My wife ah she must go to work early every day.)

Yin wei wo hsien sheng p'ing ch'ang tso shih . . . yen ma erh t'a nei jen kuai mao ping hen duo yu i tien sheng yin t'a chiu shui pu chao chiao. (Because my husband usually does research and he has many strange problems. If there's only a little noise then he can't sleep.)

So far we have noted that complaints have patterns that are influenced by the social need to maintain good relationships. That is, complaint events among working groups and family groups are likely to differ from those where the contact is perhaps only intermittent at most. If we live in a large city and do not personally know the offenders and are unlikely ever to interact with them again, the directness of our complaints is likely to be more forceful. (It's also interesting that Americans have a saying, "The squeaky wheel gets the grease," which almost always refers to people we do not interact with on a friendship level, and other sayings about "nagging wives or husbands and whining children," for whom the squeaky wheel should but is unlikely to get the grease!)

Most people avoid complaint situations because it is difficult to complain and still maintain and give face. However, when we do indulge in complaint making, the complaints are usually addressed to those *not* responsible for the offense – we gripe. As an indication of how pervasive this behavior is, I timed griping sequences in the talk of persons around me on the deck of the university's swimming pool one noon. Gripe sequences made up almost 87 percent of all verbal communication time. The university's pool is, of course, the perfect place for griping. There is no task to be accomplished, and something has to be talked about once noticings have been accomplished! The people talking were friends, and friends are often invited to share troubles. Sometimes the goal in sharing troubles is to obtain advice; we have a genuine advice speech event. Other times, we simply want to share our troubles – to gripe about a situation in which we find ourselves, expecting our listener to listen and share rather than give advice. In fact, when listeners interpret our troubles sharing as a request for advice and begin to give it, we often snatch back the turn by disagreeing with the advice. This, in turn, may begin an argument speech event.

To discover the structure of the complaint speech event, complete the following practice.

Practice 4.8   Structure of complaints

In your class or study group, complete the following role play activity in pairs. Record the role play and then use the data to answer the questions that follow. Please do not read the questions until you have finished taping.

Role 1: You've arrived home from work rather late and decide to play a new CD a friend just loaned you. It's a great CD and you assume your neighbors will like it too if they happen to hear it. You hear a knock at the door.

Role 2: Your neighbor is playing loud music at night when you need to sleep. You neither feel like ignoring it nor calling the police. You knock on your neighbor's door.

First, transcribe the role play (a rough transcription will suffice).

a. Identify the actual complaint statement. Where in the sequence does it appear?

b. To give face, did the complainer give a justification for the loud noise (e.g., ''I know you don't realize how late it is, but . . .'')? If so, does this justification occur after or before the complaint statement?

c. Did the noisy neighbor apologize? If so, did he or she save face by giving an explanation? Where in the sequence does the apology appear? Does the self-justification appear before or after the apology?

d. If either side suggested a remedy, what was it? Which side made the suggestion? Where in the sequence does the remedy appear?

e. Was a threat used ("I'm gonna tape-record this racket and play it back under your window at 6:30 in the morning when I gotta get up!!)? If so, by whom, and where does it appear?

f. If the noisy neighbor decided that the complainer's reaction didn't match reality ("Why are you getting so upset? It's my newest CD."), where did this denial of the problem occur?

g. If the noisy neighbor accepted the complaint, was the acceptance one of personal blame ("I didn't realize how late it was"), one that refused responsibility ("It's not my fault you can't sleep"), or one that referred to personal relationships ("Hey, I thought you were my friend"). How does the acceptance relate to face saving and face giving?

h. Is there a request for or promise of forebearance ("Won't happen again")?

i. Describe the opening, preclosing, and closing moves. Do you consider them part of the complaint event? Why or why not?

Complaint speech events typically contain an opening that includes an identification of the complainer and an explanation of why he or she is entitled to complain (i.e., a self-justification for the complaint), the complaint act, a possible justification of the addressee's action, an apology, a negotiated remedy, and a closing (or bridge to another topic). While other parts may be optional or not verbally expressed, the complaint act is obligatory. With the exception of an apology, these parts are shown in the following short complaint:

(E approaches counter. C looks up.)

E: //Hi

C: //Hi* what k'n I do for yuh?

E: I'm returning this "grolit." It doesn't work.

C: Yeh? What's wrong with it?

E: Don't know. I plugged it in and it just didn't work. Not your fault //but

C: //you buy it here? You got your receipt?

E: Yeh. Here.

C: Uhh okay. You wanna get a new one or you want your money back?

E: No, I want another one (.2) that works.

C: Yeh, okay, so go back and get another one and bring it up here and I'll write it up for you.

E: Okay, thanks.

C: Yeh.

Complaints are often presented to service agencies and businesses in written form. Writers of complaint letters typically spend a lot of time showing how the agency or business is at fault. In face-to-face communication, however, much less time is spent assigning fault and more time typically is spent negotiating a remedy.

Practice 4.9 Complaints

1. Make a list of situations that you think require a complaint speech event. Ask your language learners to do one event; videotape the role play. Then ask two native speakers to role-play it as well. List the components for each. What similarities or differences do you see in how learners and native speakers carry out the event? (If your teaching methodology encourages students to be "language researchers," show them the two videotapes and have them identify the structure of the event and any differences that exist between the complaint event structure of native and nonnative speakers.)
2. Complaints are one event in which we are working against ritual constraints – that is, it is difficult to give face to someone who has acted in a way that begs complaint. Here are examples of complaint statements made by English learners in a role play in which they had to wait an inordinate amount of time – three hours – in a doctor's office for a scheduled appointment. In the role play, they complained to the receptionist as follows:

    a. Thank you for calling me in a few hours!
    b. I have been waiting for three hours. Every time you just tell that I can see the doctor in a few minutes. Is the time scale of you different from mine? – or is your watch manufactured on the moon?
    c. I have waited for two hours. It's beyond my endurance.
    d. I've been waiting here too long. What's going on here?

    (Data source: Hawkins)

    The language learners then collected data on complaints from native speakers and critiqued their performance. If you try this situation with your students, how similar are the results in terms of politeness to those given in (a)–(d)?
3. As a research project, tape-record yourself and a friend during a troubles sharing (rather than a complaint) session. What components can you discover in the event? How does a troubles sharing session differ from a complaint event? Notice what happens if advice is actually offered.
4. Read through the following polished complaint letter. Locate

each component of the speech event. Comment on the deference and the demeanor shown in the letter.

Dear Manager:

Yesterday afternoon I bought a piece of pie at your cafeteria. I thought it was apple pie – it *looked* like apple pie. When I took a bite, it was pineapple. I can't eat pineapple.

I brought the pie over to the manager's desk. A man named Stuart was there. He refused to give me a different piece of pie or refund my money because he said it was not his fault that I made a mistake. He said that if he gave me another piece of pie, he would be "out" 95 cents. I left the pie with him and did without; but I lost my 95 cents.

Leaving aside the fact that you have the poor taste of even selling pineapple pie – how gastronomically inappropriate – I will concentrate on my "mistake," or rather your mistakes. People are apt to make mistakes when you don't label your pies. Your sign says "assorted pies." What would happen if you had signs saying "assorted sandwiches" or "assorted spaghettis"? Chaos, that's what would happen. You as manager keep chaos in its rightful place by (1) labeling your sandwiches or spaghetti of the day, and (2) having a server give the proper sandwich or spaghetti to the customer. So why not either label or serve the pies, especially when you have pies that look alike? When you serve carob cake, you label it "carob cake" so customers won't think that it's chocolate chip cake. Why not the same for pineapple pie?

Stuart informed me that chunks of pineapple look different than chunks of apple. I agree, but you can't see the chunks until you lift the top of the pie crust to view the chunks. My mother told me never to lift the top of pie crusts when I was in a restaurant. Stuart informed me that the glaze in a pineapple pie looks different than the glaze of an apple pie. I agree, but I agree only when you have an apple pie nearby to compare glaze colors. I was not working with such an advantage yesterday. The proof of the pudding, my grandmother used to say, is in the tasting. There was no way I could tell the difference by looking; I had to taste it. And by doing that, I made my "mistake" and lost my money.

Another thing. Stuart's excuse that he would be "out" 95 cents implies that you have strict inventory control over every piece of food that you make and sell. I don't believe that, not when I see workers take food for their personal use, and not when you fail to count plates or cups used and compare that number to the amount of money you take in. If you would do those two things, as they do in some restaurants, you would have a strict inventory accounting system. Then I could believe that Stuart might be "out" if he gave me a different piece of pie. But you don't do that. I think Stuart used that excuse to get rid of me. Stuart is not a vending machine which I madly kick and pound to get my money back. He should be a reasonable human being, but he did not play the role of manager vis-à-vis customer.

Obviously I'm upset. Your staff hasn't followed normal procedures regarding labeling and refunds. If a customer isn't satisfied or has been misled about a food, that customer should get a refund or different food. I'd like to see two things: (1) labels on your pies, (2) a refund or gift certificate valued at 95 cents. Sincerely awaiting your reply,

(signature)

(title)

cc: RW, Director of Food Services

(Data source: Kaiser)

Advice

An analysis of advice speech events shows that here, too, a template or script is easily discernible. For example, a set of components for seeking and giving advice that fits radio call-in shows includes the following:

Opening
Participant identification
Problem statement
Symptom negotiation
Diagnosis
Advice
Advice negotiation
Advice acceptance (thanks)
Preclosing
Closing

The opening, preclosing, and closing moves are easily identified. In the opening, the caller (C) does a brief self-introduction that establishes his or her right to call, as in this example from a garden advice show:

LS: But, let's go to the phones first. Hi, you're on the air.
C: Hi, Lily. This is Marie and I live in Little Rock where we're really having problems with this drought. . . .

(Data source: *The Garden Show* 1990)

In car shows, the caller identification may be, "Hi Bud, I'm a Honda owner and . . ."; for a health show, "Hello, Dr. Lesser, I'm one of the MSO users you talked about last week . . ."; for an astrology show, "Hi X, I'm Betsy – a Libra – an' . . ."

After the opening, the caller poses a question that reveals the problem that must be solved by the expert. If the question is not immediately asked, the expert often prods, "and WHAT is your QUEStion?" In the garden show, the problem might be the following:

147

C: (I have about fourteen bushes that uhmmm were in the house when I moved in it and they're doing pretty well.) HOWEVER + + I'm not real experienced at at pruning and I was wondering if there is a good book with like good illustrations that shows you exactly how to do it.

In most advice contexts, the symptoms of the problem are negotiated between the caller and the expert. In a car show, callers are asked to explain a variety of symptoms; in a health show, callers and experts spend much time in negotiating the accuracy of the callers' descriptions of the problem.

C: an' I'm following my normal healthy diet =
DL: = uh-uh wait a MIN – that normal healthy diet may not be so healthy given your problem.

(Data source: *The Health Connection* 1990)

Following a negotiation of the symptoms (if there is such negotiation), the problem is usually diagnosed and the advice-giving sequence begins. This may be a straightforward set of procedures or it may, again, require much negotiation as the caller rejects all or parts of the advice.

Example 1 (Data source: *The Garden Show* 1990)
LS: So water deeply – use those soaking hoses – and water deeply.
C: But won't that use up a lot of water? I mean, the drought and all?
LS: Not as much as you might think. You only need to do this maybe twice this summer but DEEP watering is the key.
C: Oh, okay

Example 2 (Data source: *The Health Connection* 1990)
DL: an so you're takin so MANY precautions that =
C: = not REAL/ly. I mean
DL: //precautions that may*, in fact, work against your recovery.
C: I don't see that. I'm trying –
DL Didn't you just say – now wait a minute, didn't you just tell me . . .
C: Yeh, I gue::ss.

Advice acceptance may be no more than the reluctantly voiced "Well th::nks" to an elaborate acceptance that leads into a preclosing. The preclosing is almost always an elaborate compliment to the expert.

C: Oh thanks so much. I just love your show. You've done more to promote peace than most people, I'm sure.
PS: Thank you, that's very nice to hear. Call back and let me know how it works out.
C: I will I will. Thanks again.
PS: Thank you for your call.

In call-in shows, the expert often closes off the caller and then "preaches" a bit to the listening audience – a sort of second closing of the communication channel to listeners before the commercial break.

Contrast the preceding radio advice sequence with the following written personal advice event.

Dear Abby:

My mother-in-law just left after one of her surprise visits, and I am ready to explode. Mummy has no husband and can come and go as she pleases. She lives 20 miles away and we never know when she's coming or how long she'll stay. (Overnight? For the weekend? A week? Two?) It's maddening!

Arthur and I work different shifts. We have two children and our free time is limited. I work from 11 p.m. until 7 a.m., so I need to sleep in the morning. Mummy always brings her dog, who barks all morning and ruins my sleep. I've asked her to please not bring him, but she brings him anyway.

Yesterday, Arthur and I spent our only day off together in two weeks entertaining her. We had made other plans, but had to cancel them when she showed up.

How can we tell Mummy to back off without offending her? Arthur is her only child. Lord have mercy on us! We've begged her to please call and let us know when she's coming, but she says, "I'd rather 'surprise' you – that way I'm sure you won't go to any extra trouble."

Abby, can you – or perhaps one of your readers who has had to handle this problem – help me? Arthur says, "Just don't pay any attention to her." But you know that can't be done.

Hates Surprises

Dear Hates:

There appears to be a communication gap here big enough to jump a horse through. Sit down with Mummy and stress the inconvenience and unfairness of her surprise visits.

If your pleas are ignored, then your husband's solution seems the most practical. Don't change your plans; just go about your business as though she weren't there and spend whatever time you have available with her.

The barking dog problem is one Arthur should handle – and firmly! Dogs can be trained to be quiet, you know. And if this one isn't, he should be banished from the premises.

(Taken from a "Dear Abby" column by Abigail Van Buren
© 1989 Universal Press Syndicate. Reprinted with permission.)

Advice-seeking letters on personal matters almost always include a complaint event within them, as in the first two paragraphs of Hates Surprises' letter. The complaint is, thus, in the form of a gripe since it is not addressed to the culprit (so there is usually little attempt to give the culprit face). Nevertheless, there is ample opportunity for the writer to give an introduction and state the problem before asking for advice. In Hates Surprises' letter, the advice request is stated in the first sentence of the fourth paragraph and again in the concluding paragraph. Care, however, must be taken to show that one is not a crank or troublemaker. Paragraphs two and three give self-justifications for the complaint, and some face giving is done for the erring mother-in-law in paragraph 4. The problem must also be stated as one shared by the reading audience (paragraph 5), a problem worthy of advice.

In advice-seeking letters, there is no opportunity for the expert to negotiate symptoms or for the writer to argue about the advice given (although the expert is forewarned that one solution – "Ignore her" – can't be done). This is not the case in call-in radio programs, where personal, medical, or monetary advice is sought, negotiated, and often fiercely argued.

Practice 4.10   Advice

1. Here is an abbreviated transcript of one advice event. The three dots identify where parts of the transcript have been deleted to save space. Identify each of the advice components within the transcript.

LS: Hi, you're on the air.

C: Hi, umm I live in Eagle Rock hhh and I have about fourteen bushes that uhmm were in the house when I moved in it and they're doing pretty well. HOWEVER + + I'm not real experienced at at pruning and I was wondering if there is a good book with like good illustrations that shows you exactly how to do it.

LS: Umhum well, I would say that any of the more popular uhhm publishers that have rose books out + I would recommend highly and that would include Sunset or Ortho or HP.

C: Yeah, I have the Sunset + but their pruning instructions are just I I don't think they are real sufficient I've uh I pruned mine last year and I have a good growth

LS: Umhum. . . . Well, let me give you just a couple of hints that may simplify what they say in there.

C: Yeah.

LS: First, it is very simple and so maybe their simplification is is very apt uhhm two basic rules + + when you are pruning, you want to prune above uh bud. . . . Keep one thing in mind, the farther back you prune it the less roses you're going to have next year.

C: uhmh

LS: . . . and if you want to have a lot of roses with not quite as long stems, you can prune about 18, 24 inches.

C: umhmm. . . .

LS: . . . and you make a nice clean cut about a quarter inch above at an =

C: = uhh uhh oh at an angle huh =

LS: = and you do it about a quarter inch high so you don't damage the bud.

C: okay uhhm I uh one bush I have which is just exquisite are are some peace roses

LS: uhmh yeah it's a real good strong rose that's one of the ones that isn't on patent anymore and you can get fairly inexpensively.

C: yeah okay thank you, Lily, I enjoy your show.

LS: ok thank you bye bye uhm + + I hope the caller is listening. Last year around this time or maybe it was the January or February Sunset had a real terrific article with very good pictures about local rosarians . . . you might want to head to the library and see if you can find a copy of that it's one of the best articles and explanation of rose pruning that I've ever seen.

(Data source: *The Garden Show* 1990)

Number the lines of this transcript and the advice column example. Find the line numbers for as many of the advice event components as possible: opening, participant identification, problem statement, symptom negotiation, diagnosis, advice, advice negotiation, advice acceptance (thanks), preclosing, closing. Which components appear to be optional and which obligatory? Do the components appear in this sequence? Do you think the sequence is flexible or set? Which elements seem more set than others?

2. We don't usually think of radio call-in shows as calling for a great deal of face giving. Yet, the expert on the garden show is concerned that callers not be blamed ("They're real tricky so don't be so hard on yourself if you're having trouble with it."). How do the repairs in the following examples show deference?

   a. I suspect that if it's dropping leaves you probably . . . well, obviously it is in the wrong spot.
   b. If it's planted in straight moss, you might think about changing the medium that it's growing in.
   c. Usually in this situation, you – eh, if it were mine, I'd probably cut it back.
   d. What you do with em after it starts looking really really yukky . . . what you want to do believe it or not is cut it back about four inches. . . . And then I would put it outside into the shade into a uh nice shady area in your yard.

   (Data source: *The Garden Show* 1990)

3. As a research project, tape and transcribe an event in which advice is sought in an educational setting. This might be a session where you give advice to students or seek advice from a teacher or supervisor. Is the template (the set of components and the sequence) the same? If not, why not? You might also consider how each person attempts to show deference and demeanor, protecting and giving face. Another interesting facet would be to investigate the effect

of formality of this academic situation in contrast to an
advice event among close personal friends.

4. As a research project, select one possible advice event and
contrast the structure of the event in English with that of
another language. Is the overall template the same? If not,
how does it differ? If the overall structure is similar but the
forms used or the protection of face are different, document
some of these differences.

5. Review the van Ek list of speech act functions. Select one
speech act subcategory (other than compliment, complaint,
or advice) and outline the template you believe one would
find in data for this event. Decide how you might collect
data on this event in order to test your hypotheses. In your
class or study group, discuss how variable the event
structure might be across different social or language
settings.

Speech event analysis

In speech event analysis we are concerned with how speech act functions are
realized in larger text units. The structure of the event forms a template similar to those of scripts. The script, however, is directed toward an identified
speech function. In a sense, speech event research gives us a set of function
"folders" to cross-reference with scripts. For example, in a service encounter,
EVALUATE might lead to a complaint (as in the grolit example on page 144.
The actors and the props remain the same as in the encounter, but the roles
of the actors, the goals, and DO actions would change. The similarity and
overlap of script theory with event analysis should be clear. The focus and
goals of these two analytic methods, however, differ. Script theory attempts
to build an abstract representation to memory. Work in artificial intelligence
on natural languages is based on this analysis. Speech event analysis also
attempts to build an abstract representation by identifying components, but
it is sociolinguistic in nature. In sociolinguistics, speech event analysis would
include a description of the speech setting, the participants, and the structure
of the event set in a template sequence. The ways the structure varies across
settings and participants form an important area of sociolinguistic research.

In applied linguistics, given the popularity of the notional-functional
approach to language teaching, it was only a matter of time before researchers
began to look at the cross-cultural or cross-linguistic similarities in speech acts
and speech events. For examples of research examining similarities and differences of speech acts and speech events across different language groups, see
Wolfson and Judd (1983) and Blum-Kulka et al. (1989). Such research not

only shows us that speech events have structure in all languages but also the value that discourse analysis of this type has for the teaching profession.

Research and application

A. Speech acts

1. As a research project for your study group, read and compare Austin's and Searle's functions with those of writers in applied linguistics (e.g., the notional-functional syllabus) or in developmental linguistics (e.g., Halliday's functions). How do these relate to each other? How do they link speech acts to research on human communication?

2. Jones (1977) presents materials for upper-intermediate and advanced language students using a speech act approach. Select one speech act (for example, "Asking permission," pp. 41–43) and review the presentation and expressions for the speech act. Prepare a questionnaire that asks other language teachers to rank the expressions for politeness. Do teachers agree among themselves on the continuum? Do their ratings concur with those presented in this text? In one section, Jones suggests that learners ask their teachers for information on when to use the expressions. On your questionnaire, ask the teachers to explain when they might use each expression. Again, do their explanations agree?

3. Shuy and Griffin (1981) used interesting data-collection techniques to study (among other things) children's use of directives. Could you adapt these techniques to gather data in your own classroom? What other techniques might you use if you wished to investigate other speech acts? Write out a preliminary research plan.

4. Contrast the directness of the complaint act (a) when the complaint is anonymous, (b) when it is lodged to persons not responsible, and (c) when it is addressed to the person at fault:
   a. Written entries in a campus residence book called "Gripes"
      Stop cutting our donuts and bananas in half!
      Rules! Rules! Rules!
      People who don't wash off the food left on their plates.
      People who don't rinse their dishes.
      Ditto!!
      And those who leave milk film at the bottom.
      Some people are horribly inconsiderate!

    b. Logged oral gripes (listener not responsible)
       Example 1: (The utterance occurred in a "noticing" position
       – that is, two teachers greeted each other and this was the
       next utterance.) It's a good thing you didn't come at 8:00.
       There weren't any materials.
       Example 2: (The utterance was made by a person standing
       in front of a wet sink basin in a restroom. The person was
       addressing a stranger, and no greeting was used – that is,
       this was the first and only utterance.) Why is that no one
       can make a counter that doesn't hold water? It's a pain!
       Example 3: (A student in a hallway commented to another
       student waiting to see a professor on the professor's lack of
       attention to her.) He's helping her. Why not me?
    c. Logged oral complaint to (partly) responsible person
       Gee, that truck is slow! (Passenger to driver after some time
       driving behind a truck)
       Wouldn't it be nice if there were some communication
       between the publishing houses and the schools? Then we'd
       have some materials. (Teacher to book salesperson)
       You guys coulda picked a better table. (Person sitting down
       at a table in the sun on a hot day)
       I think we have a problem here. There are three pages
       missing and, see, that makes you hafta turn the pages over.
       (Professor to clerk at photocopy center)
5. D'Amico-Reisner (1983) logged 74 expressions of disapproval
   (complaints) and analyzed their syntactic forms. She found four
   basic patterns:
    a. 8 percent were rhetorical questions – for example, What do
       you mean + S [subject]? (I mean) how can you VP [verb
       phrase]
    b. 8 percent were imperatives – for example, Getcher feet off the
       table
    c. 41 percent were declaratives, most of which were also topic
       openers – NP BE Pred [predicate], as in "That bathtub is
       filthy"; PRO [pronoun] VP, as in "You look a mess"; NP
       SHOULD VP, as in "Dishes should be emptied"; Frames, as in
       "(Hey honey) those socks are dirty" and "(Lookit) I've been
       standing here 20 minutes." Nonopeners included expressions
       such as "I just don't like it," "I told you that . . . ," and "If you're
       not *X*, just say so."
    d. 45 percent were requests for which responses were expected
       – *Wh*-questions such as "What are you eating?" "Why are you
       putting more syrup?" and "Why (the hell) did you, hon?"; *be*-
       questions such as "You gonna go or not?" "You coming?" and

"You aren't, are you?"; and other yes/no questions such as
"Do you *always* read people's mail?"

Following this analysis of logged complaint expressions,
D'Amico-Reisner compared the expressions of disapproval that
nonnative speakers of English obtained from role plays with
those in the logged data. She found no difference across
proficiency levels for her 36 ESL students (six proficiency levels).
There were differences, however, across language and culture
groups. While the expressions could be categorized, for example,
as imperatives ("Please uh Mary, don't give a knife a my son
because . . . is very danger a her.") or *Wh*-questions ("Why you
you you give the pencil a the children? No so good for him."), the
actual forms of the utterances did not match those of native
speakers.

If you have access to a corpus of spoken English, you might
want to carry out a class project where you identify and
categorize all disapproval expressions. Do the expressions fall
into the same four categories as in D'Amico-Reisner's data? Then
replicate the role play situations with your international students.
Do your findings match those of D'Amico-Reisner? Next, have
your students compare their expressions with those in your
native speaker database. Then have them carry out the role play
again. Is the method effective in changing complaint expressions
to forms more similar to native speakers?

6. Harlow (1990) compared the ways that native speakers of French
and Americans studying French carried out three speech acts:
requesting information, offering thanks, and apologizing. In a
written questionnaire, each person was asked to write what he or
she would say given a situation that called for each of these
speech acts. The items varied so that the request, thanks, or
apology was addressed to persons of different ages, gender, and
degrees of familiarity (e.g., your daughter, a new teacher). If you
teach French or another foreign language, read Harlow's study
and prepare a preliminary research plan to replicate the study
with your own students.

7. Halliday (1976) charts the steps in a child's (Nigel's) "learning
how to mean." Halliday talks about Phase II as learning to
engage in dialogue with adoption of social roles and learning
grammar. After reading Halliday's article, consider how you
might use this classification system to chart a young child's
second language learning. Give a rationale for why you think
the system will or will not be useful for your research project.

8. I mentioned before that the situational approach in language
teaching might be closely related to scripts and script theory. The

notional-functional approach includes a list of "notions," an open-ended list of what are called semantic categories that might also relate to scripts and script theory. Look closely at the notions that van Ek (1980) lists for possible inclusion in "threshold level" materials. Decide which you feel would fit with script theory. Give your rationale. Here is the list, but you will need to read van Ek for further background on this approach.

   a. Personal identification
   b. House and home
   c. Trade, profession, occupation
   d. Free time, entertainment
   e. Travel
   f. Relations with other people
   g. Health and welfare
   h. Education
   i. Shopping
   j. Food and drink
   k. Services
   l. Places
   m. Foreign languages
   n. Weather

9. King (1990) discusses ways in which functions and notions can be extracted from authentic texts for language teaching purposes. The problem of conforming to the linguistic proficiency of students is also presented. If you have an interest in the use of authentic language texts in teaching, review King's article as a basis for selecting materials for your students.

B. Speech events

10. One assumption (if we follow Goffman's ritual constraints) is that when we offer an invitation, we expect it will be accepted. One way to avoid the possibility that the invitation will be turned down is to preface it with a permission request, such as "Are you doing anything special tonight?" Some people feel that such lead-ins make it easier to turn down the request without any problem. Others think it makes the invitation that much more difficult to turn down. A question such as "What are you doing this weekend?" seems nosy, but once you respond with a vague "I'm not sure" or "Why?," you may have made it very difficult to decline the invitation that follows. Look at the pre-invitation moves used by ESL learners in Scarcella's (1979) study of politeness. Some of these moves were appropriate (e.g., "I was wondering if you are free this uh weekend."), but others were not

("I forgot sorry I forgot to tell you but I have a party this weekend. Okay you'll be one of the members."). Give these examples to your international students and ask them what signals serve as a pre-invitation move in their languages. Are these signals taught in your ESL textbooks or in the foreign language that you teach or are studying? If not, should they be? Devise a short lesson on these signals. Include both negative and positive responses to the pre-invitation moves and show what happens as a result of each in terms of the invitation speech event.

11. Cohen and Olshtain (1981) asked college students in Israel (32 intermediate learners of English and 12 native speakers of English) to write a response showing what they would say in situations that called for apologies. The responses of the Israeli EFL students differed from the native speakers in that the Israeli students acknowledged responsibility less often, offered fewer remedies, and expressed less regret than the native speakers. Olshtain (1983) followed up with a study of apologies in Israel by English, Russian, and Hebrew speakers and students from English or Russian backgrounds learning Hebrew. She found that English speakers had the highest rate of apology and Hebrew speakers the lowest. Hebrew speakers gave more offers of remedy than Russian speakers. Olshtain, however, does not believe that L1 transfer alone accounts for these differences. The seriousness of the offense, status, and so forth must also be looked at in such projects.

    Critique the method in these two studies. Are written responses and role plays efficient methods for collecting such data? What problems do you see with these methods? Develop a research plan for testing Cohen and Olshtain's findings with other language groups.

12. Beebe et al. (1990) used written responses to compare the ways Japanese ESL learners and native speakers of English turn down requests. The native speakers of English began their refusals with an empathetic statement (e.g., "I know how you must feel" or "I'd love to help you out"), then a regret statement (e.g., "I'm really sorry"), and an excuse (e.g., "I have to baby-sit that night"). Japanese ESL learners began with a statement of regret followed by an excuse, a pattern also used in Japanese. The excuses offered were also similar to those in Japanese, excuses that seem rather vague by American expectations (e.g., "Sunday will be inconvenient" or "I have things to do at home"). Yet, in American assertiveness training courses, women are taught to turn down invitations with, "I'm sorry, I have other plans," with no added explanation. This response brooks no argument

(unless, perhaps, a "Yeah, what plans?" challenge). Critique the method in the Beebe et al. study and in Kinjo's (1987) study of refusals. Develop a research plan to investigate refusals in other language groups.

13. The issue of politeness is often investigated in terms of directives and responses to directives or requests. This subject has intrigued many researchers in addition to Beebe et al. Read articles that have dealt with this issue, compare the research methodology used in each, and summarize the findings in a critical review of the literature, which might serve as the background for your own research interests. Here are a few references to start you on your way: Brown and Levinson (1978), Scarcella (1979), House and Kasper (1981), Lakoff (1973), Tanaka and Kawade (1982), Walters (1980), and two journal issues completely devoted to the topic of politeness: *Journal of Pragmatics 14*, 2, 1990, and *Multilingua, 8*, 1989.

14. Here are two "letters to the editor" from UCLA's (University of California, Los Angeles) campus newspaper. In each case, how does "what is" differ from "what ought to be"? Identify the complaint event structures within each letter. Then contrast the ways in which each writer lodges the complaint. Are these letters gripes, or do the writers hope those at fault will remedy the situation? What evidence is there to support your decision?

Editor:

Last week I locked my bicycle to the bike racks on the south side of Dodd Hall. When I returned from my class two hours later I found my bike covered with dirt, which had been caused by someone blowing leaves and dirt with a high-powered blower. My bike was filthy and my week-old tune-up was shot because my gears became gummed up from the dirt on them.

I didn't lock my bike to a signpost, parking meter or stairway – I lock it where UCLA requests bikes to be locked, a bike rack, only to find my bike completely filthy.

In addition, I'm paying more money for 8 units of summer session than for 16 units of regular session. Dodd Hall, where my classes are held, is a construction zone. Loud construction noise occurs throughout all of my class time and I would imagine other students feel the same way. The noise is so bad that students constantly ask our professors to speak up or repeat something because the tractors, bulldozers, pounding and other loud noises disturb our lectures.

This situation is ridiculous! How are we students supposed to learn if we can't hear our professors teach? Will our UCLA administration do anything about it? I doubt it; after all, we're just students. Oh yeah, that's what the university's for, students.

Why do summer school students pay more money to get less of an education while UCLA cleans up the campus? This unfortunately seems to be the case.

D. R. Senior, Economics

Editor:

I would like to complain about my treatment at Central Ticket Office. I had exactly $7 in my pocket to purchase a ticket to the Tibetan Dances. CTO told me that their price had changed to $8, and that they would not sell me one for the listed price. In their brochure the price is listed as $7 for students, and there is no warning that prices are subject to change.

P. M. Graduate, Indo-European Studies

15. Boatman (1987) looked at the effect of gender and status on giving unsolicited advice in a campus residential hall. Among the many interesting findings was that often the advice form was followed with a justification tag (Advice + I've found it's easier that way, or Advice + I learned the hard way). Here is an example showing students in a classroom giving unsolicited advice without a softening tag. Do you think tags might be less common in the classroom? If so, why?

Stephi:	John, you should write that down.
John:	Huh?
Stephi:	Write it down, write it down, write it down . . .
John:	Why don't you write it down?
Stephi:	Mrs. Eardley is writing on mine, so . . .
Teacher:	I'll write it down.
John:	So I don't need to.
Stephi:	But it makes it easier.
Teacher:	Zapisi, zapisi. (Write it down, write it down.)
John:	Pocemu? (Why?)
Teacher:	Because you'll need to for the test. You need to study and it always helps to have the stuff in front of you. ((laugh))

(Data source: Eardley 1985)

Do you think that second language learners ever give unsolicited advice to native speaker colleagues? If so, in what settings? What linguistic form is used for the advice? Develop a preliminary research plan that would allow you to answer these questions. You might want to develop the analysis to cover the complete advice-giving event rather than just the speech act.

16. Nunan (1990) provides a sample chart used as an aid in curriculum development for the Australian Adult Migrant Education Program. The chart includes information on each student: age, time in Australia, the first language, level of education, occupation, English proficiency level, aptitude, and goal. The goals of students include such things as mixing with parents of children's friends, getting a better job, talking to

159

grandchildren, talking to doctors, making Australian friends, talking with employers, and so forth. Prepare such a chart for your students (or for yourself if you are learning a new language). What types of scripts and speech events might be included in instruction, given this information on goals?

17. The lyrics of popular songs can be described in terms of either scripts or speech events. For example, country and western songs have complaint or gripe themes about "cryin' over lovers who done me wrong" or of "the lonely life on the highway or country road." As soon as we hear the rhythm of a country and western song, we can call up these popular themes and predict lyrics. The political themes of reggae music (popular music of Jamaican origin) were identified by Winer (1990). In this study, students from different backgrounds (Jamaican secondary students living in Toronto, Canada; non-Jamaican West Indians in Toronto, black U.S. college undergraduates, and white U.S. and Canadian citizens) were asked to transcribe the lyrics to several reggae songs. As Winer predicted, only the Jamaican students (who knew the speech event themes of the songs and who were also familiar with the dialect) could transcribe the songs accurately – even though most of the students had heard them before.

   Rap songs are very popular now and center on a number of speech event themes. Identify the themes and, using Winer's study as a guide, design a research project to test how well the lyrics are understood by students from different ethnic backgrounds.

18. Write a series of test items that set up a situation for which language learners must select the most appropriate response. Write one for each of the three events (compliment, complaint, advice) presented in this chapter. To get you started, here are some examples.

Multiple Choice
1. You and your friend go to a very nice restaurant for supper. You order soup first. The waiter brings it to you, but it's cold. What do you do?
   a. You eat it and say to your friend, "This soup is terrible."
   b. You complain very loudly to your neighboring tables, "My soup is cold. Isn't the service terrible here!"
   c. You get up and leave the restaurant.
   d. You tell the waiter, "Will you please bring me another bowl of soup. This one is cold."
   e. None of the above.

2. When your teacher says your term paper is very good, you should say:
   a. Thank you.
   b. No, really, it's terrible.
   c. I know.

Completion

As you leave a party, your host says, "Come back again soon." You would reply _____.

True-False

1. Professor *X* says he will not accept late papers. You can't get yours in on time. You should say:
   T   F   Professor *Y* lets everyone turn in their papers late.
2. Your roommate always borrows your class notes. To say "no" next time, you would say:
   T   F   Okay, but it will cost you $50.00 (laugh).

References

Austin, J. L. (1962). *How to do things with words.* Cambridge, Mass.: Harvard University Press.

Beebe, L.; Takahashi, T.; and Uliss-Weltz, R. (1990). Pragmatic transfer in ESL refusals. In R. Scarcella, E. Andersen, and S. Krashen (Eds.), *On the development of communicative competence in a second language* (pp. 55–73). New York: Newbury House.

Blum-Kulka, S.; House, J.; and Kasper, G. (1989). *Cross-cultural pragmatics: Requests and apologies.* Norwood, N.J.: Ablex.

Boatman, D. (1987). A study of unsolicited advice. In C. Micheau (Ed.), *Working papers in educational linguistics* (pp. 35–60). Graduate School of Education, University of Pennsylvania, Philadelphia, Pennsylvania.

Bolinger, D. (1967). The imperative in English. In M. Halle, H. Lunt, H. McLean, and C. von Schooneveld (Eds.), *To honour Roman Jacobson: Essays on his 70th birthday* (pp. 335–362). The Hague: Mouton.

Brown, P., and Levinson, S. (1978). Universals in language usage: politeness phenomena. In E. Goody (Ed.), *Questions and politeness: Strategies in social interaction* (pp. 56–310). Cambridge: Cambridge University Press.

Cohen, A., and Olshtain, E. (1981). Developing a measure of sociocultural competence: The case of apology. *Language Learning, 31,* 1: 113–134.

D'Amico-Reisner, L. (1983). An analysis of the surface structure of disapproval exchanges. In N. Wolfson and S. Judd (Eds.), *Sociolinguistics and language acquisition* (pp. 103–115). Rowley, Mass.: Newbury House.

van Ek, J. A. (1975). *The threshold level.* Strasbourg: Council of Europe. Also published in 1980 as *Threshold level English.* Oxford: Pergamon.

(1976). *The threshold level for modern language teaching in schools.* London: Longman.

Ervin-Tripp, S. (1972). On sociolinguistic rules: alternation and co-occurrence. In J. Gumperz and D. Hymes (Eds.), *Directions in sociolinguistics* (pp. 213–250). New York: Holt, Rinehart & Winston.

(1976). Is Sybil there? The structure of American directives. *Language in Society, 5,* 25–66.

The Garden Show, with Lily Singer, KCRW, Santa Monica, Calif., September 1990.

Halliday, M. A. K. (1975). *Learning how to mean: Explorations in the development of language.* London: Edward Arnold.

(1976). Early language learning: A sociolinguistic approach. In W. McCormack and S. Wurm (Eds.), *Language and man. Anthropological issues* (pp. 97–124). The Hague: Mouton.

Harlow, L. L. (1990). Do they mean what they say? Sociopragmatic competence and second language learners. *Modern Language Journal, 74,* 328–351.

The Health Connection, with Dr. H. Lesser, KCRW, Santa Monica, Calif., September 1990.

Herbert, R. K. (1990). Sex-based differences in compliment behavior. *Language in Society, 19,* 201–224.

House, J., and Kasper, G. (1981). Politeness markers in English and German. In F. Coulmas (Ed.), *Conversational routine. Exploration in standardized communication situations and prepatterned speech* (pp. 157–185). The Hague: Mouton.

Jones, L. (1977). *Functions of English.* Cambridge: Cambridge University Press.

King, C. (1990). A linguistic and a cultural component: Can they live happily together? *Foreign Language Annals, 23,* 1: 65–70.

Kinjo, H. (1987). Oral refusals of invitations and requests in English and Japanese. *Journal of Asian Culture, 11,* 83–106.

Lakoff, R. (1973). The logic of politeness: Or, minding your p's and q's. *Papers from the 9th Regional Meeting of the Chicago Linguistic Society* (pp. 292–305). Chicago: Chicago Linguistics Society.

Manes, J., and Wolfson, N. (1980). The compliment as a second language strategy. *Papers in Linguistics, 13,* 3: 391–410. See also (1981). The compliment formula. In F. Coulmas (Ed.), *Conversational routine. Exploration in standardized communication situations and prepatterned speech.* The Hague: Mouton.

Nash, T. (1983). American and Chinese politeness strategies: "It sort of disturbs my sleep" or "Health is important." *University of Hawaii Working Papers, 2,* 2: 23–39.

Nunan, D. (1990). Using learner data in curriculum development. *English for Special Purposes, 9,* 1: 17–32.

Olshtain, E. (1983). Sociocultural competence and language transfer: The case of apology. In S. Gass and L. Selinker (Eds.). *Language transfer in language learning* (pp. 303–325). Rowley, Mass.: Newbury House.

Scarcella, R. (1979). On speaking politely in a second language. In C. Yorio, K. Perkins, and J. Schachter (Eds.), *On TESOL '79: The learner in focus* (pp. 275–287). Washington, D.C.: TESOL.

Searle, J. R. (1969). *Speech acts: An essay in the philosophy of language.* Cambridge: Cambridge University Press.

(1976). A classification of illocutionary acts. *Language in Society, 5,* 1: 1–23.

Shuy, R., and Griffin, P. (1981). What do they do at school *any* day. In W. P. Dickson

(Ed.), *Children's oral communication skills* (pp. 271–286). New York: Academic Press.

Tanaka, S., and Kawade, S. (1982). Politeness strategies and second language acquisition. *Studies in Second Language Acquisition, 5,* 1: 18–33.

Walters, J. (1980). The perception of politeness in English and Spanish. In C. Yorio, K. Perkins, and J. Schachter (Eds.), *On TESOL '79: The learner in focus* (pp. 288–296). Washington, D.C.: TESOL.

Winer, L. (1990). Intelligibility of reggae lyrics in North America: Dread in a Babylon. *English World-Wide, 11,* 1: 33–58.

Wolfson, N. (1981a). Compliments in cross-cultural perspective. *TESOL Quarterly, 15,* 2: 117–124.

(1981b). Invitations, compliments, and the competence of the native speaker. *International Journal of Psycholinguistics, 24,* 4: 7–22.

Wolfson, N.; D'Amico-Reisner, D.; and Huber, L. (1983). How to arrange for social commitments in American English: The invitation. In N. Wolfson and E. Judd (Eds.), *Sociolinguistics and language acquisition* (pp. 116–128). Rowley, Mass.: Newbury House.

Wolfson, N., and Judd, E. (1983). *Sociolinguistics and language acquisition.* Rowley, Mass.: Newbury House.

5   Rhetorical analysis

To review, system constraints set a framework for analysis of all communication. Within that system, communication events take place in ways that follow ritual, or social, constraints. Scripts help us understand how communication events that might be represented in memory have structure. In speech event analysis, we discussed event components as templates similar to those of scripts, but the focus of the analysis was on a particular speech function. In this chapter, we move to *rhetorical genre analysis,* which reveals templates or scripts in the organization of discourse that is primarily monologic.

Genres

The genres that appear in the classical literature on rhetoric, from Aristotle to modern day rhetoricians, are those of narrative, descriptive, procedural, and suasive discourse. Language teachers have long followed these classifications, providing model essays that purport to demonstrate the structure of each genre. Shaughnessy (1977) writes about five basic goals or types of rhetorical organization:

1. This is what happened (narrative, temporal organization).
2. This is the look/sound/smell of something (description).
3. This is like/unlike this (comparison/contrast).
4. This (may have, probably, certainly) caused this (causal and evaluative).
5. This is what ought to be done (problem solving including effects, causes, possible solutions, the assessment of solutions, the prediction of side effects, and the suggestion of one or some combination of elements as the best solution).

Linguists, too, have found rhetorical analysis of interest, although this interest has a much stronger focus on the link between rhetorical form and syntax.

This chapter discusses text genre and also briefly acquaints you with work on rhetorical structure from a process standpoint. In this first section on genre, we will look at narrative, descriptive, procedural, and argumentative text genres, which are (along with comparison and contrast) the types most frequently presented in language arts and foreign language textbooks. Each genre has a slightly different structure, which can be described; in addition, each genre gives writers and speakers considerable flexibility in structuring

164

text. To express their intent, writers and speakers typically employ certain syntactic structures. The identification of such structure has led to interesting work on the connection between the description of discourse and syntax.

Narrative text

Narration is thought to be the most universal genre, because all cultures have storytelling traditions. Storytelling episodes have been collected in many languages, and, based on such data, researchers claim that there is some basic universal template for the narrative. (The December 1982 issue of the *Journal of Pragmatics* is devoted to descriptions of the universals of narrative text.) The template given here draws from the work of Labov (Labov 1972, Labov and Waletsky 1967) in linguistics and Mandler (Mandler 1978, Mandler and Johnson 1977, and Mandler et al. 1980) in cognitive psychology.

In order to inform listeners or readers about the world of the story, narratives usually begin with an *orientation*. This includes the *time* of the story (e.g., "Once upon a time . . .") and its spatial *setting* (e.g., "in the kingdom by the sea . . ."). In addition to the setting of the story world, the *characters* and their roles must be set up (e.g., "there lived an old, old woman named Omi . . .").

Such openings or orientations of traditional folktales reveal how syntax can be used to establish the story world. In English narratives, copula sentences (use of *be*), presentatives (*there is/there are* sentences), and identifying or descriptive relative clauses are often used to establish characters within the setting. These grammatical features are underlined in the following examples. (The twins text is taken from Mandler 1978; the farmer story is from Hunt's clause-combining book, and the third is a typical folktale opening.)

1. Once there were twins, Tom and Jennifer, who had so much trouble their parents called them the unlucky twins.
2. There was once a farmer who lived all alone. He bought a hen for company.
3. Once upon a time in a land far away there lived an old woman who had three sons.

While these examples are quite stereotypic, it is still possible to discern the parts of the orientation of narratives when such overt signals are not used.

"Where oh where has everyone gone," wondered Alice. She shifted on the rickety steps and listened to them creak in reply. The wind howled around the ranch house, blowing up dust devils on the desert floor that stretched out in all directions in front of her. But Alice didn't notice. She kept her eyes on the door of the barn. Last night it had been closed but now it swayed with each gust of wind.

Time orientation: Today versus last night (or "one morning as the wind blew up dust devils and caused the door to sway")

Place orientation: On the porch of a ranch house next to a barn located in the high desert.

Character/role identification: Alice, a girl left alone in this place (or "there was a girl named Alice who had been left all alone").

Note that there is only one participant. Nothing is happening; no action is passing from one person to another. The verbs are statives ("be," "seem," "wonder") or intransitives ("shift," "listen," "howl," etc.) that describe the setting and the main character rather than report actions.

Once the story world setting is complete, the storyteller can begin to set up the story line. Most stories involve a hero who has a *goal* (just as in scripts). There is usually some *problem* that prevents an easy attainment of the goal. The hero develops a plan for solving the problem and achieving the goal. Since, in the orientation, we – as listeners or readers – have already identified the hero, we begin to search the story for the goal and the problem in relation to the goal. In westerns, we know that the cowboy must defeat the "bad guys" so that good triumphs over evil. In mystery stories, we know that the detective will go through many trials on the way to finding the murderer. In narratives, then, focus is on the hero (actor) and on the actions the hero uses to solve problems so that a goal can be achieved.

Let's look at these in a traditional folktale.

Orientation: Once upon a time there were three Billy Goats
Goal: who wanted to cross over the bridge to eat the grass on the other side.
Problem: But, under the bridge, lived an ugly old troll.

When the listener (or storyteller) has identified the hero, the goal, and the problem, the next part of the narrative shows how the hero works out the problem to reach the goal. This usually consists of a set of action clauses arranged in temporal order (first, and then, and then, and then, finally . . .). So, the remainder of the Billy Goats Gruff story consists of a set of actions used to achieve the goal. The *resolution* of the story shows the goal attained:

Resolution: And so the three Billy Goats Gruff crossed over the bridge and ate grass to their hearts' content.

Just as we need an orientation to place us in the story world, we also need a bridge to bring us back. This concluding part is called a *coda*. The coda may also contain a moral that summarizes or evaluates the story's relevance. Do you remember the moral at the end of the "Three Billy Goats Gruff"? It was something like "Do you think the grass always looks greener on the other side?"

Good storytellers tell stories that have some meaning for their audience. To help listeners or readers understand why this story is being told and why it is worthy of telling, *evaluation* comments are woven into the story line.

These evaluative comments may be summarized in the moral (if one is present). Evaluative comments may also be phrased as bracketed asides (e.g., "this is just like what happened to your dad last week"; "and you know how deadly rattlesnakes can be") that serve to involve the audience more fully into the story. Good storytellers also use intensifiers of all sorts – gestures, changes in intonation, repetition for intensity, superlatives, sound effects, and so forth – to involve their audience even more. All storytellers must dread the "So what?" question that might be asked if the listener or reader doesn't understand why the story is interesting, what the story means, why it was told at this particular time, or why it was addressed to him or her.

Finally, the narrative may include an *abstract,* a sort of title for the story. For example, someone might ask you if you heard the news about the plane crash. "The plane crash" serves as a sort of title or abstract of the story that follows.

The narrative template, then, may include the following components: an abstract, the orientation (including time, place, and character identification), the goal and the problem, the steps to resolve the problem (a set of temporally ordered clauses), the resolution (or climax), and a coda (including a possible moral). The evaluative component may occur at various points throughout the narrative and might be summarized as a moral in the coda section.

Good storytellers, however, often embellish the template. They may give additional background information about the actors and their motives, about other activities that may be going on in parallel with the story. They may also include asides. Somehow the storyteller and the audience must keep the foreground of the story in mind while allowing for shifts of focus to other information and elaboration. Asides, as we have already seen, can be bracketed using nonverbal signals, by special intonation, and by explicit reference to their noncentral quality. Ongoing parallel action can also be marked in special ways. One way is to mark the major story line using verb tense (simple past or simple present). Verb aspect, then, can locate parallel ongoing actions (continuous or progressive aspect) or present old background information (perfective aspect) for the story line. Copula sentences and relative clauses can be used to continue setting up descriptions as they are needed to flesh out the story. We also expect that the story line will consist of *actions* carried out by heroes and adversaries. These verbs typically are highly transitive. Actions are taken and completed, the action is strongly transmitted from the agent to the object(s). Clauses that show strong transitivity are used for the main story line; and stative clauses are used for the orientation and background of the story.

Now let us connect this information on narratives with what we know about Goffman's system constraints. We know that once the storyteller has asked permission to tell the story (e.g., "Did you hear what happened to Harry?" "No, what?"), the storyteller has the floor. Others may backchannel, say some of the characters' lines, or do collaborative completions, but they cannot easily take the floor away from the storyteller. Even in cooperative storytelling, one person has the major responsibility for moving the story along. Once the story is completed, the listeners can then complete the narrative event with expressions of appreciation and use these to bridge into storytelling sequences of their own.

Practice 5.1 Narrative structure

1. Read these story excerpts, and identify the hero (actor), the goal, and the problem:

> One day, Jennifer's parents gave her a dollar bill to buy the turtle she wanted, but on the way to the pet store she lost it.
> (Data source: Mandler 1978)

> There was once an old farmer who owned a very stubborn donkey. One evening, the farmer was trying to put his donkey into its shed. The farmer pushed the donkey, but the donkey wouldn't move. Then the farmer pulled the donkey, but the donkey still wouldn't move.
> (Data source: Rumelhart 1975)

> Like I rimember when I wuz ten years old climbing over some cliffs n I wuz trying tuh get from (.1) one end of this big beach in La Jolla ((cough)) n'kay here's like the Cove n here's this beach called La Jolla SHORES, n usually ya jes' WALK ACROSS, but it was high TIDE (.1) so I had tuh go over some cliffs.
> (Data source: Bennett 1977)

2. Write out a series of temporally ordered clauses to show how each hero might have solved the problem.
3. The resolution, or climax, of the story shows the goal attained. What is the resolution in the following story segments?

> She finally found the dollar bill in the grass. But when Jennifer got to the store, the pet store man told her that someone else had just bought the last turtle.
> (Data source: Mandler 1978)

> . . . as soon as the cat scratched the dog, the dog began to bark. The barking so frightened the donkey that it jumped immediately into its shed.
> (Data source: Rumelhart 1975)

> . . . filled my lungs, and leaped upwards, catching the patch of grass at its base, where it was strongest. My faith in nature was my salvation: the grass did not uproot, and I was able to pull myself to safety, and continue on to La Jolla Shores.
> (Data source: Bennett 1977)

4. What is the coda in the following example? Write a moral of your own.

   Tom's parents said he was even more unlucky than Jennifer and made him stay in bed until he got well. So y'see, you're not so unlucky after all.

5. Bennett, who told the story about climbing the cliffs at La Jolla beach, also wrote out a version of the story and entitled it "A Clump of Grass." Give an example of how Bennett might have included "A Clump of Grass" as an abstract prior to the orientation of the oral version of her story.

6. As a group research assignment, give the storybook *Good Dog, Carl* (Day 1985) to native-speaker elementary school students to read. Explain that you want them to remember as much of the story as possible so that you can tape-record their retelling to play for someone who has not read the book. Be sure to tell them exactly who this person is. When the students have finished reading, have them close the book and tape-record their retelling of the story. Repeat this procedure with nonnative students. (If you do this as a group project, you may want to plan what level(s) of proficiency you would like your nonnative speakers to have.) Each person in the study group should transcribe two narratives: one native and one nonnative; you will be able to use these data again for projects in later chapters. First identify all the template components of narratives in the two versions. Discuss any differences that you find. Then underline the clauses with simple tense verbs, and circle those that show continuous aspect. Star those that have perfective aspect. Place a check by those that contain the simple present or past of *be*.

   a. If you pull out all the simple tense clauses, would you have a reasonable summary outline of the story? If not, what additional clauses are needed? What aspect do the clauses you pulled out show?

   b. Note the sentences that include a simple *be* ("is," "am," "are," "was," "were") link. What function(s) do these sentences fulfill in the story?

   c. Locate the sentences in which the verb is in the progressive form (uses *be* plus an *-ing* ending). What function(s) do these sentences fulfill? Then locate those with perfective aspect (uses *has/have* or *had* as an auxiliary). What function(s) do these fulfill?

169

7. We expect the set of temporally ordered clauses that show the steps in solving the hero's problem to contain transitive verbs. Transitivity, as Hopper and Thompson (1980) pointed out, is not an all-or-nothing phenomenon. That is, depending on a number of features, verbs transfer action in strong to weak ways. In the following pairs, each verb would be classified as a transitive verb in school grammar terms. That is, each takes an object. However, the transfer of action is stronger in some clauses than in others. For each pair, identify the sentence that has the stronger transitivity.

   a. I hugged Sally.
      I like Sally.

   b. I carried it.
      I kicked it.

   c. The picture startled me.
      George startled me.

   d. I bumped into Fred.
      I bumped into the table.

   e. I ate it up.
      I am eating it.

   f. I forgot your name.
      I wrote your name.

   g. I shot a squirrel.
      I shot some squirrels.

   h. I drank some of the milk.
      I drank up the milk.

   Check the verbs that form the story line (those in simple tense) in *Good dog, Carl* as narrated by your students. Are the verbs used highly or weakly transitive? Is there any difference in verb selection by the native versus nonnative students?

8. As a research project, ask a *group* of children to tell you a well-known story (e.g., "The Three Bears"). Tape-record the story. Who is the major storyteller? How do the other children cooperate in building the story? How successfully do they weave parallel events, background information, and asides into the story line?

9. If you teach a language other than English, have your students carry out the research project described in item 7 or 8. Do you believe the narrative template is the same in this language as that described for English? What similarities and differences can you discover? How skillful are your learners in telling the narrative? What problems do they encounter in the telling? If you are interested in testing the template against written narrative text, ask for a written version of the story instead.

10. Choose one narrative collected by yourself or others in

your study group. Check all the evaluative devices used. Evaluative devices include, among other things:

a. Nonverbal gestures [e.g., "so he kinda looks around *like this ((gestures))*]
   Expressive intonation [high pitch, groans, giggles]
b. Lexical intensifiers ["they spoke with an English accent, *really really* charming," "She was *all* tuckered out"]
c. Repetitions ["getting a little *whoopie whoopie* there," "and it knocked *and it knocked and it knocked*"]
d. Mimicking or direct quotes ["so we started talking, 'Hey, well, we're in the U.S. Navy, man. Can't put us in jail' "]
e. Direct evaluative pointers [e.g., "an' *all of a sudden* here's this guy," "I said to myself *this is it!*," "*I crossed myself and said a prayer*"]
f. Rhetorical questions to the listener ["And why do you suppose he said that?"]
g. Relative clauses or other embedded asides [". . . Punchbowl Park, you remember that place where you saw that rattlesnake . . ."]

Give examples of as many of these devices that help involve the audience as you can from the narrative you have selected. Do you think the story would have been more "successful" if more evaluative devices were used? Why or why not? At the end of the narrative, does the teller state a moral that summarizes why the story was worth listening to or why it was important that it be told? If so, note this as well.

Narratives have been analyzed in many different languages, and claims have been made for the universality of this particular genre. Certainly the story-telling tradition is strong in most cultures. But, if there is a universal structure of narratives, why are stories that are translated from other languages often very difficult to understand and recall? The universal template should make it easy to find the various parts of the narrative.

Some research shows that parts of the template are not always included in the narrative of other language groups. Shaul et al. (1987), for example, found that Hopi Coyote stories do not contain an evaluation, and the moral is unstated. One reason that the evaluative section is missing might be that these stories are told within a small cohesive group, among whom the point of the story is known and shared. Matsuyama (1983) claimed that while English stories tend to center on actions, Japanese stories are much more concerned with the development of characters, motives, and the relationships between characters. Schaefer (1981) suggested this may be true of Vietnamese narratives as well.

In recall experiments, Americans have not easily applied the template to stories translated from other languages. Carrell (1981, 1983), for example, found that college students had difficulty recalling the gist of American Indian folktales. Kintsch and Greene (1978) and other researchers have reported similar findings regarding the recall of stories translated from other languages. While translated stories may be difficult to understand, it is not clear whether the difficulty is due to the structure of the narrative (i.e., the template is *not* really universal) or a discrepancy in what constitutes a hero, the motives of the characters, the seriousness of the problem, the rightness of the plan to overcome the problem, the correctness of the solution, and the value of the moral. The overall evaluation (i.e., the answer to "Why am I being told this story?") may simply not be obvious to persons who are not members of the cultural group that first formed the story.

Sometimes it is difficult to process stories because the storyteller is not yet proficient in the language. Of course, it is more difficult to tell a story in a language that you do not know well. Consider the following story told by a beginning-level English learner from Japan:

S: Today my sister go to field trip and my- my mom have to pay five dollar.
NS: Oh. Where did she go?
S: She go skate. I know how skate but-but I cann go. Uh . . . she go skate and she turn around and she-she um . . . she-she and h- everybody do like "woo woo" and she WAY around she fell (back?) ((laughs)) And she um ca-um came home di (=she?) told my mom she say "Mom today I go to skate I very very" ((laughs)) and my mom say "Why you do like that?" And she say "I have to run with my – my friend. And she run and she drop I(m) know she drop and she tell me.

(Data source: Kuwahata 1984)

The locutionary meaning of the story can be paraphrased as: "My sister went on a field trip that cost my mother five dollars. She went skating. I know how to skate but I couldn't go. My sister skated and did a spin and everyone exclaimed 'woo-woo,' but then she went all the way around and fell down. She came home then and told my mother about it. My mother asked her why she wanted to do that. She said that she has to go with her friends. She went with her friends and she fell. I know she fell because she told me so." The illocutionary meaning, however, is much less clear. What message is the storyteller trying to give us? The evaluative component of why this story is being told isn't obvious. Is the story that of five dollars unnecessarily wasted? That the storyteller is more talented than her sister? That flattery causes a fall? Is it a call for sympathy for her sister's embarrassing moment, or what? The true meaning of the story is missing.

The problem, however, is not necessarily that of limited language proficiency. Other learners with similar proficiency levels (or even this same language learner telling a different story) may tell stories where the point of the story is very transparent. The following story was told by a person also described as at an early stage of acquisition (although she has lived in the United States much longer). This story is much clearer because the teller follows the narrative template and uses the evaluation component to effectively involve the listener in the story. (The slash (/) is used to show intonation groupings of words.)

A little DUCK was there/ my landlady DUCK/ she gotta little PIpi/ on Eastertime for her children/ grow UP/ come over EVery morning/ bout FIVE o'clock/ I turn light ON/ duck come inna window HOLLer at me/ Kwe: kwe: kwe:/ so I used to give a BREAD/ for all time/ she never go HOME/ STAY with it/ one morning she don't CRY/ si I was WORry/ look at WINdow/ I can't SEE nothin/ SNOW/ so I open-dupa DOOR/ duck was stuck to PATio frozen STIFF/ so I told my HUSBAND I say duck is STUCK/ maybe DYin/ he HEAD was moving/ but FEET was frozen/ so my HUSband told me she say/ get WARM WAter/ pour inna FOOT/ and so I DID/ my HUSband give me more water/ and POUR in/ and pretty soon duck MOVE ((laugh))/ he was all RIGHT/ but he come down EVery day/ messing up my PATio/ I didn't like d'ALL/ AFter that ((laugh)).

(Data source: Kumpf 1986)

The stories of professional storytellers, those of language learners, and those of young children will, of course, differ. Any storyteller can run into problems in delivering the best possible reflection of happenings in the story world. Nonetheless, we recognize when a story is well done and when it is not. This means that we must have in mind some ideal model of narration as a genre form.

Practice 5.2   Comprehension of narratives

1. As a research project, look carefully at a set of folktales translated from another language group. Do the stories contain all the structural components of the narrative template? If the stories are difficult to understand, what causes this difficulty? Folktales are often used to teach other languages. Give one reason why this should be a good approach. Give one reason why the approach might not be successful.
2. Write out a running paraphrase of the "Stuck Duck" narrative. Identify each of the structural components of the narrative. Are all the components present?
3. Here are two stories written by a Spanish-speaking ESL child to English-speaking adults.

Dear Barbara and Vanesa.

I jope you enjoy your class because I am going to tell you a Story. Ones upon a time theyr was a man. This man was happy he lived near the street. He oned a flower chop. He hade a pony a foke it was out side hes flower chop. He jate noisy people. One day kids came and ride this pony. They liked to pretend that they were cowboys. But the man send them away. Because they were making alot of noise. One day later a little girl came and ask the man. Please let me right the pony. And the man said OK. Then the man cunt right the pony and he jump and he kik it but it not work. Then it work and he was happy. Then the man put a sing it seld PONY RIDE FREE. And all of the children came to ride that pony.

Here's A picture of the

Did you like my pony? I am going to tell you another story. One upon a time theyr were two best friends. One was a frog and one was a Toad. The frog was not feling well. So he ask the Toad to tell him a story. Sou he said Okay. Onec upon a time theyr was a Toad and a frog. The frog was not feling wel he ask tha Toad to ask him as he was sleeping. Sou he said Okay. He walked one the front porth but he can't not think of a story. Then he said I got it. But the frog was asleep. How did the frog felt? Thid you like my story? Did I did well. Did you like my pony? Please right me at leas one story. Because I don't know any more storyes. Your friend G. Do you like righting? Hows your friends? Whats your favorite book? Is my rithing bad ore good? How is Vanesa? How are you. Whats your favorite pencil Whats your favorite game? Do you know how to be a teacher? Do you knou hou to use a computer. Barbara and Vanesa we mest you alot. Do you mest us? Good by your friend G.

(Data source: Hawkins and Flashner Wenzell)

In your class or study group, decide how to divide up and carry out the following tasks. (a) Comment on the overall communication system constraints shown in the text. (b) Comment on the structure of each narrative in terms of narrative components (i.e., the template). (c) Comment on the locutionary message of each story by preparing a paraphrase of each. (d) Comment on the illocutionary message of each story. Finally, (e) decide whether or not you would attempt to instruct this writer on ways to improve the stories. If you would, what suggestions do you have?

Description

In English textbooks, the two most popular writing assignments calling for description are "my favorite person" and "describe a building." Less common assignments are "describe your house or block," "describe an object seen through a magnifying glass," or even "write a work song" that describes an activity, as illustrated by this poem written by an elementary school child:

Dish washing

Dishes, swishes
   Look what we just ate.
Dishes, swishes
   Rinse away the plate.
Now the plates
   Are nice and clean
Cleanest plates
   I've ever seen

(Data source: Wolsch 1970)

There are other assignments like "describe an object and what it is used for" that join description and procedural genres. Description does not appear to have a set template. Components could be described for certain types of descriptions – for example, descriptions of objects are usually in terms of their parts and the functions and appearance of these parts. If you were to describe a plant, you would likely include mention of the roots, the stem, and the leaves and, perhaps, buds and flowers as well. You might also give the functions of these parts (transporting water and nutrients, support of the plant, etc.). Color and shape of leaves might be mentioned too. Your description would probably start at the "bottom" with the roots and end at the "top" with the leaves. If you were to describe your apartment, you might start at the door and gradually work your way through the apartment to the back. Or, you might think of the apartment as though it were viewed from above – like an architect's plan – and describe the space from that perspective.

Linde and Labov (1975) analyzed apartment descriptions and found that many of their subjects gave listeners a walking tour, pointing out their own likes and dislikes in terms of layout and furnishing as they went along. They also found (as we did in describing scripts), that much of the information about apartments is a "given." This leads to the use of definite articles in talking about, for example, *the* refrigerator (kitchens have refrigerators) or *the* sink. It would be a bit odd to say "There is *a* kitchen and the kitchen has *a* refrigerator and *a* sink," because we already have this information in our apartment schema. If we were talking about an apartment in another country, however, we might include this information to assure listeners that the script is the same.

Sometimes when we are asked to describe a room or an apartment, we describe our *feelings* about the rooms, other people we associate with the

175

apartment, and so forth (instead of describing the apartment). This may be because we are usually more interested in people than rooms, and so we talk about the rooms in relation to people. When we describe a person, we don't usually start at the top of the head and begin describing parts as though they were rooms. People are not objects. However, we probably know more about ourselves and our relationships with the people we describe so, again, the focus may not really be on the person but on ourselves.

In descriptions, we do expect to find certain types of syntactic structures. For example we expect to see many copula (*be* link) sentences, relative clauses, and prepositional and adverbial phrases (e.g., in locating objects within a room or in shifting focus from one part of the room to another). Presentatives (*there is/there are* sentences) and descriptive adjectives of shape, size, color, and number are also common in this genre.

The following description, written by a Chinese student studying English in China, shows many of these structures.

A Certain room

The paper will introduce my room to you. – I mean I will talk about my dormitory (at follows: I call it room).

The room is at 104 on the ground in building 3. Mr. Y (my classmate) and I live in the room. There are two beds in it. and there are two desks. a bookshelf and two chairs in it. The door opens to the South. Mr. Y's bed, desk and chair are in the right. Mine are in the left. There is a lamp under the ceiling. The bookshelf stands near the window in the middle of the wall. The bookshelf has six stories. No. 1. 3. 5 belong to me. the rest belong to Mr. Y. The bookshelf is filled fully with books. There are dictionaries, major books. novels. magazines and other books on the bookshelf.

There are two pictures on the left wall a Chinese picture and a famous picture in the world. There is a calendar on the wall near the window. There are many postcards on the wall below the Chinese picture.

There is a table lamp, which was assigned by the college. On the desk. and also there are books. radio. recorder, box pencil and some industrial art goods on the desk.

This room is very tidy and clean. we clean and mop the room every day.

Notice that this essay focuses on the objects and possessions in the room. *Presentatives* are used to list the objects. We are not taken on a tour of the room. The door, rather than opening to us, opens to a geographic direction. Two persons live in the room, yet the room doesn't seem to include them. The objects themselves do not seem to belong to the room (note the use of indefinite articles) but appear in certain spaces. The essay gives a picture of a well-organized, neat space where objects are physically contained. To discover whether this essay (and especially the use of presentatives) is characteristic of descriptions of Chinese apartments or simply the outcome of an assignment in an English class would, obviously, need a full research effort.

If you are especially interested in Japanese, consider the following apartment description. It has been suggested that "wa" has a discourse as well as a syntactic function – that of placing a noun phrase into high focus. Look at the underlined noun phrases (those marked with "wa") in the following oral description:

<u>watasi no apaato wa</u> sangai ni arimasite + + EE beddo-ruumu to basu-ruumu to ribingu-ruumu desu ka ANOO daidokoro mo issyo ni hitotu no heya ni natte ite + EE saate doo ittara ii desyoo ne + + <u>sono ribingu-ruumu tte iu no wa</u> + daitai + + roku-zyoo no heya ga hutatu gurai no hirosa desu ka sore yori tyotto hiroi gurai desu + + kanari hiroi desu + + de <u>sinsitu wa</u> hatizyoo kurai no ookisa desyoo ka ne beddo o singuru no beddo o mittu <u>narabete</u> hairu gurai no haba to + + sukosi nagame no yoko to + + de <u>basu-ruumu wa</u> syawaa to ANO nagasiba to otearai ga atte AA nante iun desu ka monoire ga ne sukosi knogurai no haba no doa to + + hukasa ga konogurai no monoire ga arimasu ne + ano ima iroiro + + sono basu-ruumu de tukau mono taoru to ka ne ato + + otearai no kami to ka sekken to ka sonna mono o irete irun desu keredomo ANO yuka kara zutto ue made + + tenzyoo made no ookina monoire kanari hairimasu kedo ne.

(*Translation:* <u>My apartment</u> is on the third floor. It has a bedroom, a bathroom, and a living room together with a kitchen in one single room. How shall I explain? <u>The living room</u> is about twice as large as a six mat room, a little bigger than that. It's quite large. <u>The bedroom</u> is about the size of an eight mat room. The width is three single beds long and has a rather long side. And <u>the bathroom</u> has a shower, a sink, and a toilet. And what do you call it? a closet, with, I wonder how much, about this width of a door and this much depth, we have this closet. We put in stuff we use, towel, toilet paper, and soap, and things like that, that kind of stuff. It is from the floor to the ceiling. It's a big closet. You can put a lot in it.)

(Data source: Iwasaki 1984)

Iwasaki suggests, from a collection of such apartment descriptions, that the "wa" marker puts the noun into high focus – that is, nouns marked with "wa" (and underlined in the transcript) become the center of the description in that segment of the discourse – the apartment, the living room, the bedroom, and bathroom. As in the Chinese data, this description appears to focus much more on space and less on the relationship of the people to the apartment and its contents. A discourse analysis of descriptions, therefore, can reveal interesting syntactic information not only for English (as our discussion of definite articles suggests) but also for Japanese (description focus attached to "wa").

I have already noted that when students are given an assignment to write a description, they often write a narrative instead. They tell a story about themselves in relation to the object they have been asked to describe. The reverse also happens. Sometimes when we ask people to tell us what happened, they tell us, but the result is less narrative than descriptive. That is, the focus is not on a hero who wishes to reach a goal and therefore goes through

177

a series of actions to reach the goal. The focus is more a description of a scene in which an action happens.

Practice 5.3   Description

1. In your class or study group, tape-record one person giving a description of his or her apartment. Then listen to the tape. How is the discourse organized? Are listeners, like prospective buyers, taken on a grand tour of the apartment? In general, what kinds of syntactic structures are used? What types of clauses or phrases are used to shift the listener's attention from one part of the apartment to another? What is emphasized, the general physical layout as a walking tour or a visual plan for picturing the rooms in terms of an architect's drawing?

2. Transcribe the oral description of the apartment and study its organization. If it is organized as a "walking tour," does it start at the front entrance? Are spatial expressions in relation to the location of the "walkers" (e.g., "on the left," "at the end of the hall")? Are the rooms described in the order in which they are "entered"? What comments are made to connect the tour takers and tour guide to objects in the apartment? Once the tour has been concluded, how is the description closed? Is the closing in terms of people and their relationship to the apartment or in terms of the apartment itself? Try to prepare a template that shows the components of the description. Do you think the template could be used for descriptions of other buildings – for example, a city hall, an opera house, a university building? How might the template be changed for such descriptions?

3. Ask a language learner to give an oral or written description. You might want young children to describe their favorite toy or pet, their bedroom, or their neighborhood. You might ask older students to describe their best friend or the kind of housing they think should be provided for homeless people. If you obtain an apartment description in a language other than English, compare the results with the information given in this section on description. Do your data appear similar or different from the descriptions provided here? Why do you think this is the case?

4. Here are two descriptions. The first is a 10-year-old child's description of a grasshopper seen through a magnifying glass. The second is an 11-year-old's description of his neighborhood.

Here is a colossal monster. Its eyes glare at you, they look as though they are on fire. It could cull houses and villages and put them in its mouth and still lurk about for more prey. It is like a cyclone gathering all in its path. But when you take away the magnifying glass, there is a little creature which is only a microscopic particle to what I have imagined.

(Data source: Haggitt 1967)

The place I live is terrible. There is about 20 narcartic people in our street. We watch the cars come and buy stuff across the street. We call the cops sometimes but they don't do nothing. My mom is scared too becus they could maybe reck our house.

How do these two descriptions differ from those provided by your own students?

5. Review the introduction transcript that you prepared for Practice 2.10. During the introduction, a description of a person is given. Can you identify the parts that are purely descriptive? Notice the syntactic structures used in this section. Are there a large number of *be* copula sentences and relative clauses? If not, what types of structures are used? How do you account for these? How complete is the description?

6. If you have never done so, you might want to write an essay about "the most unforgettable person you've ever met." Look at the opening and closing segments (in a Goffman system constraint way). What do you say about the person? How have you structured the description? Have you succeeded in describing the person? How much of the description relies on your relationship with the person? In these sections, is the focus on the person or on yourself?

7. The following three descriptions of California homes were written by a Japanese student and two Chinese students, respectively.

The inside planning of most houses is composed of a couch, sofa, dining table, beds, bathrooms, etc. One main thing that all houses must have is a TV. A house without a TV is like having a child without its brother.

Most of the new houses come complete with a fireplace for the winter, air-conditioning for the summer, garbage disposal, built-in ranges, and dishwashers. Boy, what a life for the wives!

Upper-class families have built-in intercoms and/or a speaker in every room for music.

All of this may not be so exciting as it seems in the long run, for all the luxury may make the wife, especially, become slow and weak.

A kitchen is furnished remarkably well but too much unnecessary furniture is displayed. All the luxury that is in the bathroom, with carpeting, towels – different ones for baths, drying your hands, or washing your face. Most California houses have dogs and/or cats. Dogs usually bark rather irritatingly as if the house is not welcoming the visitor. Cats approach the visitor with suspicious eyes as if they're going to attack. Of course for animal loves, it is a different story. But for the people who are allergic to dogs or cats, or for the people who weren't raised with animals in the house, it will be rather an embarrassing experience.

A Californian house is rather complicatedly organized, and rather difficult to understand. In a house one feels uncomfortable by thinking about spilling the red punch on the yellow carpet or whether a mean dog is going to bite a visitor or not.

It is well-designed and well-constructed. A fair sized front yard is almost standard equipment, along with a backyard as an option depending on the financial situation of the individual. On a nice sunny day, the front yard is a multi-functional field, it is a good place for a water fight between neighboring children. Also it can serve as a battlefield for the boys, or a padded field for a game of football. While the children are at play, their mothers can take some time off for over-the-fence type of gossip. Meanwhile, the master of the house sits comfortably on the sofa having a can of cold beer while watching the Los Angles Lakers having it out with the New York Nicks.

(Data source: Heaton)

Notice that in these essays the writers use a description of a place to comment on American family life. Compare these descriptions with the template given to account for the apartment descriptions of Linde and Labov (1975). How do they differ? How might you account for these differences?

8. Consider the following oral "narrative." Look for linguistic clues that mark this as a narrative or as a description.

PH: This is just about + Chinese New York. We just look + like someone look at the moon. Like + what year uhm + just two month + January or February. And any kind of day. Like today. Then + yesterday I didn't came because it's Chinese New Year. Annd + we just have to buy new CLOTHES. DECORATE the HOUSE + and clean up the HOUSE. Then you have a uhm + like you have OWED + now owe some money, you had to pay it to s- + pay it + the person. Then you have to buy new food for + Chinese New Year for the God. And you have to go + + Yesterday I went to + four church. Chinese church. First – what's the, uhm + incense?

BH: Uhhuh

PH: umm. You pray + of the God. Then the second church, you
see the dragon; that mean it's + It's mean uhmm + good
luck, the dragon mean. And you went to + then we eat
Chinese food. Then the third church we went to Ital – Italian
church. It's SO big! We ha- we saw + the s-statue + + Like
it's a + GOLD + gold statue. Then, the fourth + church is
+ like a PALACE. SO big. It's + beautiful. Wait + it's near in
uhm, what's a that called? I forgot it, the street + the street.

BH: Uhhmm

PH: ((laughs)) Then + it t- + + We have red envelope. That mean
we have money inside.

BH: Lucky money.

PH: Yeah, good luck, It stand for good luck. Then + the chi- the
children is + the + LUCKY. And adult is + just bad luck.
Because they had to + pay money + for the children. Then
+ I got 73 dollar + for the + Chinese New Year.

BH: You keep them all?

PH: ((laughs)) Yeah! Uhm, in the morning + + we just put + we
just say, "Good morning," then we put – we say Chinese
word. It's called "Gong Hay Fat Choi." Then ((laughing)) then
we have money. + + That's IT!

BH: Okay! GREAT!

RG: That was a good story!

(Data source: Hawkins)

(a) What evidence is there that the passage is a narrative?
(b) What evidence is there that the passage is a description?
How frequently do you suppose speakers and writers
combine these two genres? Would you argue for analyzing/
teaching these two genres in combination?

Procedure or process

A third genre is that of "how to" discourse. We often are called upon to explain how to accomplish some task. People ask advice on how to set up a computer, how to get to the airport, how to operate a video camera, or how to analyze a narrative. Much of instruction consists of "how to" discourse. Advice giving can also be framed in procedural discourse.

When I unpacked my personal computer, I found three sealed envelopes labeled "Open me first," "Open me second," and "Open me third." My immediate assumption was that the manufacturer had easily determined that I had a goal of setting up my computer and that these three packages, if opened in the proper order, would tell me how to do this. This should give you a hint that procedural or process rhetorical genres are meant to tell one how to meet a goal through a process of ordered steps. Opening the first package, I found a large number 1 and the title "Set up your [brand name]" – the first of a set of imperatives to accomplish this goal. These included a series of directions to "Plug A to B" and finally, "Press the on/off switch" and "turn on your personal computer by pressing the keyboard's Power On key." The second and third packages showed me how to install various software programs and offered me a guided tour on how to use the computer.

In all these directions, I knew that I was to be the actor, though the discourse itself was "neutral" in terms of agency. When the agent is "neutral" – that is, anyone rather than a specified person can carry out the task – we can predict that imperative and passive constructions will be used. Certainly this was the case with the computer instructions. When the passage is neutral in terms of the actor, it is also likely that the time of the action is not specified. The procedure will work at any time. Notice that the imperative construction shows a verb that has no tense marking.

In procedural discourse, to acquaint new users with their computers, the goals of the user were known. It wasn't necessary for the writers of the pamphlets to say, "In order to set up your computer . . ." or "To connect the cord . . ." If part of a procedure was not clear, these writers might have said, "To understand how to connect A to B, consult diagram C." They didn't, though, perhaps because pictures accompanied text throughout. Nevertheless, Thompson (1985) found that speakers and writers use more "purpose" clauses in procedural discourse than in other forms of rhetorical organization. For example, in a recipe, you might find an initial purpose clause "*To cool,* place the loaf on a wire rack." These "in order to " clauses state a subgoal or subproblem within a context and then follow it with a solution. Such clauses guide the reader to look for a solution in the next clause.

If you want to catch a leprochaun you must go to a dark woods. Plant a mousetrap. Put hay over it. Then he will get caught in the trap.

(Data source: Golub 1971)

As the analysis of narratives and descriptive discourse showed, there are interesting connections between discourse type and our choice of particular syntactic structures. This is true of procedural discourse as well. However, it is possible to produce a piece of procedural discourse that does not have imperatives (neutral actors, neutral time), a set of procedures in a set temporal order, or purpose clauses. That is, as with all genres, it is not that the genre uses certain grammar forms but rather that writers and speakers select certain forms more often than others to carry out the storytelling, the description, or the procedure.

As an example, consider the following short text:

Evelyn,
These are second generation giants. Their parents got to be about 8 feet tall. I dug a ditch about 3″ deep and 5′ long and buried them about ½″ deep in the center.

[At this point one of my graduate students exclaimed "Oh it's a murder mystery!"]

Then, as they grew I shoveled the dirt back into the ditch. So the roots would not be exposed. I may have used a small amount of rose food fertilizer too.

Best wishes,
Grant

Notice that there is no overt mention of a request for procedure (i.e., an advice seeking request) such as, "If you want to grow some plants to be about 8 feet tall, you need to do the following." Except for the information on fertilizing, each step *is* mentioned in the order in which it is to be carried out. Notice that the words "seeds" is missing from the first sentence, and yet I was able to interpret the following "them" without difficulty simply because the set of instructions was attached to a present of sweet pea seeds. The syntactic forms show no imperatives; instead each sentence appears to be a statement of fact. Yet, we know the function is directive rather than representative. In addition, the agent in each case is the giver of the instructions rather than the person who is to carry out the procedure. And, finally, the closing "Best wishes" differs from the "good luck" that we might wish for someone who is to follow the procedure. In spite of all these obstacles, we immediately interpret the note as procedural discourse. Again, the meaning comes from the fact that the note is attached to a gift of seeds, and seeds are normally a part of a planting script. The fact that a list of actions is described in the order in which the actions should be carried out also allows us to recognize the procedural nature of the text.

Practice 5.4 Procedure or process

1. If you had lots of sweet pea seeds and decided to sell them at a boutique, you might design a card of instructions to include in the envelope of seeds. What "title" would you use for the card? Write out the rest of the card and compare it to the example I gave. Discuss any differences that you find.
2. Write out your favorite recipe. Does this recipe show the "classic" attributes of procedural discourse? Is agency neutral in the recipe? Is time also neutral (not in the sequence of events but, rather, with regard to when the procedure can be carried out)? Did you use any modals? What impact do they have? Did you use purpose clauses? If so, are they sentence initial? Compare your analysis with that of other students in your class or study group. Can you draw up a template that covers all the recipes?
3. Compare the procedural discourse of the sweet pea card

and the recipe. What similarities and differences do you see? One area you might look at has to do with the actors or doers of the actions (i.e., "I," "you," "people," "one," or some unspecified neutral actor).

4. As a research project, test your "procedural discourse competence" in another language. Select a simple useful procedure. Tape-record yourself explaining how to do it. Give the tape to a native speaker of that language, asking for a critique of your performance. You might ask the native speaker to give you his or her version of the same task. Compare versions. What differences and similarities do you find? (Be sure to specify the audience in each case.)

5. Most people find procedural discourse easier to do than either narrative or descriptive discourse. Perhaps this is because the procedure is the focus rather than the doer. Discuss any presentation of self or of other in the procedural examples you have collected.

6. In traditional ESP (English for Special or Specific Purposes) courses, procedural discourse is often presented by asking students to look at an object specific to their field (such as a tool or machine) and to explain how to use the object. Collect compositions where such an assignment has been given. Compare these in your study groups. What do the compositions show about how these students organize procedural discourse?

7. QuickLetter, a computer software program, includes a one-page handout entitled "The Secrets of Writing Business Letters." The introduction includes the following paragraph: "Letter writing is not a lost art, just a forgotten one. The principles still exist. If you try them, you'll see improvement in your very next letter." Four headings are given: "To Begin With," "No Business-ese," "Be Positive," and "Write for Power." Under "To Begin With" are three imperatives: Start from the end (decide what you'd like to happen as a result of your letter; make a list of all the things you'd like to say), get to the point early, and put yourself in your reader's place (be friendly, be nice, and be positive). The subheadings under "No Business-ese" are also imperatives (say it plainly, keep sentences short, clear the deadwood, use active verbs, use pronouns or the addressee's name). "Be Positive" includes never write in anger, end with an action step, resist the hat-in-hand exit of "Thank you . . ." or "If you have any questions . . . ," be professional, write often, and respond quickly. "Write for

Power" discusses the special features of this particular software program. Would you say that this handout is an example of procedural discourse? Why or why not?

8. Young children are often taught how to get to and from school. This instruction consists of walking the route many times, but it also can include asking the child to explain how to get home. If you teach young children, ask them to tell you how to get to school from their homes. Tape-record the data for analysis. If you teach older children, you might ask them for directions to some other place (how to get to the beach; how to get to the ballfield; how to get to their favorite movie theater). If you are interested in children's understanding of their geographical location and spatial relations, ask them to draw a map that includes their home and a location you have selected. Then have them write an essay on how to get from their house to that location. (It's fun to see how they expand and contract space according to places of interest to them.) Your analysis could, of course, become a dissertation!

Argumentation

Argumentation has often been defined as the process of supporting or weakening another statement whose validity is questionable or contentious. The structure of argumentative text is even more flexible than the rhetorical modes presented thus far. However, there is a classical description of the structure of this genre that includes introduction, explanation of the case under consideration, outline of the argument, proof, refutation, and conclusion. You can see that this structure differs somewhat from that of Shaughnessy's "this is what should be done" genre, which includes problem to be solved, effects, causes, possible solutions, assessment of solutions, predicted side effects, and selection of one or some combination of solutions as the best solution.

There are many variants other than the "classic" form for the argumentative genre. In examining a series of articles and news reports, Maccoun (1983) found several patterns for organizing argumentative discourse in written prose. She calls one such pattern a "zig-zag" solution. That is, if the author is a proponent of a position, the outline would be pro, con, pro, con, pro. If the author is an opponent, the pattern would be con, pro, con, pro, con. A second pattern found by Maccoun consists of the problem and refutation of the opposition's argument, followed by a solution. The solution, if not the problem, suggests the author's bias. Like the zig-zag pattern, it requires refutation of the opposition's argument. The author must show that alternative solutions are unacceptable.

A third pattern is the "one-sided argument," where one point of view is presented and no refutation is given. A fourth pattern is an "eclectic approach," where the author may choose to reject some points of view and accept another or some combination of them all.

A fifth pattern contains the opposition's arguments first, followed by the author's argument. "Pointers" are used to identify the first position as the argument of the opposition. "Conventional wisdom," "A common prescription," "Traditionally, it has been believed" are examples of such pointers.

A sixth pattern is the "other side questioned" pattern. This involves the questioning, but not direct refutation, of the opposition's argument. A seventh pattern discussed by Maccoun is one that does not contain a refutation, but it does show disagreement from within the same camp. In other words, there are two points of view expressed and, while one is favored, both are within the same general point of view regarding the argument.

In order to follow the argument elements, the reader must identify the type of pattern, locate the author's major claim and assumptions, locate the opposition's arguments, note concessions and direct refutations, recognize pointers, and correctly read the author's tone of sarcasm or seriousness.

Consider the following opening paragraph from an article entitled "The Ozone" (in Maccoun 1983).

Remember the skepticism last year when the United States banned most aerosol sprays containing chlorofluorocarbons? People found it hard to believe that squirting deodorant out of a can was jeopardizing the stratospheric ozone layer, which protects the earth from excessive ultraviolet radiation. It was like finding out that eating candy causes earthquakes.

As native speakers of English, we know immediately that we are about to be told that, indeed, fluorocarbons are destroying the ozone layer and that the doubters were wrong. We can check this assessment in the next paragraph. Some of the signals of the author's point of view have been underlined.

But now almost all experts agree that the ozone-eating aerosol gases do indeed rise slowly into the stratosphere, where sunlight breaks them down and releases chlorine that does in fact erode the ozone layer. Even worse, the ozone seems to be eroding much faster than originally believed. The threat has not been eliminated, only postponed, by the American ban.

Such markers help us keep track of the development of the argument. By attending to such cues, Reichman (1985) suggests, we can trace the argument structure.

We need to remember that argumentation is accomplished in different ways in different cultures. Interestingly, most textbooks say that the one-sided argument is unacceptable in English, and yet Maccoun found examples in published articles. Many rhetoricians consider the zig-zag pattern unacceptable as well (though, again, many of the articles Maccoun collected were developed in this way). In reading Maccoun's collection of articles, her international students showed that the argument pattern chosen by the author affected the ease with which students could identify the author's point of view. This may be due, in part, to cultural differences in values placed on different patterns of argumentation. For example, some cultures develop arguments through repetition. The beauty of an argument is judged on how these repetitions are accomplished. In American culture, such arguments are not highly valued. In some cultures, it is considered a great mistake to recognize the arguments of the other side. In American culture, all arguments are to be raised and disposed of by counterarguments. In some cultures, it is a weakness not to completely destroy an opponent's arguments; in others, it is acceptable to see some merit in the argument of one's opponents. Finally, in some language groups, subtlety is the key to argumentation. Rubin et al. (1990) noted that Japanese students learning to write English avoid sharply defined argumentative positions – an avoidance that teachers equate with equivocation. In support of their contention that such students systematically avoid explicitly expressing a point of view, they quote one such student:

Most Japanese like to be ambiguous for everything even if they really have clear ideas or attitudes, because we Japanese believe ambiguity as a virtue. I have been discipline to be fair to everything or everyone since I was a child. But this custom means "fair" as "not clear or not strong." Even in my school days, teachers used to instruct us such type of "fair" things: for example, when they discuss about differences between A and B, they like to value both advantages, not to disagree A or B strongly . . . So when I have to write some paper, I often struggle to choose my hopeful idea from among a lot of general ideas an my honest emotional ideas!

(Data source: Rubin et al. 1990)

Practice 5.5   Argumentation

1. As a research project, collect two editorials or short articles that have a definite author bias. Identify the pattern of argumentation, showing how the author presents the argument and how the arguments of the other side are conceded or rejected. Ask your students to identify the patterns too, and compare their responses with yours. How do you account for differences in interpretation?
2. Collect two similar articles in another language of your choice. How similar or different are the patterns of argumentation?
3. In face-to-face arguments, the highly structured presentation of arguments and counterarguments is dropped for more emotional responses. Even very young children soon master the template for arguing with their parents (often degenerating into: "Why?" "Cuz" "Why?"

"Cuz" "Why?" "Just because I say so!"). Young second language learners, too, soon master the "unhn"-"nuhuh" exchanges of argument.

(The children are playing on the schoolyard swings)
L1 child: I'm the strongest!
L2 child: nuh-uh
L1 child: uhhuh
L2 child: nuh-uh
L1 child: I can beat your brother up. I can beat him up.
L2 child: (gradual build in volume over talk turn)
　　　　　You can beat him up huh I can beat him to my party n
　　　　　you can beat my brother n he beat you up ((noises)) it. I
　　　　　CAN BEAT YOU UP!!

(Data source: Young 1974)

Here, the validity of the "contentious claim" is argued on the authority of who can beat up the other side. Note that the L2 child, though still at the beginning stages of language learning, already knows that arguments must build over time and in volume and pitch. That is, he has the intonation needed for the argument template, but not the words. There are valued and nonvalued forms of argument, even in face-to-face encounters. Teachers work hard to help students use words instead of fists to settle arguments. Verbal argument is a sign of willingness to solve problems and conflicts without force, but it may also evolve into a physical argument. Note the ways teachers scaffold arguments – that is, help students verbalize arguments. (If you are interested in studying interpersonal conflict from a discourse perspective, you might consult Bavelas et al. 1985. If your interest is in how young children develop this genre, see Brenneis and Lein 1977, and Genishi and De Paolo 1982.)

4. In a formal debate, one may be arbitrarily assigned to take one side or another on some point (e.g., "It is resolved that *X* should/should not be allowed."). There are definite rules as to precisely how the debate may progress and what each side is expected to present at each point. If you have participated in debates, outline the process for the members of your class or study group. Then consult your international students to discover whether the debate structure and the goals of practice debates are similar or quite different in their languages.

5. In ESP, we talk about the rhetoric of special knowledge communities (such as economics, psychology, and so

forth). Each field has its journals, which shape this rhetoric. The rhetorical organization of most research journals in our field (e.g., *Language Learning, TEXT, Discourse Processes*) follows a set pattern. If the journals adopt a rhetorical organization that determines how research is reported, how evidence is presented, and how evidence is interpreted, the rhetoric, in turn, shapes the field. Select a leading journal from a specific content field. Describe the template for research reports in this journal. Compare the rhetorical organization with that of research in our own field.

Text structure theory

A number of researchers have looked at the structure of text in a rather different manner. Text "theories," such as Grosz and Sidner's (1986) discourse theory, Mann and Thompson's (1987) rhetorical structure theory, and Meyer's (1975, 1984) adaptation of Grimes's (1975) framework of text structure, have been proposed. Meyer's work has been very influential in the field of reading research, Mann and Thompson's is best known in linguistics, and Grosz and Sidner's is from artificial intelligence computation and natural languages. These researchers have developed ways of characterizing text in terms of the relations between parts of the text, rather than starting with an overall template as in genre analysis.

The goal of text analysis in at least some of this work is to show how the structure of discourse reflects the intentions and goals of the speaker or writer. There are, as we saw in speech act analysis, no particular linguistic structures that uniquely match these goals or intentions. It is possible, however, to examine text for both linguistic forms and writer's intentions in ways that capture some aspects of text structure. Let's look at how this works for one such proposal – that of Mann and Thompson's rhetorical structure theory (RST).

RST analysis highlights *relations*. The relations show the type of connection between two portions of text. The relationship is between two pieces of text called the nucleus (N) and the satellite (S). The function – the plausible reason why the author or speaker chose to place these two pieces of text together – is called an *effect*. Mann and Thompson have identified many types of relations; the list is open-ended, so the following is not necessarily complete.

Relations

Circumstance	Antithesis and concession
Solutionhood	Antithesis
Elaboration	Concessions

Background	Condition and otherwise
Enablement and motivation	Condition
Enablement	Otherwise
Motivation	Interpretation and evaluation
Evidence and justify	Interpretation
Evidence	Evaluation
Justify	Restatement and summary
Relations of cause	Restatement
Volitional cause	Summary
Nonvolitional cause	Other relations
Volitional result	Sequence
Nonvolitional result	Contrast
Purpose	

You will notice that some of the relations are grouped. This is because they relate to a similar function. For example, "evidence" and "justify" are grouped together. If the writer uses an evidence satellite, the intention is likely that of increasing the reader's belief in the nucleus material. If the writer uses a justify satellite, the intention may be to increase the reader's acceptance of the author's right to present the nucleus material. Both of these satellites involve the reader's attitude toward the nucleus material, and so they are grouped together.

Perhaps an example or two will make the notion of relation clearer. First, let's look at Mann and Thompson's text example from *BYTE* magazine to illustrate the evidence relation:

1(N) The program as published for calendar year 1980 really works.
2-3(S) In only a few minutes, I entered all the figures from my 1980 tax return and got a result which agreed with my hand calculations to the penny.

The statement that the program works is the nucleus (N). It is strengthened by two pieces of evidence in the satellite (S). First, the program worked quickly to give a result, and, second, the result was judged correct because it agreed with standard hand calculations. The author's intent in using these clauses is to increase the reader's belief in the N statement. Mann and Thompson formalize this information for each of the relations in chart form. Here is their chart for the evidence relation. W is the writer and R is the reader. N is the abbreviation for the nucleus, and S stands for satellite.

Relation name: EVIDENCE
Constraints on N: R might not believe N to a degree satisfactory to W.
Constraints on S: The reader believes S or will find it credible.
Constraints on the N + S combination: R's comprehending S increases R's belief of N.

The effect: R's belief of N is increased.
Locus of the effect: N

Let's look at the concession relation. Mann and Thompson's example for this relation is taken from an abstract:

1(N)   Concern that this material (dioxin) is harmful to health or the environment may be misplaced.
2(S)   Although it is toxic to certain animals,
3   evidence is lacking that it has any serious long-term effect on human beings.

As you can see, a writer who believes dioxin to be relatively harmless might want to admit its toxicity to certain animals while denying its effect on humans as a way of persuading the reader to believe in the nucleus statement. The relation used is concession. Although I have already said that these relations may not have particular linguistic forms or markers attached to them, the connectors "although," "while," "even though," and "but" are signals of concession.

Here is the formal chart for the Concession relation:

Relation name: CONCESSION
Constraints on N: W has a positive regard for the situation presented in N.
Constraints on S: W is not claiming that the situation presented in S doesn't hold.
Constraints on the N + S combination: W acknowledges a potential or apparent incompatibility between the situations presented in N and S; W regards the situations as compatible: recognizing the compatibility between the situations increases R's positive regard for the situation presented in N.
The effect: R's positive regard for the situation in N is increased.
Locus of the effect: N and S

Notice how different this type of analysis is from that of genre analysis. The focus is not on the template or overall form of the text; rather, this type of rhetorical analysis includes the writer and the reader. It is a description of a process, where the author or speaker carries out goals, selecting particular clauses and relating them in specific ways to meet those goals. In the end, the result is an overall form.

The author produces the text assuming that the reader or listener (and the discourse analyst too!) will be able to locate nucleus and satellite segments in the text. In their analysis, Mann and Thompson begin by dividing the text into units. These units are roughly analogous to a clause. Then the clauses are labeled as nucleus or satellite.

Mann and Thompson have a number of guidelines for identifying nucleus versus satellite. First, they note the asymmetry of clauses. If *A* is evidence for *B*, then *B* is not evidence for *A*. In the evidence example, the fact that the program ran and provided an answer that was the same as the one derived from hand calculation can only serve as evidence for the claim that the tax program really works. Second, one member of the pair may be incomprehensible or a non sequitur without the other (but not vice versa). Without the claim in the nucleus, the evidence would be meaningless. Third, the evidence satellite could be replaced by a different piece of evidence without changing the text. If the nucleus were changed, the change would be much more drastic. Finally, one member of the pair is more essential to the author's purpose than the other. That is, if all the satellite clauses were dropped, the nucleus clauses should contain the most important parts of the text from the author's point of view.

The order of the clauses cannot be used to locate nucleus and satellite since it is impossible to specify whether the author will place the nucleus or the satellite first. There are some relations, however, where a preferred order is apparent. This order is related to the notion of placement of new versus old or background information. That is, new information is more often in final position. Mann and Thompson suggest that the following are typical order patterns:

Satellite before nucleus	*Nucleus before satellite*
Antithesis	Elaboration
Background	Enablement
Concessive	Evidence
Conditional	Purpose
Justify	Restatement
Solutionhood	

Practice 5.6 Rhetorical structure analysis

1. Label each of the following stretches of text as either nucleus (N) or satellite (S). Then identify the relation type between them.
   a. Although much of John Cage's music is noisy and stressful,
   b. his music for the voice is lyrical.

   a. For fast delivery of SuperLaserSpool,
   b. call MacConnection 1-800-944-4444 or visit your local Authorized Reseller today!

   a. For Mildred, who had an eye for design, he tried harder.
   b. He wore a camel's hair cardigan over a white open-neck shirt and tan pants, an ensemble that enhanced the suntan he had acquired during recent months of biking.
2. Look at each of the following examples, and decide which order (*a* before *b* or *b* before *a*) seems more natural. Does

your order agree with the typical order patterns found by Mann and Thompson? If not, why do you believe yours differs?

ENABLEMENT *(effect: R's potential ability to perform the action presented in N increases)*
a. Don't miss the department's first big party.
b. Sign up before Thursday, 5:00 P.M.

a. For a catalog, write to Elderhostel, [address], Boston, Massachusetts.
b. Join one of the 50 international trips available in 1991.

a. Ask for SYNCOM diskettes, with burnished Ectype coating and dust-absorbing jacket liners.
b. What if you're having to clean floppy drive heads too often?

(Data source: Mann and Thompson 1987)

MOTIVATION *(effect: R's desire to perform action presented in N is increased)*
a. The faculty will supply the food and drinks.
b. Don't miss the department's first big party.

a. Ask for SYNCOM diskettes, with burnished Ectype coating and dust-absorbing jacket liners.
b. Easy to purchase and easy to use.

(Data source: Mann and Thompson 1987)

CONDITION *(effect: R recognizes how the realization of the situation presented in N depends on the realization of the situation presented in S)*
a. If you are a member of KCRW and have not received tickets in the past 90 days. . . .
b. Call now for free tickets for the Thursday performance of the Nutcracker.

a. Employees are urged to complete new beneficiary designation forms for retirement or life insurance benefits.
b. Whenever there is a change in marital or family status,
. . .

CIRCUMSTANCE *(effect: R recognizes that the situation presented in S provides the framework for interpreting N)*
a. Probably the most extreme case of Visitors Fever I have ever witnessed was a few summers ago.
b. When I visited relatives in the Midwest, . . .

a. . . . while lubricating it at the same time.
b. Cleaning agents on the burnished surface of the Ectype coating actually remove buildup from the head

(Data source: Mann and Thompson 1987)

Once the clauses or text spans have been identified as nucleus and satellite, the relations are identified (i.e., operational definitions are given for each). As with speech act analysis, this can be difficult because the intent of the author may differ from that shown in the analysis, and it is possible for more than one relation to appear among the clauses. Ford (1986) gives the following example.

1. No parking.
2. Violators will be towed at the owner's expense.

There is no linguistic signal to indicate that a particular relation is to be interpreted between the two pieces of text. However, we might decide that (2) *motivates* the reader not to park. It is also possible to interpret towing as the consequence of parking. This would be an antithesis relation. The questions, then, are, can relations function simultaneously, and do we choose one inference rather than the other in reading such material?

To handle these issues, Mann and Thompson note that the claim is not that the writer's intent in selecting clauses has been identified, but rather that it is *plausible* that such an intent exists. It is also not claimed that the reader will interpret the relation of parts of the text in this way, but that it is *plausible* that such an interpretation will be made.

To show relations in a more formal way, Mann and Thompson number the clauses in the text and then use diagrams to show how the nucleus and satellite are connected as spans of text. An arc with the relation name connects the underlined spans of text. For example, the concession and evidence relations discussed earlier for the dioxin example would be diagrammed as shown in Figure 5.1. The numbers stand for the clauses identified in the examples.

Each of these text spans is then connected to other spans until the set contains one final span for the entire text. Thus, the analysis covers all the relations among all the clauses in the text in a way that shows how coherence is established by the author and, hopefully, is discovered by the reader.

Connections between analyses

In Chapter 4, we talked about the structure of various speech events. In this chapter, we discussed rhetorical structure (via genre analysis and RST). Again, we can see a definite overlap among these different ways of looking at discourse. For example, the analysis of an advice speech event might be sim-

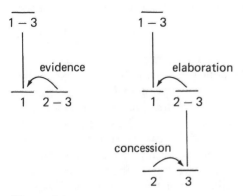

Figure 5.1

ilar in many ways to the rhetorical analysis of procedural text. A narrative analyzed as a genre could be analyzed as a storytelling speech event, or it could even be described as a script. The approach, however, as we have seen, differs because the goals of the analyses differ.

This chapter has presented two ways of thinking about the structure of text: rhetorical genre analysis and rhetorical structure theory. The two types of analyses share some of their goals (e.g., discovering structure) and differ in others (e.g., whether the analysis should center on conventions or templates, or on the intentions and goals of authors and readers, or on both).

To illustrate the overlap among these various ways of looking at discourse, let's use a longer example from Mann and Thompson, an analysis of an advertisement for computer diskettes. As you read through the text (numbered by text spans), consider how this same text might be described in terms of an advice speech event or as an example of procedural discourse.

1. What if you're having to clean floppy drive heads too often?
2. Ask for SYNCOM diskettes, with burnished Ectype coating and dust-absorbing jacket liners.
3. As your floppy drive writes or reads,
4. a Syncom diskette is working four ways
5. to keep loose particles and dust from causing soft errors, dropouts.
6. Cleaning agents on the burnished surface of the Ectype coating actually remove buildup from the head,
7. while lubricating it at the same time.
8. A carbon additive drains away static electricity
9. before it can attract dust or lint.
10. Strong binders hold the signal-carrying oxides tightly within the coating.
11A. And the non-woven jacket liner,
12. more than just wiping the surface,
11B. provides thousands of tiny pockets to keep what it collects.
13. To see which SYNCOM diskette will replace the ones you're using now,

195

14. send for our free "Flexi-Finder" selection guide and the name of the supplier nearest you.
15. SYNCOM, Box 130, Mitchell, SD 57301.

The RST diagram for this text is shown in Figure 5.2.

Obviously, there are differences among these methods of discourse analysis. The RST diagram makes it appear that this type of analysis works from the bottom up as clause units are identified and then linked according to function. The links gradually reveal the total structure. This is true in terms of the analysis itself. Of course, the writer and the reader do not make their decisions or interpretations in such a bottom-up fashion. Speech event and rhetorical genre analyses, on the other hand, work from the top down by specifying the components and their order in flexible templates. Again, this is true only of the analytic description, for no claims are made that people actually operate in this way. Another difference in methods is that in speech event analysis, the focus is on interaction: the text has been built among participants as dialogic rather than as monologic. In genre analysis, cooperatively built text is usually not selected for analysis. The focus is on the template, not on the interaction that may have produced the text. The analyses differ because of this focus.

Of course, one can argue that the text is a dialogue between author and reader and that this is captured in the "effect" statements of the Mann and Thompson method of text analysis. As you can see from the preceding example, text analysis reveals text structure by making explicit the connections among all the clauses of the text. In genre analysis, on the other hand, the text would be matched to a (flexible) template of procedural discourse (i.e., the "what to do if you're tired of cleaning drive heads" question, followed by a series of steps one might take to find relief – with neutral actor, neutral time, frequent use of imperatives and passives, the use of modals, and so forth). There are, then, major differences in the various methods of discourse analysis. These are reflections of differences in focus, goals, and range of phenomena each method addresses.

Conclusion

The structures and templates described so far are not static but flexible. They change as we put them to use in real communication. Templates are meant to capture the essence of the discourse. We can make connections between types of teaching approaches and each analysis. Goffman's system and ritual constraints relate to conversational and cross-cultural approaches to language teaching. Script theory is reflected most clearly in the situational approach. Speech act and speech event analyses relate to the notional-functional approach, and rhetorical analysis reminds us of contrastive rhetoric and ESP or content-based approaches. However, just as there is overlap in

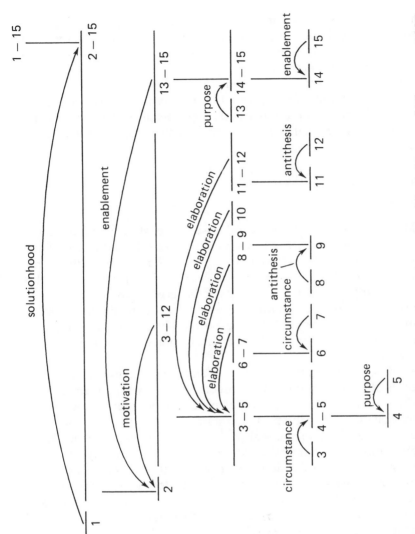

Figure 5.2 RST diagram for SYNCOM text. Reproduced from Mann and Thompson 1987 with permission from the authors and Information Sciences Institute.

each of these types of discourse analyses, there is overlap in each teaching approach. That is, knowledge of system constraints or of speech event analysis might turn out to be just as important as rhetorical analysis for the ESP or content-based language class.

In these first chapters, we have begun to move from larger overall systems, scripts, and rhetorical genres to show how each contributes to coherence in discourse. Chapter 6 will continue in that direction by looking at the multiplicity of ways we can manipulate linguistic signals to help create more coherent discourse.

Research and application

A. Narratives

1. Mandler et al. (1980) compared the recall of stories by Liberian children and adults, both schooled and nonschooled. These data were then compared to similar data from American children and adults. Since the patterns of recall were similar for all groups, the data were used to support the hypothesis of universality of narrative structure. Compare the stories used in this study with those used by Carrell (1981). Prepare preliminary notes for a research project that might help resolve the difference in findings.

2. Kindergarten and preschool children telling stories perform some parts of the narrative better than others. For instance, young children are not very successful in story orientation – they are not explicit about who the participants are and where the events occur or when. They do well in telling how the events occur in chronological order and what props were used, but they are not very explicit in explaining why these events happened. They do use extensive evaluation, but often their stories stop short of resolution so that it is not clear how or if the crisis was resolved. Analyze the following narrative cooperatively built by a bilingual child and her elementary school teacher. What marks it as a narrative? What suggests that it is not a narrative? Which features are well performed, and which are not?

BH: And now you do your story.
MM: When I went to my grandma's house . . . we had a barbeque.
BH: When did you go?
MM: uhm:: last week
BH: Okay.
MM: And++well, everybody – I had my – first we went to the market and then everybody..we::=
BH: =First you went WHERE?

MM: To the market+with my cousin an' my dad. Then me and my
cousin+went to go get everything, and my dad was getting the
meat. And that took a long time. An' then we went home. An' then
we were doing all this stuff already. Then we were getting
everything ready. An=

BH: =You went to your grandma's home?

MM: ((nods "yes"))

BH: Okay.

MM: She lives in.++she lives next – downtown.

BH: Uhhuh.

MM: Okay. An' then . . . we went in the backyard. An' then we had to
wait for everybody++because we were going to show 'em the
tape++that – when my mom and dad got married.

BH: OH!

MM: So, anyway, we're waiting for everybody to get there. We got there
at ten. An' //then

BH: //Now* who all went? Your mom, and your dad, and your
grandma, an'=

MM: =My sister, my brother.

BH: Your sister, your brother.

MM: An' my=

BH: =Robert?

MM: Uhhuh. An then++when+my Aunt Dorie came home, we looked
at the movie. Everyone was laughin at it cuz my dad, he was++
nervous. An' then we+a little while later=

BH: =Why was your dad nervous?

MM: Cuz uhm he uhm he never did that before. He, uhm++he's-=

BH: =He'd never SEEN it before?

MM: Yeah, he saw it, but he didn't – he was embarrassed because+
uhm, last time when we saw it it, everyone was laughing.

BH: Oh.

MM: An' then, uhm++a little while later we+got s – we ordered pizza.

BH: Uhhm.

MM: An then we uhm++an then, a little while later, we went home.

BH: So, wait. Now when was the barbeque?

MM: At+three or something.

BH: Oh at three. And then when everybody got there, then you showed
the movie, and then when that was over, you ordered pizza++
and then after that, you went home. ++ Well, what was your
favorite part of the day?

MM: When we+when me and my cousin-s++at the market, cuz we
were run – we were going up so fast ((zoom sound effects)). It was,
uhm+going down the aisle so fa-,+it was so fast.

BH: Uhm. Did you have fun when your whole family got together?

MM: Yeah. That was the first time we had a barbeque at my grandma's
house.

(Data source: Hawkins)

3. Hopper and Thompson (1980) list the features that determine the degree of transitivity of verbs and relate this to foreground (high focus) and background (low focus) parts of narratives. Analyze all the verbs in one of your narratives for the features they list (participants, kinesis, aspect, punctuality, volitionality, affirmation, mode, agency, individuation of object, affectedness of object). Are you able to successfully separate background information from the main story line on the basis of these features?

4. McGann and Schwartz (1988) examined linguistic markers for protagonists in narratives. The protagonist is typically the person who is more intimately involved in causing events in the story (agentive), is higher in animacy than competing characters, has a primary function of reaching a goal, is referred to most frequently, appears in more than one scene, and is usually introduced in the initial stage of the narrative. Wordless storybooks that varied in terms of agentiveness were used to elicit stories from children. Do you believe that protagonists share these features in narratives of all languages? Read McGann and Schwartz's article and prepare a preliminary research proposal to test the findings in another language or in a second or foreign language setting.

5. Hatch (1976) gives examples of various types of language mixing/switching that may relate to an "evaluation" function in discourse – that is, changing from one language to the other serves to involve the listener in the interaction or lends dramatic effect to the story line.

   a. Repetition (the same information is given in each language by the speaker)
      RR: The water leaked from all sides. Di vaser gest fan ale zeytn.
      AU: Kono mae doo natta? What happened to this last time?
      DL: But what I usually buy are those thick ones, las más gruesas.
      EH: Maleesh, maleesh, cherie, never mind, never mind.

   b. Switch for additional emphasis
      RR: I wouldn't take my dog to him, aza klug er zey (however clever he may be)
      AU: Kango fu ga iru yo (I need a nurse, you know) 'cause I've had enough good medicine, man.
      DL: Boy, you get to hurtin so bad you can't hardly even 'cer masa pa' tortillas (work the dough for tortillas)

   c. Switch to emphasize the unexpected
      RR: The kitchen is finf dolar (unexpectedly cheap)
      AU: Un, Rodan ga tabeta. Oooh, another Rodan. Two Rodans. (yeah, Rodan ate it up)
      EH: And there in the doorway was en stor mand (a big man)

d. Switch to signal parenthetical remarks

    RR: Tuesday is a busy day – leysn-kreyze, arbeterring – (reading circle, workman's circle) better another day.

    AU: Oichi-ni, oichi-ni (one-two, one-two), that's the way A walks, oichi-ni, where's she going?

e. Tags and fillers (to mark solidarity with listener?)

    AU: He's unhappy, *ne*, that's the point, *ne*.

    DL: Pero como, *you know*, la Estela.

f. Switch to highlight direct speech segments

    AU: "Oh no, D, do you think a monkey can fly?" to ettara ne.

    DL: Dice "You're gonna hit it," Le dijo, "I don't think."

    AH: "Spank you," ńii leh (he usually says)

g. Switch to show affection, teasing and swearing

    EH: Er du faerdig, you slow poke, saa kører vi. (Are you ready . . . let's drive off)

    AU: Yuki is a nut. Soo kana. Taberare soo demo nai kedo nee. (Really? She doesn't look very edible) Yuki is a pig.
    [Rest of conversation in Japanese.]

(Data source: Hatch 1976)

No one has really looked at language mixing/switching in terms of "evaluation" in narratives. If you have narrative data from bilinguals who mix and switch languages, you might carry out such a project (and publish the results).

B. *Other genres*

6. The June 1990 issue of *European Journal of Personality* (*4*, 2) is devoted to descriptive terms for personality. When students are asked to write a descriptive essay about their favorite character, they need to know the special vocabulary for particular personality traits. This issue includes articles on how psychologists group such traits and the terms they use. Authorities from different countries (particularly Germany and the Netherlands) point out that the categories are not universal across languages. Prior to assigning a "your favorite character" essay to your students, present them with vocabulary from lists included in this journal and ask them to sort the vocabulary into categories. If the categories differ among your students, how would you account for this? If they are all the same, are they the same as your own and those presented in the journal? Which terms could be appropriately used in a descriptive essay? Which are more appropriate to a psychological report? Can your students identify those that are and are not appropriate for the assignment?

7. Zuck and Zuck (1984) list the components of accident reports in newspaper articles. These include (a) nature of the accident, (b) the setting, (c) the cause, (d) the victims, (e) comparison with other accidents, and (f) public figures involved. Collect examples of such reports from your local newspaper. Do they follow this template? Would you consider this template a script or a genre? We've already noted the overlap between scripts, speech events, and genre analysis. In all cases, we attempt to see the abstract system behind the surface form. Does it matter which we call it? Why or why not? If you have access to accident reports in newspapers from other countries, compare the format to see if it is the same for other languages as well. You might like to select another type of newspaper story to see if you can discover the template (e.g., obituaries, weddings, meetings, etc.).

8. Connor and Lauer (1985) believe that argumentation is not a separate rhetorical genre but, rather, part of persuasive discourse. They define persuasive discourse as the genre that uses appeals to effect cooperation from and identification with the audience. They have identified 23 types of persuasive appeals: 4 ethical, 5 affective, and 14 logical appeals. With a database of 50 British compositions, they show that variation in the effectiveness of some of these appeals relates to overall holistic ratings of the compositions. Using Connor and Lauer's categories, identify the types of appeals language learners use in their compositions. Do they use certain types of appeals more than others? How might you use this information in teaching persuasive or argumentative discourse?

9. There are many forms of poetry where a genre template is obvious. For example, as soon as I present you with the line "There was a young linguist named Noam," you not only know this is a limerick but are able to begin the next line with a "who" and count out the beats of the remainder of the verse. Write a first line for a limerick and ask friends to add lines to it. Highlight the words that are stressed and mark the rhyming words. When we hear a limerick form, we immediately believe the author's intent is humorous (or possibly satiric). What parts of the limerick substantiate this? If you changed these parts, would the result still be a limerick? Why or why not? If you are interested in the language of humor, Nash's book (1985) will be especially helpful for this project.

10. Folman and Sarig (1990) tested the contrastive rhetoric hypothesis by looking at the rhetorical structures preferred by native Hebrew and native English writers. The preferred structures of the two groups differ, but the authors speculate that

preference patterns may be related to instruction practice as much as to transfer of the rhetorical preferences from L1 to L2. Read Kaplan's (1966) article on the contrastive rhetoric hypothesis or his 1988 reformulation toward a theory of contrastive rhetoric. Select articles from Connor and Kaplan (1987) and, along with the Folman and Sarig article, do a critical review of the studies that support or question the hypothesis.

C. Other application activities

11. Johns (1986) worked out a procedure to help language learners see the match or mismatch of their compositions with genre templates. For example, once a student has begun an essay that is a problem/solution essay, Johns gradually identifies for the student the template that is closest to the form the student has used. For a problem/solution essay, according to Hoey (1983), this could be situation (setting, time), problem, causes (often embedded in problem or situation), responses or solutions, and evaluation. Looking at the introduction to the composition, Johns shows how she expects to see a situation described (e.g., "in the past five years, Hong Kong has seen . . ."), then a problem set (e.g., ". . . a dramatic rise in crime"), followed by the responses of government and private individuals. If, instead, the writer goes off in another direction to talk about juvenile delinquency around the world, the expectations of a native-speaker reader would have to change, perhaps to a comparison and contrast template. Thus, the writer can compare what he or she has written to see how close or far off from the template the composition is. Read this article and try the methodology with one of your students who has problems with problem/solution essays. Report on how well the methodology works for you and your student. What changes or suggestions do you have for improving the method?

12. Connor and McCagg (1983) asked native speakers of English and Japanese and Spanish ESL adults to paraphrase a representative problem/solution passage. While ESL teachers rated the paraphrases quite differently according to the L1 groups, there were not many differences in the rhetorical styles of the paraphrases across the three groups. By selecting from each group the best and the worst paraphrases (according to the ESL teachers' ratings), the authors were able to show how scientific or academic tone and lack of details affected the ratings. You might like to replicate this study with your own language learners. Or you might compare the written paraphrases of students who are immigrants with those who are newly arrived international

students to see whether cross-cultural genre differences rather than style differences emerge.

13. Hinds (1979, 1983) contrasts certain features of Japanese and English rhetorical structure (procedural, expository, monologic). If you teach Japanese to English speakers or English to Japanese speakers, review and summarize these articles. Either draw implications for teaching from these descriptions or prepare a preliminary research plan to investigate these contrasts with data from your own students.

14. Olsen and Huckin (1990) found that although students understood the words of lectures, they didn't always understand the lectures. Listening to lectures organized around several main points, students who used a strategy of listening for points did well in oral recall summaries. Those who listened for information couldn't grasp the main points. The organization of the lecture was problem/solution with side references to theory. In the lecture, the professor used such cues as "The real problem is . . ." "The whole idea is . . .," "The key is . . ." to highlight main points. Review this article along with Johns' article (1986) on problem/ solution. How might this information be used in a listening comprehension class for EFL or ESL engineering students?

15. Lund (1990) presents a function-response matrix for use in planning goals, objectives, and instruction in teaching language learners *how* to listen. The six functions for academic listening are: identification, orientation, main idea comprehension, detail comprehension, full comprehension, and replication. There are also nine categories of listener responses presented in this article. Read Lund's article and decide how (or whether) this system would work for planning lessons for your students and how the system might relate to genre structure.

D. Rhetorical structure analysis

16. Mann and Thompson (1987) say that relations between satellite and nucleus need not be made explicit by linguistic markers. However, they also point out that there are connectors, such as "although" and "however," that can be used to make a relation specific. Reichman (1985) talks about these as "clue words." For example:

Support: Because, Like, Like when
Restatement and/or conclusions of point being supported: So
Interruption: Incidentally, By the way
Return to previously interrupted space: Anyway, Anyhow, In any case

Indirect challenge: Yes? Right but, Except, However
Direct challenge: (No) but
Subargument concession: All right but, Okay but
Prior logical abstraction: But look/listen/you see
Further development: Now

The clue words signal the kind of shift about to take place in the discourse. Examine a piece of text (perhaps your classroom transcript from Practice 1.2) for these clue words. Have they been used to show these particular relational functions? Examine the "logical connectors" presented in your language teaching text or in your grammar reference book. Can you assign relational functions to each of these connectors? Are some used for several functions? If you teach or are learning a language other than English, what logical connectors are presented? What relations do they signal?

17. Johns (1980) gives a number of examples in which nonnative speakers use inappropriate conjunctions in their essays. Attempt to apply rhetorical structure theory relations to Johns' examples. If this seems like a helpful task, you might want to collect examples from your own students and analyze them in this way.

Tanaka, who was once prime minister in Japan, was born in 1928. *Moreover,* his family was very poor.

Culture is transmitted from old generation by word, painting picture, and others. *For example,* the parents who live in different countries back their children in different ways.

In Japan, mainly, there are two vacations. New Year's and summer vacation; *however,* both are about four or five days in general.

Although it is difficult to define culture. *But* generally culture is everything about nations received from and possessed by different generations including education. *But* culture is not education.

Another example: if a man has stolen for three time his right hand must be cut off. *But* the same conditions which are required for death are mentioned in this case.

Reorganize the following paragraph so that the relations are more easily drawn among the segments:

During the past 30 years, many ships and airplanes have disappeared in this area. They vanished without any reason. Investigators couldn't find anything out about these strange

205

disappearing ships and airplanes. The strange phenomenon which can't be explained exists in the modern world.

If you added conjunctions, explain why you selected them – that is, what relations do they highlight?

References

Bavelas, J. B.; Rogers, L. E.; and Millar, F. E. (1985). Interpersonal conflict. In T. van Dijk (Ed.), *Handbook of discourse analysis. Vol. 1: Disciplines of discourse* (pp. 9–26). London: Academic Press.

Bennett, T. (1977). An extended view of verb voice in written and spoken narratives. In E. Ochs and T. Bennett (Eds.), *Discourse across time and space. Occasional Papers in Linguistics, 5,* 43–50. Linguistics Department, University of Southern California.

Brenneis, D., and Lein, L. (1977). "You fruithead": A sociolinguistic approach to children's dispute settlement. In S. Ervin-Tripp and C. Mitchell-Kernan (Eds.), *Child discourse* (pp. 49–65). New York: Academic Press.

Carrell, P. (1981). Culture-specific schemata in L2 comprehension. In R. A. Orem and J. F. Haskell (Eds.), *Selected papers from the 9th Illinois TESOL/BE Annual Convention and the First Midwest TESOL Conference* (pp. 123–132). Chicago, Ill.: TESOL.

　　(1983). Some issues in studying the role of schemata, or background knowledge in second language comprehension. *Reading In a Foreign Language, 1,* 81–92.

Connor, U., and Kaplan, R. (1987). *Writing across languages: Analysis of L2 texts.* Reading, Mass.: Addison-Wesley.

Connor, U. and Lauer, J. (1985). Understanding persuasive essay writing. *TEXT, 5,* 4:309–326.

Connor, U., and McCagg, P. (1983). Cross-cultural differences and perceived quality in written paraphrases of English expository prose. *Applied Linguistics, 4,* 259–263.

Day, A. (1985). *Good Dog, Carl.* La Jolla and London: Green Tiger Press.

Edelsky, C. (1982). Writing in a bilingual program: The relation of L1 and L2 texts. *TESOL Quarterly, 16,* 211–228.

Ford, C. E. (1986). Overlapping relations in text structure. In S. DeLancey and R. Tomlin (Eds.), *Proceedings of the Second Annual Pacific Linguistics Conference* (pp. 107–124). Eugene, Oreg.: Linguistics Department, University of Oregon.

Folman, S., and Sarig, G. (1990). Intercultural rhetorical differences in meaning construction. *Communication and Cognition, 23,* 1: 45–92.

Genishi, C., and De Paolo, M. (1982). Learning through argument in a preschool. In L. C. Wilkinson (Ed.), *Communicating in the classroom* (pp. 48–84). New York: Academic Press.

Golub, L. (1971). Stimulating and receiving children's writing: Implications for an elementary writing curriculum. *Elementary English, 48,* 1: 33–46.

Grimes, J. E. (1975). *The thread of discourse.* The Hague: Mouton.

Grosz, B. J., and Sidner, C. L. (1986). Attention, intentions, and the structure of discourse. *Computational Linguistics, 12,* 3: 175–204.

Haggitt, T. W. (1967). *Working with language.* Oxford: Basil Blackwell.

Hatch, E. (1976). Studies in language mixing and switching. In W. McCormack and S. Wurm (Eds.), *Language and man. Anthropological issues* (pp. 201–217). The Hague: Mouton.

Hinds, J. (1979). Organizational patterns in discourse. In T. Givon (Ed.), *Syntax and Semantics. Vol 12: Discourse and syntax* (pp. 136–157). New York: Academic Press.

(1983) Contrastive rhetoric: Japanese and English. *TEXT 3,* 2: 183–195.

Hoey, M. (1983). *On the surface of discourse.* New York: Allen & Unwin.

Hopper, P., and Thompson, S. (1980). Transitivity in grammar and discourse. *Language, 56,* 2: 251–300.

Hunt, K. (1965). *Grammar structures written at three grade levels.* Research report 3, Urbana, Ill.: National Council of Teachers of English.

Iwasaki, S. (1984). Semantic characteristics and discourse functions of the noun phrase *-wa:* A study of Japanese spoken expository discourse. Ph.D. dissertation, Linguistics Department, University of California, Los Angeles.

Johns, A. (1980). Cohesive error in the written discourse of non-native speakers. *CATESOL Occasional Paper, 6,* 65–70.

(1986). The ESL student and the revision process: Some insights from schema theory. *Journal of Basic Writing, 5,* 2: 70–80.

Kaplan, R. (1966). Cultural thought patterns in intercultural education. *Language Learning, 16,* 1–20. Reprinted in H. Allen and R. Campbell (1972). *Teaching English as a Second Language: A book of readings* (pp. 294–310). New York: McGraw-Hill.

Kaplan, R. B. (1988). Contrastive rhetoric and second language learning: Notes toward a theory of contrastive rhetoric. In A. Purvis (Ed.), *Writing across languages and cultures.* Newbury Park, Calif.: Sage Publications.

Kintsch, W., and Greene, E. (1978). The role of culture-specific schemata in the comprehension and recall of stories. *Discourse Processes, 1,* 1–13.

Kumpf, L. (1986). Structuring narratives in a second language: Descriptions of rhetoric and grammar. Ph.D. dissertation, Applied Linguistics, University of California, Los Angeles.

Kuwahata, M. (1984). The negation system in the interlanguage of a Japanese speaker. Master's thesis, Applied Linguistics, University of California, Los Angeles.

Labov, W. (1972). The transformation of experience in narrative syntax. In W. Labov (Ed.), *Language in the inner city* (pp. 354–396). Philadelphia: University of Pennsylvania Press.

Labov, W., and Waletsky, J. (1967). Narrative analysis: Oral versions of personal experience. In J. Helm (Ed.), *Essays on the verbal and visual arts* (pp. 12–44). University of Washington Press.

Linde, C., and Labov, W. (1975). Spatial networks as a site for study of language and thought. *Language, 51,* 924–939.

Lund, R. L. (1990). A taxonomy for teaching second language listening. *Foreign Language Annals, 23,* 2: 105–115.

207

Maccoun, W. (1983). On the acquisition of argumentative discourse from the comprehensive point of view. Master's thesis, Applied Linguistics, University of California, Los Angeles.

Mandler, J. M. (1978). A code in the node: The use of a story schema in retrieval. *Discourse Processes, 1,* 14–35.

Mandler, J. M., and Johnson, N. S. (1977). Remembrance of things parsed: story structure and recall. *Cognitive Psychology, 9,* 77–110.

Mandler, J. M.; Schribner, S.; Cole, M.; and DeForest, M. (1980). Cross-cultural invariance in story recall. *Child Development, 61,* 19–26.

Mann, W. C., and Thompson, S. A. (1987). *Rhetorical Structure Theory: A theory of text organization.* Information Sciences Institute, University of Southern California. See also Mann, W. C., and Thompson, S. A. (1988). Rhetorical structure theory: Towards a functional theory of text organization. *TEXT, 8,* 3: 243–281.

Matsuyama, U. K. (1983). Can story grammar speak Japanese? *The Reading Teacher, 36,* 666–669.

McGann, W., and Schwartz, A. (1988). Main character in children's narratives. *Linguistics, 26,* 215–233.

Meyer, B. (1975). *The organization of prose and its effect on memory.* Amsterdam: North Holland Publishing.

(1984). Prose analysis: Purposes, procedure, and problems. In B. K. Britton and J. B. Black (Eds.), *Understanding expository text: A theoretical and practical handbook for analyzing explanatory text* (pp. 11–64). Hillsdale, N.J.: Erlbaum.

Nash, W. (1985). *The language of humour: Style and technique in comic discourse.* English Language Series, no. 16. London: Longman.

Olsen, L., and Huckin, T. (1990). Point-driven understanding in engineering lecture comprehension. *English for Special Purposes, 9,* 33–47.

Reichman, R. (1985). *Getting computers to talk like you and me: Discourse context focus and semantics (an ATN model).* Cambridge, Mass.: MIT Press.

Rubin, D.; Goodrum, R.; and Hall, B. (1990). Orality, oral-based culture, and the academic writing of ESL learners. *Issues in Applied Linguistics, 1,* 56–76.

Rumelhart, D. E. (1975). Notes on the schema for stories. In D. G. Bobrow and A. M. Collins (Eds.), *Representations and understanding: Studies in cognitive science* (pp. 211–236). New York: Academic Press.

Schaefer, J. (1981). Coupling as text-building, myth evoking strategy in Vietnamese: Implications for second language reading. In S. Hudelson (Ed.), *Learning to read in different languages.* Washington, D.C.: Center for Applied Linguistics.

Shaughnessy, M. (1977). *Errors and expectations.* New York: Oxford University Press.

Shaul, D. L.; Albert, R.; Golston, C.; and Satory, R. (1987). The Hopi Coyote story as narrative: The problem of evaluation. *Journal of Pragmatics, 11,* 1: 3–35.

Thompson, S. (1985). Grammar and written discourse: Initial vs. final purpose clauses in English. *TEXT, 5,* 1–2: 55–84.

Wolsch, R. (1970). *Poetic composition through the grades.* New York: Columbia University, Teachers College Press.

Young, D. (1974) The acquisition of English by three Spanish-speaking children. Master's thesis, Applied Linguistics, University of California, Los Angeles.

Zuck, J. G., and Zuck, L. V. (1984). Scripts: An example from newspaper texts. *Reading in a Foreign Language, 2,* 147–155.

6 Coherence, cohesion, deixis, and discourse

So far we have looked at how coherence in talk and writing is attained via overall system constraints on communication, by calling up generic scripts that fit the communication situation, by knowing the structure of speech events, and by recognizing the ways information may be formatted in various rhetorical genres.

Many linguists believe that none of this is truly "linguistics." For them, units and structures discovered in scripts, speech events, or rhetorical organization are to be dealt with by pragmatics or semiotics, not by linguistics. In fact, the system revealed by discourse analysis is often ignored in favor of terms such as "background knowledge," "world knowledge," or "social knowledge." However, many of these linguists do believe that linguistics should be concerned with the study of text to the extent of using discourse phenomena to explain certain features of grammar. One area of interest, then, is the relation between text coherence and syntax.

Coherence in discourse is developed in many ways. If we observe Goffman's constraints on communication systems; use our knowledge of scripts, speech events, and rhetorical organization; and maintain the topic, the result is usually coherent text – text that "sticks together" as a unit. However, sometimes the connections we want to draw between various parts of the discourse are not very apparent. To guide the listener or reader through this maze, we also have at our command a wide repertoire of cohesive markers. Cohesive ties and deictic markers help make relations among sentences or clauses of the discourse more explicit.

Cohesion and deixis

Reference and deixis

Much of meaning can only be understood by looking at linguistic markers that have a "pointing" function in a given discourse context. For example, consider the following note, pinned on a professor's door: "Sorry I missed you. I'm in my other office. Back in an hour." Without knowing who the addressee is, what time the note was written, or the location of the other office, we are hard put to make a precise interpretation of the message. Those terms that we cannot interpret without an immediate context are sometimes called *deictics*. (The name comes from the Greek word "deixis," which means "pointing." So, as a linguistic term, it means "identification by pointing.") Deictic terms are used to refer to ourselves, to others, and to objects in our environment. They are used to locate actions in a time frame relative to the present. Deictic terms show social relationships – the social location of individuals in relation to others. They also are used to locate parts of a text in relation to other parts.

Deictic expressions are typically pronouns, demonstratives ("this/that," "these/those"), certain time and place adverbs (e.g., "here and now"), some verbs of motion (e.g., "come/go"), and even tenses. In fact, all languages have expressions that link an utterance to a time and space context and that help to determine reference. These are words, then, whose meanings cannot be given in any precise way in a dictionary because they are dependent on context for interpretation.

Levinson (1983) identified five major types of deictic markers: person, place, time, discourse, and social.

PERSON DEIXIS

Person deixis refers to grammatical markers of participant roles in a speech event. First person is the speaker's reference to self; second person is the speaker's reference to addressee(s), and third person is reference to others who are neither speaker nor addressee.

From your teaching or language learning experience, you probably already know that all pronouns are not acquired at the same time (even though they may be taught in the same lesson). Most learners acquire "you" – the form for the addressee – quickly. They may have more difficulty sorting out "I/ me" (partially because of the case difference). Third person pronouns – markers that point to people other than the speaker and addressee – are not so quickly acquired. However, even when the forms are acquired, there are many slips when the speaker fails to shift roles. In the following example, a psychologist discusses advice given to a client. The underline highlights the shifting pronoun choice.

P: I-I-I was talking to her about the fact that + there isn't any particular reason why you should stop loving people we're no longer with. . . .

In this transcript, consistency of person deixis was frequently violated as the psychologist tried, perhaps, to make the problem more global and the advice more neutral (i.e., advice that could be applied to all of us). At any rate, the shifting of deictic markers went unnoticed until the tape was transcribed. So, obviously, precision was not important.

Confusion in person deixis can also result when writers are unsure of the true identity of the reading audience. For example, a student was asked to read and then comment on an essay written by a classmate. The comments were then to be given to the author of the essay. Yet, as you can see in the next example, the student (a university student from Japan) seemed unsure of his true audience.

According to the organization of the "Turning Points" essay in the composition and handouts, you must have an introduction first and three different turning points in your life. Since the writer only discusses one turning point, I don't know whether this is acceptable or not. In spite of this, the writer has made his purpose of the story clear. . . . There are some times my colleague can apply to improve this article. Try to express the same notion by different words and sentence structures. You can use them one way or the other. Well, that's all.

(Data source: Wenzell)

In this, the shifting deictic markers lead to confusion, because the referent being pointed to each time should be the same person but does not appear to be.

Basham using as data letters written by Athabaskan children (grades 4, 6, 7, 11) to peers in Alaska and Arizona, reported (in an unpublished paper) the ways that children refer to themselves and others. In presentation of self, the children often referred to groups and language memberships:

I myself I am Navajo.
I'm a Navajo and half Piute Indian. I speak both language at home. At school I speak English because some teachers don't understand the language the Navajo and Piute.

In the early grades, most children use "me" in referring to themselves in relation to others (e.g., "Me and Sam are going on the playground.") In the Navajo letters, however, Basham found that children produced "me" not only in this "relation to other" meaning, but also as a topic or focus shift for the discourse:

Me I live in Kayenta, Arizona
How's life treating you. Me my life is treating me fine.
As for me nothing is going on.
Or do you have any pet like a dog or a cat. Me I don't like to have a pet.

Basham suggests that the topic shifting strategy shown in the pronouns in the examples warrants further study as a possible way in which learners adapt English to carry out functions that are present in their native culture. The "As for X," of course, occurs with this function in standard English, but there is no evidence whether Anglo children also use pronouns of the "Me I live in Kayenta, Arizona" variety for focus or topic shifts within discourse.

The letters also show a more common phenomenon – the use of second person plural for the addressee. Writers not only identified or located themselves in terms of group membership, but also talked about themselves as representing their social group. In turn, they asked about their addressees as representatives of another group. They asked for responses that would allow the addressee to give an identification that placed him or her within a membership group.

What do *you guys* eat in Alaska?
Do *you dudes* have cassette player that you can listen to.
In Alaska Do *you guys* or *people* have polar bears or seals. So what do *you guys* do for fun. As for *us we* do things *your* mother tell *you* not to do.
Do *you kids* got a gym.
How are *you people* doing.

Person deixis, then, can be expressed in a number of ways. Pronouns and expressions such as "you guys" have no precise meaning but serve the function of pointing to different people at different times in different contexts.

Practice 6.1   Person deixis

1. In some languages, it is considered polite to address other people by name (e.g., "Mister Yamaha") or role title (e.g., "Teacher") rather than with a pronoun ("you," or "he"). In the following blurb on the authors of an article in *Natural History* (September 1989), decide how you would refer to each and fill in the blank.

The River of No Return Wilderness is blanketed by several feet of snow for up to eight months a year, and Patricia H. and Gregory D. Hayward have seen much of it on cross-country skis. Alumni of the University of Idaho [PH] _____ has a bachelor's degree in wildlife ecology and [GH] _____ has just finished his doctorate. [PH & GH] _____ met on an owl study in the Rockies and from 1984 to 1988 [PH & GH] _____ persevered at the demanding task of tracking these birds. The job, says [GH] _____ was "far from work. My fondest memories are of skiing through miles of unbroken powder knowing that [PH] _____ was the only other human for more than 20 miles or listening at night to the soft call of a boreal owl." [GH] _____ intends to continue to monitor the boreal owl population and to study old-growth forests. Until recently, [PH] _____ an avid horsewoman, spent almost all of [PH's] _____ leisure time participating in dressage. But most of the [PH and GH's] _____ time now goes to [PH and GH's] _____ son, born in June. Distance running keeps [PH] _____ in shape for chasing owls, horses, and little boys. The [PH and GH] _____ recommend two books for readers who wish to learn more about boreals and other owls: Johnsgard's *North American Owls* and Heimo Mikkola's *Owls of Europe*.

The writer of this blurb does use the role title "author" on occasion. Did you? I would be surprised if you used the role titles "mother" or "father" to refer to the Haywards as the parents of their son. Why would these be inappropriate? Why is the son not named in this passage?

2. If you know American Sign Language, explain the deictic terms used to refer to persons. Compare your explanations to those given by Bellugi and Klima (1982).

3. Young children often forget to keep track of person deixis for their listeners and readers. Identify the person deictics in the following essay written by an elementary school ESL class (Chicano students) who had been learning about the influence of Spain and Mexico on life in the Southwest of the United States. The teaching unit included a section on establishment of missions and mission life.

Missions

They were built by the Indians.
They used red earth to make them into bricks and build the missions.
The leader was father Serra.
He told the Indians what to do and when to do them.
They were built to teach the Indians about God and a better way of life.
Some of the Indians wanted to live in their normal life.
There were twenty one missions.
They teach the Indians how to farm.
Priests were on the missions.
They prayed on the mission so did the Indians prayed.
The first mission was called San Diego.
They had bells to tell the Indians when to start working and when to stop work.
The Indians women cooked the food and the Indian men went hunting for food like deer, fish and buffalos.
The Indian women cooked and ground acorn, wheat, corn but they used the acorn more than the other foods.
They used the acorns for oatmeal

(Data source: Hawkins and Wenzell)

Discuss the person deixis in this composition. The essay was written for teachers who already knew all about missions. If the students were asked to write about missions for a group of elementary school children in Japan or in Germany, do you think the person deixis terms might change? Why or why not? If you teach at the elementary school level, investigate this question, and write a short research plan to gather data to answer this question.

4. Coherence is obtained not just by deictic cohesive markers but by the rhetorical organization of the text. The missions essay was elicited from students. Each made one or more contributions, which were written on a chalkboard. Thus, there was less attention to organization. Show how the essay could be improved by reorganizing the sentences that describe the missions.

SPATIAL DEIXIS

Spatial, or place, deixis refers to how languages show the relationship between space and the location of the participants in the discourse. Most languages make a distinction between close to speaker *(proximal)* and away from the speaker *(distal)*. In English, this distinction is realized in demonstratives ("this" versus "that"), or in adverbs ("here" versus "there"), or in phrases (such as "in front," "in back," "at our place," or "out back").

Children use place deictic terms very early (within the first 50 words). The meaning of words such as "this" is initially "attention directing" (in the same way as words such as "look" or "see" or "oh-oh.") to objects in view.

Paul: Oh-oh!
Jim: What?
Paul: This (points to ant)
Jim: It's an ant.

Place deictic terms may set the stage for the move from the one-word to two-word utterance stage for child second language learners:

Paul: this
Jim: A pencil.
Paul: this + + + pencil (falling intonation on each word)
                           (Data source: Huang and Hatch 1978)

Only later does the use change to include the notion of distance. The contrast of proximal versus distal then becomes included in the meanings of these words for children. Exactly when children learn to be specific in locating themselves and objects in space that are not visible depends on at least three types of abilities:

Cognitive (developing a "spatial map" that includes familiar pathways in their environment and the relationship of these paths to those still unknown)
Interactive (taking account of the listener's knowledge of these spatial relations)
Linguistic (how these are mapped on language)

All groups have ways not only of referring to themselves (e.g., "I am American," "I myself I am a Navajo"), but of locating themselves in space: We are

214

"here" while others are "there." Where I live ("here"), we refer to ourselves as "locals" (e.g., "Yeh, I'm a local here"), and we refer to Los Angeles as "down below" (e.g., "I don't understand how anybody'd want to live in all that smog down below"). This is partly because Los Angeles is south. ("Up" is often used for north and "down" for south.) It is also "down" because there is an elevation drop of about 4,000 feet to Los Angeles. "Up" and "down" for north and south, however, doesn't always work. For example, while living in Cairo, I used to talk of going "down to Alex" even though Alexandria is north of Cairo. The Nile flows south to north, and Alexandria is *down* river from Cairo.

If you think about the ways in which you locate your hometown in relation to other places, you may note similarities to the following examples, which locate places in relation to my childhood home in Iowa:

"Out west" = Southwest United States
"Back east" = Northeast United States
"Up to Waverly" = up river and north
"Over in Reinbeck" = northeast direction
"Out there in Independence" = westerly direction
"Back home" = Denmark

The here/there distinction also reflects social organization. Even within my town, we may say "across the river," "across the tracks," "the other side of town," "up on the hill," or "in the valley" to refer to our social group in relation to all others. Deictic terms, therefore, refer not only to our location in space but our social organization of that space.

Practice 6.2   Spatial deixis

1. Interview speakers of two languages other than English to discover if they have parallel terms for "this/that," "here/there," "come/go," and "bring/take."
2. We use deictic markers to show movement toward or away from persons. Log examples from phone calls of people inviting others to "come over" or people talking about being invited to "go over" to someone's house. Attempt to explain the deictic rules governing the choices of "come/go" in these data. If they offer to "bring" something, explain the deictic rules that govern the choice of "bring" versus "take."
3. Language learners also need to use the come/go categories in their new languages. Consider the following extract from a "life story" narrative told by a Japanese speaker of English:

T: ah, I came stay before New York City
   (ah, I first went to New York City)

ah, I came here to Los Angeles alright
(ah, I came here from New York City)

(Data source: Niimura 1985)

Japanese does have terms similar to "come/go." Why, then, do you imagine the speaker used the "come" form as he did in the example?

4. Fillmore (1974) noted that "come/go" differ not just in location of the speaker. He used the first sentence of Hemingway's "The Killers," changing "come" to "go":

The door of Henry's lunchroom opened and two men came in.
The door of Henry's lunchroom opened and two men went in.

Decide whether the action is viewed from inside or outside the lunchroom in each case, and decide who opens the door. Translate the sentences into either of the two languages you used in item 1. How is the difference shown?

5. Basham also analyzed the deictic terms used for spatial location in the letters of Athabaskan children. She notes that in Navajo, points west and south are "down" while points north and east are "up." She also reports that in Koyukon, "front" is toward the river and "back" is away from the river. Identify the spatial terms in the following data. Then, remembering your geography for Alaska and Arizona, draw diagrams that show how the children view their spatial orientation

Navajo
How is it thier? Is it cold? It is hot over here.
So hows life treating you over there in Alaska, here in
    Kayenta, Arizona is treating me fine.
How are you doing down in Alaska as for me I'm doing just
    great in school up here in Arizona.
Is there lots of fun up in Alaska?

Koyukon
I go swimming back at the lake.
all the kids go back to the ball park and play
I live on the front street of Kaltag.

6. Klein (1982) used a database of 40 route communications. Questions were asked about directions to places in downtown Frankfurt. Audiotape one interaction where you

ask someone directions. List the spatial deictic terms used and compare your results with those of Klein.

7. Lakoff (1974) claims that both "this" and "that" can be used to establish emotional closeness between speakers. "This" is used to achieve camaraderie, but so is "that." For example, we might say "How is *that* throat?" to a friend. Fillmore (1982) also argues that "that" serves such a function since a garage attendant might say "Check *that* oil?" to a male driver but probably not to a female driver. In these examples, the speaker cannot use "this" because the entities (throat and oil) belong to the hearer and so are farther away from the speaker. Log instances you hear where "that" rather than "this" is used for the purpose of establishing camaraderie.

TEMPORAL DEIXIS

Temporal, or time, deixis refers to time relative to the time of speaking. English, for example, uses "now" versus "then," "yesterday," "today," and "tomorrow." However, languages differ in how many deictic day names are included. According to Levinson (1983), Chinantec, an Amerindian language, has four days on each side of "today"; Hindi has the same word for both "tomorrow" and "yesterday."

Confusion sometimes occurs when units are not clearly indicated as being definite calendar times or definite in relation to the moment in which we are located. For example, "next week" or "in a fortnight" are confusing to the person who isn't sure what day it is at the moment of speaking!

While we think of time deixis as locating ourselves in terms of "now" versus "then," we use deictic time markers for additional functions as well. For example, we use them to give verisimilitude to our stories. Often it is not important that the time frame be known other than it happened "then" (i.e., once upon a time) rather than "now." Locating the time of an action more precisely makes it somehow more credible. Notice the use of time deixis in the orientations of the following oral narratives produced by ESL children. (These particular children had been identified as "at risk" children – children that the school district had identified as having little possibility of academic success – so their abilities to produce effective orientations to their narratives and to use deictic markers to promote verisimilitude are worth noting.)

1. I was like five or four years old when . . . me and my brother was taking a BATH an' we were putting all kinds of shampoo on our hair.
2. The story I'm gonna tell is the time when uhm . . . I put uhm . . . a whoopee cushion under my . . . sister's chair.

3. OK and the story's gonna begin when . . . one morning, at night . . . I didn't know if we were gonna get any presents.

(Data source: Hawkins)

Contrast these examples with the orientation of oral narratives of college professors:

1. Well it was back in let's see '64 '65 an' the students were jus' getting organized. . . .
2. Do yuh remember the time-I think it wuz the second week after school started an' . . .

In none of the examples is a specific time reference really needed. A "remember when" would do the job, but not as well in terms of validating the story that follows.

When writing, we are often confused as to how to code time deixis. Do we write to someone as though what they are reading happened in the reader's time or in the writer's time? Which seems better?

1. I am writing this letter while the women's marathon is in progress.
2. I was writing this letter while the women's marathon was in progress.

Person, time, and place deictic markers identify persons and locate them in time and space. The signals themselves have no meaning other than that carried by these functions.

Practice 6.3   Time deixis

1. Check two languages and list the relational time words (i.e., the equivalent of words such as "yesterday," "next week," and so forth) that are used.
2. Look at the orientation sections of the narratives collected by your study group classmates for Practice 5.1. Precisely how did each storyteller use time deixis in the orientation?
3. Verb tense and aspect are also deictic markers that help us keep track of time reference in relation to the discourse. Tense-aspect distinctions (as we have already noted in Chapter 5) help us keep track of ongoing actions and background information. Select one narrative composition (or one of your own in a language other than English) and analyze verb tense/aspect use. How successful is the writer in tracking time throughout the composition? Skilled storytellers often switch back and forth between simple present and simple past tenses within a narrative. The switch itself helps to highlight a change in focus, the break between plans for a solution and the resolution, and so

forth. However, such switches also show emotional attachment; present tense more often signals an emotional closeness to that segment of the narrative. Give examples to show how this information helps explain the use of tense/ aspect in the narrative you selected. What examples still present problems for the analysis?

4. A supervisor began a letter of thanks to teachers who were asked to rate a group of compositions as follows:

> Dear Rater,
> My sincere thanks for your cooperation in scoring these additional essays. I know you have a lot to do today and I hope it is not as hot there tomorrow as it is here today . . .
>
> (Data source: Gaskill)

First, explain why the writer used the demonstrative "these" instead of "the." Then, decide how you would take care of the muddled time deictics.

DISCOURSE DEIXIS

Discourse deixis, according to Levinson, has to do with keeping track of reference in the unfolding discourse. We may use phrases such as "In the following chapter" or pointers such as "this/that" to refer to large chunks of the discourse that are located within the discourse itself.

1. So okay *this* is what I'm gonna tell you.
2. *That* was awful; please try harder next time.
3. *This* will be covered in our next lecture.
4. We will *return* to *that* in a moment, *but first* . . .

Even though other languages often use such markers, they are not easily acquired in second language learning. In the following example (from a Brazilian student's composition) we can guess why the writer used "those" instead of "these."

> For two years I will have to interact with a new system, being part of it. *This* is a dilemma: on one side, I have to be prepared for a different life; on the other, I am not inclined to forget all values and tastes that I had before. The trade-off between *those* two opposite tendencies showed me that, at least, my home should reflect my personality.
>
> (Data source: Wenzell)

That is, we teach students to attend to "distance" in deciding when to use "this/these" versus "that/those." Distance includes the physical distance of arguments within the discourse. "This/these" usually refers to composite ideas just mentioned or relatively close in the discourse. "That/those" refers back to more distant places in the discourse. Distance, here, is not just physical distance but a matter of what is most in focus (and therefore likely to be mentioned more recently in the discourse). Close/far for "this/that" is also a matter of alignment. If we strongly identify with an idea, it is "close" and we are likely to refer to it as "this." With lack of alignment, we are more likely to use "that." The learner who produced the text has not been completely successful in showing this orientation via discourse deixis "this/that."

As shown at the beginning of this section, we use a variety of deictic markers to point the way to various parts of the discourse. The frequency of all such deictic terms varies across types of text. The more formal the discourse, the more markers may be needed to keep the text coherent. For example, legal reports and science reports are a rich source of guiding clauses such as "X is given in Appendix A," which direct the reader to another part of the text.

Practice 6.4 Discourse deixis

1. In the following extract from a Korean speaker's essay, the student uses the deitic terms "that" and "it." What evidence is there that the pronouns point to a noun, to a chunk of discourse, or to both? Do you imagine that difficulty with English definite articles might also play a role in this student's choice of demonstratives?

   Haagen Daazs ice cream has unique and special characterister. *That* is the design of the package. Therefore, in spite of high process of *this* cost, the sales of *it* shows to increase of 25% every year.

   (Data source: Wenzell)

2. Discourse deixis can be accomplished with clauses, phrases, single adverbs, or demonstratives. Give additional examples of your own.

   Clauses: "Before going further," "Illustrated in the following passages"
   Phrases: "In the above figure," "On page 23"
   Single word adverbs: "Here (we can locate the problem)," "(We'll deal with this) later"
   Demonstratives: "(We'll deal with) that (later)," "this (is what all of us have been waiting for)"

3. If you know Sign, describe the deictics that can be used to point back or forward to parts of the discourse.

SOCIAL DEIXIS

Social deixis is used to code social relationships between speakers and addressee or audience. Included in this category are honorifics, titles of address, vocatives, and pronouns. There are two kinds of social deixis: *relational* and *absolute*.

Absolute deictics are forms uniformly attached to a social role (e.g., "Your Honor" or "Mr. President"). In a sense, when we use these, we address the "office" rather than the "person." At press conferences, all reporters address the President of the United States as "Mr. President." In other languages, absolute deictics may involve more than just titles. For example, Japanese has an "exalted" level of language to show respect in reference to the emperor and the imperial family.

Relational deictic terms differ from absolute terms in that they locate persons in relation to the speaker rather than by their roles in the society as a whole. In English, relational deictics may be lexical items (e.g., my husband, cousin, teacher), pronouns (you, her) or particles. Social deixis is important because it concerns the coding of specific social relationships. Again, in Japanese, there are special respectful and humble forms for these relationships. When speaking of one's own father, for example, the speaker would use "chichi," a humble form. But in referring to the father of an addressee, one would use "otosan" or "oto-sama," respectful forms. In some languages, social relationships are marked in pronouns (e.g., "vous" in French; "usted" in Spanish). They can also be shown by verb inflections as in Japanese, or in verb agreement. Notice that we say "Vous parlez anglais?" when we are speaking to only one person, but the pronoun and verb agreement are in the plural form. When we are only speaking to one person, it seems strange to use plural agreement. Yet, in many languages, it is more polite to use the plural second person than the singular form.

Even in different areas of one country, we find differences in use of social deictic forms. It has been reported that in a divided Germany, "du" had been used in more and more situations in the Federal Republic of Germany. While "du" had always been used among workers, the change in other groups is reported to have originated in the student movement of the 1960s. In the German Democratic Republic, there was no such student movement, and the spread of "du" to the younger generation did not occur. Instead, "du" apparently was used to express solidarity, especially among party members. In this case, the form was used in different ways in response to pragmatic concerns. Now with a unified Germany, it will be interesting to see what changes come about in the use of "du" as a social deixis marker.

In English, social deixis is not heavily coded in the pronoun system. We do have a +powerful "we," though we don't have an +insignificant "I." Like a royal "we," the pronoun "we" is used in announcements proclaimed by company offices:

We are happy to inform you of our new. . . .
We at TRW announce the launching of. . . .

While many languages use pronouns, Levinson notes that social deixis can be

221

shown via particles (e.g., in Tamil) or prosodically (e.g., in Tzeltal). In many languages – for example, Japanese and Korean – nearly every sentence has some reference to social deixis. Speakers of these languages often mention their discomfort with the meager options available to mark social deixis in English.

Practice 6.5   Social deixis

1. In some languages – for example, Japanese – social deixis can be shown in lexical alternates. If you teach Japanese (or if you have access to a Japanese speaker), list examples of this phenomenon.
2. The *Peking Daily* published a letter from a reader who argued that "Miss" was not really an imperialist lexical item. Do you consider "Miss" to be an honorific term? Why or why not?
3. In a BBC radio broadcast, the announcer said that the "Secretary of State, Mr. Baker" had attended some meeting. Would you consider this an example of absolute deixis or of relational deixis? Why? Do you think an American broadcaster would have used the "Mr." form in talking about the Secretary of State? Listen to the news and note when (and if possible why) "Mr.," "Mrs.," "Miss," and "Ms." are used with such titles. Do German titles such as "Herr Professor" or "Professor Dr. Schmidt" work the same way? Are such double markings common in other languages you know?
4. In some languages, social relationships are well marked in the pronoun system. If you teach or have learned a language that has special honorific pronouns (e.g., "vous" in French; "usted" in Spanish), can you clearly identify what triggers the use of formal forms? Is it age, social class, gender, personal closeness, or something else? Give examples to support your hypotheses.
5. Students from other countries often address their instructors as "Teacher." If we interpret this as the use of an absolute role title, we may feel insulted ("I'm not some anonymous cut-out to be labeled teacher – Chen doesn't even know my name!"). It is likely that the student feels that it is a relational term (i.e., "my teacher") or a form that honors the person addressed. If you have students who use the term "teacher" rather than your name, ask them whether they feel this is an absolute or relational deictic

term. Can they give examples of the use of other such title terms?

6. In the following article, identify the social deictic terms that locate Ms. Velten within her social circle. Why did the author use relational deictic terms rather than names? (By the way, how many men were killed, and which were nuisances? How many husbands did Ms. Velten have? And who is the "they" in the final line?)

Pudding Poisoner Gets Life Sentences

Krefeld, West Germany – A 68 year old mother of six received three life prison sentences and an additional 15 years Thursday for poisoning two husbands, a lover, her father, and an aunt because they were a nuisance.

Maria Velten admitted killing her second and third husbands and her lover between 1976 and 1982 by feeding them blueberry puddings laced with a herbicide.

The judge said Velten killed the three men because she felt they were a nuisance. Greed was an additional motive in the case of her third husband, who left her money, they said.

(Data source: Wenzell)

Cohesive devices

Coherence of text is accomplished in many ways (e.g., using templates from scripts and rhetorical genre forms, via clause selection, and with syntactic markers of various types). Cohesive devices are also used to tie pieces of text together in specific ways. While Levinson's system applies to deictic markers of reference, Halliday and Hasan's (1976) system distinguishes five major types of grammatical cohesive ties: reference, substitution, ellipsis, conjunction, and lexical ties.

Reference

At the risk of being repetitive, let us discuss reference again. Earlier in this chapter we talked about deictic markers as pointing or referring to parts of the discourse (person, place, temporal, and discourse deixis). We will now call these markers (as do Halliday and Hasan) cohesive ties.

To establish *reference*, we may use lexical items. For example, "Mary" can be used to refer to a person named Mary. Once we establish the referent, we can also refer to Mary as "she," at least for the period of time during which our focus is on Mary. The pronoun "she," by itself, has no referent. It is a cohesive tie to the noun "Mary." In addition to lexical items, English uses pronouns, demonstratives, and comparatives for grammatical reference.

223

PRONOUNS AS COHESIVE TIES

Pronouns may be used in a way that "ties" them to certain nouns in the text. For example, "If the buyer wants to know what is covered by the guarantee, *he* has to read the fine print and consult a lawyer." Here, the pronoun refers back to a previously mentioned noun, so "he" refers to the buyer not the lawyer. Now consider the constructed example "John asked *him* to sing and so Bill sang." This time the pronoun refers forward to the noun "Bill" rather than back to the noun "John." In each case the cohesive tie is a pronoun that refers across a clause boundary to the referent noun. Ties that point back to a previously established referent, as in the first example, are called *anaphoric*. Those that point ahead, as in the second example, are called *cataphoric*.

DEMONSTRATIVES AS COHESIVE TIES

Demonstratives are also cohesive ties and either cataphoric or anaphoric. In the following constructed example, the demonstrative "this" refers to "Magic Motor's special sale is February 14": "If you are buying a car, you should know about *this*." If the author continues by telling us something related to the sale, the tie is cataphoric, and we expect that "this" will refer not to the noun "sale," but to some larger unit, such as details about special prices or factory rebates.

In the example, "*This* is why Esprit is a leader in sports fashion," we assume that the referent has already been established for "this." The tie, therefore, is anaphoric.

COMPARATIVES AS COHESIVE TIES

A comparative can also provide a tie to a referent. Most comparatives are used for anaphoric reference. For example, "I'd like *more*." It is less common for a comparative to be used for cataphoric reference (i.e., to tie the comparative to a noun in the following clause or sentence), but here is an example: "I demand *the best*. Your service leaves much to be desired."

Substitution

A second major type of cohesive tie is that of *substitution*. In contrast to reference, substitution refers not to a specific entity but to a class of items. In the constructed example "Did you find the blankets? Only the blue *ones*.," "ones" refers not to "the blankets" but to a class of blankets – those that are blue.

Substitutions can also be made for nominals, verb groups, and clauses. While Levinson would claim that such substitutions serve as deictic markers to point to these groups, Halliday and Hasan see the markers as tying the marker and group together, forming a more cohesive text. For example:

Nominal: Do you want the blankets? Yes, I'll take *one* ("one" substituted for "blankets")
Verbal: Did you sing? Yes, I *did.* ("did" substituted for "sang")
Clausal: The blankets needed to be cleaned. Yes, they *did.* ("did" substituted for "needed to be cleaned")

Ellipsis

Ellipsis can be thought of as a "zero" tie because the tie is not actually said. For example, in "Would you like to hear another verse? I know twelve (verses).," the entity ("verse") has been named but is then deleted in the second clause.

Ellipsis, like substitution, can be used to create ties to nominals, verbals, and clauses, as shown in the following examples.

Nominal: They're small; take two (cookies).
Verbal: Were you typing? No, I wasn't (typing).
Clausal: I don't know how to work this computer. I'll have to learn how (to work the computer).

Conjunction

A fourth type of cohesive tie is *conjunction.* In the example, "I was not invited. *Otherwise,* I would have been there.," the two clauses are connected by the cohesive conjunction "otherwise." The conjunction helps us interpret the relation between the clauses. There are several different kinds of conjunctive relations:

Additive: She worked on the computer the whole day without stopping. *And* as she worked, she thought about the problem.
Adversative: She was hardly conscious of her attempts to solve the problem. *Yet,* by evening the solution magically appeared.
Causal: Her work was finished, *so* she turned off the computer.
Temporal: Then as the five o'clock bell rang, she hurried out of the office building.

We may use different lexical items as cohesive terms, depending on the particular type of discourse we are creating. This is particularly true of our choice of conjunctive ties. There is, as noted in the discussion on rhetorical structure theory, no one-to-one correspondence of one conjunctive to only one function. However, there are preferential patterns. For example, Winter (1971) categorized the conjunctive ties used by writers of science texts. He found the following forms most frequently.

Logical sequence: thus, therefore, then, thence, consequently, so
Contrast: however, in fact, conversely

Doubt/certainty: probably, possibly, indubitably
Noncontrast: moreover, likewise, similarly
Expansion: for example, in particular

An interesting sidelight for English language teachers is the fact that conjunctive ties seem to differ in the distance they can span. Some cannot cross more than one clause, but others can. For example:

She failed to set a new record. *Yet,* she did her best.
Sue likes bike riding very much. She goes riding almost every weekend. *However,* she likes swimming even more.

Lexical ties

Halliday and Hasan's fifth type of cohesive tie is *lexical.* Lexical ties can be either "short" or "long" – that is, the ties can cross short or large pieces of the discourse. In some cases, the same word or a synonym is used and repeated throughout the text. In other cases, related words (such as superordinate or general words) are used, and this repetition of the same concept strengthens the text cohesion.

Repetition: Sue is in the *race* on Saturday. Everyone believes that she or Tamara will win the *race.*
Synonym: Sue hopes to set a *PR.* Her *personal best* is still 1.2 seconds off the 10K age-group record.
Superordinate: She'll win a *trophy.* The *prize* won't mean as much to her as a new PR.
General word: The *runner* needs to be well prepared to be competitive in this race.

Lexical items are also tied together simply by *collocation.* That is, when we think of a flower, we also think of the stem, the petal, the leaf, and, perhaps, even the vase that might contain the flower. When we think of a grocery store, we think of all the produce, canned goods, and other items that make up a grocery store. Each time one of the grocery store items is mentioned, we can draw a tie between it and the concept of a grocery store. Note the cohesion created by collocation in the following examples:

Great *time!* A new PR! For a *minute* I couldn't believe the race *clock.*
I couldn't *correct* anything. My *red pencil* was dull, for one thing.

In addition to grammatical cohesive ties, some languages also use clause chaining to achieve stronger cohesion in text. As an example, look at the parts of the following text reiterated in chainlike fashion:

I want to think of a good Christmas present for Dion. A good Christmas present for Dion might be Taj Mahal's new record. Taj Mahal's new record is the first he's done in eight years. Eight years is a long time to wait for a new record from the master of blues.

Such clause chaining is not conventional in English. We may find chains of phonological repetition, though, particularly in oral discourse (e.g., "What a wonderful way to lose weight." Where the /w/ sound recurs in initial position across a stretch of text). Structural repetition and parallelism are also used in chainlike fashion to add ties to build text cohesion (e.g., "And we went there and we saw the students milling in the square and we were frightened.").

Practice 6.6 Cohesive ties

1. Give an example for each type of anaphoric and cataphoric reference: nominal and clausal.
2. Give an example of each type of grammatical substitution: nominal, verbal, and clausal.
3. Give an example of each type of grammatical ellipsis: nominal, verbal, and clausal.
4. Give an example of each type of conjunctive tie: additive, adversative, causal, and temporal.
5. Can you reclassify Winter's categories of conjunctive ties so that they fit those of Halliday and Hasan?
6. Investigate the distance limit for conjunction ties, that is, whether you can cross paragraphs, sentences, clauses, or phrases, or must nothing intervene. Select three conjunctive ties and give examples to support your claims.
7. Clause chaining is not used much in English. If you teach international students who use clause chaining in their compositions, determine whether this is a common strategy for creating cohesion in their first languages.
8. Read the following selection written by a French-Canadian student. Think about what makes the text cohere so beautifully.

In Memory of Grand Father,
The person I want to introduce to you, died two years ago but he stills living in my memory. Perhaps all grand fathers of the world are famous for their own children but that one is mine.

He wasn't like old people with round shouldered complaining all the time about the sadness of life. He just thought that his mind was always young and he wistled all day. The training in the army gave him a straight position wich he was very proud of it. You couldn't ask him about the war. He became serious looking far away then he would say that he all forgot and any how he would never send his worst friend.

Like a bee, he never really stopped to work and after He retired his favorite occupations were firstly to fed the birds. That reminds me a shining morning. I was only a school girl visiting her grand parents on summer holliday. I was sleeping when I heard him calling me softly from the kitchen. I couldn't believe what I saw. Sparrows in the house! They were eating on the carpet near the kitchen's door. I rubbed my own eyes and clapped my hands but the birds flew away. Sorry I saw that wasn't a dream.

A Sunday afternoon, not so long ago, my youngest sister and me were walking with him in the garden. Suddenly she asked him what would be life after death. He took a deeply breath and answered that he wasn't quiet sure but if we will have to come back into animal's form he wished to be a bird. Also we shouldn't forget to fed them specially in winter time, because they're brave enough to stay and to enjoy us with song when it's so cold.

Most part of his time was spent in his work shop building wood toys for Xmas present or teaching us how to make little houses for birds.

Few weeks before he left he told us that he was a bit afraid for grand mother and we hadn't to be sorry. Again now when I think what I should do or not. He come to visit me in dream and you know he stills whistling.

(Data source: Hottel-Burkhart 1981)

a. List the ways that "grandfather" is referred to throughout the passage.
b. How does the writer refer to herself throughout the passage?
c. What kinds of cohesive ties are used to refer to "bird"?
d. How is the "bird" tied to the "grandfather"?
e. What temporality cohesion holds the passage together?
f. What spatial cohesion terms hold the passage together?
g. What links "grandfather," "birds," and "seasons"?
h. Does "war" link to "grandfather," "birds," or "seasons"?
i. How are posture and complaining linked?
j. Would the story be more/less/as effective if people had been given names rather than relationship terms? Why?

Conclusion

Coherence in text can be obtained by the general overall form of the discourse (i.e., the script, the rhetorical genre). Within the discourse, as we have seen in this chapter, we may also use cohesive ties or deictic markers to help guide us through the discourse maze. The analysis of cohesive ties shows how we as readers or writers use linguistic signals to promote cohesion. For example, each time a lexical item occurs in collocation with another, it allows us to draw a tie to a concept. So words such as "playground," "teacher," "student," "study," "paper," "book," and so forth allow us to draw a tie to the concept of school. The collocations are like nets that help tie the text together.

However, for many, the study of cohesive ties is a "local level" analysis; the findings are for a specific piece of text. So when we discussed lexical collocation as promoting cohesion in discourse, I used the "grocery store" example for a reason. In cohesion analysis, lexical items such as words for produce or canned goods, clerks, checkout counters, and so forth allow us to draw a tie to the concept of a grocery store. However, in script theory, the grocery shopping script (discussed in Chapter 3), once called up in memory, activates such lexical items as part of the script. The script is a mental construct that covers many instances of text, not just one.

There is, then, a definite overlap between script analysis and lexical cohesion analysis. In cohesion analysis, the analyst is building structure by working "up" from a particular text. In script theory, structure is predicted from the script to the text (although the script structure has been arrived at by the analysis of many text examples).

In addition to overall forms of discourse (communication component signals, scripts, rhetorical genre) and cohesive ties and deictic markers, we can also use syntax to do discourse work. The ways in which we use syntax may vary according to the amount of time we have to form our message, the degree of planning, and the formality of the occasion, as will be demonstrated in the next chapter.

Research and application

A. Deixis

1. Jakimik and Glenberg (1990) looked at the clarity of discourse deixis in spoken and written text. There are many times, they note, when readers zip through an article and then stop with a "thud." Because of their lack of concentration, they then have to reread the section. This seldom happens when listening to a lecture. Jakimik and Glenberg's research confirmed that it is easier to keep track of reference and discourse deixis in spoken than in written discourse. Do you think this is true for second language learners as well? Prepare a preliminary research plan to replicate this study with language learners.
2. The professional wrestling match is a charade enjoyed by wrestling aficionados. Coddington (1977) describes the structure of the wrestlers' interviews as part of the total event. The wrestlers

have names that help define their status as "good" or "bad" guys.
King Kong Bundy, Jake the Snake Roberts, and George the
Animal Steele are bad guys. Ricky Steamboat, Hulk Hogan, and
Mister T are good guys, and the interviewer himself is "Mean
Gene." Can you think of any other script or social group activity
where actors play roles with special names? Are these names
examples of relational or absolute reference terms?

3. Weissenborn (1980) had pairs of children play a hide-and-seek
game outside. One child in each pair was familiar with the
surroundings (host child) while the other was not (guest child). The
host child was asked to hide a bag of toys and then describe the
route leading to the bag to the guest child, who then went to look
for it. If the guest child could not find the toys, he or she could
come back and ask for more information.

One group, made up of four-year-old children, tried to jump to
the goal without giving route directions (e.g., "It's at the
Tuetterswall – the bag is hanging on the garbage can" or "where
the bench is"). Interestingly, the host children did have the spatial
map needed for the task. They knew the steps involved in getting
to the bag because they could answer Weissenborn's questions
about the route:

W: Where does he go first from here?
C: to the mill tower.
W: first to the mill tower and then, where does he go then?
C: to the post office.
W: and then?
C: by the trees.
W: and then?
C: and then, there is a trash can.

Although they had the mental schema for walking to the bag, the
four-year-olds did not use this as a planning device to establish a
shared context of reference for the guest child. A second group of
children, six to eight years of age, did spontaneously establish a
connection between starting point and goal. But their route
description became inadequate as soon as it left the immediate
visual surroundings of the starting point – that is, when they tried
to describe the invisible part of the route.

C: up here, through here . . . through there . . . through there . . . then in
there, into the forest, and then there in the . . . in the paperbasket.

These children likewise failed to adapt their spatial descriptions to
the listener's needs. However, children in the eight-to-ten-years-
old group were able to give good route descriptions to their guests.
Weissenborn's study suggests, therefore, that although young

children may have a cognitive "map" of an area, they have not yet developed a template for descriptions that takes into account listener or reader needs.

If you work with young children, replicate Weissenborn's procedure with your students, taping the data. After they have played the game with each other, have the students prepare and hide a special present for your teacher's aide. Then have them tape-record instructions on how to find the treasure. (Be sure to use this recording when the aide tries to find the treasure!) If the descriptions obtained by these two methods differ, explain why this should be the case.

4. Harman (1990) describes a "deictic circle" graphic that can be used to teach indirect speech. Review the article, try the technique with your students, and report the results along with suggestions for other ways for presenting these concepts.

5. Kirsner (1979) used quantitative methods to test qualitative claims made about demonstratives in Dutch. If you are preparing a research project on the use of deictic expressions, review his methodology and data analysis. Explain how Kirsner's methodology would or would not be appropriate for your research.

B. Cohesive ties

6. Tanz (1980) looked at identity and quantity in reference markers. She had young children (three-, four-, and five-year-olds) respond to stimuli such as:

Identity
Make one of the pigs go in the house. Now make (a) *it;* (b) *one* go in the truck. (Materials: two pigs, two chickens, house, truck)

Quantity
There is chocolate on the table. Give (a) *it* to me; (b) give me *some.*

Identity, plural
Drive two cars to the house. Now drive (a) *them,* (b) *two* to the edge of the cliff.

Quantity, plural
There are flowers on the table. Give (a) *them* to me. (b) me *some.*

If possible, replicate the procedure with young bilingual children. You could show how these pronoun and demonstrative cohesive ties work in the children's first language too, and collect data for both languages.

231

7. McCutchen and Perfetti (1982) gave children (Anglo second, fourth, sixth, and eighth graders) the first and last sentences of a paragraph. The sentences were "There are many things about (*X* – football, ice-skating, videotaping) that make it fun and exciting." and "So while *(X)* can be fun, we have to be careful so that the fun is not spoiled." Students were asked to add some sentences in the middle to make a good story. Read McCutchen and Perfetti's article and then use the procedure as a writing assignment for your students. Compare your results regarding coherence and connectedness with those found in the original study.

8. Johns (1984) found that the most frequently occurring error in cohesive ties in the compositions of Chinese English teachers (in China) involved what Halliday and Hasan called the adversative – where the meaning is contrary to expectation. In the following example, native speakers would find the use of "however" ambiguous or unresolved: "The audio-lingual method sees language as a collection of discrete items put together. Language acquisition becomes a matter of conditioning. *However,* after years in vogue, ALM is challenged by a new approach, namely, COG." The use of "however" suggests that the writer will continue with what is *not* expected about ALM in regard to these characteristics. But that doesn't happen. Johns found that students used "however" where a causal tie such as "thus" would be appropriate, "nevertheless" where causals would normally be used, and expressions such as "on the other hand" without an "on the one hand" for balance.

   The second most frequent type of cohesive error involved pronoun reference. The teachers produced stretches of discourse such as the following:

   a. In this paper, I examine the frequency of the passive and active forms in eight physics textbooks. I find that active verb forms also play an important part in *them.* ["them" = forms or textbooks?]

   b. Altogether, I examined 21 dialogues. As a result of preliminary study, I found complimenting appears most frequently in these dialogues. I copied each incidence *under it.* ["it" = dialogues or complimenting?]

Finally, Johns noted that the Chinese English teachers did *not* use lexical cohesion as frequently as native speakers. She attributes this to the Chinese custom of teaching vocabulary words and phrases as isolated items rather than as part of a semantically related chain. The teachers were not sure whether synonymous words were really synonymous or, if synonymous, whether they were from the same register. If you have access to a composition database from language learners check to see whether these findings can be corroborated from your data as well. Design a research proposal to investigate the connection between the ways vocabulary is taught and the use or avoidance of lexical ties in compositions.

9. Halliday and Hasan's cohesion analysis has proved useful in the study of thought disorders (sometimes called *discourse disorders*). If you are interested in language disorders, you might like to read Rochester and Martin (1979) as an example of how cohesion analysis can be applied in other fields. Alverson and Rosenberg (1990) is a good resource if you would like to see a "friendly critique" of cohesion analysis applied to language disorder data. Do you believe that the shortcomings listed by these authors are serious problems? Why or why not?

References

Alverson, H., and Rosenberg, S. (1990). Discourse of schizophrenic speech: A critique and proposal. *Applied Psycholinguistics, 11*, 2: 167–184.

Bellugi, U., and Klima, E..(1982). From gesture to sign: Deixis in a visual-gestural language. In R. J. Jarvella and W. Klein (Eds.), *Speech, place and action* (pp. 297–313). New York: John Wiley & Sons.

Coddington, L. (1987). "Well, you know, Mean Gene . . ." The professional wrestling interview. In C. Micheau (Ed.), *The Pennsylvania Working Papers in Educational Linguistics* (pp. 61–79). Graduate School of Education, University of Pennsylvania.

Fillmore, C. (1974). Pragmatics and the description of discourse. *Berkeley studies in syntax and semantics.* Linguistics Department, University of California, Berkeley. Reprinted in Cole, P. (1981), *Radical pragmatics* (pp. 143–166). New York: Academic Press.

(1982). Towards a descriptive framework for spatial deixis. In R. J. Jarvella and W. Klein (Eds.), *Speech, place, and action* (pp. 31–59). New York: John Wiley & Sons.

Halliday, M.A.K., and Hasan, R. (1976). *Cohesion in English.* London: Longman.

Harman, I. (1990). Teaching indirect speech: deixis points the way. *ELT Journal, 44*, 3: 230–238.

Hottel-Burkhart, N. (1981). Cohesion in the essays of native speakers of Canadian French. Ph.D. dissertation, University of Texas, Austin.

Huang, J., and Hatch, E. (1978). A Chinese child's acquisition of English. In E. Hatch (Ed.), *Second language acquisition: A book of readings* (pp. 118–131). Rowley, Mass.: Newbury House.

Jakimik, J., and Glenberg, A. (1990). Verbal learning meets psycholinguistics: Modality effects in the comprehension of anaphora. *Journal of Memory and Language, 29*, 582–590.

Johns, A. (1984). Textual cohesion and the Chinese speaker of English. *Language Learning and Communication, 3,* 1–92.

Kirsner, R. S. (1979). Deixis in discourse: An exploratory quantitative study of the Modern Dutch demonstrative adjectives. In T. Givon (Ed.), *Syntax and semantics. Vol. 12: Discourse and syntax* (pp. 355–375). New York: Academic Press.

Klein, W. (1982). Local deixis in route directions. In R. J. Jarvella and W. Klein. *Speech, place, and action* (pp. 161–182). New York: John Wiley & Sons.

Lakoff, R. (1974). Remarks on this and that. *Papers from the Tenth Regional Meeting* (pp. 345–356). Chicago, Ill.: Chicago Linguistics Society.

Levinson, S. (1983). *Pragmatics.* New York: Cambridge University Press.

McCutchen, D, and Perfetti, C. (1982). Coherence and connectedness in discourse production. *TEXT, 2,* 1–3: 113–139.

Niimura, T. (1985). The English interlanguage of a native Japanese speaker: Temporality and transfer. Master's thesis, Applied Linguistics, University of California, Los Angeles.

Rochester, S., and Martin, J. (1979). *Crazy talk: A study of discourse of schizophrenic speakers.* New York: Plenum.

Tanz, C. (1980). *Studies in the acquisition of deictic terms.* Cambridge: Cambridge University Press.

Weissenborn, J. (1980). Children's route descriptions. Paper presented at the Language Society of America Summer Meeting, August 1980, Albuquerque, New Mexico. Paper obtained from author: Max Planck Institute, Nijmegen, Holland.

Winter, E. (1971). Connection in science material. Proposition about the semantics of clause relations. Science and technology in a second language. *CILT Reports and Papers, 7,* 41–52.

7 Discourse mode and syntax

In order to capture the range of syntactic structures used in discourse in various settings and modes, educators and sociolinguists have tried to describe language in terms of dichotomies. As you will have noted from the transcripts presented in this book, the language of oral and written modes differs – this is the *oral versus written dichotomy*. For example, in school, students and teachers must use the language of academic life. While we often speak of this as specifically related to written language (reading and writing), academic life also calls for expertise with oral language. Thus, some researchers have struggled to demonstrate explicit differences in the language of oral versus written discourse.

However, some talk (e.g., prepared lectures) shares many features with written language, and some written language (e.g., notes) shares features with spoken language. Therefore, other researchers prefer to describe an *unplanned versus planned dichotomy* where spontaneous language performance, whether spoken or written, is unplanned and revised and polished language is planned. With time and the opportunity to organize our performance (writing our thoughts down or rehearsing our talk), we can expect to produce final results that differ from spontaneous or first-draft output. This second dichotomy suggests that life requires expertise with highly planned as well as unplanned discourse modes. That is, academicians must be able to use highly planned language in writing technical reports, but they must also be able to interact with colleagues using unplanned forms of both oral and written discourse.

A third option used by researchers is to describe language as *contextualized versus decontextualized*. Oral language is said to be highly contextualized. It is situated in a shared context; it refers to real objects present in the environment; it is based on shared, common sense experience; and so forth. Written, academic text is said to be decontextualized, because the information presented is not necessarily shared, and the reader or writer is thought to rely much more on specialized lexicon and syntax than on context to discover meaning in such "decontextualized" academic situations. Reference may be to abstract entities rather than to objects physically present in time or space.

The oral versus written and unplanned versus planned dichotomies have also been characterized as *informal versus formal* and, in the field of language teaching, as basic interpersonal communication skills (BICS) and cognitive academic language proficiency (CALP). The BICS/CALP terminology comes from Cummins (1979, 1980, 1981, 1984). While each dichotomy differs in some respects from the others, all have the same goal – matching language forms to each pole of the dichotomy. Each serves as a heuristic in the attempt to describe and explain differences in linguistic choice related to discourse setting.

As with all dichotomies, it is very easy to assume that one side or the other is "good" or "better" than the other. Planned language is "better" than unplanned; use of decontextualized language is somehow a "higher" skill than the use of contextualized language; language groups that lack a written mode are somehow not as "good" as language groups with strong traditions of written literacy. It is always dangerous to play "dichotomy." If you attended to the preceding chapters on ritual and system constraints, you know that planned is not necessarily better. For example, disfluencies are "good" in oral conversations where they project appropriate demeanor and deference but "bad" in written discourse. Tight syntactic organization is "good" in formal, written discourse but "bad" in informal conversations (we don't want our friends to sound like talking books). There is also the danger of thinking that one side of each dichotomy is "easier" than the other. Again, this is not the case. For example, when we argue a case orally, we must not only present all the arguments in a well-organized way (as in written argumentation), but we must also worry about the ritual constraints of face-to-face communication. This complicates rather than simplifies the task. Conversely, when we want to convince readers of arguments, we do not have the benefit of face-to-face communication, and therefore must constantly think about whether or not our points are coming across. Again, we could say the task of convincng readers is complicated, rather than simplified, by the written mode.

Nevertheless, we know that oral versus written, unplanned versus planned, informal versus formal, contextualized versus decontextualized, and BICS versus CALP language differ in some way. If this is the case, then those differences would assist us in assigning coherence to text. That is, the different signals used in discourse at each side of the dichotomy should aid us in comprehension and production of such text. Let us first consider a number of linguistic distinctions that have been drawn for oral and written modes. Then, later in the chapter, we will consider how these might relate to the other dichotomies. You may want to check the data you have collected for some of the projects in this book and note which features that distinguish each side of the dichotomies are and are not found in the data.

Features of planned and unplanned language

Many books and articles have been written about the ways in which speech and writing differ. Collected articles, such as those in Horowitz and Samuels

(1987), Kroll and Vann (1981), Olson et al. (1985), and Tannen (1982a), offer strong claims about linguistic and cognitive demands of speaking and writing. Edelsky (1986), Farr and Janda (1985), Rubin (1987), Kroll (1981), and Zamel (1987) are sources that give a more pedagogical perspective on differences. The contrasts between speaking and writing have also been identified for other languages (see, for example, Zellermeyer 1988 on Hebrew and Clancy 1982 on Japanese).

Many of the differences discussed in these sources have to do with the amount of time and space available for communication in each mode and the effect that this has on how tightly or loosely organized the text will be. As writers revise their work and speakers polish their performance, the language they use changes. Spontaneous talk and polished writing differ syntactically. In discussing the differences between unplanned and planned language, Ochs (1979) identified six features:

1. Clausal or phrasal versus sentential organization
2. Left dislocation and topic-comment structures
3. Nextness
4. Parallelism
5. Repair
6. Conjoined versus embedded clauses

Clausal or phrasal versus sentential organization

Interactive talk is often clausal or phrasal in structure. In the following example, a psychologist (P) is advising a client (C) on how best to break "writer's block." Note that P is not speaking in complete sentences.

P: take a tape recorder an+that y'just punch+an:: y'work on the tape recorder+an:: y'talk to the tape recorder.
C: mmhmm
P: and the other thing you you+when y'wanna+when y'wanna ask+ that+ +just play a little of the tape+n listen to yerself talk+an talk back to it the second time+on the typewriter.

A written version of the oral message might be something like this:

To solve writer's block use a tape recorder as a partner. Tell the tape recorder what you want to write. Then play back this message. As you listen, type out your message. Continue this process until the block disappears.

In the written version, the organization is sentential rather than phrasal. In a sense, we could say we have "improved" on the message by changing it in this way. However, the written, planned version would not be appropriate or better in soothing the ritual constraints of face-to-face communication. Rather, it would come across as stuffy, pompous, opinionated, or preachy. The message is not negotiated, and negotiation is central to the success of interpersonal communication in general.

Practice 7.1   Clausal or phrasal versus sentential organization

1. You might think that only "some people" use clausal or phrasal organization in their face-to-face unplanned talk. Select any of the transcripts that you have prepared and used in previous chapters of this book. Listen again to the tape as you reread your transcript. Can you justify the capital letters and periods you may have used to make the transcript look more like sentences? Give examples to show how accurate you have been in showing the true nature of the data in this respect.
2. Teachers often instruct language learners to "speak in complete sentences." The drills used in language classes are sentential in nature. Does it matter that the language being modeled does not really reflect the face-to-face communication of native speakers? At what stage do you think it might be helpful to make students aware of the true nature of spontaneous oral discourse?
3. Native speakers as well as language learners are often shocked when they first read oral language transcripts. If you were interviewed for an article in a newspaper or journal, would you be willing to allow a transcribed record of your responses stand as is? If the nature of the talk is changed to agree more closely with that of the written mode, what would be lost and gained?
4. As a group research project, interview four students on some topic of importance to your school or program. Conduct an oral interview with two of the students and use a written interview with the other two. Use the same set of interview questions with each. When the two oral interviews have been transcribed, compare the texts in terms of phrasal, clausal, or sentential organization.

Left dislocation and topic-comment structures

In spontaneous talk, we frequently introduce a new topic, shift the focus, or shade into a new topic by using topic-comment structures. Instances of each are underlined in the following examples. The fourth example shows a left dislocation of the subject ("John"), lending it topic status. ("C" stands for different clients; the data were obtained from personal counseling interviews.)

1. C: Uh, <u>about money</u>, uh he has a darn good job+makes good money.
2. C: ... y'know, <u>things with the kids</u>, they need this, they need that.
3. C: OK, let's say <u>like vacation</u>+ +well, y'know+I haven't taken a vacation+I can't tell you how many years.
4. C: <u>John</u> he's like about twice my age.

A planned, written version for each of these utterances might be:

1. As for money, we don't have to worry because he has a good job.
2. ... and then there are the children who need so many things.
3. A vacation is one example of what I would like to have.
4. John is about twice my age.

In the written versions, I have tried to preserve the topic-comment nature of the talk by using an "as for" and a presentative "there is/there are" in the first two sentences. However, the outcome is less than satisfactory. While the sentences look more like standard written language, and the first two do use standard topic-comment devices, they are not "better." They do not convey the emotion of the oral versions, and they are not as successful in showing topic focus.

Practice 7.2   Left dislocation and topic-comment structures

1. In the data you used in Practice 7.1.1 or the oral interviews in 7.1.4, check for topic-comment structures. List any examples you find and compare the frequency of such structures with those found by other members of your class or study group.
2. Language learners (both first and second language learners) are said to use large numbers of topic-comment structures in their early language production. Later it is said that they use fewer and fewer of these structures as they "progress" by widening their repertoire of syntactic structures. If adult native speakers use topic-comment structures frequently in spontaneous talk, should learners be discouraged from using such forms? Why or why not?
3. Many languages have been classified as topic-comment languages, but English has been classified as a subject-prominent language. Japanese and Chinese students continue to use many topic-comment structures in writing

even though they may be quite advanced learners of English. For example:

Beginners, oral mode
Sunday is I'm working.
American car is too much y'know gasorin. Japanese car is uh very long.

(Data source: Niimura)

Advanced, written mode
How to use variable English sentences to express myself exactly, that is the main problem I faced when I picked up my pencil.
For more complex feeling, I had trouble to write it down.

(Data source: Wenzell)

First, write out a standard English sentence for each example. Since we use many more topic-comment structures in oral than in written discourse, how might you go about encouraging students to use forms closer to those you produced for the written mode?

Nextness

In unplanned talk, phrases are often produced one after another, and it is this "nextness' that shows they are related. In written discourse, syntactic structures and explicit cohesive ties can mark these relationships.

C: As I said+I can't discuss-very few things can I discuss with him++"I don't want to talk about it"+he walks outta the room.
P: all you do when you trap y'know an animal+they fight back + that you lie+get angry+whatever.

A planned, written version might be:

There are very few things I can discuss with him. When I try, he says that he doesn't want to talk about it and leaves the room.

Animals, when you try to trap them, fight back. If you try to trap a man, he will become angry, say that you lie, and so forth.

The planned, written versions are more explicit in drawing connections between the clauses. This makes the written text more comprehensible to the reader, but such organization is unnecessary when speakers are interacting with each other and already focused on the topic.

Practice 7.3 Nextness

1. Consult the data you used for Practice 7.1 for examples of nextness. Rewrite these examples in the written mode.

What syntactic means did you use to show the relationships among the clauses?

2. When writing notes to yourself and personal notes to your close friends, you may use phrasal or clausal organization (rather than sentential), use topic-comment structures, and rely on nextness to make connections among clauses. Ask your students or friends if you may borrow notes from one of their content classes. Prepare photocopies of the data and, as a research project, describe the data using these first three features from the oral versus written dichotomy. How closely do the notes fit the descriptions of oral versus written modes?

Parallelism: phonological, lexical, and syntactic

In spontaneous talk, words and phrases are repeated, and words seem to touch off the use of words having similar sound sequences. In Chapter 6, we noted that this is one way of promoting cohesive text.

C: nn I find this is a wonderful way to keep your weight down
C: you-you should be nominated for the Nobel Peace Prize + you're so mar-velous + you cause more peace in people's lives than + any person I'm sure.
C: it-it was a very strange situation uh + uh he starts saying-this is the shocker ((ha-ha)) he starts seeing other men + strange.

Repeated words and parallel phrases also promote cohesion in the following oral discourse:

P: . . . doing it all, being it all, y'know the Superwoman uh + having a career, a husband, children, everything + n I'm not saying we have the answer either + + but but we as a culture here y'know + we have been involved and are + guess are still having it + something of a feminist revolution + where women have been REALLY examining + themselves n how they wanna live + and what they wanna do + and how they wanna be treated.

Strong lexical association links are also frequent in spontaneous talk, although I have no such glorious examples as those reported by Goffman in his analysis of radio talk interviews (e.g., "Leo Lebel has been competing with a pulled stomach muscle, showing a lot of guts" and "May the winner emerge victorious"). Repetition of sounds and words, and lexical collocations across turns, give the text extra cohesion.

In written text, we try to use parallelism while avoiding too much repetition. One might, therefore, think that we improve text in the written mode by deleting the ties that appear with such frequency in oral data. However, consider the similarity between the devices used in the preceding oral language examples and those used in poetry. Poetry is the ultimate example of effective parallelism (rhythm, rhyme, alliteration, and lexical, phrasal, and syntactic parallelism). Poetry is also, perhaps, the ultimate example of planning. Face-to-face interaction and poetry are most successful when they establish a shared rhythm of verbal involvement among people. When the focus is involvement, all the devices align the participants in a common rhythm of interaction. It is difficult, then, to say that oral discourse would somehow be improved if this difference between oral and written modes were changed.

Practice 7.4   Parallelism

1. Examine the data used in Practice 7.1 – this time for examples of parallelism. Categorize them as phonological, lexical, or syntactic.
2. As a class or study group assignment, review two of your favorite poems. List examples for each type of parallelism (phonological, lexical, and syntactic). How do these parallelisms work with the rhythm of the poem?
3. As a research project, analyze the forms of parallelism in Martin Luther King's "I Have a Dream" address. How do these help create a spirit of involvement in the dream?

Repair

As the preceding examples show, unplanned discourse is heavily marked by repair. Few utterances beyond the phrase level are given without either hesitation markers (giving time for planning) or some correction work.

Example 1
C: Okay, if I-if I don't-if I don't-if I'm not sure I like them I can-I can-I can (pray?)+I can be what I'm supposed to be.

Example 2
P: I-I sorta saw him as a hedonistic+but but in those days+ everybody seemed hedonistic to me+I was s-so worth uh work eth-oriented.

From the standpoint of ritual constraints, these utterances would not be more appropriate if the repairs were removed. However, in written text such repairs are edited. The feelings of inadequacy projected by the repairs in the first example could be turned into a subordinate clause. The repairs in the second example could be deleted and the aside (I was so work-oriented in those days that I saw everyone as hedonistic) placed in parentheses. That is, special syntactic measures rather than repairs can be used in written text.

Practice 7.5   Repair

1. Check the transcript you used in Practice 7.1 for repairs. Give examples that show the appropriateness of the repairs in the discourse. List any examples for which you believe fewer repairs might have made the discourse more effective (i.e., more intelligible and more appropriate from the ritual aspect of communication).
2. Repair also occurs in written text. In Chapter 1, we talked about the use of parentheses as bracket signals. However, not all material inside parentheses are asides or side sequences. Some seem to function as repairs to the material in which they are embedded. Find three such parenthetical examples in this book and show how they function as repairs.

Conjoined versus embedded clauses

Unplanned talk is often delivered clause by clause or phrase by phrase. Nextness may show the relationship among the clauses, and temporal organization may also help make the text cohesive. In addition, when people are telling what happened (narration), the temporally ordered clauses are frequently connected with the conjunction "and."

C: When I was 18 I got pregnant and + it was with a + a boy I'd been going with a + a year and a half an:: we decided to get married + + an:: I went home to tell my parents + and my dad said, "No, it will send your mother over the edge."

In some oral data, it is difficult to tell whether "and" actually connects text or whether it serves some other system need, such as holding a turn against interruption or continuing a turn when the addressee does not pick up his or her turn.

C: uh that's my uh + fear of snakes (.1) annnd (.1) well uh–my mother always said + uh we should take care of animals (.2) annd (.2) who know what's gonna happen these days (.4) annd (.6) I dunno what YOU think + it seems kinda strange.

Note the series of sound stretches on "and." The longer and longer gaps suggest that the speaker has wound down and is using these signals to indicate a transition-relevant place. A planned written version would need to capture these functions in some other way: The "ands" would probably be deleted, and subordinate or embedded clause constructions would be used to connect the clauses. It has been suggested that such clauses are too difficult to produce in the oral mode. It might also be suggested that using coordinating clauses is an appropriate way to mark the temporal succession of events in such stories. Whatever the reason, speakers do not normally produce subordinate and embedded clauses in spontaneous, unplanned talk.

When speakers use clause markers for subordinate or embedded clauses (e.g., *if, that, because* clauses) during talk, the clause that follows the marker is often ungrammatical. Perhaps more telling is the long pause that separates the marker from the so-called *if*-clause, causal clause, relative clause, or complex nominalization. It is as if the speaker is ready to produce such clauses, places the relative pronoun in the correct position, but then does not yet have the clause ready in its proper form.

P: The point is <u>that</u>+ +you're+ you're at a place now <u>where</u>+ +he doesn't wanna give <u>you</u> ANYthing.

P: Yah well I think <u>that</u>+I think <u>that</u> y'need to tell your son <u>that</u>+we+ <u>that</u>+that's just+it's stupid.

Pawley and Syder (1976) have proposed a one-clause-at-a-time hypothesis to account for the nonfluent speech we use when producing novel material or when we are unprepared to express our thoughts on an unfamiliar subject. They note that even when speakers know their subject well, once they begin to use a "subordinating style," they are noticeably less fluent. The style is seldom if ever maintained beyond two or three clauses. They give interesting examples of "errors" when speakers adopt this style.

Adjoined raw clauses
1. I was goin' with a girl she was a bloody opera singer.
2. Those are the three kids their parents died.

Lingering pronouns
1. I only know this one girl that she went to New York.
2. The man who this made him feel sad.

Delayed relatives
1. Because I played in his garden all the time which was 5 acres.
2. He drove through the town yesterday where I went to school.

Prenominalization
1. She talks about somebody that she doesn't clarify who he is for about three pages.
2. The child points to the tape recorder which the parents tell him what it is called.

Getting out on a Wh-*limb*
1. This flight goes to Hilo which I'm not sure if it goes in the summer.
2. I've seen people elaborate on them by means that I'm not sure where they find them.
3. I got if from a map which I've seen lots of them.

4. They've developed a specific series of linguistic textbooks which we haven't used any of them so far.

(Data source: Pawley and Syder 1976)

Practice 7.6 Conjoined versus embedded clauses

1. Using the data from Practice 7.1, examine the ways in which the clauses have been connected. If you find examples of embedded clauses, note whether there are pauses and other disfluency markers between the conjunction or relative pronoun and the clause that follows. Are the embedded clauses grammatically correct?

2. Some composition books follow a sequence that asks students to change oral text to written text. I know of no textbook that uses authentic spontaneous oral text for such purposes. Rather, the text has been doctored to make it look more like written text to begin with. This means that the data are sentencelike, disfluencies and repairs may have been removed, and problems with embedded structures have been eliminated. The result is a "sanitized text." Since the focus is not on oral language but on written text, how might this be justified? Select one small section from the data you used in Practice 7.1 and show what things you might change if you wished to use it as a basis for teaching composition.

3. The language experience approach to reading instruction begins with oral language data produced by the learner. This is usually a story that the child (or adult learner) wants to make into a storybook. The teacher transcribes the story with the help of the storyteller. The teacher and student read the story together until the learner feels that he or she is ready to read it alone. The story then becomes part of the learner's library. If you have used this approach, how accurate must the transcription be to obtain results? Give an example of some of the problems involved with such transcriptions.

4. Here are some examples of talk in oral discourse. Discuss them in terms of Pawley and Syder's one-clause-at-a-time hypothesis. If they fit the hypothesis, can you categorize them in some way?

   a. We always congregate in the kitchen but we have a big

living room which, y'know, we use it for just when we
have a meeting or something like that, or the neighbors
all come over.
b. . . . and the women that are working on the quilt project
who by just being so dedicated we're very happy about.
c. I see a lot of Arien's age group and some of the seniors
that they're not into track or wrestling or any of that jock
stuff.

The six features which Ochs identified to differentiate oral and written (or,
more specifically, unplanned and planned) do help us see the tighter organization of written language. However, there are times when we want our writing to sound and look more like oral language. We can, of course, use the six
features, but we can also use punctuation to put back some of what has been
lost in changing talk to writing. Punctuation – capital letters and periods –
is actually more useful for "reading aloud" than for syntactic decoding. Com-
mas, semicolons, and colons all help us hear the intonation of the text. For
extra emphasis, some writers put spaces between the letters of important
words; others underline, italicize, or capitalize words. Quotation marks, single quotes, dashes, and dots lend a voice quality to text.

In addition to punctuation, as Chapman (1984) has pointed out, our word
selection helps to bring an oral sound to writing. Instead of "he said," we may
use "muttered," "whispered," "gasped," "grunted," and so forth. Synaesthe-
sia, the borrowing of other senses for sounds, gives us expressions such as "in
a bitter tone," "in a sweet voice" – all of which help bring the oral sound of
language to text. Some authors use modified spelling (e.g., "sez," "wanna")
to give the sound of talk. While these are actually more accurate than regular
spelling as reflections of pronunciation and are used for that reason by
researchers for conversational analysis, they are most often used to represent
lower-class or regional accents in ordinary writing.

In speech, our attitudes about what we say are shown by prosodic features
such as intonation, stress, and pitch and by facial expressions as well. In writing, as Tannen has often said, you can wrinkle your face till it cracks while
you write, but this will not show up on the page. You can yell or whisper or
sing as you compose, but the words that fall on the page, unless you circle
them with smiles or something, will not reflect this. Feelings must be lexical-
ized in some ways. You can write "I don't mean this literally," but you can't
smile and wink.

Ochs' features have been presented in many linguists' discussions of differences between oral and written language modes. Halliday (1987), however,
argues that oral language, contrary to what most people think, is at least as
complex or "grammatically intricate" as written language. The major difference he sees in the two modes is that written language is lexically denser (i.e.,
there are more content words per clause than in spontaneous oral language).

246

Features of involvement and detachment

Like the oral versus written and the unplanned versus planned dichotomies, the dichotomy of *contextualized versus decontextualized* language highlights differences, but in a slightly different way. For many educators and researchers, the language required in school is the ultimate example of decontextualized language, while language outside school is said to be contextualized. Of course, all language is contextualized in that it relies on shared knowledge of many types. Perhaps a more helpful way of looking at this dichotomy is to think of it as focused and nonfocused interaction, sometimes called *involvement versus detachment*. We would expect differences in the language used in conversations among friends and that used to write a technical report to be read by strangers, where supposedly less interpersonal involvement is required. Tannen (1979) identified a number of features of interpersonal involvement that could be associated with oral strategies.

One pattern of interpersonal involvement identified by Tannen is that of overlap or simultaneous speech. Although speakers may talk at the same time, this doesn't mean they aren't listening to each other or that they want to "grab the floor" or interrupt each other. The overlaps show encouragement much as backchannel signals do. Speakers will often tell ministories to demonstrate their understanding of the other's point. They do collaborative completions to demonstrate they know where the speaker's utterance is headed. They may ask questions that the speaker clearly would have answered anyway. All this, Tannen says, assures the speaker that he or she isn't in the conversation alone.

In high involvement conversations, more stories are told about personal experiences. The point of these stories is more likely to be about feelings, and this may be made clear not by direct statement but by dramatization or re-creation of voice qualities relating to people in the stories. There is no need to state the obvious point since it is made by mimicking voices. For example:

K: I have a little seven-year-old student . . . a little girl who wears //those . . . She
T: //She wears those? ((chuckle))*
K: is TOO much. Can you imagine? She's seven years old, and she sits in her chair and she goes ((squeals and squirms in chair))
T: OH:: Go::d . . . She's only SEVen?
K: And I say well . . . how about let's do so and so. And she says . . . "Okay" ((squealing)) Just like that.
T: Oh::::
D: What does it mean.
K: It's just so . . . she's acting like such a little girl already.

(Data source: Tannen 1979)

D asks that K state the obvious – that the little girl is a coquette, a point made by K's intonation and mimicry. Tannen suggests that we all have our own

247

oral strategy styles. By expecting the story point to be made explicit and by finding events more important than character's feelings, D showed a more literate or detached style of speech. By expecting the point of the story to be dramatized by the speaker and inferred by the hearer, and finding feelings more interesting than events, K showed features of involvement as an oral strategy. Of course, neither D nor K are to be classified as "oral, involved" or "literate, detached"; rather, we have at our disposal and use, according to individual habits and social group conventions, strategies that are associated with either or both.

Moving to written text, Tannen suggests that literature shares more of the interpersonal involvement features used by friends in conversations than the literate, noninvolvement features of expository text. Creative writing is best when it suggests the most to the reader with the fewest words. The goal of the writer is to have the reader fill in as much as possible. The more the reader supplies, the more she or he will believe and care about the message. The features that are thought of as literary are basic to spontaneous conversation, not to expository prose. We've already noted such features as sound repetitions, repetition of words, parallel syntactic constructions, and the general rhythm of conversation; these are basic to literature as well.

In order to promote the ritual side of communication, we can mark discourse for involvement. This includes many of the features already discussed, but Chafe (1982) has listed others as well:

Involvement
Concreteness and imageability (use of details)
Personal quality (use of first and second person pronouns)
People and their relationships highlighted
Actions and agents emphasized more than states and objects
Feelings and thoughts (evaluation) reported
Hedged and aggravated signals used (e.g., "sorta," "really")
Feedback signals checked and repairs used where needed

At the other end of the involvement-detachment continuum is detachment, where the involvement features are no longer crucial. Consider, for example, a science report (one where the authors are *not* using features of involvement to convince readers of their arguments). What features would we expect to find? Chafe suggests that text not focused on interaction will show the importance of complex syntax in integration of ideas. The types of complex structures he has in mind include:

Detachment
Relative clauses
Complement clauses
Sequences of prepositional phrases
Nominalizations

248

Attributive adjectives
Passive voice
Subordinate conjunctions
Complex morphosyntax

Practice 7.7   Involvement versus detachment

1. Using Chafe's list of features of involvement and detachment, analyze the following research report written by a first-grade child. Identify involvement features and detachment features within the text.

> By Kelly Hunt
> The pets on half of my street
> We have 116 pets on my street. I have 88 thats what made so much. 2 Houses I inculoodid suffed andamals. I even did resuch on this. I went up and down half of my street and whot it down. My friend Nicole S. helped me do this and her dad helped us with 1 math problom. We cecked him on it. So don't you think that's alot for just half?
>
> ---
>
> This is Dedacated to my friend Nicole: because she helped me with the job. P.S. I whot this wal waiting for Didner.

> (Data source: Hunt)

2. Select a paper that you or one of your students has written as an academic course paper. List the features of involvement and detachment shown in the paper. Comment on the use of involvement features in academic writing.
3. Give two examples of involvement features that you believe should not be used in academic writing. If and when these appear in students' compositions, what explanations do you give regarding their inappropriateness?

Identifying BICS versus CALP

Researchers and educators have searched for dimensions that are important in understanding language needed for academic success. In all the dichotomies, one side describes language where the participants have optimal opportunity to interact and negotiate their meanings. Often the communication is face to face, and the participants cooperate in building communication and the content of the communication. On the other side of the dichotomy, there is little opportunity for the participants to interact in order to negotiate form or content. The participants may never see each other (as when a writer prepares a paper for publication), there may be strict rules about who gets to talk (as when a speaker gives a lecture to an audience), or the writer may have little if any idea why his or her language is being solicited or who the reader will be (as when a child takes a language proficiency test in school). In the literature that relates bilingualism and academic achievement, the two sides of this dichotomy are called *BICS versus CALP*, BICS shows the learner's basic interpersonal communication skills, and CALP reflects the learner's cognitive academic language proficiency.

If we look at the ordinary, everyday work that takes place in classrooms, we see that we cannot easily assign a BICS versus CALP identity to each activity. Nor can we say that the language required in the activity is unplanned versus planned or contextualized versus decontextualized. If you doubt this, consider the following set of activities an elementary school child might reasonably be expected to participate in. How would you rate each in terms of unplanned versus planned, contextualized versus decontextualized, involved versus detached, and BICS versus CALP dichotomies?

Talking with friends while eating lunch in the cafeteria
Talking to your mom on the phone
Listening to the teacher tell you how to do fractions
Reading a story without pictures about the latest space mission
Reading a comic about astronauts
Hearing a classmate tell what the teacher said about the space mission
Reading a play about travel in space
Listening to a story about travel in space
Listening to someone read a play about the astronauts' trip to the moon
Reading a note left on the kitchen table
Having a conversation on linked computer terminals
Listening to a conversation between the teacher and your best friend
Drawing a comic strip story about the astronauts' trip
Writing an essay on "the moon"
Writing a letter to your best friend
Reading a letter from your best friend
Making a poster about the moon for "share and tell"
Writing on linked computer terminals about being an astronaut
Writing in your diary about being an astronaut
Writing words in blanks on an exercise sheet (seat work)
Writing a message to put in a time capsule for school
Writing a message to put in a bottle
Writing instructions on how to use the video camera
Preparing a poster on how to do fractions for "parents' night" at school
Explaining the poster to parents as they visit the classroom during "parents' night"
Taking a test (short answers) on "the moon"

Again, it's important to remember that all the dichotomies are only heuristic terms to illuminate the language choices available along different but similar continua. A balanced language curriculum needs to offer learners opportunities to practice language all along the continua. It's also important to realize that learning of all kinds could first be accomplished in a cooperative face-to-face interactive setting. That is, teachers should not assign a "good" value to planned, written forms of language and devalue as "unimportant" the language of social interaction, because learning may take place in either mode.

Practice 7.8   Dichotomies reviewed

1. Stubbs (1980, 1986) gives examples of events that are carried out in either written or oral modes. For example, promises in marriage ceremonies – the "I do" and "I will" statements – are oral contracts given before witnesses, family, friends, and the entire congregation in my community. Promises to purchase a house, however, are written contracts where the buyer and seller may never even meet each other. List examples of other events that are typically carried out in either oral or written modes.
2. Make a list of all the activities that occur in the classroom you videotaped for data in Chapter 1. Attempt to classify each activity in terms of the type of language required using the dichotomies discussed in this chapter. How balanced are the demands for oral versus written modes for each of the other dichotomies?
3. Examine the corrections and suggestions that you (or your teacher) make on student compositions. Would these suggestions apply if the student gave an oral report on the same material? Why or why not?
4. In Chapter 2, we talked about Tannen's claim that each of us evolves a personal style as we balance the demands for involvement and autonomy. How might this be related to Chafe's notions of involvement and detachment? Do you believe that the discourse context itself determines the degree of involvement and detachment, or do you feel that each of us evolves a set of personal styles and selects from them according to the need at the moment for involvement or autonomy? State your position and give two examples in support of that position. (In teaching argumentation, teachers always ask students to give three supporting arguments. You might add a third example and turn this into a term paper for this course!)

Conclusion

In this chapter, we have looked at several dichotomies that reveal differences in how texts are organized in different modes and, perhaps, in different tasks. These differences are important because they add to the repertoire of signals forming the discourse system. These are heuristic dichotomies, and we might feel more comfortable if they were called continua. The continua, to my way of thinking, are not features of the text; rather, they represent choices that writers and speakers have at their disposal to communicate in the most effective way within any given context. Thus, when speaking of "discourse markers," I do not mean to imply that these markers belong to the discourse. Rather, they belong to the speaker or writer and may or may not be selected to enhance communication.

Research and application

1. Brown and Yule (1981) give an example of a speaker's description of a rainbow and a famous author's written description. Read their descriptions of the phrasal, clausal, and sentential nature of the data. If possible, replicate the study by asking language learners to do both tasks. Compare your results to that of Brown and Yule.

2. Ochs (1977) had graduate students in linguistics tape-record their "danger of death" stories, a procedure used by Labov (1972) to collect narratives. The students later produced written versions of the stories. The list of features given for oral versus written discourse come, in part, from Ochs' discussion of the differences found in the written and oral data sets. Replicate this methodology with your own students. Compare your results in terms of these categories. If your results differ, hypothesize why this should be the case.

3. Chafe (1980) asked students to watch a silent film (*The Pear Story*) and then retell the story. Replicate this study with your students using any silent film that is available. Analyze the data in one of two ways: according to the six features discussed as separating oral versus written modes or according to features of involvement and detachment. What problems do you see in the film in terms of the types of language structures it might require? That is, do the events require that several characters be distinguished from each other via minimal visual cues so that you will find many relative clauses in the data – clauses that are not supposed to appear with high frequency in oral language data?

4. Halliday (1987) notes that both oral and written language are

structurally complex. His analysis shows that written language is *lexically* more dense and *grammatically* less intricate than oral language. He maintains that "contrary to what many people think, spoken language is, on the whole, more complex than written language in its grammar; and informal, spontaneous conversation is the most grammatically complex of all" (1979: 47). Examine Halliday's analysis of grammatical intricacy and lexical density of oral and written language. Explain how the analysis can be integrated with those presented in this chapter. What insights does the analysis provide regarding each of the dichotomies presented here?

5. To capture the sound of oral language, comic strip writers commonly use large letters, surround letters with jagged graphics or smooth bubbles, and employ a variety of foreigner talk and dialect markers. A few writers use a very odd mix of hypercorrect language and the language of ordinary talk. Collect comic strips and cartoons from the language you teach or are studying. How do these strips characterize spoken language? Note instances that seem to differ radically from that of normal talk.

6. The notion that much of the language we use in communication consists of "chunks" or "speech formulas" has influenced our notion of language units. Review some of the articles and books that have been written on the notion of a phrasal lexicon. (See Pawley and Syder 1976; Becker 1975; Coulmas 1979, 1981; Peters 1983; Krashen and Scarcella 1978 for a start.) While such "chunks" are more obvious in talk, they also are used in writing. Design a preliminary research proposal to investigate such forms in the writing of native speakers and of language learners.

7. Kreeft Payton et al. (1990) considered a range of factors that make up the context of writing in elementary school classrooms: purposes (to communicate, to be evaluated), topic choice (writer-chosen or assigned), knowledge about topic (extensive to limited), audience (familiar to unspecified), and response (genuine message or for grade/correction). The data, the written materials of limited English proficiency (LEP) students, was collected in four contexts that could be classified according to the preceding system: dialogue journals and three assigned tasks (letter to a friend, letter of thanks to a teacher, and a comparison/contrast essay on grasslands and the desert). These were analyzed for quantity (number of words during the sample week), syntactic complexity (T units and clause connectors), focus (involvement or personal and noninvolvement or nonpersonal measures), and cohesiveness (number and type of

cohesive ties). The results showed that students had substantially more practice time in journal writing than in assigned writing. More complex syntax was used in the letter to a friend, the next most in dialogue journals, and the least in the essay on desert and grassland contrasts. More impersonal subjects occurred in the essay, and more personal subjects in the other tasks. There was no difference in the data for cohesive ties, although the variety of ties was greater in the dialogue journals and the letter to a friend than in the other task. Read this article and explain its implications for the dichotomies presented in this chapter as well as for Halliday's claims. Then classify the types of writing assignments you give your students using Payton et al.'s system. Design a research plan to investigate the range of language complexity and expressiveness in the writing of your students.

8. Sigel and Cocking (1977) talk about "distancing" behavior and the mental demands placed on the learner by events. Examine each of the following demands on the learner to determine whether you agree that they are arranged in ascending order of cognitive difficulty. The examples are those typically used in elementary schools. Write another example for each that would be typical for secondary or tertiary levels. Then decide which of these demands are typical of BICS, CALP, or both.

To observe: "Look at what I am doing."

To label: "What color is the star?"

To describe: "What did the boy look like?"

To sequence: "First we will look at the pictures and then we will make up a story."

To reproduce: "How do you do that?" (i.e., reconstruct experience)

To compare: Note (describe, infer) characteristics or properties using following categories: (a) describe similarities ("Are these the same?"); (b) describe differences ("In what way are the truck and airplane different?"); (c) infer similarities ("Would it be like last year?"); (d) infer differences ("This egg is cracked. How about this one?")

To propose alternatives: "Could we lift it instead?" "How else could we fix it?"

To combine: (a) symmetric ("Why did you put those two together?"); (b) asymmetric ("Can you put these in order by size?"); (c) enumerating ("Count how many there are." "Is this bigger than that one?") (d) synthesizing ("Can you summarize the whole thing?")

Sigel and Cocking also note that the form used by the teacher can be classified as demanding more or less active participation of learners.

Less: The boy is upset because his dog ran away.
More: There are other ways the boy could feel when his dog ran away.
Less: How did the boy feel when his dog ran away?
More: What can you tell me about how the boy felt?
Less: I wonder if the boy was sad when the dog ran away.
More: The dog ran away. I wonder how the boy feels.
Less: Tell me why the dog ran away.
More: Tell me more about the story.

Do you believe that the cognitive complexity of these demands might also be reflected in BICS versus CALP?

9. Schwartz (1990) describes a communication exchange program similar to that described by Basham in Chapter 6 (Navajo and Koyukon pen pals). High school students in Montana, South Dakota, and Pennsylvania linked their computers to communicate with each other. More than learning about "preppies" versus "cowboys," the program was set up to move through a series of activities toward formal writing. The sessions started with pen-pal–type letters with interviews and self-portraits. This moved to questions about the community and community life, to essays on the community, followed by a final evaluative essay. In addition to the electronic mail exchange, photos, handwritten notes, and local and school papers were exchanged. Read Schwartz's article and draw up a research proposal to link your classroom with the "ideal" classroom of your choice. Justify the choice in terms of what you think your students could learn or teach students in the ideal classroom. (You might be surprised to find a grant available to actually carry out the project. Distance education has finally come of age in the United States as distance education programs link U.S. foreign language classes with EFL language classes in other countries. For example, there are students at the University of California, Los Angeles, studying Japanese, Spanish, and Korean who are linked with students learning English in those countries. Half the communication period is devoted to one language and half to the other, so both sides have the opportunity to work on developing language skills.)

10. Traugott (1987) argues that we should not make claims about specific differences in mode as arising out of a change from orality to literacy or the period of "Enlightenment" without

looking at the complete context of language use over time. For example, it is claimed that assertive speech acts ("observe," "state," "claim") are linked to literacy and the written mode. However, Traugott found that such speech act verbs were more related to the language of law courts, feudal practices, and rhetorical debate in the Middle Ages than to a shift from orality to literacy. That is, these specific forms are not linked just to literacy but to particular uses of language at that time. As evidence, she presents a table of assertive speech acts verbs in Old English (600 to 1130), Middle English (1130 to 1480), Early Modern English (1480 to 1700), and Modern English (1800 to present). After reading Traugott's article, prepare a research paper regarding the ways in which historical linguistics might be used to readdress the issue of orality versus literacy.

References

Becker, J. (1975). The phrasal lexicon. In R. Schank and B. Nash-Webber (Eds.), *Theoretical issues in natural language processing* (pp. 60–63). Boston: Bolt, Beranek & Newman.

Brown, G, and Yule, G. (1981). *Discourse analysis.* Cambridge: Cambridge University Press.

Chafe, W. (1980). *The pear stories: Cognitive, cultural and linguistic aspects of narrative production.* Norwood, N.J.: Ablex.

(1982). Integration and involvement in speaking, writing, and oral literature. In D. Tannen (Ed.), *Spoken and written language: Exploring orality and literacy* (pp. 35–53). Norwood, N.J.: Ablex.

Chapman, R. (1984). *The treatment of sounds in language and literature.* London: Basil Blackwell.

Clancy, P. M. (1982). Written and spoken styles in Japanese narratives. In D. Tannen (Ed.), *Spoken and written language: Exploring orality and literacy* (pp. 55–76). Norwood, N.J.: Ablex.

Coulmas, F. (1979). On the sociolinguistic relevance of routine formulae. *Journal of Pragmatics, 3,* 239–266.

(1981). *Conversational routine: Exploration in standardized communication situations and prepatterned speech.* The Hague: Mouton.

Cummins, J. (1979). Linguistic interdependence and the educational development of bilingual children. *Review of Educational Research, 49,* 2: 222–251.

(1980). The construct of language proficiency in bilingual education. In J. Alatis (Ed.), *Current issues in bilingual education.* Washington, D.C.: Georgetown University Press.

(1981). The role of primary language development in promoting educational success for language minority children. In California State Department of Education, *Schooling and language minority students: A theoretical framework* (pp. 3–

49). Los Angeles: California State University, Evaluation, Dissemination, and Assessment Center.

(1984). *Bilingualism and special education: Issues in assessment and pedagogy.* San Diego: College-Hill Press.

Edelsky, C. (1986). *Writing in a bilingual program: Habia una vez.* Norwood, N.J.: Ablex.

Farr, M., and Janda, M. A. (1985). Basic writing students: Investigating oral and written language. *Research in the Teaching of English, 19:62–83.*

Halliday, M. A. K. (1987). Spoken and written modes of meaning. In R. Horowitz and S. J. Samuels (Eds.), *Comprehending oral and written language* (pp. 55–72). San Diego: Academic Press.

Horowitz, R., and Samuels, S. J. (1987). *Comprehending oral and written language.* San Diego: Academic Press.

Krashen, S., and Scarcella, R. (1978). On routines and patterns in language acquisition and performance. *Language Learning, 28:* 283–300.

Kreeft Payton, J.; Staton, J.; Richardson, G.; and Wolfram, W. (1990). The influence of writing task on ESL students' written production. *Research in the Teaching of English, 29,* 2: 142–172.

Kroll, B. M. (1981). Developmental relations between speaking and writing. In B. Kroll and R. Vann (Eds.), *Exploring speaking-writing relationships: Connections and contrasts* (pp. 32–54). Urbana, Ill.: National Council of Teachers of English.

Kroll, B. M., and Vann, R. (1981). *Exploring speaking-writing relationships: Connections and contrasts.* Urbana, Ill.: National Council of Teachers of English.

Labov, W. (1972). The transformation of experience in narrative syntax. In W. Labov (Ed.), *Language in the inner city* (pp. 354–396). Philadelphia: University of Pennsylvania Press.

Ochs, E. (1977). *Discourse across time and space. Occasional Papers in Linguistics, 5,* 1–42, Linguistics Department, University of Southern California.

(1979). Planned and unplanned discourse. In T. Givon (Ed.), *Discourse and syntax* (pp. 51–80). New York: Academic Press.

Olson, D.; Torrance, N.; and Hildyard, A. (1985). *Literacy, language and learning.* Cambridge: Cambridge University Press.

Pawley, A., and Syder, F. (1976). The one clause at a time hypothesis. Paper presented at the First Congress of New Zealand Linguistic Society, Auckland.

Peters, A. (1983). *The units of language acquisition.* Cambridge: Cambridge University Press.

Rader, M. (1982). Context in written language: The case of imaginative fiction. In D. Tannen (Ed.), *Spoken and written language: Exploring orality and literacy.* Norwood N.J.: Ablex.

Rubin, D. L. (1987). Divergence and convergence between oral and written communication. *Topics in Language Disorders, 7,* 4: 1–18.

Schwartz, J. (1990). Using an electronic network to play the game of discourse. *English Journal, 79,* 3: 16–24.

Sigel, I., and Cocking, R. (1977). Cognition and communication: A dialectic paradigm for development. In M. Lewis and L. Rosenblum (Eds.), *Interaction, conversation, and the development of language* (pp. 207–226). New York: John Wiley & Sons.

Stubbs, M. (1980). *Language and literacy: The sociolinguistics of reading and writing.* London: Routledge and Kegan Paul.

(1986). *Educational linguistics.* Oxford: Basil Blackwell.

Tannen, D. (1979). *Processes and consequences of conversational style.* Ph.D. dissertation. University of California, Berkeley.

(1980). Implications of the oral/literate continuum for cross-cultural communication. In J. Alatis (Ed.), *Georgetown University Round Table on Language and Linguistics, 1980, Current issues in bilingual education* (pp. 326–347). Washington, D.C.: Georgetown University Press.

(1982a). The oral/literate continuum of discourse. In D. Tannen (Ed.), *Spoken and written language: Exploring orality and literacy.* Norwood, N.J.: Ablex.

(1982b). Oral and literate strategies in spoken and written narratives. *Language, 58,* 1: 1–21.

(1985). Relative focus of involvement in oral and written discourse. In D. Olson, N. Torrance, and A. Hildyard (Eds.), *Literacy, language and learning* (pp. 124–148). Cambridge: Cambridge University Press.

Traugott, E. (1987). Literature and language change: The special case of speech act verbs. *INTERCHANGE, 18,* 1/2: 32–48 (OISE, Ontario, Canada).

Zamel, V. (1987). Recent research on writing pedagogy. *TESOL Quarterly, 21,* 4: 697–715.

Zellermeyer, M. (1988). An analysis of oral and literate texts: Two types of reader-writer relationships in Hebrew and English. In B. Rafoth and D. Rubin (Eds.), *The social construction of written communication* (pp. 287–303). Norwood, N.J.: Ablex.

8 Pragmatics, prosody, and contextual analysis

In discourse analysis, as in phonology, lexicon, and syntax, the linguist's task is to identify structural units and the processes that operate on those units. For many linguists, the most interesting relationship included in this book is the one between discourse and syntax.

From the analysis of rhetorical structure, we can make predictions about the types of syntactic structures that will appear in certain types of discourse. We can predict, for example, that in narrative discourse storytellers will use a series of temporally ordered clauses with highly transitive verbs. Tense/aspect may separate the major actions of these clauses from ongoing parallel actions or clauses giving background information. In procedural and advice-giving discourse, we also expect speakers and writers to select a series of temporally ordered actions, but the agent is more likely to be neutral. Therefore, we can anticipate a large number of imperative and passive constructions, and introductory phrases such as "in order to X" and "to X" may set the stage for the focused action. Time in such discourse is also usually neutral, so there is much less focus placed on the use of tense/aspect to precisely locate time relationships. In descriptive discourse, we expect speakers to use introductory presentatives (e.g., "*There are* 27 students in Taro's school."), identification through BE copula and possessive HAVE (e.g., "Father Serra *is* the leader" and "We *have* science fourth period"), and spatial relationships via prepositional phrases (e.g., "We have fun *out here in Rosamond*"). Also, we have seen that the mode (oral versus written) or degree of planning (unplanned versus planned) in discourse may influence the types of syntactic structures we choose. We can expect more complex verb morphology and more explicit marking of embedded and subordinate clauses in planned written discourse than in unplanned talk. An analysis of discourse data, then, reveals the selections we typically make in using syntax to carry out our discourse intent.

If, however, our primary interest is in syntax, we may approach our analysis in a very different way. Rather than analyzing discourse to discover the types of syntactic choices that might be made for particular functions, we might begin by posing an interesting question about syntax and then trying to answer the question by looking at the discourse context in which the structures occur.

Thus, there is a difference in asking "How is 'and' used?" and saying "narratives include a series of temporally ordered clauses that show the steps in solving a problem, and these clauses are often connected by 'and' or 'and then.'" A study that asks "How is X used?" calls for a combination of syntactic, pragmatic, and context analyses. Celce-Murcia (1980) calls this combination *contextual analysis.* The result of a contextual analysis might show that while descriptive grammars tell us something about when forms are used, the choice of form is influenced by genre, the purpose of the communication, the relationship of writer and reader or speaker and listener, the message content, and the context in which the communication takes place. In the language classroom, the teacher's expectations and the talk that surrounds the writing task might cause students to use particular structures for particular purposes. Pragmatics also helps to explain why and when particular language forms, rather than others, are selected. Before we turn to the methods used in contextual analysis, let us review some of what we already know about pragmatics.

Pragmatics

In linguistics, we often talk about meaning that derives from syntax and semantics. Meaning, however, is more than syntactic form and semantics. Pragmatic meaning is that which comes from the context rather than from syntax and semantics. The study of what speakers mean to convey when they use a particular structure in context is called the study of *pragmatics.* (See Levinson 1983 for a historical view of the scope of definitions of pragmatics.)

We have already talked about pragmatics to a certain extent when speech act analysis was described. Chapter 4 discussed the general classification of speech acts as representatives, directives, commissives, declaratives, and expressives. Searle (1975, 1976), from whom this classification was drawn, also talks about speaker intent. For example, the sentence "I didn't see you" has truth value and so can be classified as a representative. However, it could also have a pragmatic meaning of an excuse or apology. A seeming representative such as "I lost my purse" might have the pragmatic meaning of a directive, a request for a loan. How do we know what pragmatic meanings, rather than literal meanings, are conveyed by these utterances?

Grice (1975) claimed that what is conveyed by an utterance falls into two parts: what is *said* and what is *implied.* He uses the term *"implicature"* to cover what is implied (i.e., what is conveyed minus what is said). In Grice's system, there are two types of implicature: *conventional* and *conversational.*

Conventional implicature

Through experience, we learn the conventions that govern our use of expressions on certain occasions for certain purposes. Philosophers and linguists categorize some of these conventions in terms of entailment, paraphrase, conventional metaphorical meanings, presupposition, and implicatives.

Philosophers interested in the logic of conventional implicature look at how we use *entailment* in attributing meanings to utterances. For example, if I say "Oh, I thought you meant he was a good student when you said he always volunteered in class," it shows that I believe that being a good student entails volunteering in class. Entailment means that both propositions are true in the world being described. Since utterances can be relevant to more than one state of affairs, entailments are dependent on the context. For example, in some countries where students are not encouraged to volunteer, one would not expect that being a good student entailed volunteering in class. In that case, an utterance such as "Oh, I thought you meant he was a real troublemaker when you said he always volunteered in class" would show that I believe that being a troublemaker entails volunteering in class.

Philosophers also use *paraphrase* as a method to determine conventional implicature when assigning appropriate speaker meaning to an utterance within a context. We may use linguistic signals of paraphrase to make our meanings clear within a context. When we read or hear "what I mean is," "in other words," "to rephrase," "in essence," we know, by convention, that a paraphrase is about to happen. The writer or speaker is asking us to be sure consensus has been reached on the meaning of the previous utterance. (The notion that there may be many paraphrases possible that do or do not reflect writer or speaker intent, however, is not a happy one for second language acquisition researchers who try to write transliterations for interlanguage data. And it is a problem faced by every translator.)

Philosophers also include *metaphorical* meanings as conventional implicature for assigning meaning to speech acts. By convention, we know that "He's such an old fox" is not to be processed in a literal syntactic and semantic way. A metaphor brings together two distinct concepts in a way that lets us see similarities. Metaphors can also summarize and synthesize meaning. A good metaphor can make clear a whole argument, because it calls up or invokes a much larger context. If we say, "Our research went *off track*," we call up a conventional metaphor of work as a journey down a path or, in this case, a train track. When we leave that path, we need to get *back on track*. The journey metaphor is needed in order to analytically account for the fact that the meaning does not match that of conventional linguistic analysis. To some extent, at least, the use of metaphor asks us to use conventional implicature to give an altered meaning to a speech act.

We've said that representatives as speech acts have truth value. If I say, using the example from Chapter 4, that "I went to the Amish quilt exhibit," there are many *presuppositions* that are made in bringing meaning to the utterance. We assume that such an exhibit was held, that I found transportation to get to the exhibit, that I was able to obtain admission, and so forth. For linguists, however, presupposition does not refer to all the possible knowledge within which we interpret propositions but *only* those that are encoded in the linguistic syntactic system.

There are a number of syntactic features that relate to presupposition. Karttunen (1971), for example, identified a group of *implicatives* – verbs like "manage" that indirectly convey both a presupposition and an implication. If I had said, "I managed to go to the Amish quilt exhibit," the implicatures that can be drawn from the verb "manage" let us presuppose that I made an effort to go to the exhibit, and, since the effort was "sufficient," it also implicates truthfulness to the proposition "I went to the Amish quilt exhibit." If I had said, "I didn't manage to go the Amish quilt exhibit," the presupposition is that the effort was not "sufficient," and so the proposition "I went to the exhibit" is implicated as not true.

Thus, by using a conventional syntactic signal, the truth claims of representatives can be modified or the signal can show that something more than a representative is being said. In addition to implicative verbs, sentential adverbs can change the degree of truthfulness to be given to utterances. If I say, "Maybe I went to an Amish quilt exhibit," the previous presuppositions no longer hold. By adding one word, I have told you not to interpret the following proposition as strictly true. I may or may not have gone; I can't remember.

In Chapter 4 we talked about hedges that weaken the strength of speech acts. In effect, these are syntactic signals of pragmatic intent, because they tell us to reinterpret either the truth value of the utterance or the presuppositions that go with it. Modals have this function. For example, each of the following types of modals serves as a signal that the usual presupposition – that speakers sincerely believe the truth value of the representative – is modified and that a special judgment about the speech act is to be made.

Modal auxiliary: I *may* have gone to the exhibit.
Modal lexical verb: I *think* I went to the exhibit.
Modal sentence adverbial: Perhaps I went to the exhibit.
Modal adjective: It's *possible* that I went to the exhibit.
Modal prepositional phrase: As far as I know, I went to the exhibit.

Conversational implicature

Grice's second type of implicature differs in scope. Called *conversational implicature,* it contrasts with conventional implicature in that the meanings of utterances are only indirectly associated with their linguistic content. According to Grice, these implications are drawn from the principles of cooperative conversation. We've already noted in Chapter 1 that we can violate Grice's maxims and still be a cooperative conversationalist. For example, if it's clear to both of us that the music we are listening to is horrendous, and I say "What a lovely melody," Grice's maxim of quality (i.e., truthfulness) is violated, and the conversational inplicature is that the utterance is meant in irony. Thus, it is possible that the representative "I didn't see you" may have the pragmatic meaning of an apology, which comes from the conversational context (even though this is not obvious in the linguistic content of the utterance). And the representative "I lost my purse" might have the pragmatic meaning of a directive – a request for help in finding it or a request for a loan – even though this is not contained in the form of the utterance itself.

Of course, it is not always easy to determine whether meanings come from conversational or from conventional implicature. For example, if my boss says, "Mail this, please" and I reply, "I'm not your slave!" the reply shows that something has gone wrong. Perhaps the problem is one of entailment. Being a boss may not entail ordering employees around, or being an employee may not entail mailing things for the boss. There are also *felicity conditions* – conditions regarding when it is or is not appropriate to make such a request. The speaker must sincerely believe the addressee *can* do the action, is *willing* to do the action, and so forth. The presupposition is that these felicity conditions have been met or the request would not be made. These are shown in the syntactic signals of tag questions:

Mail this, *could/can't* you? (presupposes the felicity condition of ability has been met)

Mail this, *will/won't* you? (presupposes the felicity condition of willingness has been met)

Since entailment and presupposition are involved, we might, then, say that meaning here is derived from conventional implicature. However, these implications are also based on Goffman's (1976) ritual, or social, constraints for conversation. When we make a request, we assume that the request will be granted, that we will not be thought rude or pushy, and so forth. In this case, a conversational convention ("be polite") is being violated, and the meaning of "I'm not your slave" in the exchange relies on conversational implicature. Thus, it becomes difficult to assign meanings exclusively to one or the other type of implicature.

Practice 8.1 Pragmatics and syntax

1. Give an example where context and intonation show listeners that the speaker's intent is one of irony. Give an additional example for sarcasm.
2. Karttunen (1970) subdivided implicative verbs into presuppositions that hold in both affirmative and negative contexts ("full implicatives") and those that hold for either an affirmative or negative context but not both. For example, "Zeinab was able to study," does not absolutely

guarantee that she did, but "Zeinab was unable to study," guarantees that she did not. For each of the following, decide whether or not the implication holds for both the affirmative and the negative:

a. I discouraged Zeinab from studying.
b. I stopped Zeinab from studying.
c. I persuaded Zeinab to study.
d. I saw Zeinab studying.

3. What entailment holds in the following examples? What happens if you don't believe that "a" entails "b"?

He can't be a distance runner; he's too heavy.
She's a good teacher; she never returns our papers.
"You get what you pay for."

4. When a response to a question does not seem immediately relevant (as in the "Do you do buttonholes?"/"She'll be back in an hour" example from Chapter 1), we search for relevance at some deeper level of meaning. We assume that seemingly irrelevant responses must somehow be relevant – that is, cooperative conversationalists give relevant responses. When we can't find relevance, we are puzzled or think that we have misheard. Language learners often respond with answers that are topic relevant but not directly relevant to the question. The teenager Ricardo (see Hatch 1978) often gave such responses:

Q: Why are you going to the Chili Pepper.
A: (= who) Mr. L., Mrs. D, ten boys and girls.
Q: How long to go home?
A: (= how) In bus.
Q: When do you watch cartoons?
A: (= which) Aquaman.
Q: Are you sleepy?
A: (= where do you sleep) In mi house?

What arguments can you give for accepting such responses as if they were completely relevant? How might you show that they are partially relevant?

5. In the classroom data you collected for Chapter 1, look for examples of paraphrase. Are the examples all from the teacher, or did students also paraphrase? Did the teacher ever ask students to paraphrase information? What pedagogical purpose(s) might paraphrase serve?

6. Lakoff and Johnson (1980) have shown how very pervasive metaphor is even in ordinary everyday talk. It seems unlikely

that many of these metaphors actually cause us to call up two different concepts. For example, if I say I really stewed over some idea, it's unlikely that you will think about cooking (even if I say the idea was half-baked to begin with). If I tell you I turned the idea over and over in my mind, you are unlikely to think of the idea as some sort of an object that physically revolves. If the idea finally blossoms, you are not likely to think of a flower. If I shoot down your pet ideas, you may want to go to war but it's unlikely that you would do it to defend your goldfish. Conceptual everyday metaphor is such a basic process in language that it goes largely unnoticed. New examples, however, stand out. You can become "famous" if you create a new metaphor that can conventionally stand for a much larger idea. Think about the metaphor involved in the following terms and explain why they have become so widely used in studies of language learning: "scaffolding," "cooperative learning," "fossilization."

7. We can analyze sentences for their semantic and syntactic meaning, and we can analyze them according to their conventional uses in particular contexts. Ask your international students to tell you the conventional formulas for greeting and taking leave and then ask them to translate the expressions literally. How many are expressions of concern about health or about blessings from some higher being? Why do you suppose these particular expressions became conventional expressions of greeting and leave taking? Is presupposition, entailment, paraphrase, or metaphor involved? Do you believe that any of these cognitive comparisons are actually made by speakers of these languages? Would you use such processes in trying to build a model of how second language learners acquire these forms? Why or why not?

8. In your own words, summarize the differences between conventional and conversational implicature. How might each be important in language instruction?

Contextual analysis

In applied linguistics, Celce-Murcia (1980) has renewed interest in using context to understand how and when we select particular linguistic forms. She calls this method of discourse analysis *contextual analysis*. Teachers are often asked to explain why a particular grammatical form is used in a particular place. The explanation may be based on pragmatics, it may be based on differences between oral and written forms, it may have to do with formality, or it may be a syntactic requirement. Students, for example, often ask whether "when" and "if" can be used interchangeably ("When/if a million stars guide your way, you're in Kentucky, sure as you're born."). What difference does it make if we select "To water, run the soaker hose overnight" or "Run the soaker hose overnight to water"? When would you say "I like to run" rather than "I like running"? We can always consult reference books to see what linguists have discovered about such questions. Jespersen's *Essentials of English* (1964) is a traditional source. However, the information given in traditional references comes from scholarly observation and may not reflect that of real life use by present-day native speakers. (Better sources are Celce-Murcia and Larsen-Freeman's *The Grammar Book* 1983, M. Frank's *Modern English* 1972, and Leech and Svartvik's *A Communicative Grammar of English* 1975.) Although good reference manuals are an important resource, the information needs to be checked against real language use. This can be done using contextual analysis.

The first step in any contextual analysis is to find an interesting question to research. Many linguists, including Bolinger and Celce-Murcia, have been very interested in accounting for seemingly synonymous syntactic forms. For example, we might think of active versus passive voice as a choice between parallel forms. What in the context leads us to select one over the other? Another example of synonymous forms is that of optional adverbial clause placement. Is there any contextual explanation for the choice between:

Example 1
High on the bluff stood Sergeant Begay.
Sergeant Begay stood high on the bluff.

Example 2
There at the end of Box Canyon was the bullet-ridden jeep.
The bullet-ridden jeep was there at the end of Box Canyon.

The change in clause order shown in the first line of each example signals that something unexpected has happened. The switch causes us to change our focus to the second clause. Imagine, in example 1, that you had scanned the horizon with little hope left of finding anyone to help you. You would more likely choose the first alternative. Now imagine that you had located Prissie Lovejoy on a small mud flat and wondered where the Sergeant was. In this case, you would be more likely to select the second alternative. The new information, the information in focus in each situation, is in the second clause. (If you have studied syntax, this should agree with what you already know about topic-comment, old-new information, theme-rhyme.) To carry out a contextual analysis, the most typical method is to set up a questionnaire and present native speakers of the language with a forced choice as to which of two forms is best given the question context. If most native speakers select the first alternative when the context shows that the information regarding the *person* or the *car* is new or unexpected and select the second alternative when information on *place* is new, then the researcher has evidence in support of the claim.

The placement of adverbial clauses may be very much conditioned by what we hope to accomplish in the discourse. Recall Halliday and Hasan's distinction between anaphoric and cataphoric reference (see Chapter 6). In a sense, an adverbial clause in initial position serves as cataphoric framework for what is to come. When we need to prepare the listener or reader for what is about to be explained, we may select an initial adverbial clause, as shown in these examples from *The Garden Show* transcript (see Chapter 4):

when you're pruning, you want to prune above . . .
if you want to have a lot of roses with not quite as long stems, you can prune
  about eighteen, twenty-four inches.

Perhaps the relation between initial versus final clause placement and the principle of guiding the reader or listener are clearest when we are being taken on a tour:

As we top the crest, the desert fans out below us.
Entering the master suite, you will be pleased to find generous closet space.
From the patio you can watch the sun setting behind the mountain range.
As the sun sinks slowly into the west, we enter the charming village of
  Inyokern.

In all these examples, the initial clause builds a framework for what is to follow. We don't expect the information in this initial clause to be challenged. It is shared knowledge between the writer/speaker and reader/listener.

The claim about initial versus final adverbials rests on example data, linguistic conjecture, and on questionnaire data. Since questionnaires ask for preference judgments, Celce-Murcia believes they are suspect. She points out that it is important to check natural language texts to see whether generalizations drawn from questionnaires occur in real data. With the help of computers and the availability of large text corpora, this is no longer an impossibly tedious pursuit. It is a simple matter to search for certain types of items when you have a database and a computer to assist you. You may even be fortunate enough to have a concordance program (e.g., the Oxford Concordance Program or Wordcruncher) and a large database such as the Brown corpus ready to use. If you do not, all software programs have ways of searching and finding material for you from a data file. For example, when I did a cursory search of *if/whether*-clauses in this book, I found many more *if*-clauses than *whether*-clauses. Moreover, most of this *if*-clauses occurred before *then*-clauses. L. Ronkin (personal communication) suggested that *if*-

clauses will come first when sarcasm is being used and when the sentence is a tautology:

Sarcasm: If he's intelligent, then I'm Albert Einstein.
Tautology: If she says she's the leader, she's the leader.

Neither explanation holds for the *if*-clauses in this book; another account is needed. Ronkin noted that when a deduction is made on the basis of information in the *if*-clause, the *if*-clause usually appears first. The *if*-clause "guides" the listener or reader to what follows in the discourse.

If they went there last night, they saw what happened.
If you've already learned to use the computer, this should be easy for you.

This is a much better explanation for the position of *if*-clauses in this book. And there is more evidence for this hypothesis. Haiman (1978) claimed that conditionals ("if/then" constructions) are topics: They give the speaker's perspective and point of departure for the following message. Ford and Thompson (1986) decided to test this claim using a large written and oral database. The written database consisted of 854 pages from three texts: one argumentative, one procedural, and one narrative. The oral data, 56,460 words, included samples from conversations and lectures. More conditionals were found in oral (7.2 per 1000 words) than in written samples (4.6 per 1000 words). Initial *if*-clauses outnumbered final placement of *if*-clauses by three to one. The findings supported the "framework" or "topic" explanation. The authors then considered how initial *if*-clauses do this. They discussed four ways: (1) by repeating an assumption present earlier in the text; (2) by offering a contrast to an earlier assumption; (3) by providing exemplification of an earlier generalization; and (4) by exploring options made available by earlier procedural or logical steps. The findings for their oral data show these same four uses in addition to the use of initial *if*-clauses with polite directives. Thus, contextual analysis can validate and elaborate on claims initially based on insights from examples and linguistic analysis.

A second method, then, for carrying out a contextual analysis is to look for examples of particular structures within a discourse database. It can validate findings of the first method of creating minisituations that ask native speakers to decide which of seemingly synonymous structures they would prefer. Each of these methods has been widely used by Celce-Murcia and her students. Using questionnaires, they have shown that shifts in the formality of discourse register may cause a shift in choice between "if" and "whether" (e.g., "I wonder if you have time to help out" versus "I wonder whether you might be willing to assist the department in this matter"). Register formality also appears to influence native speakers' choices of either an apostrophe or an "of the" form to show possession (e.g., "Shakespeare's plays" versus "the plays of Shakespeare"), and between "there is" and "there are" (e.g., *"There's* lots of ways to do this"; *"there are* natural processes for getting sulphur out of water").

As already mentioned, modality is used to signal special meanings for speech acts. Celce-Murcia and her students have also linked the choice among the modals to formality. A quick computer search of this book showed the following frequencies for the modals "may," "will," "should," "must," "going to," "ought to," and "have to."

0 may (permission)	33 should
93 may (hedged probability)	3 ought to
40 will	20 going to
26 must	16 have to

According to findings of contextual analysis, the regular modals ("will," "should," and "must") are more formal than their "periphrastic" modal equivalents ("going to," "ought to," "have to"). If you believe this book is informal in tone, then you would expect to find fewer "will," "should," and "must" entries. If, on the other hand, you believe that all written prose is fairly formal, then there are too many periphrastic modals (especially "going to" and "have to"). However, a closer analysis shows that "will" appeared frequently in "Do I need a lawyer" (see Practice 1.4) and the section that describes ritual constraints (e.g., "will be greeted in return") (see Chapter 2). "Will" was also used for discourse deixis (e.g., "you will notice," "we will turn now to . . .") (Chapter 6). These portions of the text are, perhaps, somewhat more formal than other portions. The "going to" modals appeared in two different contexts – in created example sentences (e.g., "Sue is going to win the race") and in examples drawn from talk. Thus, depending on interpretation, this search further validates the notion of formality as accounting for selection of modal forms.

A contextual analysis can also illuminate differences due to oral versus written mode. Chafe (1982), for example, found that the adverb "just" is used in informal spoken data seven times more often than in formal written text. His informal spoken and formal written database consisted of approximately 10,000 oral and 12,000 written words. Hulquist (1985), looking at a broad spectrum of formal and informal oral and written discourse – approximately 100,000 words in each mode – found the occurrence of "just" to be four times greater in spoken data.

Language teachers and writers working on language teaching materials often need to know how native speakers use particular language structures. Certainly this has been a central concern in preparing materials for ESP (English for special or specific purposes) and EST (English for science and technology) courses. The answer is to be found in context within discourse data. If you have access to the Brown corpus or the Lund corpus, or if you have computer-stored language data, then the feasibility of contextual analysis will be greatly enhanced. As more and more researchers enter their students' data into computer files, it may be possible to ask these same questions about grammar and lexical usage of language learners as well as native speakers. You might want to inquire whether researchers at your institution have computer files for learner data as well as that of native speakers. Information on how students from various first language backgrounds or from various proficiency levels use a particular structure would also be extremely valuable for pedagogical purposes.

"Context" in contextual analysis is a very broad term. It could include all the areas of discourse mentioned in this book. Scripts call up context, speech events set context, rhetorical forms provide context, cohesion and coherence constrains choice of language forms and therefore also reflect context. So, in a sense, contextual analysis is another way of looking at discourse analysis. Before we close this section, let us consider how contextual analysis relates to other types of discourse analysis and how it might be linked to the other analyses we have discussed.

For example, contextual analysis might be linked with rhetorical analysis. It is important, as contextual analysts have noted, to be specific about what types of materials are being used in contextual analysis. A text search of written data might yield different results if two different genres – say, narrative and then descriptive text – are analyzed. Many studies take samples from several different genre categories in the Brown corpus to see whether there are similarities and differences in how particular forms are used. One might contrast science texts with novels or science texts with science fiction for a particular structure. However, if general claims are made, then a very broad range must be searched.

Contextual analysis has been linked to studies of mode (oral versus written text). Yet most of the text searches of oral language have been from monologues. It's important that conversational data be included too, because quite different functions for a form might be found in conversation and monologic texts. Ford (1988), for example, looked at how initial adverbial clauses might function in conversations to project the length of a turn. If you begin a turn with "When . . ." or "If . . ." the turn is not complete until the second clause has been delivered: the initial adverbial clause allows you to claim an extended utterance turn. Maynard (1989) noted that the Japanese conjunction "dakara" has a turn signal function in Japanese conversations in addition to its traditional "cause and result" grammar function. "Dakara" may be used to claim a turn (it signals that the speaker has something relevant to add to the prior discourse) or to end a turn (a turn-yield signal). Ford argues that contextual analysis be combined with conversational analysis to help us understand why speakers select certain forms when other options are available.

Contextual analysis can also be combined with speech act and speech event analyses. For example, Chang (1988) examined oral and written text for the use of "should" and its periphrastic forms "ought to" and "supposed to." Her findings on frequency of each form and the effect of mode on the various functional meanings of the modals were interesting. However, the data in which these modals occurred most frequently were those of advice giving and procedural text. Thus, her work could appropriately relate contextual analysis and both speech event and rhetorical analyses. The high frequency of "just" mentioned by Hulquist and Chafe for the oral mode may reflect its use as an evaluative device in spoken narratives. An analysis that looks at evaluative devices in narratives might, then, enhance a contextual analysis in much the same way as Hulquist's pilot study linked contextual analysis of "just" with speech event analysis in doctor-patient advice giving. Another example is Lee's (1990) contextual analysis of sentential adverbs (especially, "perhaps," "maybe," and "sometimes"). Again, the findings were of interest, especially the predicted high frequency of "maybe" in spoken data. The examples, however, show that the contextual analysis of "maybe" could be supplemented by a rhetorical structure analysis. Many of the examples given show a concessive relation (in rhetorical structure parlance) as much as a pragmatic meaning of possibility.

Example 1
Maybe these sound like old-fashioned ideas, *but* I'm not exactly a dried-up old prune . . .

Example 2
Female: Do you have one?
Male: No
Female: *Maybe* that's too personal. Ha, ha, ha.
Male: Yeah, let's stay away from personal stuff. Ha, ha, ha.

(Data source: Lee 1990)

In the first example, the speaker concedes that the ideas may sound old-fashioned and, in the second, the speaker takes back her question, conceding it would have been inappropriately personal.

A third type of extension of contextual analysis is illustrated in the work of Watabe et al. (1991). They followed a contextual analysis of passive constructions in both English and Japanese with an analysis of passives used by Japanese EFL and American JFL students in their compositions. Thus, three types of contexts were combined. The first two analyses showed that while many of the same functions for the passive can be found in the two languages, Japanese has an additional "adversity" or "affected" passive.

Mary wa sasimi o tabe-rare-ta.
Mary TOPIC raw fish DO eat-PASSIVE-Past
"Unfortunately for Mary, the raw fish was eaten."

The adversity passive shows that the subject of the sentence has been "adversely affected." They then turned to a third context – 40 compositions written by English speakers learning Japanese ("advanced" learners who had

271

lived in Japan for at least 18 months). They found examples of inappropriate use of passives, such as the following:

Nikkoo mo onazi zidai ni deki-masi-ta. Tokugawa Ieyasu ni tate-rare-masi-ta.
The Nikko shrine came to be (was built) at the same time. It was built by Tokugawa Ieyasu.

Watasi wa otoosan no kuruma o tukat-tei-ta toki aru otoko ga watasi ni untens-are-tei-ta otoosan no kuruma ni butukat-ta.
When I was using Dad's car, a man ran into his car which was driven by me.

1492 nen Korombusu ni hakkens-are-te kara samazamana kuni no hito-tati ga Amerika tairiku ni watatte ki-masi-ta.
After it was discovered by Columbus in 1492, people from various countries came over to the American continent.

Although the translations look acceptable in each case, the passive in Japanese causes them to take on the adversity affectedness meaning. So, the meanings are "Unfortunately for the Nikko shrine, it was built by Tokugawa Ieyasu"; "When I was using Dad's car, a man ran into his car which, unfortunately for it, was driven by me"; and "After it was unfortunate enough to be discovered by Columbus in 1492, people from various countries came over to the American continent." Also found were examples where an adversity condition was being expressed, yet the learners inappropriately used an active verb. Watabe et al. also examined 80 compositions written by Japanese ESL students and found examples in which Japanese ESL learners tried to use passives in English to show the affectedness function.

Contextual analysis methods can be layered with other types of discourse analysis to reveal the many ways that context influences our choice of syntactic forms.

Practice 8.2   Contextual analysis

1. Review the classroom data you collected for Chapter 1. Are there instances where the students request an explanation or where the teacher offers an explanation regarding "when" a particular structure is used? If so, check the explanation against that offered by Jespersen (1964) and by Celce-Murcia and Larsen-Freeman (1983). Then plan a research project to confirm or discomfirm these explanations. List texts you would analyze or types of questionnaire items you would prepare for the study. How extensive a database or how many items would you want in the questionnaire?

2. Hulquist (1985) did a contextual analysis of an oral database of callers to a medical advice radio program. She found that

the doctor used many more "just" adverbs in his advice to women than to men:

To woman caller: It's <u>just</u> early . . . I would <u>just</u> give it another couple of years.

Even though male callers used "just" in their speech (e.g., "It's *just* terrible, *just* terrible"), this doctor did not use "just" in his replies. Hulquist does not claim that the doctor necessarily responded to male and female callers with different styles. What she suggests is that perhaps the seriousness of the ailment triggered more abrupt, direct advice to males. For example, heat rash was one problem presented by a male. It is possible that the doctor felt this was a problem an adult male should have learned how to deal with and therefore was not so sympathetic or indirect in giving advice (i.e., the use of "just" adverbs was included as a feature of sympathetic involvement). It has also been suggested that "just" marks a contrast with the expectation of "more" or "something else too" and so may seem to belittle what does occur. If you have an oral database, do a contextual analysis to see how you might account for the use of "just."

3. Here is a piece of data in which a daughter (D) asks her mother's (M) advice on what to do about her roommate. Notice the use of "just" and "really."

D: You want me to <u>just</u> say, "YOU clean it"?
M: Yeah! If they say "No," <u>just</u> say "Why?"
D: You can't-it's not like somebody you <u>really</u> know. You can't <u>just</u> say-you can't say "YOU do this and you do that."
M: Go ahead and <u>just</u> ask them.
D: Well, they're not <u>really</u> dirty+ + +but they're not <u>really</u> clean. It's not like with someone you <u>really</u> know.

(Data source: Hamada 1985)

A few more examples from my computer database include:
a. . . . I <u>really</u> have a lot of respect for those French. [oral]
b. . . . I met this <u>real</u> creep. [oral]
c. I <u>really</u> like the way the writer 'quated his thoughts in with the government to let this great plan <u>really</u> effective [EFL oral]
d. It was a <u>really</u> exciting experience . . . [oral]
e. I <u>really</u> like it; it's beautiful [oral]
f. Do you <u>really</u> eat turkey for Thanksgiving? [oral]

The examples of "really" are almost exclusively from oral examples in this database; this is not the case with "just." If you have access to a database, locate all the examples of "really" and compare it to the findings for "just." Do you see any evidence that these expressions have an evaluative function (i.e., work to involve the participants in the material or point out parts of the discourse to which the listener or reader should pay particular attention – the "listen up; this is important!" function)?

4. Formality and the oral versus written continuum may not completely account for the use of structures. Consider the following sentences:

Karl sat at the computer, working on his thesis.
*Karl sat around at the computer, working on his thesis.

The first sentence seems preferable, and so the second is marked with an asterisk to show that it is less acceptable. Can you think of an explanation for this choice that would also account for the following hypothetical data?

What did you do yesterday?
  I hung around the university.
  Nothing. I just walked around.
  I stuck around campus waiting for Cece.

If your analysis of "around" works for these sentences, can you extend it to sentences with "push around," "boss around," or "order around," – expressions that show a power differential? Fillmore's explanation (Fillmore et al. 1983) is that being at a place (hanging around, sitting around) keeps the person from doing something else. What is your hypothesis?

5. In the last chapter, we talked about various cohesion markers used to promote coherence in writing. Jisa and Scarcella (1982) give examples of some substitutions used by adult ESL students for these markers:

To shorten: (= in brief?) "they become to be similar to Western people"
In my thought: (= in my opinion? to my way of thinking?) "this is the most imperative thing in our economic history"

If you have access to a database, call up all instances of these three connectors ("in brief," "in my opinion," "to my way of thinking"). How frequent are they in the database? Are they always in initial position? Look for such connectors in the compositions of your students. Do you have or know of teaching materials that present these particular expressions? Give an explanation of when and why they are used based on your intuition and on the database.

6. Merritt (1980) discussed the ways in which "OK" is used in service-encounter scripts. I have already noted that "OK" is used for special functions in classroom discourse. Using the data collected by members of your study group for Chapter 1, perform a contextual analysis of "OK" and compare the results to those of Merritt for service encounters. What other contexts might you include if you wished to do a larger scale study of the use of "OK"?

7. Astington and Olson (1990) asked eighth-to-twelfth-grade students and adults to read 12 stories where characters *said* or *thought* something. The task was to replace the general words "say" and "think" with more appropriate words – for example, "assert," "concede," "imply," "confirm" for "say" and "remember," "doubt," "hypothesize," "assume" for "think." How might you carry out a research project using contextual analysis to see whether native speakers use these words in academic contexts?

Prosody and context

When we listen to speakers, we obtain much more information than what is actually given in the words uttered. We get information on personal variables such as age, gender, and perhaps temperament and character; sociolinguistic information such as where speakers are from, their social membership, their status, or the formality they think situations have. Much of this information comes from *prosody,* the suprasegmental system made up of intonation, stress, rhythm, and pitch. At the discourse level, this system also gives us information on the speaker's emotions, feelings, moods, convictions, sincerity, and so on. The suprasegmental system may also give message-bound meanings – for example "oops" as meaning an accident has happened. In each of the previous chapters, we have seen that intonation, stress, pitch, and rate play a role in discourse analysis.

Chapter 1 noted that falling intonation and slowing of rate may signal the end of a speaking turn. Pauses and rising intonation may elicit collaborative completion of turns or completion of a turn by others in a conversation. To help learners understand our talk, we may use slower rate, heavy stress on content words, a rising "checking" intonation to be sure our message is understood, and so forth. We signal brackets by intonation, by pauses, and by nonverbal means. Preempt signals include nonverbal signals and special breathy or exclamatory intonation. In Chapter 2, we talked about the social constraints on the communication system. Again, prosodic features were shown to play an important role in smoothing social interactions. False starts, repairs, and other seeming disfluencies may be used to portray "self" with appropriate demeanor or to give others face through proper deference.

In the discussion on scripts (Chapter 3), we noted that intonation is used by teachers to frame the end and beginning of activities and topics. That is, a slowing of rate and falling intonation marks the end of an exchange, and a switch to rapid rate and louder speech marks the beginning of the next one. Intonation may also help learners decide how to process the meanings of words (as in the "rip you off" example). We also talked about the special intonation teachers use when directing class activities, in switching topics, and in evaluating student responses.

The meaning of speech acts (Chapter 4), too, is linked to intonation. Intonation tells us about the pragmatic meaning of an utterance. We've already mentioned that sarcasm and irony are signaled not by the words of the utterance but by the special intonation used in saying the words. To use Crystal's (1969) example, the utterance "This is the third time he's been to see me this week" may be a complaint, an announcement, a doubt, a suspicion, and so on. The pragmatic meaning comes from the intonation used with the utterance.

As language teachers, we might wonder whether these suprasegmental meanings are recognized by second language learners – are they universal? Language learners may feel fairly certain that they recognize question intonation and intonation that marks surprise or pleasure. But how do they feel about other intonation patterns? Gumperz (1977) and others have suggested that we need to look at the connection between intonation and discourse meaning. If second language learners do not acquire the appropriate intonation for functions, there can be serious social consequences:

The . . . incident . . . took place in London on a bus driven by a West Indian driver/ conductor. The bus was standing at a stop and passengers were filing in. The driver announced periodically, "Exact change, please," as London bus drivers often do. When passengers who had been standing close by either did not have money ready or tried to give him a large bill, the driver repeated, "Exact change, please." The second time around, he said "please" with extra loudness, high pitch, and falling intonation, and he seemed to pause before "please." One passenger so addressed, as well as several following him, walked down the bus aisle exchanging angry looks and obviously annoyed, muttering, "Why do these people have to be so rude and threatening about it?" (1977: 199)

The bus driver, as it turned out, wasn't really annoyed nor did he intend to be rude. The intonation was, according to British English rules, interpreted as excessively direct and rude.

Another example from Gumperz shows how important the connection between prosody and pragmatic meaning is:

In a staff cafeteria . . . newly hired Indian and Pakistani women were perceived as surly and uncooperative by their supervisors as well as by the cargo handlers whom they served. Observations revealed that while relatively few words were exchanged, the intonation and manner in which these words were pronounced were interpreted negatively. For example, a person who had chosen meat would have to be asked whether he wanted gravy. A British attendant would ask by saying "Gravy?" with rising intonation. The Indian women, on the other hand, would say the word using falling intonation: "Gravy." . . . The falling intonation means "This is gravy" and is not interpreted as an offer but rather as an announcement. (1977: 208)

For the women, falling intonation was the normal way of asking questions to make an offer, and no rudeness or indifference had been intended. Happily, following practice and change in intonation, improvement was also found in the attitudes of the clients toward the workers, and the women no longer felt they were being discriminated against (a natural reaction to the behavior their "rudeness" provoked).

In speech events, special intonation is used for pragmatic function. Observing a two-year-old named Beth, Miller (1982 a, b) traces the development of the ability to respond to and initiate teasing sequences – sequences that require special intonation to mark the teasing quality. These include emphatic stress, rapid delivery rate, and singsong intonation. At 25 months, Beth displayed none of these except rate. Once she began to use singsong intonation in teasing sequences, she overextended it to other contexts. She used this intonation with formulaic teasing utterances (e.g., "yeayeayea"). Less frequently, she used this intonation for defiance or as she seized possession of some object. At 28 months, Beth narrowed down the contexts in which she used this intonation. In the final months of her second year, Beth used dispute tactics with her mother, including emphatic stress and rapid delivery, appropriate voice quality (giggles and laughter to show the play quality of teasing), seized possession of disputed objects, and made fighting gestures.

Chapter 5 on rhetorical organization showed how special intonation, pitch, and stress are used as evaluative devices. They are used to involve the audience in our personal stories. Prosody is an important part of oral argument, whether it is a debate or personal argument. Hortatory text – religious, moral, and political urgings – requires great skill in control of prosodic features.

Among the many cohesive devices discussed in Chapter 6 is rhythm. The rhythm of repeated parallel structures, the touching off of similar sounding phrases with the same stress patterns give an added cohesion to coherent text. For example, Sacks (1971) showed that context influences the choice of the phonological variants of "because," "cause," or "cuz." The choice, he found, was sound coordinated with sounds of other words in its environment. For example, speaking of a fish he was eating, a speaker said; "cause it comes from cold water." Sacks' explanation of the selection "cause" is related to the initial /k/ sounds of "come" and "cold" in the rest of the utterance. A moment later, the same speaker said, "You better eat something because you're gonna be hungry before we get there." Sacks attributes this choice of "because" to a phonological match with that of "be hungry" and "before." Notice that the choices also maintain the rhythmic pattern of the utterance. Rhythm is a powerful force on spoken language and on written language as well. Poetry, of course, relies heavily on the prosodic system of the language.

In contextual analysis (Chapter 7), it is also clear that prosody interacts with message content to determine meaning. For example, stressed information is usually the "new" or "comment" part of a message. In English, the stress pattern follows the discourse organization of sentences: New information is located at the ends of sentences, and the highest pitch and stress point is located near the end of the utterance – usually on the last content word. Old information receives little stress and occurs first in the utterance. The "given→new" order matches the intonation pattern. The contextual analysis studies of changes in clause order, or the position of the indirect object (She gave HIM the book" and "She gave the book to HIM" versus "She gave 'im the book" and "She gave the book to 'im") show how stress, pronoun reference, and the given→new order interact.

In most respects, the place of prosody and its relation to discourse has been largely ignored in second language acquisition and teaching. In the literature on first language acquisition, however, the development of intonation and of prosody for discourse functions has been an important issue. Studies suggest that young children acquire the intonation patterns of their first language relatively early. It has been difficult, as Crystal (1979) noted, to work out procedures that allow us to reliably test when infants first begin to use prosodic features for discourse functions. However, a number of researchers have attempted to test this. The general consensus (see studies in the Research and Application section) is that children gradually develop a powerful knowledge about the use of the system during the two-to-three-year-old stage.

While lip service has always been paid to the importance of the suprasegmental system in language acquisition and instruction, the volume of studies that relate phonology and discourse, at least on the American continents, is still fairly scant. Yet, anyone who works with language learners knows how important discourse phonology is in cross-cultural communication. Gumperz's (1977) examples show that this is indeed the case. For further examples, see Gumperz et al. (1975) on crosstalk. All of us can add our own examples. One of mine is that of a Chinese student from Singapore who enrolled in one of my classes. At the beginning of the semester, he seldom talked in class. During a conference, I was bewildered by his apparent anger at me. I asked him why he was so angry, and he replied that he wasn't. I was puzzled. In class, as he began to talk more, I noticed that he invariably got into confrontations with his fellow students. I listened carefully, trying to understand this. It wasn't really *what* he said but the *way* he said things that brought a defensive reaction from other students in the class. He spoke in a very staccato style, using syllable timing with large pitch fluctuations between syllables. The highest pitch points (and, in general, his pitch was much higher than that of a native speaker of English) were at the beginnings of utterances. Remember that the highest pitch and stress point in English is located near the end – not the beginning – of utterances. And, with the staccato timing, all words seemed to be given equally high importance. That is, even "known" information at the beginning of the utterances received stress. This made him sound arrogant, as though others in the class didn't know this information or that each of his words were important and should receive attention. He sounded angry and accusatory given the high pitch overall and gradual fall of the intonation curve. He used non-English fillers and backchannel signals and an inbreath /h/, which made him seem impatient.

At out next conference, I asked this student how he was adjusting to life on campus. He said he did not understand Americans; that they weren't friendly and, if they talked to him, they always seemed to get angry. Needless to say, he was very upset that he had not made friends even though he and his family lived in student housing surrounded by other student families. I wish that I could say that a study of his discourse phonology solved the problem. He did sign up for an elective phonology class, but most of the work in the class was geared toward segmental phonology. Over the two years he spent in our program, he gradually improved – his overall pitch lowered and sentence initial high pitch and stress changed, but the move away from staccato delivery and toward final sentence stress did not change. He gradually acquired a few friends but spent most of his time studying in the library and learning computer skills.

Given this experience, Pennington's (1990) paper on building a system for communication in a second language proved extremely interesting. She described the many differences in Japanese and English. In Japanese, phrase accent is initial rather than final. Japanese students beginning English often start their English utterances with high pitch, transferring the L1 pattern. Timing in Japanese is also syllabic so that parts of their English utterances receive stress-timing regardless of their informativeness. This, combined with non-English fillers (e.g., "ano," "etto," "ee," and inbreath /h/) and differences in segmental patterns, sounds similar in some respects to the patterns used by my Singapore student. In my student's case, rapid pitch fluctuations added to the general staccato delivery. Pennington talked about the connection between phonology and other aspects of discourse development as a set of interlocking systems such that "L2 phonology and discourse must be investigated as an integrated whole."

Practice 8.3 Prosody and discourse

1. Much of the work on suprasegmentals and pragmatic meaning relates to individual utterances. Show how stress, juncture, and intonation could change the meaning of the following sentences.
   a. What did she find out there?
   b. They arrived late today.
   c. I couldn't recommend him too highly.
   d. We prefer dancing to music.

2. Labov and Fanshel (1977) noted that the meanings of utterances are seldom clear or unambiguous and that this is an advantage. "Speakers need a form of communication which is *deniable.*" This allows us to express hostility, affection, friendliness, and so forth in a way that we can always deny. If our message is not well received, we can always say we didn't mean it the way it sounded. Say the sentence "I'd like to talk to you" in as many different ways as you can. What meaning is conveyed by each? Which do you think would be deniable, and which are so obvious that you might have difficulty denying the meaning?

3. Second language learners are sometimes puzzled by the reactions of native speakers to what they have said. The form and the content seem normal and correct. The intonation, however, may have been at fault. Document an instance from your own language learning. Compile these in your class or study group. What common threads do you see running through the examples?

4. Holmes (1990) noted that we can't perform contextual analysis by simply adding up the number of occurrences of a structure across many text types. Not only may text type be an important variable that relates to frequency of a form, but a form may also have many different meanings, some of which are signaled by changes in stress and intonation. In her work on differences in use of forms by men and women in different culture groups, Holmes noted that intonation often marks differences in meaning. For example, "I think" is said to be a mitigating or weakening signal often used by women. However, "I think" can be either tentative or deliberative depending on intonation. "You know" (another hedge claimed to be prevalent in women's speech) can be either a hedge or an intensifier or booster. "Of course" is always a booster of the affective quality of the utterance,

but it can be used as marking consensual truths and shared knowledge when used with falling intonation. It can also be used as a confidential function with the meaning of "as you know on the basis of information or attitudes that we share." Holmes also found that "sort of," which is claimed to occur with high frequency in spoken (but not in written) text, actually occurs in narratives or sustained accounts that are meant to amuse and amaze but not in argumentation or in phatic talk. It also occurs more often in picture descriptions than in relaxed conversation. Thus, text genre and intonation need to be considered in such studies. Use Holmes's comments on intonation to determine the intonation curve for each of the following utterances.

I think I have everything well under control. (said by a
    veteran teacher; said by a worried, novice teacher)
I expect you to appear at nine o'clock sharp, *you know.*
    (said by a judge to a negligent clerk)
He's *you know* always late. (said to your best friend about
    another friend)
The software can be used for other purposes, *of course.*
He's too conceited *of course* to ever let on.
And it was getting *sort of* dark, like *kind of* dark and foggy.
The picture is *sort of* depressing; it's so dark and dreary.

Research and application

A. Pragmatics of speech acts

1. Brown (1980) questions the notion that only representative speech acts can have ironic meanings. He gives examples of expressives ("Congratulations on the IRS audit") and directives ("Give me another hit of that fantastic wine," where no such request is intended and the quality of the wine is in doubt) with ironic meanings. If you have access to data where ironic utterances are used, check the type of speech act and determine if it is an illocutionary act with a "felicity condition."

2. Rintell (1983) looked at the expression of emotion as a pragmatic function and at the sociolinguistic constraints that affect it. She also reported a study of second language learners' ability to use contextual and intonational cues to identify speaker emotion. Among her many findings, Rintell noted that positive emotions such as pleasure were easier for learners to identify. She raised the interesting question of whether this is because positive

emotions are usually attached to grammatically less complex sentences than negative emotions (a claim attributed to Collier who is cited in the article), or whether it is due to the difficulty of recognizing different types of negative emotional content. Read Rintell's article and prepare a preliminary research plan to investigate this question further.

B. Contextual analysis

3. Levy (1990) discusses ways learners might use on-line computer programs as an exploratory device when they want to know more about how and when particular structures or vocabulary items are used. He discusses the use of corpora that vary in size from large (e.g., the Brown corpus, the Lancaster-Oslo-Bergen corpus, the Australian corpus project) to small databases (Sinclair's TEFL corpus, Inman's English for business corpus, the Melbourne-Surrey corpus). When concordance programs are integrated with dictionary, thesaurus, and style checkers, the resources, Levy says, become a powerful resource for learners as well as teachers and textbook writers. If you are interested in the use of such databases, read Levy's article, and see Sinclair (1987), for a description of the TEFL corpus and its uses and the COBUILD English course. Develop an outline for a materials project that would allow your students to use such resources.

4. Fox and Thompson (1990) looked at relative clauses used within conversations. The use of relative constructions related to information flow, including information status, grounding, definiteness, and the function of the relative clause. That is, the researchers began with a syntactic structure of interest (i.e., relative clauses) and then described which forms of the structure are used and for what function or purpose within conversations. If you have access to a spoken language database, pull all samples of relative clauses and check to see whether the choices in the database coincide with those found for conversational data. If there is agreement in some instances and not in others, can this be accounted for by the negotiated or cooperative nature of conversation building versus that of less interactive talk?

5. Greene (1980) used three methods to determine the uses of "which": She did a contextual analysis of Shuy's Detroit dialect study tapes, logged sentences she heard, and used example

sentences. Her analyses showed five conceptual relations between "which" and its antecedent: (a) relation of result of an action to the action that brings it about (e.g., "Those are my initials there in the top righthand corner which is about all I do in this damned place."; "I like to wear socks because they soak up sweat which happens inside these boots."); (b) relation of one or more parts of a thing to the whole (e.g., "My idea at that time was that I would go to the University of Michigan for two years and then become a service representative for the telephone company which was what their requirement was at that time."; "I would never give anyone a canary or a parakeet for a wedding present which is what happened to me."); (c) relation of doers to what is characteristically done (e.g., "Fred gave up his academic career in order to write which is what he always wanted to be."; "Most teachers, which is an underpaid profession, don't belong to unions."); (d) the notion of using something (e.g., "His grandmother bought him a finger painting set which shot the laundry bill way up."; "Hula hoops, which I was pretty good at when I was a kid, are now made out of cheap plastic."); (e) relation where the inference includes the antecedent with some sort of comment on the saying of it (e.g., "Well, diet schmiet, which means I'd like you to start acting like a human being again."; "You know the old saying about sleeping dogs, which is my advice to you right now."). Study the classifications given in Greene's article and then do a contextual analysis of "which" in the classroom data you and your classmates or study group collected. How do teachers and students use "which" in classroom discourse (if they do)? Review the one-clause-at-a-time examples (Pawley and Syder) from spoken discourse, presented in Chapter 7. How would you account for the apparent contradiction between that claim and the extremely complex uses of which-clauses in Greene's data?

6. Schmerling (1978) gives examples of sentences with "prefer," "expect," "allow" of the sort "I allowed the doctor to examine John" versus "I allowed John to be examined by the doctor." Most people would agree that these two sentences are not synonymous. Schmerling concludes that synonymy judgments may not be a reliable research method. Review this article. Do you feel that questionnaire research might be more reliable than synonymy judgments? Why or why not? Could you use text searches to examine "prefer," "expect," and "allow" utterances? If so, what type of corpus would you need? Would the corpus allow you to avoid the problem raised by Holmes (Practice 8.3.4)?

7. Lakoff (1973) compared the acceptability of "well" and "why" in questions and answers:

   (Well/Why) who is going to take out the garbage?
   Who is buried in Grant's tomb? (Well/Why) General Grant.

   Read Lakoff's article and then perform a contextual analysis to see whether the explanations given for the constructed examples work with real data.

8. Byrnes and Gelman (1990) found that third-, fourth-, and fifth-grade children associate "if" with unexpected content and "when" with ordinary content. For example, they might say "This is a teeter-totter. *When* I put a weight here (near the fulcrum), nothing happens."; "This is a sound box. *When* I pull this lever, it makes a noise. *If* I pull this lever, nothings happens." The *if*-clauses plus unexpected content were often followed by an explanatory *because* statement. Read Byrnes and Gelman's article and then perform a contextual analysis to see whether their finding can be applied to whatever written data you have on file. Or, construct an *if/when* questionnaire where expected versus unexpected content follows. Administer the questionnaire to international students and to a native speaker control group. Do the findings agree with those of Byrnes and Gelman?

9. Side (1990) summarized information from grammar reference books and teaching materials to arrive at suggestions for teaching phrasal verbs. Compare the findings of Side's article with the contextual analyses that have been done on phrasal verbs mentioned in Celce-Murcia and Larsen-Freeman's *The Grammar Book*. List the phrasal verbs included in your teaching text and decide whether these particular verbs fit in well with the statements given in these sources. How might you carry out a contextual analysis that would give you valid information on the use of these particular verbs?

10. Mitchell (1990) contradicts Jespersen's claim that the comparative "as . . . as . . ." expresses a notion of equality. Read Mitchell's article and review Jespersen's (1964) and Celce-Murcia and Larsen-Freeman's (1983) descriptions of the comparative. Then do a contextual analysis to see whether your findings support Mitchell's claims regarding comparatives, expecially the "as . . . as . . ." comparative.

11. Fillmore et al. (1983) suggested that lexical phrases such as "let alone" can be understood only by hypothesizing a context where comparative likelihood is taken into account.

Vanessa read Chapter 8 again.
   She wasn't satisfied let alone delighted.
   She wasn't happy let alone ecstatic.
Context: My boss was coming to dinner and I wondered if I
   should prepare a Chinese specialty that I love. My husband
   said, "Are you kidding! He won't eat shrimp let alone sea
   cucumber."

Prepare a research plan for a contextual analysis of "let alone,"
"much less," "barely," and "not to mention." In addition to a
contextual analysis, you might include in your plan a way to test
whether ESL/EFL students can distinguish contexts where these
choices are appropriate.

12. Another example from Fillmore et al. is the use of "that"-
quantifier expressions:

Context: At dinner, Sue refused to eat my tuna casserole.
I say: "I thought you were hungry."
She says: "I'm starving but I'm not that hungry."

Context: Sam asked a cheerleader for a date.
She said: "I'm not that desperate."

Prepare a research plan for a contextual analysis of the "that"-
quantifier structure. The analysis should be broad enough to
include examples such as "that much of a problem," "that big a
difference," "that forgetful." Include a description of this structure
from your grammar reference books. Be sure to justify your
selection of discourse texts for the analysis.

13. Hughes (1990) gives a brief review of the history of the term
"register" and a general definition: "Certain levels of usage are
considered appropriate to particular topics or social situations."
The examples given in the article are primarily lexical. In this
chapter, though, register is claimed to have an effect on syntactic
choices. Hughes's article includes a diagram from the preface of
the *Oxford English Dictionary,* a diagram that relates lexical
choice to register (see Figure 8.1). Read Hughes's article and
compare the classification with that given in Joos's classic work
(1967) on register. Notice that of Joos's five registers, the
oratorical-frozen and deliberative-formal registers seem to
appear mainly in monologues while the consultative, casual, and
intimate registers seem to relate to dialogue or multiparty talk.
Attempt to find a definition of "register" that pleases you, is useful
in terms of contextual analysis, and which is not circular in
nature (i.e., we use structure X in formal register : the register is

Scientific   Foreign

    LITERARY

    COMMON

Technical   Dialectal

    COLLOQUIAL

      Slang

Figure 8.1 Reproduced from the *Oxford English Dictionary* by permission of Oxford University Press.

formal because it contains structure X). Demonstrate the usefulness of your definition for contextual analysis.

C. Phonology in context

14. Dowd et al. (1990) reviewed the research linking pronunciation and social marking and wrote an excellent article on ethnic identity in L2 pronunciation, the effect of listener on the L2 learner's pronunciation, Giles' accommodation theory, and even the effect of emotional questions on the phonology of L2 learners. Use this article as a foundation for a research proposal investigating the connection between phonological variation and discourse context.

15. Egan (1980) asked native speakers of English to listen to the utterance "On Sunday" with 17 different intonation curves and judge the intonation as appropriate for the expression of particular meanings. Read Egan's article and decide whether this would form a good test of pragmatic meaning via intonation for language learners. If you think it would be interesting to replicate Egan's study with language learners, prepare a preliminary research plan. If you think it would not work as a test of intonation and pragmatics, justify your decision.

16. Menn and Boyce (1982) found that children age 2 to 5 differentially use peak frequency at points in their discourse where new topics are introduced. Furrow (1984) found that two-year-olds use a greater pitch range and greater intensity during periods when they maintain eye contact with their communication partners. The two methods (prosody and eye contact) work together to show which parts of the communication are most important for the child. Marcos (1987) examined the use

of pitch in young French children between the age of 1 and 2. The findings showed that higher pitch as well as rising intonation were used when the child made requests. Finally, Furrow et al. (1990) used very complex procedures to look at clusters of prosodic features used by young children for two speech acts: directives and representatives. The procedure included offering the child an object contained within a plastic purse that was difficult to open. The child would try to open the container to get the object and, on failing, would issue a directive to the adult (asking him or her to open it). In the representative task, the child was presented with a toy, such as a block, to put into a pail. The experimenter would say "Here's a block to put in the pail." Then a second block would be offered as the experimenter said, "Here's another block to put in the pail." On the third trial, the experimenter would present a doll rather than a block to the child, naming it again as a block. The child would challenge this with a representative about the block. A very complex analysis of the child's use of prosody (beginning, end, peak, frequency range, contour, etc.) showed that children's prosody patterns differed according to discourse function. Review these articles and those on the acquisition of prosody by L2 learners. Prepare a preliminary research plan to look at the acquisition of suprasegmentals by young L2 learners.

17. Shen (1990) contrasted the prosody patterns for questions in French with tonal patterns for questions in Chinese. Statements versus questions in French are accompanied by falling versus rising final intonation. In Chinese, the contrast is between lower versus higher pitch at the beginnings of utterances. Higher pitch is used to mark questions in both languages, but there is a difference between high final for French and high initial for Chinese. Shen's description reinforces those given by Pennington (1990) for Japanese speakers. Read Shen's and Pennington's articles and attempt to draw parallels and differences. How might the language typology distinction of topic-comment languages such as Chinese versus subject-prominent languages such as French and English be related to predictions about phonological patterns in discourse?

References

Astington, J., and Olson, D. (1990). Metacognitive and metalinguistic language: Learning to talk about thought. *Applied Psychology: An International Review*, *39*, 1: 77–87.

Brown, R. (1980). The pragmatics of verbal irony. In R. Shuy and A. Shnukal (Eds.), *Language use and the uses of language* (pp. 111–127). Washington, D.C.: Georgetown University Press.

Byrnes, J. P., and Gelman, S. A. (1990). Conceptual and linguistic factors in children's memory for causal expressions. *International Journal of Behavioral Development, 13,* 1: 95–117.

Celce-Murcia, M. (1980). Contextual analysis and its application to teaching English as a second language. In D. Larsen-Freemen (Ed.), *Discourse analysis and second language research* (pp. 41–55). Rowley, Mass.: Newbury House.

Celce-Murcia, M., and Larsen-Freeman, D. (1983). *The grammar book: An ESL/EFL teacher's course.* Rowley, Mass.: Newbury House.

Chafe, W. (1982). Integration and involvement in speaking, writing, and oral literature. In D. Tannen (Ed.), *Spoken and written language: Exploring orality and literacy* (pp. 35–53). Norwood, N.J.: Ablex.

Chang, L. (1988). *SHOULD and its periphrastic forms in American English usage.* Master's thesis, Applied Linguistics, University of California, Los Angeles.

Crystal, D. (1969). *Prosodic system and intonation in English.* London: Cambridge University Press.

(1979). Prosodic development. In P. Fletcher and M. Garman (Eds.), *Language acquisition.* Cambridge: Cambridge University Press.

Dowd, J.; Zuengler, J.; and Berkowitz, D. (1990). L2 social marking: Research issues. *Applied Linguistics, 11,* 1: 16–29.

Egan, R. (1980). Intonation and meaning. *Journal of Psycholinguistic Research, 9,* 1: 23–39.

Fillmore, C.; Kay, P.; and O'Connor, M. (1983). Regularity and idiomaticity in grammatical constructions: The case of *let alone.* Paper presented at Center for the Study of Language and Information, Stanford University, Palo Alto, California.

Ford, C. (1988). Grammar in ordinary interaction: The pragmatics of adverbial clauses in conversational English. Ph.D. dissertation, Applied Linguistics, University of California, Los Angeles.

Ford, C., and Thompson, S. (1986). Conditionals in discourse: A text-based study from English. In E. Traugott, A. ter Meulen, J. Reilly, and C. Ferguson (Eds.), *On conditionals.* Cambridge: Cambridge University Press.

Fox, B., and Thompson, S. (1990). Relative clauses in English conversations. *Language, 66,* 2: 297–316.

Frank, M. (1972). *Modern English.* Englewood Cliffs, N.J.: Prentice-Hall.

Furrow, D. (1984). Young children's use of prosody. *Journal of Child Language, 11,* 203–213.

Furrow, D.; Podrouzek, W.; and Moore, C. (1990). Children's use of prosody. *First Language, 10,* 37–49.

Goffman, E. (1976). Replies and responses. *Language in Society, 5,* 3: 254–313.

Greene, J. (1980). Which. In R. Shuy and A. Schnukal (Eds.), *Language use and the uses of language* (pp. 143–161). Washington, D.C.: Georgetown University Press.

Grice, H. P. (1957). Meaning. *Philosophical Review, 66,* 377–388.

(1975). Logic and conversation. In P. Cole and J. N. Morgan (Eds.), *Syntax and semantics. Vol. 3: Speech acts* (pp. 41–58). New York: Academic Press.

Gumperz, J. (1977). Sociocultural knowledge in conversational inference. In M.

Saville-Troike (Ed.), *Linguistics and anthropology* (pp. 191–211). Washington, D.C.: Georgetown University Press.

Gumperz, J.; Jupp, T.; and Roberts, C. (1979). *Crosstalk*. London: Centre for Industrial Language Teaching.

Haiman, J. (1978). Conditionals are topics. *Language 54*, 564–589.

Hamada, R. (1985). Code-switching: A case study of two Japanese-English bilinguals. Master's thesis, Applied Linguistics, University of California, Los Angeles.

Hatch, E. (1978) Discourse analysis and second language acquisition. In E. Hatch (Ed.), *Second language acquisition: A book of readings* (pp. 401–435). Rowley, Mass.: Newbury House.

Holmes, J. (1990). Hedges and boosters in women's and men's speech. *Language and Communication, 10*, 3: 185–205.

Hughes, G. (1990). What is register? *English Today: The internation review of the English language, 6*, 2: 47–51.

Hulquist, M. (1985). The adverb *just* in American English usage. Master's thesis, Applied Linguistics, University of California, Los Angeles.

Jespersen, O. (1964). *Essentials of English grammar*. Tuscaloosa: University of Alabama Press.

Jisa, H., and Scarcella, R. (1982). Getting it together: An analysis of written discourse markers. Paper presented at TESOL 1982.

Joos, M. (1967). *The five keys*. New York: Harcourt Brace Jovanovich.

Karttunen, L. (1970). On the semantics of complement sentences. In *Papers from the 6th regional meeting of the Chicago Linguistic Society* (pp. 328–339). Chicago: Chicago Linguistic Society.

Karttunen, L. (1971). Implicative verbs. *Language, 47*, 340–358.

Labov, W., and Fanshel, D. (1977). *Therapeutic discourse*. New York: Academic Press.

Lakoff, G., and Johnson, M. (1980). *Metaphors we live by*. Chicago, Ill.: University of Chicago Press.

Lakoff, R. (1973). Questionable answers and answerable questions. In B. Kachru, R. B. Lees, Y. Malkiel, and S. Saporta (Eds.), *Issues in Papers in linguistics: Papers in honor of Henry and Reneee Kahane* (pp. 453–467). Urbana: University of Illinois Press.

Leech, G., and Svartvik, J. (1975). *A communicative grammar of English*. London: Longman.

Levinson, S. (1983). *Pragmatics*. Cambridge: Cambridge University Press.

Levy, M. (1990). Concordances and their integration into a word processing environment for language learners. *SYSTEM, 18*, 2: 179–188.

Marcos, H. (1987). Communicative functions of pitch range and pitch direction in infants. *Journal of Child Language, 14*, 255–268.

Maynard, S. K. (1989). Functions of the discourse marker Dakara. *TEXT, 9*, 4: 390–414.

Menn, L., and Boyce, S. (1982). Fundamental frequency and discourse structure. *Language and Speech, 25*, 341–383.

Merritt, M. (1980). On the use of OK in service encounters. In R. Shuy and A. Schnukal (Eds.), *Language use and the uses of language* (pp. 162–172). Washington, D.C.: Georgetown University Press.

Miller, P. (1982a). Teasing sequences. *Bulletin of Cross-Cultural Human Cognition and Development* (University of California, San Diego), *6*, 169–183.

  (1982b). *Amy, Wendy, and Beth: Learning language in South Baltimore.* Austin: University of Texas Press.

Mitchell, K. (1990). On comparisons in a notional grammar. *Applied Linguistics, 11,* 1: 52–72.

Pennington, M. (1990). The context of L2 phonology. In H. Burmeister and P. L. Rounds (Eds.), *Variability in second language acquisition: Proceedings of the 10th meeting of the Second Language Research Forum,* vol. 2 (pp. 541–564). Eugene: University of Oregon, Department of Linguistics.

Rintell, R. (1983). "But how did you FEEL about that?" The learner's perception of emotion in speech. *Applied Linguistics, 5,* 3: 255–264.

Sacks, H. (Unpublished). *Lecture Notes (1967–1972),* 11 March 1971. Department of Sociology, University of California, Irvine.

Schmerling, S. (1978). Synonymy judgments as syntactic evidence. In P. Cole (Ed.), *Syntax and semantics. Vol. 9: Pragmatics* (pp. 299–313). New York: Academic Press.

Searle, J. (1975). Indirect speech acts. In P. Cole and J. Morgan (Eds.), *Syntax and semantics. Vol 3.: Speech acts* (pp. 59–82). New York: Academic Press.

  (1976). *Speech acts.* Cambridge: Cambridge University Press.

Shen, X. S. (1990). Ability of learning the prosody of an intonational language by speakers of a tonal language: Chinese speakers learning French prosody. *IRAL (International Review of Applied Linguistics in Language Teaching), 28,* 2: 119–134.

Side, R. (1990). Phrasal verbs: Sorting them out. *ELT (English Language Teaching) Journal, 44,* 2: 144–152.

Sinclair, J. (1987). *Looking up–An account of the COBUILD project.* London: Collins.

Watabe, M.; Brown, C.; and Ueta, Y. (1991). Transfer of discourse function: Passives in the writing of ESL and JSL learners. *IRAL, 29,* 2: 115–134.

9 Layers of discourse analysis

The preceding chapters have shown how researchers have searched for *system* in discourse. The various methods developed in this search reveal different aspects of discourse. When we follow one method, adopting the units and processes described by that method, we arrive at one picture of what discourse is. When we follow another method, the picture changes as the units and processes change and the focus of the research changes. Each new method adds another layer to the total discourse picture.

In deciding which methods to include in this book and what kinds of practice activities to offer, I became concerned that you might see each method as doing the same thing albeit in a slightly different way. However, none of the methods discussed so far covers everything that is included in the next method – layered analysis. Moreover, none of the methods seems more "correct" than the others; each has its own purpose – some focus on writer intent, others on component forms or templates, and others on more abstract notions of how discourse and language might be modeled or mapped as a cognitive system.

To show that this is the case, we could roughly divide the various methods into three groups: those that describe the structure of text, those that show text structure to be the result of speakers' or writers' goals and intents, and those that show structure as evolving from socially and cooperatively built communication. In the first group, the structures are properties *of* the text. Goffman's (1976) universal system components would fall into this category, as would Labov and Waletsky's (1967) narrative structure components and Halliday and Hassan's (1976) cohesive ties. The description is static. The second group would include such analyses as Schank's (1975) and Shank and Abelson's (1977) script theory and Mann and Thompson's (1989) rhetorical structure theory. It's true that these analyses describe structures, but the structures are seen as arising out of selections made by speakers and writers as they produce text to meet their goals. The third group would include such methods as Schegloff's (1968, 1979) and Schegloff and Sacks's (1973) conversational analysis, Tannen's (1985) involvement, and Labov's (1972) evaluation components. Here the text is seen as cooperatively built among participants engaged in communication. Arguably, this three-way classification might, then, look something like the following:

A. *Linguistic and cognitive templates* (text characteristics)
   1. Goffman's system components
   2. Labov and Waletsky's (versus Mandler's 1978 and Rumelhart's 1975) narrative structures

3. Levinson's (1983) deictic and Halliday and Hassan's cohesive ties
4. Analysis of differences in features across modes
5. Speech act analysis

B. *Linguistic and cognitive processes* (text structure results from selection/ activation based on speaker's/writer's goals and intents)
   1. Schank and Abelson's script analysis
   2. Mann and Thompson's rhetorical structure analysis
   3. Participant cohesion
   4. Pragmatics of speech acts
   5. Celce-Murcia's (1980) contextual analysis

C. *Social, linguistic, and cognitive processes* (text structure evolves from socially built communication)
   1. Schegloff's conversational analysis
   2. Goffman's ritual constraints; the playing of "self"
   3. Labov's evaluation component
   4. Tannen's and Chafe's (1982) involvement features
   5. Speech event analysis

Although each type of analysis has its own goals, each can be used for many different purposes. Throughout this book, I have asked you to apply methods to various types of data while considering the implications for cross-cultural understanding, for teaching, and for research. In some practices, you have been asked to think about what alternative methods of analysis might be used. However, you have not been asked to apply all the methods in sequence to a piece of data. We will do that now. I will give you one more example and use a layered analysis to demonstrate more convincingly that language use is a structured social, cognitive, and linguistic enterprise.

One of the times a layered approach might be used is in the study of case data. In all research, there are always a few people who perform in ways that differ from the norm or in ways that do not fit our classifications. In experimental studies, these are called *outliers* – subjects whose scores differ vastly from others in the group. Typically, such data are set aside for separate case study. Such data also occur in discourse analysis. Some learners produce language texts that do not fit with the rest of the data. These too can be set aside for separate case study.

The example I will use to demonstrate the layered approach is from Hatch and Hawkins (1991), a study of 64 spoken and written narratives. The stories were collected at a school that qualified for special funding because of low student scores on state-mandated tests. The children in this study scored at or below the thirty-ninth percentile on these tests and were designated as having limited English proficiency ("LEP" is a school designation arrived at via a series of English language tests). Their average age was 10, and the first languages of the children included Spanish, Vietnamese, Chinese, and Korean. Each child told a story about a personal experience.

292

The stories the children told varied in length. Some were very long and involved while others were quite brief. There were also differences in how effectively the children involved the audience in their stories via evaluation or involvement features. In terms of components, all 64 children produced an orientation, temporally ordered clauses, and evaluation components, but they differed in terms of explicitly stating a problem and resolution. This final difference was accounted for by an analysis of story topic and the relative power of the protagonist storyteller within the theme.

There were three "outliers" in the database. One story was told by an emotionally disturbed child and consisted entirely of problems with no plan or hope of solution. The other two were stories that were impossible to classify in terms of relative power of the protagonist storyteller within the story theme. I have selected Mario's story to demonstrate how a layered discourse approach might be used with outlier case data – in this case to help explain why the power issue was so ambiguous.

Oral Version

1	MA:	My name is Mario A ——
Today is (+) February 6th, 1989.
		This story's about when Fabian got –
I – when I got mad at Fabian
5		and Fabian got mad at me. (+ +)
H-he got mad at me
because me and Joe were just passing the ball to each other
and we didn't pass it to him (+ +)
in basketball.
10		And (+ +) just me and Joe were working on our shots, an' (+ +)
after the bell rang,
he got mad at me an'
he was gonna hit me an' (+ +)
I just hit him back,
15		an' Mr. L came (+ +)
	T:	He was GONNA hit you and you hit him before he hit you?
	MA:	Yeah (+ +)
Then – then he – he uses – he just (+ +) got me and pushed me.
Then Mr. L came an'
20		– before Mr. L came (+ +)
I pushed him back, and (+ +)
Mr. L just (+ +) told us to stop it an'
		– Then in the classroom when we were walking back (+ +)
Umm Fabian – Fabian just (+)
25		I wa – just sat in my seat an' Fabian (+)
Fabian got me an' (+ +)
he threw me against the chalkboard an' then (+)
I just got back up
an' next (+) I started (+) I started hitting him, an'

30		Mrs. D told us to stop it, but
		Fa-Fabian didn't let me go
		so I kept on hitting him, too.
		An' (+ +) ummm (+ +)
		we got suspended for (+) f-f-for a week, I think.
35		St-we had to stay up in the office.
	T:	How come uhm (+)
		How come you and Joe wouldn't let (+ +)
		wouldn't let Fabian play?
	MA:	Cuz he can't shoot ((nervous laugh))
	T:	Well how do you KNOW that
40		if you don't give him the ball?
	MA:	I know.
		We pass to him, but (+ +)
		he-he just (+ +) he won't – he can't –
		he can't dribble or anything.
		He just would like let the ball roll (+) or something.
45		That's why me and Joe would pass it to each other.
	T:	Okay ((sighs while talking)) Any other questions?
	Other Ss:	No. No.

(Data source: Hawkins 1990)

Please note that the following analyses are not complete. They are simply brief lists of findings relevant to the points raised by each method of discourse analysis. A full analysis would fill another book! Since the data form a monologue, some of the analyses will be less revealing than others. My intent, however, is to show that each analysis gives us valuable information about the data. Let us begin with analyses that fit into the first category – that is, those that describe cognitive or linguistic templates as characteristics of text.

Linguistic and cognitive templates

In this group of analyses, the goal is to describe the structure as a template that belongs to, or is a characteristic of, the text.

1. Goffman's system components

This analysis includes the signals for each of the components that Goffman believes are universal in communication. Together the components form an overall template for communication.

OPENING/CLOSING SIGNALS

The actual opening move has not been transcribed, but in it, the teacher, Barbara, nominates Mario to tell a story. However, there are two other sets of opening signals: an opening for the recording with self-identification and the date (lines 1 and 2), and the opening for the narrative (lines 3–5). Mario performs a precloser "an' (+ +) ummm (+ +)" (line 33) and then ends the narrative section of the text (lines 34 and 35). Barbara provides a preclosing move for Mario's recording (line 46). Her final "okay" serves as a boundary marker for Mario's story as she turns to elicit further preclosing moves from the other students. The actual closing move and transition to the next storyteller are not on the tape.

BACKCHANNEL SIGNALS

There are no transcribed backchannel signals. The storyteller has received the floor with permission to tell a narrative. Nonverbal backchannel signals may have been given but they have not been transcribed. (This absence of backchannel signals will be discussed again later.) We know that the communication signal has been received because Barbara responds to the message.

TURN-TAKING SIGNALS

Some of the other stories (particularly those of shier, newly arrived children) show many turn exchanges as the teacher helps the child structure the narrative. Here there are few exchanges. The teacher uses one pause in Mario's performance (line 15) to take a turn. Mario takes a response turn (line 17) before returning to his story. At the conclusion of the narrative (line 36), Barbara takes back the floor with a question directed to the storyteller. There are two turn exchanges – question and answer adjacency pairs – at lines 36–37 and 38 and at lines 39–40 and 41–45. Within his final turn (lines 43–45), Mario uses disfluencies to hold onto the turn long enough to give a summary of the cause of the fight. Barbara acknowledges the answer with a neutral evaluation marker "OK" and then takes back her turn-allocation role, asking other students for their questions.

ACOUSTICALLY ADEQUATE AND INTELLIGIBLE MESSAGES

Mario does a good deal of repair work to make his message intent clear. The repairs are self-identified and self-corrected. The reasons for the repairs are not clear at this stage of the analysis. The "clarification questions" asked by the teacher are not for the purpose of clarifying intelligibility but to offer clues about social behavior in the school setting. At this point, the message appears to be adequate and intelligible.

BRACKET SIGNALS

Utterance 10, "just me and Joe were working on our shots," could be thought of as a side sequence bracketed by pause signals. However, the information in this line is not different from the ongoing narrative. Rather, it seems to give additional information on what "me and Joe" were doing. We will return to this line again in later analyses.

Discourse and language education

NONPARTICIPANT CONSTRAINTS

Mario has been given the floor for an extended period of talk. The teacher has set up the situation where others participate as an audience – they cannot enter the communication channel without either her permission or that of the storyteller. In other stories, however, students gave verbal backchannel signals, asked clarification questions, and in some instances engaged in cooperative storytelling.

PREEMPT SIGNALS

No signal is shown in the transcript. However, the teacher's first question (line 16) preempts the story or at least interrupts the flow of the story to the extent that Mario must do a repair to rework the actions that took place prior to Mr. L's appearance (lines 18–22).

GRICEAN NORMS

Each utterance is *relevant* within the segments. Segment 1 (lines 3–15) and the restatement repair (lines 18–22) are about the fight on the playground after the bell calling students back to class has rung. Segment 2 (lines 23–32) is the continuation of the fight in the classroom. Segment 3 (lines 33–35) is the outcome – a trip to the office and the suspension. The quantity and quality maxims are sufficient for the story, although the restatement repair after the teacher's interruption does not improve the clarity of the storyline. There is some confusion about who struck the first blow (lines 13, 14, 18, and 21). Were there three pushes or blows before Mr. L arrived to break up the fight or only one? This evidence is not clearly or convincingly presented. The speaker seems to appeal to the audience to believe that his account is "true," or at least that the evidence he presents for his claims is relevant and truthful.

2. Rhetorical genre analysis

Our first question might be whether this text is narration or description. The story does fit Shaughnessy's (1977) narrative category of "what happened" for narration rather than the "this is the look/sound/smell of something" of description. The story components are as follows:

Abstract: An abstract is presented: "This story is about (a fight)." (lines 3–5)
Orientation: The two major protagonists, Mario and Fabian, are introduced in the orientation (lines 3–5). Other secondary characters (Mr. L and Mrs. D) are introduced at the point where each enters the story. The setting is not directly established in the orientation but is implicit in lines 7–9. Later the story setting shifts. First the fight is situated on the playground as the bell rings and then in the classroom.

296

The problem: The story has no explicit statement of the problem. A reasonably implicit problem is, How will the fight be resolved?

Temporal clauses to solve the problem: The steps in solving the problem are shown in temporal order. To obtain the story line, we can divide the clauses into foregrounded, simple tense clauses, background actions where the verbs are marked by aspect, and the statives of description and setting. The narrative section in lines 3–15 and 19–35 forms the following display.

Foreground tense	Setting, time, place statives	Background aspect
	I got mad at Fabian	
	Fabian got mad at me	
		me and Joe were just passing the the ball to each other and . . .
we didn't pass it to him in basketball		
		me and Joe were working on our shots
	After the bell rang	
	He got mad at me	
		he was gonna hit me
I just hit him back		
Mr. L came		
He got me and pushed me		
Then Mr. L came		
	Before Mr. L came	
I pushed him back		
Mr. L said to stop		
	Then in the classroom	
		when we were walking back
Fabian just		
I sat in my seat		
Fabian got me and		
he threw me against the chalkboard		
I just got back up		
		I started hitting him
Mrs. D said stop		
Fabian didn't let me go		
		I kept hitting him too

Resolution: "We got suspended [agentless passive] for a week." The resolution is not brought about by the major character but by others.

Coda: Mario does not provide a coda, an optional element that brings the listeners out of story time and back to the present. The teacher's "okay" (line 46) could be classified as a coda because it brings us out of the story world and into the here and now of the classroom.

Because I believe the evaluation component is not a text feature, we will discuss it later along with involvement features.

3. Cohesion analysis – deixis and cohesive ties

In this analysis, we will look at Mario's narrative in terms of how deictic terms and cohesive ties promote coherence.

PERSONAL DEIXIS

Pronouns as cohesive ties refer back to the major characters (*Fabian,* he, him; *Mario,* I, me and Joe). At line 21 there is a potential reference problem because "he" could refer either to Mr. L or to Fabian. This potential problem, however, is not real, for on the tape, stress clarifies the reference.

TEMPORAL DEIXIS

Time clauses such as "when (I got mad and Fabian got mad)" and "after (the bell rang)," and temporal adverbs or adverbial phrases such as "then – then," "an' then," "when (we were walking back)," and "for a week" show the change in time throughout the narrative. Verb tense and aspect also show the order of actions within the temporal framework of the story and in relation to the moment of speaking.

SPATIAL DEIXIS

"In basketball" is the only hint that the outbreak of the fight took place on the playground. "In the classroom" and "walking back" shifts the setting to the classroom. "In my seat" and "against the chalkboard" also place the continuing fight. "Up in the office" sets the final stage of punishment.

DISCOURSE DEIXIS

"That's why (line 45) points back to a series of "reasons" (he can't dribble and he rolls the ball) within the discourse.

SOCIAL DEIXIS

Mr. L and Mrs. D are referred to by name rather than by role. Their roles are well known by the audience, so specific names without role designation are appropriate.

In addition to these deictic cohesive ties, there are numerous lexical ties to the *school* (classroom, chalkboard, seat, bell, office, suspension), and to *basketball* (ball, shots, shoot, pass, dribble). Overall, the cohesive devices promote story coherence.

4. Discourse mode and syntax

There is evidence of some of the six linguistic differences for the oral versus written mode presented in Chapter 7. (1) For the most part, the talk is *phrasal or clausal rather than sentential* in organization. There is one more tightly organized segment (line 23): "Then in the classroom when we were walking back." However, upholding Pawley and Syder's (1976) one-clause-at-a-time hypothesis, this linguistic complexity leads to "error." The order within this segment is reversed (i.e., students walk back *to* the classroom, not the reverse) and this utterance is followed by disfluency fillers and repairs. (2) There are no *left dislocations* or *topic-comment* structures. (3) Interestingly, definite links (e.g., "because," "but," "cuz" in lines 7, 30, and 38) are used in addition to *nextness* (e.g., "he threw me against the chalkboard and then + + I just got back up" where the information about falling to the floor, which necessitates getting up, is missing). (4) There are some examples of phonological parallelism ("pass," "basketball"; "we were working," "we were walking"; "sat in my seat"; "cuz he can't shoot"; "like let the ball roll"). There are repeated words and phrases (e.g., "got mad," "hit me," "hit him," "pushed me," "got me") and parallel syntactic forms ("*were* work*ing*," "*were* walk*ing*"). (5) As one would expect, there are many *repairs* in this short transcript. (6) Most of the clauses are *conjoined* (e.g., "an'," "and then," "next") though, as already noted, there is one embedded clause that is not carried through. None of Chafe's (1982) attributes of detachment appear in the story. Thus, the language of the narrative is typical of speech rather than written text.

Linguistic and cognitive processes

In this group of analyses, text structure results from selection or activation of forms based on the speaker's or writer's goals and intents.

5. Process cohesion – participant tracking

In Chapter 6, we talked about the use of pronouns for person deixis or reference. Here we will look at such cohesive ties in a slightly different way – we will trace reference in order to answer the question, Who is this story about? To do this, we need to look at the ways the storyteller places focus on the major and minor protagonists. One way is already shown in the series of temporally ordered clauses previously displayed. The hero of the story line is usually the person who carries out the actions in the foreground; the hero is also supposed to have high "agency." If we look at the clauses that occur in the foreground and those that have highest transitivity (terms used by Hopper and Thompson 1980), you will discover that the majority belong to Fabian. The majority of those in the background with lower transitivity belong to the storyteller, Mario:

Fabian: He got me; pushed me; got me; threw me; didn't let me go
Mario: I just hit him; pushed him back; sat in my seat; just got back up; started
   hitting him; kept hitting him, too

Mario's actions are weakened by making them serial and by the use of the hedge "just." (Although no contextual analysis has been performed on the data, one could compare Mario's use of "just" with the findings of Chafe 1980 and Hulquist 1985.)

Another way of establishing "agency" is to count the number of times the major and minor protagonists are mentioned and whether they have agent or patient status (i.e., whether they are the more powerful actors in subject slots or whether they are relatively weak receivers of actions in object slots). In the story, Mario mentions himself as an agent 8 times and as a patient 9 times. He mentions Fabian as an agent 11 times and as a patient 6 times. (In addition, "me and Joe" are in subject position 3 times, and Fabian and Mario or "we" appear twice as agents and 3 times as patients.) We begin to see, then, why it was so difficult to classify this narrative in terms of storyteller power.

Karmiloff-Smith (1986) has analyzed children's stories in terms of protagonist tracking too. She notes that repairs are one important source for our interpretation of who a story is about. The major protagonist usually occurs in subject slot. If a secondary protagonist is moved to the subject slot, a full noun phrase or a stressed pronoun is used to show that, even though the person is in subject slot, he or she has secondary status in the story.

Notice Mario's repairs as he begins the story (lines 3–6):

MA: This story's about when <u>Fabian</u> got –
   I – when <u>I</u> got mad at <u>Fabian</u>
   and <u>Fabian</u> got mad at <u>me</u>. (+ +)
   H-<u>he</u> got mad at <u>me</u>

In line 3, Mario starts the story by saying that it is about Fabian. In line 4, he repairs this start by placing himself in the subject slot, saying, in effect, that the story is about himself and that Fabian is in the patient status of the secondary participant. Mario continues this in line 5. Although Fabian is in subject slot, he is still the secondary participant because a full NP (Fabian rather than an unstressed "he") is used. Following a pause, however, Mario reverses himself and puts Fabian back in major protagonist position with an unstressed pronoun and places himself in the less powerful patient slot of the secondary protagonist.

This happens again in lines 24 and 25, where the two boys are walking back to the classroom. Line 24 makes Fabian the major protagonist. At the start of line 25, Mario repairs this to claim major protagonist status for himself.

We see, then, that the linguistic choices Mario makes contribute to our uncertainty (at this point) as to who the story is really about.

6. Script analysis

Script analysis attempts to model communication that arises from speaker goals and intents. The text that results as the speaker develops plans to meet goals can be described in terms of its script form. What scripts would be needed in order to understand Mario's story? What scripts would we need to program if we wanted a computer to be able to display understanding of the story? At least four scripts would be needed: the school script, the playground script, the fight script, and the classroom script. Some of the components for each are outlined very roughly as follows.

School script: SCHOOL HASA (*actor roles:* TEACHERS, STUDENTS); HASA (*parts:* PLAYGROUND, CLASSROOMS, OFFICE); HASA (*props:* BELL); *actions:* RULES, DO, etc. Barbara, Mrs. D, Mr. L ISA TEACHER. Mario, Fabian, Joe ISA STUDENT. STUDENTS NEG FIGHT ISA RULE. STUDENTs DO share PROPS ISA RULE. STUDENTs NEG DO RULE, TEACHER MOVE STUDENT to OFFICE. OFFICE DO PUNISH STUDENTs. Suspension ISA PUNISHMENT.

Playground script: PLAYGROUND HASA (SUPERVISOR, GAMEs). Basketball ISA GAME. BASKETBALL HASA (*props:* BALL, HOOP; *actions:* DO ATRANS BALL). Mr. L ISA SUPERVISOR. STUDENTs DO GAMEs.

Fight script: (The playground fight would draw from a fight MOP) Fabian and Mario ISA COMBATANTs. COMBATANT ANGER TAU. Mr. L ISA REFEREE. Fabian MOVE Mario and Mario MOVE Fabian. REFEREE DOes STOP FIGHT. (Note the nice double-script use of the bell: the bell of the school and a metaphorical fight bell!)

Classroom script: CLASSROOM HASA (*props:* BLACKBOARD, BELL). STUDENTs HASA DESK. Barbara HASA (*prop:* TAPE RECORDER). Barbara DOes (nominate STUDENTs). Barbara ATRANS tape recorder to STUDENT. Mario DOes (tell story). Barbara DOes evaluation (MBUILD-TAU) for STUDENT.

Using these scripts, we can account for many of the cohesive and deictic devices that appear in the text. Now, however, these ties are seen as arising from the speaker's goals and intents as Mario tells the story, rather than as characteristics of the text itself. For example, once Mario activates and uses the four scripts, his choice of definite and indefinite articles comes from the script. We are not surprised to see definite articles used, for example, in lines 11 and 23. Since schools have bells and classrooms, a definite article can be used for "the bell" and "the classroom." Since schools have playgrounds and playgrounds have basketball hoops, a definite article can be used for "the ball" in line 7. The classroom has a chalkboard and the students have seats, so these too can be used with definite articles (lines 25, 27). Schools also have offices, so Mario can activate "the office" from the script (line 35). Evaluation in the school script ensures that bad behavior means being sent to "the office," and especially bad behavior calls for school punishment such as detention or suspension. The script for playground basketball is also well known by Mario's listeners allowing for activation of "working on shots" and "passing" and "dribbling" the ball (line 6–10, 43–44).

The story begins on the playground with a game script and ATRANS moves as "me and Joe" pass the ball to each other but refuse to share "ownership" with Fabian. An MBUILD or affective TAU (thematic affect unit) is evidenced by Fabian and is responded to in kind. At this point, a fight script is activated. The combatants are identified and they do a number of MOVEs as pushes and blows are exchanged. Fight and playground scripts overlap as Mr. L takes on the role of fight referee at the sound of "the bell"! A recent National Public Radio news program reported that part of the elementary school fight script for males is that much pushing and shoving is supposed to go on and that others will separate the posturing combatants. If this report is correct, then pushing and shoving would be part of the script. The fight is first stopped by Mr. L (lines 15, 19, 22) and later by Mrs. D (line 30). Two more negative actions (lines 31 and 32) result in a MOVE (who CAUSEs to MOVE is not specified) of the boys to "the office" and a suspension punishment.

In this script analysis, Mario's reason (goal) for selecting and telling the story is not entirely clear. One goal, of course, is to complete a task set by the teacher and to show himself as a competent storyteller. This goal and the goal of entertaining or showing self in a positive light are characteristic of most of the stories in this database. A more important goal is for Mario to establish himself within his social group by telling a story that involves him in two ways. First, this particular story has the potential to show him as a "macho kid," a strong fighter. Second, the story can also show him in the role of the "picked-on kid," one who is not at fault. The teacher does not buy the no-blame evidence presented in the story, and we can only guess how the children reacted to Mario's recount of his physical prowess and (as I read it at this point in the analysis) pride in being suspended.

In addition to rethinking where cohesive ties and deictic markers originate, we might integrate still other types of discourse analysis methods with script analysis. If we turn to ethnography (in the Gumperz 1982, Saville-Troike 1982, and Tannen 1982 tradition of discourse analysis), we can ask many other questions that relate to understanding Mario's narrative. Do school storytelling scripts match those of storytelling outside school? Do school playground scripts match those of playground scripts in general? Does the school fight script match that of fights among children outside the school setting? Do male fight scripts (on and off the playground) match those of female students? Which parts of the scripts are "givens" and which are "mentionable" because they are the focus of the script in a particular setting?

It should be noted that this particular school has a rule that students solve their arguments without physical fights. It also has a rule that games and game props be shared. These rules are in sharp conflict to Mario's life outside of school. Who does or does not get to play games is determined by a social hierarchy determined in part by gang membership. In gangs, all methods are used to solve arguments. And, in Mario's story, as we shall see in a moment, these differences are in conflict.

Before turning away from scripts, I want to point out that much of the work on pragmatics could be carried out effectively within script theory. Conventional implicature (presupposition, implicatives, entailment, paraphrase, and metaphor) and, at least to some extent, conversational implicature could be seen as the effect of script activation. "After the bell rang," for example, presupposes schools have bells and implies that lines 6–10 are located at school on the playground. Line 38, "he can't shoot," entails (whatever the Los Angeles Lakers think) "he can't dribble." Metaphors such as "shoot" the ball can be seen as coming out of some higher classification of games, war, and contests. Thus, it could be argued that many of the analyses described in earlier chapters could be nicely assumed under script analysis.

7. Rhetorical structure analysis

Rhetorical structure analysis is primarily a cognitive processing model. The analysis also attempts to show what the speaker may reasonably be expected to have had in mind in relating spans of the text. While we will only do a partial analysis, just looking at Mario's story using Mann and Thompson's (1989) rhetorical structure theory (RST) analysis presents us with some interesting alternatives.

Let us see first how lines 6–10 relate to lines 3–5. If we look at the span of clauses numbered 6–10, we find the cause of Fabian's anger and perhaps the cause of Mario's anger as well. A possible elaboration relation holds between clauses 9 and 7 (remember that N and S stand for nucleus and satellite):

N: me and Joe were passing the ball to each other (7)
S: (specifically) in basketball (9)

Clauses 7 and 9 show a background relation to clause 8

N: we didn't pass it to him (8)
S: (when) me and Joe were passing the ball to each other in basketball (7, 9)

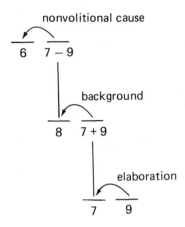

Figure 9.1

Then clause 8 together with attached clauses 7 and 9 form a causal relation to clause 6:

N: he (Fabian) got mad at me (6)
S: Because (when) me and Joe were passing the ball to each other, we didn't pass it to him, (specifically) in basketball.

This relation is shown in Figure 9.1.

The next clause (line 10) poses a dilemma and, I think, shows why Mario's intent is not clear. There are two possible relations that might hold for this clause and the previous clauses. It may be just a last-minute repair or bracket, an elaboration that describes the game.

Elaboration relation
N: me and Joe were passing the ball to each other (# 7)
S: (actually) it was just me and Joe were working on our shots (# 10)

This possibility is formalized in Figure 9.2.

If, however, Mario's intent is to show that, according to regular playground rules if not school rules, Fabian had no right to be angry, the relation might be a justification relation for not passing the ball.

Justify relation
S: (since) just me and Joe were working on our shots (# 10)
N: we didn't pass it to him. (#8)

If Mario wants us to explicitly contrast school playground rules and outside playground rules, we need another set of clauses to show that, playing by nonschool rules, Joe and Mario belong to a group that works on shots, and

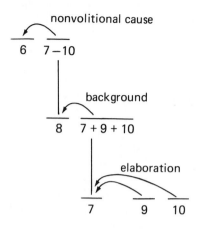

Figure 9.2

that this contrasts with a group that does not – a group to which Fabian belongs. If this antithesis holds, then Fabian should not expect to receive the ball and has no justification for getting mad. A demand for the ball, in these circumstances, would explain why Mario got mad at Fabian. See Figure 9.3 for possible relations for these spans of text.

The next group of clauses (lines 11–15) shows the first fight segment in a series of causal relations. Mario claims that lines 12 and 13 are causally linked.

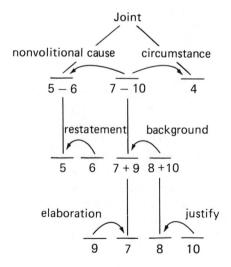

Figure 9.3

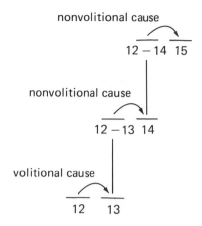

nonvolitional cause

12 – 14 15

nonvolitional cause

12 – 13 14

volitional cause

12   13

Figure 9.4

S: (because) he got mad at me (12)
N: he was gonna hit me (13)

(However, the action does not take place, as shown by his use of "gonna." Thus, we could read this as Mario's attempt to motivate our belief that Fabian would have hit him if he had not hit Fabian first.) These two clauses, in turn, form a causal relation to Mario's "first" blow:

S: (because) he got angry and was gonna hit me (12–13)
N: I just hit him back. (14)

The ruckus leads to Mr. L's appearance on the scene (line 15).

S: (given) I just hit back (14–18)
N: Mr. L came. (15)

Figure 9.4 shows these relations for lines 12–15.

At this point, Barbara, the teacher, interrupts and expresses her belief that Mario has hit the first blow without justification. By school rules, there is no justification for Mario's side of the story; he failed if his intent was to justify his anger at Fabian and his striking the first blow. The teacher's chiding question may have led to the repair sequence in lines 18–22, a repair regarding the physical events that took place prior to the arrival of Mr. L. Again, it is not clear whether the intent is simple elaboration or "filler talk" while Mario gets himself organized to continue the story, or a reorganization of the story so that no blow was struck and Mario merely returned Fabian's pushes.

The next repair segment shows that Mr. L is still the arbiter in this scene:

S: (when) Fabian got me and pushed me
N: Mr. L came.

But the scene now consists of shoves and pushes. The relation between lines 18 and 21 is cause and result:

S: (because) he just got me and pushed me (18)
N: I pushed him back (21)

The altercation seems less serious. The repair sequence serves less as a cause of Mr. L's arrival than as background to the restatement of his arrival.

S: (after) Fabian got me and pushed me and I pushed him back.
N: Mr. L came. (19)

With the first fight sequence linked to the arrival of Mr. L, the next clause is linked to all the previous clauses in a solutionhood relation:

S: (lines 6–21)
N: Mr. L just told us to stop it. (22)

This ends the first segment of the fight story. The fight, however, is not over. Line 23 might be divided into two clauses with an elaboration relation:

N: In the classroom
S: (specifically) when we were walking back

The classroom is the background setting for Mario's normal behavior of sitting down in his seat:

S: In the classroom (repair elaboration dropped) (23)
N: I just sat in my seat. (25)

Such a normal action could have a (non)enablement relation to Fabian's action:

S: (even though) in the classroom I just sat in my seat (23, 25)
N: Fabian got me. (26)

(At some deeper interpretive level, it is also evidence for Mario's implicit claim that he is the innocent party.) Fabian's action is elaborated in the next clause.

N: Fabian got me. (26)
S: (specifically) he threw me against the chalkboard. (27)

The next nucleus is missing (though usually the nucleus cannot be deleted without affecting coherence).

S: (as a result of) he threw me against the chalkboard (23–27)
N: (I fell down)

The next might be an adversative (although) relation or a temporal (after) relation.

S: (although or after) he got me and threw me against the chalkboard (causing me to fall down) (23–27)
N: I got back up (29)

Getting up enables Mario to fight back. Or, again, it could simply be a temporal (after) relation.

S: (after) I got back up (enabling) (28)
N: I started hitting him. (29)

If we understand these clauses as enabling relations, then Mario is seen as
aggressively fighting back. If we interpret them as temporal relations, Mario
seems like a hapless victim carried along by the action.
   Clauses 23–29 culminate in clause 30, causing Mrs. D to intervene.

S: (given or since) (lines 23–29)
N: Mrs. D said to stop it. (30)

The next relation could be adversative:

S: (even though) Mrs. D said to stop it (30)
N: Fabian didn't let go. (31)

And, since Fabian doesn't allow the two to stop, another (non)enabling relation holds between lines 31 and 32.

S: Fabian didn't let go (31)
N: So I kept on hitting him, too. (32)

Finally, the result of all these clauses is punishment. The agent involved in
solutionhood (perhaps "the office" came?) is not given. The relation is volitional cause.

S: (because of all the preceding clauses)
N: We got suspended. (34)

The punishment may be all one span – that is, suspension and staying in the
office for a week – or, staying in the office may be an elaboration.

N: We got suspended for a week (34)
S: (specifically) we had to stay up in the office. (35)

To complete the RST analysis, we would need to link the first two parts of
the story: (a) the fight begins on the playground (lines 4–15 and the repair
segment 16–22), and (b) the fight continues in the classroom (lines 23–32).
Then we would have to show how, as a result of (a) and (b) (lines 4–32), the
boys are suspended (lines 33–34). The title of the story might be "Suspended."
   Although this completes Mario's story, the following clauses (lines 36, 37)
are interesting for at least two reasons. First, they show that the teacher did
not perform the same rhetorical structure analysis as shown here. Second,

they reinforce our interpretation that Mario is reasoning with outside-school rules while the teachers and the office are using school rules. When Barbara asks Mario why he broke the school rules, he gives an outside-school rule where he determines who can play according to expertise (among other things). In addition, he gives evidence (lines 42–45) that Fabian doesn't qualify.

N: He can't dribble
S: He just would just like let the ball roll or something.

Mario also draws an interesting equivalence relation between not being able to dribble the ball and not being able to shoot. These clauses are evidence of Mario's belief that Fabian was not justified in expecting to be included in the practice and, therefore, not justified in getting mad – the anger that "provoked" the fight.

In contrast to the genre analysis, RST reveals Mario as the major protagonist. He demonstrates that within his rules, Fabian had no right to be angry. When Fabian began a physical fight, Mario acted and acted firmly. Fabian responded in kind, and the two were suspended. If the storyteller had been successful in making these relations more explicit, it is possible that his story would have been more "convincing." However, it is also possible that he would have been challenged even more strongly for not playing by school rules.

Social, linguistic, and cognitive processes

In this group of analyses, text structure is described as evolving from socially built communication.

8. Conversational analysis

In Chapter 1, we talked about Goffman's system components and then illustrated how these components were cooperatively managed in communication with examples from conversational analysis. There are several points in Mario's story where our understanding could be strengthened by looking at the cooperative nature of communication. The two most obvious are the absence of backchannel signals from Mario's audience and Mario's relatively poor use of evaluation or involvement features.

In conversational analysis, the absence of a component is as telling as its presence. Silence, for example, has perhaps a stronger meaning in communication than the presence of such backchannel signals as "um hm" or "yeh" – signals that encourage the storyteller to continue. The lack of such signals and the children's refusal to ask Mario questions or make comments at the end of his story is particularly noticeable. In all the other stories, the children not only gave backchannel signals but asked clarification questions during the story as well as at the end of the story. Here, the children sat in silence. The teacher, in our retrospective discussions of the story, said there was an incredible amount of tension in the air throughout the story. In a moment, we will look at why this should be the case.

In addition to selecting a personal topic, Mario used intonation and the power of the fight scenes rather than evaluation to involve his listeners. The text is amazingly free of repetition, sound effects, direct quotations, stress, and direct evaluation comments. Why Mario did not use such devices to entertain and involve his audience is not clear at this point. Given their volubility in responses to many of the other stories, the students seem a bit stunned.

9. Speech event analysis

If we look at each utterance in the narrative to determine its speech *act* function, we find that the text consists primarily of representative speech acts. That is, each gives information that has truth value in the world Mario is telling us about. There are a few expressives that give "emotional values" information (e.g., "He got mad"), but they are not delivered in an emotional way. There are two embedded directives – commands from Mr. L and Mrs. D to "stop it" – but again, these are given in a nonevaluative manner. The pragmatics of many of the speech acts are not clear.

It is difficult to determine a speech *event* structure within the story. If we believe that Mario's goal is to complain, or gripe, or share his troubles, it is difficult to see how his story fits the structure that usually results from such events. Complaints are addressed to the trouble source – to persons responsible for the trouble – and a remedy is negotiated. If Fabian is the trouble source, he has not been addressed. Gripes are brief complaints addressed to persons not responsible for the trouble. Mario does not really seem to be griping about Fabian's behavior. Troubles sharing is usually addressed to friendly persons not responsible for the trouble and sympathetic to the complainer's point of view. The listener is expected to offer sympathy and encouragement or perhaps to reciprocate with similar stories of trouble. At this point there is little in our analysis of the story that allows us to make a successful match with these three types of "complaint" speech events.

A second possibility is that this is a "fight report" speech event. We could look for similarities with play-by-play reports of sports, fights, and war. Mario does, indeed, use metaphors from fight scripts, and he does show surprising impartiality in giving the play-by-play report of the fight itself. Still, as a combatant in the fight, his intent to play the reporter role seems in doubt.

Speech event recognition can, however, be enhanced if we turn to an analysis of ritual constraints and the playing of self.

10. Ritual constraints and self

In communication analysis, we examine the ways in which the system is manipulated to smooth social interaction and the ways in which deference and demeanor are handled. In narratives, the storyteller's major theme is that of portraying or establishing "self" in Goffman's definition of that term (i.e., "not an entity half concealed behind events, but a changeable formula for managing oneself during them"). Storytelling may be one of our favorite universal social activities, because it allows us to pretend that there *is* a half-concealed self behind events that we narrate while it also allows us to display self as we manage ourselves in the telling of our thoughts and actions.

In Chapter 2, we talked about Goffman's ritual constraints as related primarily to deference and demeanor, so we will begin with that. We might say that Mario wants to show two half-concealed entities, successively characterizing himself as the macho kid and as the picked-on kid in the fight. Macho kids don't pick on weaklings, so Mario must give his opponent Fabian face as a competent, persistent fighter (lines 12–13, 18, 26–27, 31). While Mario may also mark Fabian as an incompetent basketball player (lines 8, 38, 42–44), notice that the phrase "Cuz he can't shoot" is accompanied by a nervous laugh, a disfluency to soften the criticism of a worthy opponent. Line 44 shows further softening of the criticism. The repairs and "or something" and "or anything" further weaken the criticism given in the message. Mario is willing to share the glory of being suspended (a mark of the macho kid) with Fabian – the camaraderie of tough guys sent to "the office."

Simultaneously, Mario tries to show himself as a blameless participant in the fight. He does this linguistically with his shifts in agency and his weakly transitive actions ("just hitting back"), and by setting up text relations that work according to his rules (but not by school rules). The teacher, however, asks questions that reject this portrayal. The questions imply that one does not strike the first blow and that no one should be excluded from play among friends. The teacher's sigh in line 46 suggests that she feels she has failed in getting Mario to concede that he may not have acted wisely, but we will question that interpretation later.

In an analysis of Mario's portrayal of himself as a half-hidden entity, we can see that there are many different Marios that he may wish to show:

Mario the *storyteller*
Mario the *basketball captain* (ruler of the playground)
Mario the *macho kid*
Mario the *picked-on kid*
Mario the *troublemaker*

In initial readings of his story, it seemed that fitting at least one of these portraits was Mario's goal or intent in telling the story. However, given our analysis to this point, none of these seem right. In terms of the storyteller, Mario chose a story, "Suspended," that seems to be an unlikely source of entertainment for his audience. Further, he neglected to use the range of evaluative devices to enhance that role. As Mario the macho kid, he used too little agency and allowed Fabian too much power. As the picked-on kid, he used strong clause relations that undermined weak agency. As ruler of the playground, Mario neglected to point out that his rules and the rules of playground in the world outside the school are ones that any rational person would adopt. In the role of the troublemaker, Mario, indeed, had a fight and further selected this – a near taboo topic – for his story. He rebuffed the teacher's challenging questions. That sounds like a troublemaker, but the teacher does not view him as such.

If we turn to Goffman's notion of self as the changeable formula for managing oneself during events, there are other possibilities:

Mario the *angry kid*
Mario the *troubled kid*

A retrospective analysis of Mario's performance from the teacher's point of view and an analysis of Mario's prosody shows Mario as managing himself with a great deal of frustration and anger. He performs as the kid who is angry at school rules and angry at rules outside school. The anger, confusion, and conflict show in his reshaping of the storytelling assignment. The narrative, in effect, is addressed not to the other students in the classroom (they are like a silent radio audience in call-in programs) but to Barbara, the teacher – a representative of the school that imposes rules he doesn't want to follow and a caring person whom he admires and from whom he wants to win approval. This need for approval disappears in his anger as Mario selects the story and chooses to tell it in front of the other students as a challenge to the teacher – a representative of the school. Ultimately, his story is a complaint at his own lack of power in the school setting. Complaints, by their nature, are face-threatening to the receiver of the complaint. In our retrospective discussion, Barbara listened to the sigh (line 46), which I had interpreted as a mark of her unhappiness at not convincing Mario of the error of his ways. She, however, said that she sighed at the moment when she realized Mario had trapped her. She said that, by not thinking quickly on her feet, she had responded using his rules rather than by school rules – she had lost her chance to juxtapose the two sets of rules and justify Mario's punishment. Further, she felt she had been manipulated by his choice of telling the story in front of an audience, caught between her wish to talk about the problem with him privately and to carry on her teacher role, evaluating and turning the microphone over to the next storyteller. Perhaps, then, Mario succeeded if his goal was to display anger at his teacher as a representative of the school and to "pay back" that school for punishing him.

While this layered analysis is only a rough overview, it reveals the participants' abilities to use the system components of communication (turn taking, openings/closings, and so forth). It shows awareness of the need to project deference and demeanor, particularly in a story that has self as its central theme. The school script, the storytelling scripts, and the fight script are all well known to the participants. Mario, the teacher, and the other children all play their roles with ease. Rhetorical analysis shows Mario's abilities to use the narrative template effectively. Rhetorical structure theory highlights the possible relations among the clauses Mario used.

We have seen then, that Mario has impressive abilities to use linguistic and cognitive templates (system components and narrative templates). His choices of deictic and cohesive ties add to the general coherence of the text, which is obtained from the templates. He shows skill in the cognitive processes that participant tracking, script theory, and rhetorical structure theory are meant to describe. On the social side, Mario selects a personal story, provides what he believes is a socially acceptable rationale for his behavior, and even uses ritual markers to give his fight opponent face. To reveal self, he chooses a story that most children would normally not select for this task. His reasons for doing so must ultimatley be ambiguous. Perhaps Mario wants to leave his intent unclear – and therefore deniable. What he does not do is give face to his listeners – the teacher and the children in the classroom. Had he explicitly asked them to judge his "reasons" for the fight, made his intent clear from the beginning, it is just possible that he might have succeeded in showing himself as the picked-on but competent macho kid, someone to be admired or, at least, understood and forgiven.

You can see that the layered approach has allowed us to understand why Mario's story is so difficult to classify. Thus, the decision not to include it in the narrative database is justified. The layers of analysis have shown a wealth of possible interpretations for the story. Linguistic features serve as clues to these interpretations. They do not, however, completely justify any of the interpretations we have imposed on the data. Although the story seems to be a very powerful complaint against being powerless in school, we may have pushed the interpretation too far. Further evidence for the interpretations can come only from retrospective interviews, an ethnography of the classroom, and the cumulation of observations of those who know Mario best.

Practice 9.1 Layered analyses

You might want to replicate the process of layered analysis in your class or study group. I have randomly selected one written narrative from the database in Hatch and Hawkins (1991). The written stories are the final, edited versions that appear in a book of short stories produced by the children's Writing Laboratory.

The Rotten Fence
by PL

I want to tell this story because this is how I felt when something scary happened to me when I was five years old. Actually, I was very scared, but then something happened that changed my fear to happiness.

   The story began when my brother, Julian, and I decided to go to Thrifty's and buy an ice cream sundae. After we bought the ice cream sundaes, we went back home. We sat on the fence that divided our yard from the next door neighbor's yard. There were two mean looking bulldogs on the neighbors' side of the fence. When we sat on the fence, the dogs started barking at us. All of a sudden the fence started moving. Before we knew it, the fence fell down. Julian and I both fell down hard. He quickly got up and ran into the house and locked the door. I was mad at him because he left me sitting there crying and wouldn't help me. Then I got scared because the dogs were coming across the fence toward me. They had their mouths open as if they were going to bite me. I was really scared now! But all of a sudden, I relaxed and became happy. The dogs didn't want to bit me; they only wanted to lick my ice cream sundae. Then I felt good because I knew everything would be all right and that I had two new friends. When it was all over, my brother came outside and started laughing at me. I hit him because I was still mad at him for not helping me. So in one afternoon, I was mad, scared, and happy.

Before you assign parts of the analysis to each person, be sure there is sufficient data or evidence for a particular method. For contextual analysis, select a lexical or syntactic feature of interest and compare it to that found in other narratives collected by your classmates for previous exercises.

1. *System and ritual constraints*
    Opening/closing signals
    Backchannel signals
    Turn-taking signals
    Acoustically adequate and interpretable messages
    Bracket signals
    Nonparticipant constraints
    Preempt signals
    Gricean maxims
       Relevance, truthfulness, quantity, clarity
    Demeanor, face, self-presentation
    Deference, other presentation

2. *Scripts*
   Goal, actors (roles), props, actions
   Evaluation regarding meeting goal
3. *Speech act and speech event analysis*
   Speech acts
     Directives, commissives, representatives, declaratives,
     expressives
   Speech event components
4. *Rhetorical analysis*
   Narrative
     Orientation, pròblem, temporal steps to solution, solution,
     coda, evaluation
   Foreground and background
   Participant tracking
5. *Rhetorical structure analysis*
   Nucleus and satellite spans
   Relations between spans
6. *Cohesion analysis*
   Deictic markers
     Person, spatial, temporal, social, discourse deixis
   Cohesive ties
     Reference
       Pronouns, demonstratives, comparatives
     Substitution
     Ellipsis
     Conjunction
     Lexical ties
7. *Mode and syntax*
   Clausal or phrasal versus sentential
   Left dislocation and topic-comment structures
   Nextness
   Parallelism (phonological, lexical, syntactic)
   Repair
   Conjoined versus embedded clauses
8. *Mode*
   Involvement and detachment
9. *Contextual analysis*

Once you have decided which of the analyses would be most
appropriate for the data, divide up the remaining work so that
each person does one analysis. Do each analysis
independently without concern for overlap. After you have
discussed each analysis in class, present the findings in an
integrated paper. When you have finished, decide whether this

paper gives evidence that you have met many of the objectives for this course.

Discourse as a social and cognitive enterprise

In no area of linguistics is it clearer that language use is a social and cognitive enterprise than in our search for system in discourse. Part of the work in this book has emphasized the cognitive and linguistic aspects of discourse. Attempts to describe system constraints, the structure of scripts and the components of speech events and rhetorical genre emphasize flexible templates that might be mentally represented in some way in the cognitive system. The pragmatic analysis of speech acts and the work on rhetorical structure theory emphasize the cognitive processes used as we select from the available means of showing intent. The study of deixis and cohesive ties could also be interpreted in terms of the cognitive processes involved in making linguistic choices that promote coherent messages in communication. All these systems and processes arise out of, and are tempered by, the social aspects of discourse. Since a whole chapter (Chapter 2) was devoted to the social constraints on the system components of communication, it might appear that this is true mainly of the overall communication system. But, in fact, each of the analyses in Chapters 3 to 6 showed the power of social patterns on the organization of scripts, speech events, genre analysis, and even the more local analysis methods of cohesion and deixis. Social organization is also behind the ways in which written and spoken discourse are organized across language groups. Contextual analysis, too, reveals social factors at work in terms of differences found for mode, formality, register, and power.

It is difficult to separate linguistic, social, and cognitive factors in the discourse system; they are tightly interwoven. However, as we have seen, different schools of discourse analysis may emphasize one or another factor depending on the goal. If the goal is to describe or model the abstract system behind parts of the discourse, cognitive aspects of the system will be emphasized. If the goal is to describe or model the output of language users, researchers may emphasize the cognitive processes that may be at work in accounting for linguistic choices made by the speaker or writer. If the goal is to understand the interaction of people in social communication (as in our analysis of Mario's story), the emphasis will be on social processes that influence the system of communication and the choices available to express social and personal as well as intellectual meanings.

Anyone who studies discourse analysis soon becomes aware of the overlap of work within these different methods of analysis. Although we understand how and why the overlap occurs, there should be some way of bringing all these various ways of analyzing discourse into a more coherent whole. Perhaps that can be a goal for you in the future.

316

Meanwhile, as teachers and practitioners of applied linguistics, we must determine what role discourse analysis should and could have for our work with the design of language teaching curricula, syllabi, teaching methods, teaching materials, and testing and evaluation. We know that ritual and system constraints reflected in conversational analysis can be applied to courses in intercultural communication and conversation. Script analysis calls to mind the situational approach in foreign language teaching, where scripts such as a visit to the museum, a trip to the market, and holidays are the focus of lessons, and in survival language learning where the newly arrived learn the everyday scripts of getting a driver's license, opening a bank account, applying for a job, and so forth. Speech event analysis is an outgrowth of the notional-functional approach to language teaching. The goal of the analysis is to discover how people really do such functions as inviting, complaining, and asking permission so that teaching materials would match real practice as closely as possible. The variations across languages in terms of rhetorical genres is of great interest not only to composition teachers but to those involved in cross-language transactions of all sorts. ESP practitioners are especially concerned with ways in which specific fields (such as engineering, economics, medicine) develop a special rhetorical style with its own use of cohesive ties for coherence. The analysis of oral and written modes of language use has been valuable in the promotion of literacy at all levels of education. How strong a connection we need between discourse analysis and materials selection is not clear. The current arguments about the use of authentic language materials in classrooms is a case in point.

We also need to consider how discourse analysis (as well as lexical analysis, phonological analysis, and syntactic analysis) relates to a theory of language acquisition and language learning. While there are some attempts to move in this direction – that is, work that informs both theory and practice – there is still much to be done. This, too, can be your goal.

Meanwhile, here in the present, let us stop and reconsider the goals I set in the introduction to this book and those that you may have formed as you worked through the practice exercises.

Review and application

My objectives for this book are listed in the introduction. Review each one and decide whether you can or cannot give evidence of meeting them. Your objectives and those of your teacher may differ from those in the list. Compile a list of the objectives you have evolved for your own study of discourse. Decide how each might be evaluated (i.e., what evidence you would need to show that they have been met). Be sure you feel confident that you have met each of these objectives.

Language teachers often state that their major goal is to help students develop communicative competence. "Communicative competence" and "discourse analysis" are both very broad terms. They mean different things to different people. In this introduction to discourse analysis, I have attempted to show that discourse can be systematically described. I have shown that the analysis can be done at many different levels, some of which overlap. The system is revealed as we look at the universals of all communication systems, at the structure of conversations, the structures shared in scripts, the underlying structure of rhetorical genres, the structure of speech events, and the linguistic signals (of syntax, deixis, cohesive ties, and prosody) used to promote coherence within discourse at a more local level.

How does this description of system relate to communicative competence? It shows us the choices that learners have at their disposal in creating text. Communicative competence is the ability to manipulate the system, selecting forms that not only make for coherent text but also meet goals and fit the ritual constraints of communication. That is, communicative competence is the ability to create coherent text that is appropriate for a given situation within a social setting. Discourse analysis is a description of the many subsystems that promote coherence and the social constraints that operate on those subsystems.

Just as we have found it difficult to talk about discourse analysis without discussing each of the subsystems within it, it is difficult to define communicative competence without turning to the competencies that are nested within it. However, when we use these terms, it is assumed that we are talking about *all* these subsystems. You would rightfully be surprised, then, if an introductory class in discourse analysis covered only the relation between syntax and discourse or between rhetorical analysis and discourse. In the same way, you would be surprised if a curriculum that purports to promote communicative competence only covered a small list of speech acts or focused only on turn taking in conversations. It is important, therefore, that we are clear in our definition of "communicative competence" and "discourse analysis," because these definitions have important consequences for both language analysis and curriculum design.

I expect you have been given adequate practice to allow you to make a connection between the objectives of this course (and the information in the text that addresses each) and practical application of that information to the kinds of everyday issues learners and teachers confront in their classrooms. As a review, several such situations are included in this final practice.

Practice 9.2 Application practice

1. Discuss each of these situations in your class or study group. How does the material in this book help you solve these problems?
    a. You feel fairly fluent in Swedish, but you are puzzled about the way your colleagues react to you. They seem

to think you are pushy and aggressive, but that isn't the way people react to you when you speak English. Has your personality changed?

b. International students tell you that Americans are so insincere. As evidence, they say that as soon as Americans greet each other, they start offering compliments. Are Americans insincere compliment givers?

c. You have taught your students all about the English verb system and yet their writing still seems unnativelike regarding their choice of verb tense/aspect. Can discourse analysis shed any light on this problem?

d. You like using a role-play approach in your teaching, but your supervisor says that role plays are too specific: They can't be generalized and they can't be used to teach "grammar." What can you do to convince your supervisor that both of these objections can be met?

e. You notice that your students rely mainly on lexical cohesion to tie compositions together. Although this is a useful technique, you'd like them to expand their repertoire. What might you do?

f. Some of your students misread the author's intent when text begins with a presentation of a counterargument to the author's main point. The same students never seem to give counterarguments when they write on topics that require persuasive discourse. How do you explain this?

g. Your teachers have attended a special in-service workshop on the differences between BICS (basis interpersonal communication skills) and CALP (cognitive academic language proficiency). They are inspired, ready to make changes so that ESL and bilingual children in their classrooms do less "BICS" and more "CALP." What might this entail, and how could you argue for balance?

h. Students ask you how to make offers and invitations politely but also in a way that ensures they will not be accepted. They also ask why Americans often inquire if they are busy at some set time and, if they are busy, go on to tell them about a party they could have gone to. This seems very rude to them. What can you tell these students about the structure of invitations?

i. Teachers in your school feel that the students do not seem to be able to organize compositions in a "logical" way. In writing descriptions, they jump from one facet to another. You look at the compositions and agree that the descriptions are difficult to follow. How can you teach students to shift focus in a way that teachers would find "logical"?

j. At a local conference, proponents of a notional-functional approach and those of a situational approach get into a heated argument. Each side accuses the other of having no "foundation in theory." What do you know that shows both sides are wrong?

k. A student shows you a composition in which you have circled "jùst really too" in the phrase "this was just really too difficult." First you say that it's redundant; then you decide it's too informal; and then you say that it is only used in spontaneous talk or that it is only used by teenagers. Your grammar reference book is no help. What might you and the student do to decide when the use of this phrase is appropriate?

l. The teachers in your school often use the language experience approach as an aid to reading instruction. They have a debate over whether revisions should be done by the teacher to make the learner's original text more like written language. Which side would you be on? What information would you give in support of your position?

2. List two situations in which an understanding of discourse system would be valuable. Compile these situations in your class or study group and discuss how discourse information would help in solving the problem.

Conclusion

In applied linguistics, we continually search for *system* in language acquisition and language use. In this book, we have looked for system at the discourse level of language. The goal of finding order is one shared by most fields of inquiry. Here is a quotation from the translation of Italo Calvino's *Invisible Cities*. Marco Polo and the emperor Kublai Khan are trying to understand how we explain the order and diversity of form in the natural world.

"From now on, I'll describe the cities to you," the Khan had said, "in your journeys you will see if they exist."

I have tried to do the same thing – describe discourse for you, and in your journeys, you will see if they exist. The cities visited by Marco Polo were always different from those thought of by Kublai Khan. The discourse that you encounter will also differ from that presented here.

"And yet I have constructed in my mind a model city from which all possible cities can be deduced," Kublai said. "It contains everything corresponding to the norm. Since the cities that exist diverge in varying degree from the norm, I need only foresee the exceptions to the norm and calculate the most probable combination."

We, too, have talked about the variation that is possible within the patterns, templates, and systems that have been proposed. Still, we see these systems as possible underlying representations of discourse.

"I have also thought of a model city from which I deduce all the others," Marco answered. "It is a city made only of exceptions, exclusions, incongruities, contradictions. If such a city is the most improbable, by reducing the number of abnormal elements, we increase the probability that the city really exists."

Whenever we talk about system, it is possible that no such "city" really exists. However, in discourse analysis, we begin with real language used in human communication. We begin with all the exceptions, exclusions, incongruities, and contradictions already there, and we try to understand why these features occur – what function they serve with the discourse. Thus, we agree (as in the interpretation of Mario's story) with Marco Polo's conclusion:

"I cannot force my operation beyond a certain limit: I would achieve cities too probable *to be real*." [italics added]

Still, if we side with the Khan, we might discard all the turrets, gazebos, and patios (e.g., backchannel signals, cohesive ties, pragmatic entailment) as just oddities that need not be included in our invisible system. If, like Marco Polo, we start with data on a real city, then *all* parts of the data must be analyzed, evaluated for function, and emphasized according to their importance in the invisible system that underlies all communication. That continues to be our goal in describing language communication.

I hope this introduction to discourse analysis will serve as a guide in your journeys through discourse. An introduction, however, is only an introduction. I urge you to travel on *and* to share your ideas, your data, and your analyses. From your work will come new and better descriptions of the underlying, invisible system of discourse and new and better evidence of the importance of that system in language learning and cross-cultural communication.

References

Calvino, I. (1974). *Invisible Cities*. Translated by W. Weaver. New York: Harcourt Brace Jovanovich.

Celce-Murcia, M. (1980). Contextual analysis and its application to teaching English as a second language. In D. Larsen-Freeman (Ed.), *Discourse analysis and second language research* (pp. 41–55). Rowley, Mass.: Newbury House.

Chafe, W. (1980). *The pear stories: Cognitive, cultural, and linguistic aspects of narrative production*. Norwood, N.J.: Ablex.

——— (1982). Integration and involvement in speaking, writing, and oral literature. In D. Tannen (Ed.), *Spoken and written language: Exploring orality and literacy* (pp. 35–53). Norwood, N.J.: Ablex.

Goffman, E. (1976). Replies and responses. *Language in Society, 5*, 3: 254–313.

Gumperz, J. (1982). *Discourse strategies*. Cambridge: Cambridge University Press.

Hatch, E., and Hawkins, B. (1991). Power in children's narratives. Paper presented at the Second Language Research Forum, University of Southern California, Los Angeles.

Halliday, M., and Hassan, R. (1976). *Cohesion in English*. London: Longman.

Hopper, P., and Thompson, S. (1980). Transitivity in grammar and discourse. *Language, 56*, 2: 251–300.

Hulquist, M. (1985). The adverb *just* in American English usage. Master's thesis, Applied Linguistics, University of California, Los Angeles.

Karmiloff-Smith, A. (1986). From meta-processes to conscious access: Evidence from children metalinguistic and repair data. *Cognition, 23*, 95–147.

Labov, W. (1972). The transformation of experience in narrative syntax. In W. Labov (Ed.), *Language in the inner city* (pp. 354–396). Philadelphia: University of Pennsylvania Press.

Labov, W., and Waletsky, L. (1967). Narrative analysis: Oral versions of personal experience. In J. Helm (Ed.), *Essays on the verbal and visual arts* (pp. 12–44). Seattle: University of Washington Press.

Levinson, S. (1983). *Pragmatics*. Cambridge: Cambridge University Press.

Mandler, J. (1978). A code in the node: The use of a story schema in retrieval. *Discourse Processes, 1*, 14–35.

Mann, W., and Thompson, S. (1989). *Rhetorical structure theory: A theory of text organization*. Information Sciences Institute, University of Southern California.

Pawley, A., and Syder, F. (1976). The one clause at a time hypothesis. Paper presented at the First Congress of New Zealand Linguistic Society, Auckland.

Rumelhart, D. (1975). Notes on the schema for stories. In D. Bobrow and A. Collins (Eds.), *Representations and understanding: Studies in cognitive science* (pp. 211–236). New York: Academic Press.

Saville-Troike, M. (1982). *The ethnography of communication*. Baltimore, Md.: University Park Press.

Schank, R. (1975). *Conceptual information processing*. New York: North Holland.

Schank, R., and Abelson, R. (1977). *Scripts, plans, goals, and understanding*. Hillsdale, N.J.: Lawrence Erlbaum.

Schegloff, E. (1968). Sequencing in conversational openings. *American Anthropologist, 70*, 6: 1075–1095.

——— (1979). The relevance of repair to syntax-for-conversation. In T. Givon (Ed.), *Syntax and semantics. Vol. 12: Discourse and syntax* (pp. 261–268). New York: Academic Press.

Schegloff, E., and Sacks, H. (1973). Opening up closings. *Semiotica, 8*, 4: 289–327.

Shaughnessy, M. (1977). *Errors and expectations*. New York: Oxford University Press.

Tannen, D. (1982). Oral and literate strategies in spoken and written narratives. *Language, 58,* 1: 1–21.

(1985). Relative focus of involvement in oral and written discourse. In D. Olson, N. Torrance, and A. Hildyard (Eds.), *Literacy, language, and learning* (pp. 124–148). Cambridge: Cambridge University Press.

Appendix   Selected journals on discourse analysis

The major journals for articles on discourse analysis are *Language and Communication* (articles on functional syntax), *Language in Society* (discourse analysis from a sociolinguistic perspective), *Journal of Pragmatics* (speech acts and functional syntax), and *TEXT* (rhetorical analysis and functional syntax). All of the following journals, however, carry articles on selected topics in discourse analysis. In addition, the proceedings of the Georgetown Roundtable and of the Berkeley Linguistics Society often contain papers on discourse topics.

American Annals of the Deaf, Gallaudet University
Applied Linguistics, Oxford University Press
CALICO, Brigham Young University
Discourse Processes, Ablex Publishers
ELT Journal (English Language Teaching), Oxford University Press
English for Specific Purposes, Pergamon Press
English Today, Cambridge University Press
First Language, Alpha Academic
IRAL (International Review of Applied Linguistics), J. Groos Verlag
IAL (Issues in Applied Linguistics), Applied Linguistics, University of California, Los
    Angeles
Journal of Child Language, Cambridge University Press
Journal of Classroom Interaction, University of Houston
Journal of Communication, University of Pennsylvania
Journal of Language and Social Psychology, Multilingual Matters
Journal of Multilingual and Multicultural Development, Multilingual Matters
Journal of Pragmatics, North Holland Publishing Company
Journal of Research in Reading, Basil Blackwell
Language, Linguistics Society of America
Language and Cognitive Processes, Lawrence Erlbaum Associates
Language and Communication, Pergamon Press
Language and Education, Multilingual Matters
Language in Society, Cambridge University Press
Language Learning, University of Michigan
Lingua, North Holland
Reading in a Foreign Language, College of St. Mark and St. John
Reading Research Quarterly, International Reading Association
RELC Journal, SEAMEO Regional Language Center, Singapore
Research in the Teaching of English, National Council of Teachers of English
Semiotica, Mouton de Gruyter
Studies in Second Language Acquisition, Cambridge University Press

Selected Journals

SYSTEM, Pergamon Press

Teaching English to Deaf and Second-Language Students, Gallaudet University English Department

TESL Canada Journal, TESL Canada Federation

TESOL Quarterly, TESOL, Inc.

TEXT, Mouton

The Writing Instructor, Writing Programs, University of Southern California

Written Communication, Sage Publishers

Index